Breverton's
FIRST
WORLD
WAR
Curiosities

TERRY BREVERTON

First published 2014

Amberley Publishing
The Hill, Stroud
Gloucestershire, GL5 4EP

www.amberley-books.com

Copyright © Terry Breverton, 2014

The right of Terry Breverton to be
identified as the Author of this work
has been asserted in accordance with
the Copyrights, Designs and Patents
Act 1988.

British Library Cataloguing in
Publication Data.
A catalogue record for this book is
available from the British Library.

ISBN 978 1 4456 3341 1 (paperback)
ISBN 978 1 4456 3352 7 (ebook)

Typesetting and Origination by
Amberley Publishing.
Printed in Great Britain.

Contents

Preface

This book attempts to cover a global war, but inevitably much of it is devoted to the ghastly trench warfare in Europe. In 1915 the first British Army chief, John French, was sidelined, to be replaced by General Haig, responsible for Western Front strategy. Also in 1915, Field Marshal Douglas Haig, 1st Earl Haig of Bermersyde, KT GCB OM GCVO KCIE AFC noted that 'the machine gun is a much overrated weapon' and that 'bullets have little stopping-power against the horse'. In June 1916, just before the terrible Somme Offensive, he stated that 'the nation must be taught to bear losses. No amount of skill on the part of the higher commanders, no training, however good, on the part of the officers and men, no superiority of arms and ammunition, however great, will enable victories to be won without the sacrifice of men's lives. The nation must be prepared to see heavy casualty lists.'

On the first day of the Somme, 1 July 1916, Haig considered the worst British battle casualties ever seen as good for hurting the enemy's morale. On the day after the debacle, when discussing continuing the offensive, Haig said that the enemy 'has undoubtedly been shaken and has few reserves in hand'. The 'few days' campaign lasted fourteen weeks, with 420,000 British casualties. The much-honoured Douglas Haig, who never ventured to the front lines, features throughout this book. The American General Pershing called Haig 'the man who won the war', but to his troops he was 'the Butcher of the Somme'.

History has thankfully not been kind to Haig. 'In a situation demanding the military equivalent of wit and invention ... Haig had none' – Paul Fussell. Haig 'wore down alike the manhood and the guns of the British Army almost to destruction' – Winston Churchill. 'On the Somme, [Haig] had sent the flower of British youth to death or mutilation; at Passchendaele he had tipped the survivors in the slough of despond' – John Keegan. 'To persist ... in this tactically impossible battle was an inexcusable piece of pigheadedness on the part of Haig' – J. F. C. Fuller. 'He [Haig] was a man of supreme egoism and utter lack of scruple – who, to his overweening ambition, sacrificed hundreds of thousands of men. A man who betrayed even his most devoted assistants as well as the Government which he served. A man who gained his ends by trickery of a kind that was not merely immoral but criminal' – B. H. Liddell-Hart.

Upon 4 June 1925, the sixty-four-year-old Douglas Haig was given an honorary diploma at the annual meeting of the Royal College of Veterinary Surgeons. He addressed the group and spoke about the future use of horses during warfare. The next day *The Times* reported Haig's remarks:

> Some enthusiasts to-day talked about the probability of horses becoming extinct and prophesied that the aeroplane, the tank and the motorcar would supersede the horse in future wars. But history had always shown that great inventions somehow or other cured themselves; they always produced antidotes, and he believed that the value of the horse and the opportunity for the horse in the future were likely to be as great as ever. How could infantry, piled up with all their equipment, take advantage of a decisive moment created by fire from machine-guns at a range of 5,000 to 6,000 yards? It was by utilizing light mounted troops and mounted artillery that advantage could be taken of these modern weapons. He was all for using aeroplanes and tanks, but they were only accessories to the man and the horse, and he felt sure that as time went on they would find just as much use for the horse – the well-bred horse – as they had ever done in the past. Let them not be despondent and think that the day of the horse was over.

Generals, like politicians, seem to have a non-existent learning curve.

Introduction

French Second Lieutenant Alfred Joubaire wrote in his diary about the First World War just before he died that 'humanity is mad! It must be mad to do what it is doing. What a massacre. What scenes of horror and carnage! I cannot find words to translate my impressions. Hell cannot be so terrible! Men are mad!' Front-line German officers also despaired, like their French and British counterparts, that generals far from the front line did not realise the futility of their outdated concept of war. For instance, the German Paul Hub wrote to his wife, 'Our blood is flowing in torrents. All around me is the most gruesome devastation. Dead and wounded soldiers, horse cadavers, burnt-out houses, churned-up fields, vehicles, clothes, weapons. I didn't think war could be like this.'

This book is written as a tribute to the men on all sides who suffered in 'the War to End Wars'. It is written to be entertaining and informative, and the underlying terrible sadness of war is alleviated by the humour and good nature of front-line soldiers, airmen and seamen. Only with a sense of 'gallows humour' could they exist with any semblance of sanity in the conditions they faced. This author wishes that politicians of his lifetime would realise that conflict – in Korea, Vietnam, Africa, Serbia, Iraq, Libya, Afghanistan, etc., etc. – should always be avoided. If generals and politicians had to serve in the front line, there would have been hardly any bloodstained disputes in the last few decades. We have not learned anything from this first global war, a century ago.

We believe, even now, that the Allies won the First World War, but it was only 'won' by starving the German nation and its troops, not in battle. It cost over twenty Allied Powers an estimated $125,690,477,000, compared to around $60,643,160,000 for the four Central Powers, with Britain and Germany being virtually bankrupted in suffering the highest costs on either side. As well as costs, casualties were 43 per cent higher for the Allies, with 22,104,209 military casualties compared to the Central Powers' 15,404, 477. If we examine actual military deaths, at 5,152,115 for the Allies and 3,386,200 for the Central Powers, the Allies had 52 per cent more deaths. The Central Powers had around half the manpower of the Allied Powers. Does this sound like the successful war portrayed in the history books and peddled by politicians?

However, the truth is that no one won. Germany was simply exhausted by fighting on two fronts against Russia and on the Western Front. No sooner had Russia collapsed into communism than the USA entered the war – very late – with countless supplies and fresh troops. French troops mutinied. Starving German soldiers stopped fighting. If there was a winner, it was America, which gained international and economic trade dominance, taking British markets and becoming the acknowledged leader of the Western political world. Britain was severely financially indebted to the USA, a situation exacerbated by the horrors and costs of another world war just two decades later. A very brief timeline of this first global war gives us an initial perspective.

1914

June	Archduke Franz Ferdinand, heir presumptive to the Austro-Hungarian throne, is assassinated by a Serbian nationalist
July	Austria-Hungary declares war on Serbia; Russia mobilises its troops to defend Serbia
August	Germany declares war on Russia; Germany declares war on France and invades Belgium; the First World War breaks out when Britain declares war on Germany; Japan joins the Allies; the Western Front reaches a virtual stalemate
November	Turkey joins Germany and Austria-Hungary

1915

February	Germany begins unrestricted submarine warfare
May	Italy joins the Allies

1916

The Arabs revolt against their Turkish overlords

1917

January	The Bolshevik communists come to power in Russia after overthrowing the government of the Tsar

April   The United States declares war on Germany
June   The first US troops arrive in Paris, France, on 13 June

1918
March   Russia and Germany sign the Treaty of Brest-Litovsk
October   Germany asks President Wilson to begin peace
               negotiations; Wilson rejects Germany's request for
               peace talks
November   The US Army begins its final advance on 1 November;
               Germany requests an armistice on 6 November; Kaiser
               Wilhelm II abdicates on 9 November; Germans revolt
               and take over government; Germany signs the armistice
               on 11 November, ending the First World War

1919
The countries that ratify the Treaty of Versailles on 28 June become
the original members of the League of Nations; the US Senate rejects
the treaty

1

The Causes and Nations Involved

Europe today is a powder keg and the leaders are like men smoking
in an arsenal … A single spark will set off an explosion that will
consume us all … I cannot tell you when that explosion will occur,
but I can tell you where … Some damned foolish thing in the Balkans
will set it off.
Prince Otto von Bismarck, Congress of Berlin, 1878

A total of twenty-eight nations (twenty-four Allied and four Central
Powers) participated in the First World War. If we add new nations
that came into existence as a result of the war, those who were neutral
but lost civilians and those French, German and British colonies and
dependencies which are now nations, around seventy nations were
affected directly. The world would never be the same after this first
global 'modern warfare'. Conflict had been coming for some time,
with Germany building its navy and seeking a new 'empire in the sun'.
Britain resented the growing threat to its naval superiority. Growing
alliances came about for many reasons, but the flashpoint came on
28 June 1914. The Archduke of Austria-Este, Franz Ferdinand, was
the heir presumptive to the Austro-Hungarian Empire. He and his
wife were on an official visit to Sarajevo in Bosnia-Herzegovina, a
Serb-dominated province of Austria-Hungary. Serbian militants,
seeking independence, made two attempts on the archduke's life.
In the first attempt they threw a grenade at his car shortly after he
arrived in Sarajevo, but the bomb bounced off the car. Later that day,
the archduke asked to go to a hospital to visit those wounded by the
bomb. Leaving for the royal palace, the driver took a wrong turn down
a side street and stalled the car. Gavrilo Princip, a nineteen-year-old
militant Bosnian Serb who had been part of the assassination attempt

that morning, just happened to be in the street. Taking the unexpected opportunity, Princip stepped up to the car's window and shot both the archduke and his wife at point-blank range. Both died, with the archduke saying to his wife, 'Don't die, Sophie, for the sake of our children.'

Perhaps this driver's error altered history and caused millions to die and four empires to fall. Another two, the British and French, were fatally weakened. However, Europe was ripe for another war. More likely Princip's actions merely brought forward an inevitable conflict. The assassination inflamed tensions between Austria-Hungary and Serbia, which been growing for several years over territorial disputes. Without any real evidence, Austria-Hungary blamed the Serbian government for the deaths. The Austro-Hungarian government also blamed Serbia for causing unrest among ethnic Serbs in Bosnia-Herzegovina, the province of Austria-Hungary that shared a border with Serbia. It was decided to invade Serbia, a policy which many, including Count Conrad von Hötzendorf, Chief of the Austrian General Staff, had argued forcibly for years. Von Hötzendorf had formally proposed a pre-emptive war with Serbia at least twenty-five times, in his wish to 'crush the Serbian skull'.

However, the Russian Empire had close ethnic, religious and political ties to Serbia, and had a huge army. Thus on 5 July 1914, Austria-Hungary sent an envoy to the German emperor, Kaiser Wilhelm II. Wilhelm believed that Russia was unlikely to respond to an Austro-Hungarian invasion of Serbia, as the Russian armies were unprepared for war. He was also personally close to his cousin Tsar Nicholas II, and felt that he could smooth a diplomatic path with Russia. However, Germany promised that if Russian troops did in fact advance on Austria-Hungary, Germany would help fight them off. The German guarantee to the Austro-Hungarians is often referred to as their 'blank cheque'. Assured by German promises, on 23 July 1914, the Austro-Hungarian government issued an ultimatum to Serbia containing ten demands. They insisted that Austria-Hungary be allowed to participate in Serbia's investigation of the assassination and take direct part in the judicial process against the suspects. They also required Serbia to stamp out all forms of anti-Austrian activism and propaganda. The ultimatum was specifically written to be humiliating and unacceptable to Serbia.

On 25 July, Serbia accepted Austria-Hungary's demands almost entirely. There were just a few simple caveats about Austria's participation in the judicial process against the criminals. Despite this, Austria-Hungary had decided upon war. Its embassy in Serbia closed within a half-hour of receiving Serbia's answer, and just three days later, on 28 July, Austria declared war on Serbia. On 29 July, the first Austrian artillery shells fell on Serbia's capital, Belgrade. Russia ordered a general mobilisation of its troops on 30 July. Germany believed that Russia was intending to go to war to defend Serbia, and immediately ordered its own mobilisation. The Tsar and the Kaiser were in constant communication by telegraph, but failed to convince each other that they were only taking precautionary measures. Tsar Nicholas II, who was personally hesitant about joining the war, briefly changed his mind over ordering mobilisation. Ultimately, however, he caved in to pressure from overly optimistic Russian military leaders and advisers who had strong nationalistic leanings.

Britain made an attempt to intervene diplomatically, but on 1 August, the German ambassador to Russia handed over a declaration of war. German military leaders felt that war with Russia was inevitable at some point. They argued that it would be far better to fight Russia now, while its army was still poorly armed and untrained, rather than to wait until it could pose a greater threat. Some historians claim that Germany deliberately encouraged Austria to go to war with Serbia in order to set off a war with Russia.

Upon 1 August, feeling threatened by German mobilisation, the French now ordered a general mobilisation. In 1871, France had lost the territories of Alsace and Lorraine to Germany, a humiliating blow that left France desperate to regain these lands. While fearful of an all-out German invasion, some French leaders felt that if Germany was distracted by a war with Russia, France might have a chance to seize Alsace and Lorraine. However, on 3 August, Germany, in accordance with its Schlieffen Plan, declared war upon France and began its invasion. Germany had been developing plans for invasions into every European country for three decades, since the time of Bismarck. Their Schlieffen Plan called for quick, encircling movements that would surround and destroy the enemy. On 3 August Germany began to cross neutral Belgium in order to reach France's least fortified border, in violation of its own treaty in respect to neutral countries. Britain, which had a defence treaty with Belgium, declared war on Germany the next day, 4 August, bringing the number of states at this time involved up to seven – the British Empire (with its many nations), France, Belgium, Serbia and Russia against Germany and the Austro-Hungarian Empire. More and more countries joined in, from across the world, either seeing opportunities or threats, and fighting spread on land and at sea across the globe.

German military leaders had believed there was a good chance that Britain would remain neutral, but Churchill and others had warned about Germany's intentions towards the British Empire. For centuries, Britain had been the greatest naval power in the world, with the largest collection of colonies. Germany made a massive and costly effort to build up a comparable naval fleet of its own, with the Kaiser having the specific goal of matching Britain on the high seas. Germany also wanted new colonies, their 'place in the sun'. Britain saw these developments as a dangerous threat to the balance of power in Europe.

With the Schlieffen Plan, it was absolutely necessary to put all possible force behind the invasion of France and not to hold any soldiers back in reserve. Germany's expectation was to end the war quickly by attacking France immediately and overrunning it before Russia had a chance to properly mobilise. The plan involved attacking Belgium and then proceeding south into France, but Belgium fought back, making it much harder for Germany to carry out the Schlieffen Plan. Also, Germany made the fatal mistake of becoming involved on two fronts, against Russia and France. If it had concentrated all its forces upon France, the plan would probably have worked. Aside from their war plans, Germany also tried to stop Allied countries from getting involved in the war by starting revolutions in them, for example, India, Russia and Ireland.

Footnote:
More than seventy of today's nations were involved. An incomplete list includes Belgium and Belgian colonies of Belgian Congo, now Democratic Republic of the Congo; France and French colonies now called Algeria, Vietnam, Mali, Morocco, Senegal, Guinea, Madagascar, Benin, Burkina Faso, Republic of the Congo, Ivory Coast, Tunisia, Chad, Central African Republic, Niger, Gabon; British possessions and colonies of Ireland, Ghana, Kenya, Malawi, Nigeria, Sierra Leone, Uganda, Zambia, Zimbabwe, Australia, Canada, India, New Zealand; Germany and German colonies of Tanzania, Namibia, Cameroon, Togo; Austria, Hungary, Poland, Germany, Russia, Romania, Albania, Bulgaria, Macedonia, Greece, Egypt, China, Japan, Slovenia, Croatia, Bosnia, Serbia, Montenegro, Macedonia, Italy, Israel, Syria, Nepal, Iraq, Czechoslovakia, Estonia, Luxembourg, Portugal, states formerly in the Ottoman Empire and new states from the Russian Empire such as Ukraine, Latvia, Estonia, etc.

2

The First World War on Land: Global Conflict

Captain Henry Dalton described a German night attack:

> A great grey mass of humanity was charging straight on to us from 50 yards off. We fired our rifles and I saw the great mass of Germans quiver. Some fell, others fell over them, and others came on. I have never shot so much in such a short time. My right hand is one huge bruise from banging the bolt up and down. The firing died down and out of the darkness a great moan came. People in grey uniforms with their arms and legs off were trying to crawl away. Others who could not move gasped out their last moments with the cold night wind biting into their broken bodies. Some would raise themselves on one arm or crawl a little distance. It was a weird, awful scene.

Armies	Standing Armies & Reserves in August 1914	Mobilised Forces in 1914–18
Russia	5,971,000	12,000,000
France	4,017,000	8,410,000
British Empire	975,000	8,905,000
Italy	1,251,000	5,615,000
[United States]	[200,000]	[4,355,000]
[Japan]	[800,000]	[800,000]
Romania	290,000	750,000
Serbia	200,000	707,000
Belgium	117,000	267,000
Greece	230,000	230,000
Portugal	40,000	100,000
Montenegro	50,000	50,000
ALLIES	14,141,000	42,189,000
ALLIES w/o USA/JAPAN	13,141,000	13,141,000

Germany	4,500,000	11,000,000
Austria-Hungary	3,000,000	7,800,000
Turkey	210,000	2,850,000
Bulgaria	280,000	1,200,000
CENTRAL POWERS	7,990,000	22,850,000

The Race to the Sea and the Beginning of Trench Warfare

Despite its relative lack of troops, a blockaded navy, poor supplies and being surrounded by enemies, it is amazing how close Germany and Austria-Hungary came to winning the war. The Central Powers had only 35 per cent of the war's troops, and 41 per cent of its casualties, yet the war is somehow regarded as a resounding Allied success. Germany, in particular, lost the war because of a lack of supplies and the sudden entry of the USA with seemingly limitless supplies of arms and food, not because of any great strategy by the Allies. It had soon developed into a war of attrition, but the Germans had a more suitable phrase, *materialschlacht,* a war of material. The sudden availability of fresh war materials and men from the USA broke the bloody stalemate of four years.

Germany had counted on a short war, taking Paris and overrunning France, as the only way to achieve victory. After being halted at the Marne, on 14 September 1914 General Falkenhayn had replaced von Moltke, and by 15 September Germany's western line had been stabilised. By this time the German Army was so hurt that even if they could have reached Paris, they could never have taken it. After the battle, the two lines entrenched themselves around 800 yards away from each other, forming the 'Western Front'. Germany chose the best positions on ridges and uplands, so the Allies were disadvantaged by groundwater and mud in their trenches. Also, the German trenches, dugouts and shelters were built to be defended and were much stronger than those of the Allies, who used theirs as places from which to start attacks. When the Germans failed to break through at the Marne, it was the failure of the entire Schlieffen Plan, and ended any prospect of a short war. The failure occasioned the 'Race to the Sea', which ended at the North Sea coast after each army attempted to outflank the other by moving north and west. Flanders in Belgium was the last gap through which either side could launch a decisive thrust.

By October 1914, the Allies had reached Nieuwpoort, on the North Sea coast. The Germans, as a prelude to Falkenhayn's Flanders Offensive, had captured Antwerp and forced its Belgian defenders back to Nieuwpoort, near Ypres. Ypres was strategically located along the roads leading to the Channel ports in Belgian Flanders.

Under Field Marshall Sir John French, the British Expeditionary Force had retreated to Ypres after Antwerp fell, arriving between 8 and 19 October to assist the Belgian and French defence. The BEF held a 35-mile line in the centre while Foch's French Army defended the flanks to the south of the city. At the outset of the battle, both John French and Foch believed a coordinated attack would enable the Allies to recapture the industrial city of Lille in French Flanders, followed swiftly by Brussels. Lille was taken by the British on 17 October, but Brussels remained in German hands for the entire war.

Falkenhayn's Flanders Offensive began on 18 October when he ordered an advance to smash through the Allied line and capture the ports of Dunkirk, Calais, and Boulogne. From 18–30 October the Battle of the Yser was fought in a great effort by the Germans to break through Belgium. British warships off the coast fired upon the German Fourth Army, and when Franco-Belgian troops were wavering, the canal locks at Niewepoort were opened on 25 October. This flooded the Lowlands from the sea and covered the railway lines essential for German supplies. There was now a 20-mile strip of land between Dixmude and Nieuwpoort with a 2-mile-wide water barrier that forced Falkenhayn to halt.

The second phase of the Flanders Offensive was a series of assaults on Ypres against the much smaller BEF, from 31 October until 22 November, when winter made fighting difficult. More than half of the 160,000 men the BEF sent to France were wounded or killed at this First Battle of Ypres. After November 1914, the British called these trenches 'the Salient', and there were another two major battles at Ypres, the third being known as Passchendaele. The Germans committed all of their last resources to launch this first attack on the Western Front, but the battle proved costly and ineffective. The attacks lasted until Falkenhayn was convinced that breaking through in the west was hopeless, and that the only place to secure a victory was in the east against Russia.

Von Falkenhayn understood that there was no way to win a war against England, France, Belgium and Russia together, so adopted the defensive policy of attrition to try and exhaust the Allies on the Western Front. He allowed the Allies go on the offensive, which in general cost far more men and supplies than defending strong, fortified positions. At the same time he attacked Russia on the Eastern Front. However, the German economy was also going through more and more of a strain as the war went on. In 1914 the German economy was almost completely reliant on outside trade and was not prepared for a protracted war. Germany had no large stocks of guns or ammunition, and was forced to employ chemists to find replacements for substances that were made scarce by the war and the blockade by the Royal Navy. Their scientists discovered a replacement for gunpowder ingredients and synthetic rubber, and began using oil instead of coal in machinery. The armed forces took all the hired labour out of the economy, and there were such shortages that food riots began in 1916.

Unfortunately there is no room in a volume like this to describe the heroism of the men and the stupidity of some generals in the following battles, but the following chronology gives some idea of the geography, timescale, advances and reverses of the war. We tend to think of this war as one fought mainly in the trenches in France and Belgium, but it was in fact fought globally, and the following shows the deployment of British forces in the main British campaigns:

Theatre of war	British Army max. deployment	Men who saw service in this theatre
France and Flanders	2,046,901	5,399,563
Mesopotamia	447,531	889,702
Egypt and Palestine	432,857	1,192,511
Salonika	285,021	404,207
Italy	132,667	145,764
Gallipoli	127,737	468,987
Other theatres	293,095	475,210

Chronology of Major Battles and Events

1914

'THE RAPE OF BELGIUM', 4 August 1914–September 1918
This description initially had a propaganda use, but was then justified by the German policy of 'frightfulness', especially in the first few months of the war. The German Army engaged in atrocities against the civilian population, killing and deliberately destroying homes and buildings. Around 1,500,000 Belgians, a fifth of the population, fled. On 25 August 1914, the German Army ravaged the ancient city of Leuven, deliberately burning the university's library of 300,000 medieval books and manuscripts with gasoline, killing 248 residents and expelling the entire population of 10,000. Before the war Belgium was the sixth-largest economy in the world, but the Germans destroyed it by dismantling industries and transporting the equipment and machinery to Germany. The Belgian economy never returned to its pre-war levels. More than 100,000 Belgian workers

were forcibly deported to Germany to work in the war industry and to Northern France to build roads and other military facilities for the benefit of the German military. At least 32,000 civilians were killed.

THE BATTLE OF GALICIA, 23 August–11 September 1914
At Lemberg in the Austro-Hungarian Empire, now Lviv in north-western Ukraine.

There were four major conflicts where the Russians forced the Austro-Hungarian Army out of Galicia. By the time the battle ended, 130,000 prisoners had been taken by the Russians, while they inflicted 324,000 casualties. The Russians suffered 225,000 casualties, including 40,000 captured. The Russians had pushed the front 100 miles into the Carpathian Mountains. The battle severely damaged the Austro-Hungarian Army, destroyed a large portion of its trained officers, and crippled Austria.

THE BATTLE OF MONS, 23 August 1914
On the Franco-Belgian border, south-west of Brussels and south-east of Lille.

After completing their occupation of Belgium on 20 August 1914, two German armies moved quickly upon France. The French Army and BEF came under heavy fire from long-range German artillery at Mons. With the German armies outside the range of their own guns, the Allies had to quickly fall back. Their fighting retreat covered 120 miles in fourteen days, to the River Marne on the outskirts of Paris.

THE BATTLE OF TANNENBERG, 26–30 August 1914
On the Lyna River in Prussia, now north-eastern Poland.

Two German armies, under the command of General Paul von Hindenburg, faced an overwhelming Russian invasion force of the First and Second Armies. However, Germany discovered that the Russian General Rennenkampf, who had been slapped in the face by General Alexander Samsonov, would be reluctant to support Samsonov's army. Hindenburg thus attacked Russia's Second Army, led by General Samsonov. Weakened by constant pounding from German artillery, Samsonov's poorly equipped troops were forced to retreat. As they did so, the Second German Army cut off their path, and they were surrounded. Over 50,000 Russian soldiers were killed or wounded and 92,000 were taken prisoner. Samsonov committed suicide that same day.

THE BATTLE OF THE MARNE, 5–9 September 1914
A tributary of the Seine, south-east of Paris.

The Second Reich's fortunes started to turn on the Western Front just weeks after the war began. Papers detailing a planned German drive on Paris by General Alexander von Kluck's 1st Army were captured by a French patrol. Using the papers, the French 6th Army initiated a counter-attack that stopped the German advance. On 4 September, the Allies halted their retreat from Mons at the River Marne. The exhausted German troops had out-advanced their supplies and faced a strong Allied defence reinforced with fresh troops from Paris, determined not to let the capital fall. More than a million troops fought on each side as the Allies made their stand. A gap emerged between the German First and Second Armies, and British and French commanders seized the opportunity to split the German forces apart by moving into the gap. French reservists were ferried in to fill the breach using streams of taxicabs. On 9 September, after four days of intense fighting, the German armies were ordered to fall back, and staged a fighting retreat over 45 miles to the River Aisne. The Germans managed to dig in successfully and hold their position, and railways were now better able to supply them. The Western Front remained centred near this position for the rest of the war, but the German trenches and firing positions had a geographical advantage.

THE BATTLE OF THE MASURIAN LAKES, 9–14 September 1914
Near Tannenberg, in Poland.

Hindenburg had crushed Russia's Second Army and now attacked its First Army, commanded by the incapable General Paul von Rennenkampf. Rennenkampf had virtually refused to assist the more capable Samsonov at Tannenberg owing to long-standing hostility. Rennenkampf's army retreated, but suffered 125,000 casualties. In the battles of Tannenberg and the Masurian Lakes, Russia lost around 300,000 soldiers in less than a month of fighting.

FIRST BATTLE OF YPRES (THE FIRST BATTLE OF FLANDERS), 31 October–22 November 1914
In West Flanders, north-west Belgium.

Ypres occupied a strategic position because it was central to many roads, and it stood in the path of Germany's planned invasion across the rest of Belgium and into France from the north, following the Schlieffen Plan. The land surrounding Ypres to the north is flat and canals and rivers link it to the coast. To the south the land rises to about 500 feet with the Messines (Mesen) Ridge, which would give a significant advantage. Fierce fighting took place around the town and neither the British nor the Germans could claim to control the area, but the British took control of the town. Each day Ypres was heavily shelled and civilian casualties were high. By the winter, the Germans had not taken Ypres and heavy rain meant that any movement was impossible as the roads turned to mud. The first battle at Ypres ended in stalemate, but the BEF was almost wiped out of existence. The situation was so desperate that Sir John French, the BEF's Commander-in-Chief, was forced to signal, 'I have no more reserves. The only men I have left are the sentries at my gates. I will take them where the line is broken, and the last of the English will die fighting.' The British lost 7,960 killed, 17,873 missing and 29,562 wounded. The French had between 50,000 and 85,000 killed, wounded and missing, and the Belgians 21,562. Against these Allied losses of between 126,957 and 161,951, the Germans had 134,315 losses. The days of mass casualties had arrived.

THE BATTLE OF ŁÓDŹ, 11 November–6 December 1914
Around 80 miles south-west of Warsaw, in central Poland, then a client-state of Russia.
The survivors of the Russian First and Second Armies joined the Fifth Army to fight the German Ninth Army in terrible winter conditions. Russia had halted the German advance 12 miles from Warsaw at the Battle of the Vistula River, with 65,000 casualties against 139,567. General von Hindenburg now saw an opportunity to attack the Russian flank as it moved into Silesia. The results of the Battle of Łódź were inconclusive. The Russians repulsed the Germans and saved Warsaw, and the Germans caused the Russians to abandon their offensive into Silesia. The Russian Empire saw 120,000 troops killed, wounded or captured, against Germany's 160,000.

1915

THE SECOND BATTLE OF YPRES, 17 April–31 July 1915
Flanders, Belgium.
Historians often include four to six engagements, but this seemed to consist of seven battles: at Hill 60, 17 April–7 May; Gravenstafel, 22–23 April; Saint Julien, 24 April–4 May; Frezenberg, 8–13 May; the First Battle of Bellewaarde, 24–25 May; the Battle of Hooge, 30–31 July; the Second Attack on Bellewaarde, 25 September.
   Hill 60 is about 3 miles south-east from Ypres, and with a height of 150 feet became a prime target for both Allies and Germans. Hill 60 changed hands on a number of occasions throughout the war. The

Germans first captured it in December 1914. The British responded by digging four tunnels into the hill, detonating massive mines and taking the hill easily on 17 April. The Germans retook it on 18 April, and then the British gained it on 19 April. On 21 and 22 April, the Germans used poison gas. Though tear gas had been used against the Russians in January, the Second Battle of Ypres would mark the debut of the lethal chlorine gas.

On 22 April 1915, the German 4th Army began releasing chlorine gas towards the French troops at Gravenstafel. Unprepared for such an attack, the French troops began retreating as their comrades were blinded or collapsed from asphyxiation. A gap of around 8,000 yards opened in the Allied lines as French soldiers died and fled from the gas. To seal the breach, the 1st Canadian Division of General Sir Horace Smith-Dorrien's Second British Army was shifted to the area after dark. The Canadian troops used handkerchiefs soaked in urine as gas masks, and launched a counter-attack on the Germans. In a brutal battle, they succeeded in reclaiming the area, but sustained high casualties in the process. As fighting spread down the Ypres Salient, the Germans again attacked with gas near Hill 60. The British had developed new tactics such as shelling behind the gas cloud to strike at the advancing German infantry. On 24 May the German assault sought to capture Bellewaarde Ridge, but the Germans brought the battle to a close with insignificant gains owing to a lack of supplies and manpower. The British suffered around 59,275 casualties, the French around 10,000, while the Germans endured 34,933.

THE GALLIPOLI CAMPAIGN, 25 April 1915–6 January 1916
The Gallipoli Peninsula is in the European part of Turkey, with the Aegean Sea to the west and the Dardanelles Strait to the east.
Turkey's entrance into the war in November 1914 had placed the Dardanelles in German hands, separating the Russian and Allied naval forces. German control of the strait also meant that Russian wheat could not be shipped to Britain and that British military equipment could be shipped only by means of a treacherous northern route to the Russian ports of Murmansk and Arkhangelsk. Britain invaded the Gallipoli Peninsula as part of its effort to force open the Dardanelles, the strait between Europe and Asia. The operation failed and cost hundreds of thousands of lives, before the British abandoned the operation and evacuated their forces at the start of 1916. Allied troops, including major contingents from Australia and New Zealand, had launched a ground attack after a naval failure where U-boats began torpedoing the British fleet. Turkish forces attacked and pushed the

Allied troops back to the beaches, where they were trapped with their backs to the sea. The Allies incurred 252,000 casualties and the Turks 218,000–251,000.

THE SECOND BATTLE OF ARTOIS, 9 May–18 June 1915

The interior of the Pas de Calais département, northern France, which includes the battle sites of Arras, Lens and St Omer.

This occurred at the same time as the Second Battle of Ypres, and was the final Allied offensive of spring 1915, ending inconclusively. Casualties were 75,000 German, 74,000 French and 5,000 British.

THE GORLICE–TARNÓW OFFENSIVE, 1 May–19 September 1915

South-east of Krakow, south-east Poland.

In April 1915 the German 11th Army was transferred from the Western Front. It joined the Austro-Hungarian IV Army to attack the Russian Army. The Central Powers shattered the Russian defences, and the Russian lines collapsed. The Russian Army lost about 100,000 killed and wounded, along with about 140,000 prisoners, and almost ceased to exist as a fighting unit. Central Powers casualties were only around 90,000. The Central Powers recaptured most of Galicia, and the Russian threat to Austria-Hungary was averted. Warsaw was evacuated and fell on 4 August to the Germans. At the end of the month Poland was entirely in Austro-German hands, and 750,000 Russian prisoners had been taken

THE LOOS–ARTOIS OFFENSIVE, THE THIRD BATTLE OF ARTOIS, 25 September–15 October 1915

Loos is in the Pas-de-Calais, just north of Lens in northern France; Artois is a former province in the centre of Pas-de-Calais.

This was a joint operation of the French and British to cut off supplies to the German troops by capturing the railway centres at Douai and Attigny. On 25 September 1915, the French 10th Army attacked the German 6th Army at Arras, and the battle remained indecisive. Haig launched an offensive at Loos on the same day, but General French called off the offensive on 13 October 1915. The BEF registered over 50,000 casualties in the Loos–Artois Offensive; the French recorded a loss of 48,000 soldiers, and the Germans lost 24,000 soldiers. The inconclusive offensive was meant to complement the Champagne Offensive, by using the Allies' numerical advantage. At the same time the Italians attacked along the Isonzo River to try and stretch the Germans.

THE SECOND BATTLE OF CHAMPAGNE, 25 September 1915–6 November 1915
North-east France, 100 miles east of Paris.
This was a French offensive to complement that at Arras, and the Germans initially lost ground, but counter-attacked on 30 October. They managed to reclaim all the territory lost to the French. The offensive was finally abandoned on 6 November. The French lost 145,000 troops, while the Germans lost 72,500–97,000.

THE SERBIAN CAMPAIGN OF 1915, 7 October 1915
The Kingdom of Serbia suffered proportionately more than any other country. The front ranged from the Danube to southern Macedonia and back north again, involving forces from almost all of the combatants of the war. If Serbia was taken, then the Germans would have a rail link from Germany through Austria-Hungary and down to Istanbul to support the Ottoman Empire. However, von Hötzendorf of Austria was also fighting Russia and Italy. The Bulgarians saw an opportunity and entered the war for the Central Powers after the Allied defeats at Gallipoli and Gorlice. Germany and Austria-Hungary now attacked the depleted Serbian Army, crossed the Danube, and took Belgrade on 9 October. Bulgaria then attacked and won two battles and the Battle of Kosovo. This was a nearly complete victory for the Central Powers at a cost of around 67,000 casualties as compared to around 90,000 Serbs killed or wounded and 174,000 captured. The vital railroad from Berlin to Istanbul was finally opened.

1916

THE BATTLE OF VERDUN, 21 February–18 December 1916
Verdun straddles the River Meuse in north-eastern France.
This was the longest and one of the deadliest battles of the war, with Germany hoping to wear France down and break the stalemate. Von Falkenhayn wrote that his objective was to see the forces of France 'bleed to death'. The fortified town of Verdun guarded the German Army's path to Paris. There was a massive artillery bombardment and both sides employed shells filled with poison gas on a large scale. The Germans used flamethrowers and initially had massive aerial superiority. From 24 June the French heard the welcome sound of the British guns attacking at the Somme. The Germans almost made it within 2 miles of Verdun and France lost its two defensive forts but regained the forts by the battle's end. After ten months, the fighting ceased, with both sides back where they had started, but with a

staggering 650,000 soldiers dead. The French lost between 315,000 and 542,000 men at Verdun, with 156,000 killed between February and December. Germany lost between 243,000 and 434,000 troops, with 143,000 deaths in the same period. This battle is said to represent the highest density of fatalities of the war.

THE SURRENDER AT KUT, 29 April 1916
Kut-al-Amara, on the Tigris River in the Basra province of Mesopotamia, modern Iraq.
Under the command of Sir John Nixon, British troops enjoyed early success in their invasion of Mesopotamia. Forces led by Sir Charles Townshend reached and occupied the Mesopotamian province of Basra, including the town of Kut al-Amara, by late September 1915. From there, they attempted to move up the Tigris and Euphrates toward Baghdad, but were pushed back by Turkish troops at Ctesiphon in late November. Despite outnumbering the Turks two-to-one, Townshend's troops, made up partially of soldiers dispatched from India, were forced to retreat to Kut, where on 5 December Turkish and German troops began to lay siege to the city. Problems with illness plagued Townshend's forces and morale sank along with dwindling supplies. They could not be relieved due to the heavy winter rains, which had swollen the Tigris River and made it difficult to manoeuvre troops along its banks. The British attempted four times over the course of the winter to confront their opponents, only to suffer 23,000 casualties, almost twice the strength of the entire remaining Kut regiment, without success. After five months, General Townshend was forced to surrender all 13,000 of his starving troops, the largest surrender of British troops in history up to that time. Townshend was treated with splendid hospitality in captivity. Meanwhile his troops were largely subjected to barbaric treatment, including rape. Two-thirds of the prisoners died while being marched into captivity.

BATTLE OF ASIAGO, BATTLE OF THE PLATEAUX, THE TRENTINO OFFENSIVE, 15 May–2 June 1916
Near Asiago in the province of Trentino, then in the Kingdom of Italy. This counter-offensive was nicknamed *Strafexpedition*, 'Punitive Expedition' by the Austrians. It was an unexpected attack after the Fifth Battle of the Isonzo on March 1916. Von Hötzendorf had wished to attack Italy, as well as Serbia, since well before the war, and asked Germany for help from the Eastern Front, but this was denied because Germany was not yet at war with Italy. Around 2,000 Austrian artillery guns opened a heavy barrage against the Italian lines, then

the Austrian infantry attacked along a 30-mile front. The Austrians broke through, reaching the beginning of the Venetian plain. However, on 4 June, Russia unexpectedly managed to enter Austrian territory in Galicia. Although they were effectively countered by German troops, Hötzendorf was forced to quickly withdraw half of his divisions from Trentino. The *Strafexpedition* could no longer be sustained and the Austrians retired from many of their positions. The Austrians lost 150,000 men, and the Italians 147,000.

THE BRUSILOV OFFENSIVE – THE BATTLE WHICH WON THE WAR, 4 June–late September 1916

Around the towns of Lviv, Kovel and Lutsk, in what is now Ukraine.

Also known as 'the June Advance', this was the Russian Empire's greatest victory, and one of the most lethal battles in history. Professor Tunstall has called the Brusilov Offensive of 1916 the worst crisis of the war for Austria-Hungary, and the Triple Entente's greatest victory. The extremely competent General Aleksei Brusliov amassed four armies totalling forty infantry divisions and fifteen cavalry divisions. He faced thirty-nine Austrian infantry divisions and ten cavalry divisions, formed in a row of three defensive lines, although German reinforcements were later brought up. Brusilov, knowing he would not receive significant reinforcements, moved his reserves up to the front line. He used them to dig entrenchments about 300 yards long and 90 yards wide, all along the front line. These provided shelter for the troops and hindered observation by the Austrians. The Russians secretly crept to within 100 yards of the Austrian lines and at some points as close as 75 yards.

Brusilov prepared for a surprise assault along a 300-mile front. The Russians opened the offensive with a massive artillery barrage against the Austro-Hungarian lines. The key factor was the brevity and accuracy of the bombardment. The normal protracted barrages gave the defenders time to bring up reserves and evacuate forward trenches, while damaging the battlefield so badly that it was hard for attackers to advance. The initial attack was successful and the Austro-Hungarian lines were broken, enabling three of Brusilov's four armies to advance on a wide front. Their success was helped in large part by Brusilov's innovation of 'shock troops' to attack weak points along the Austrian lines to effect a breakthrough, which the main Russian army could then exploit. Brusilov's tactical innovations were copied for the German 'stormtrooper' tactics used later in the Western Front.

Within four days the Russians had taken over 200,000 prisoners. All forces involved were now reaching exhaustion and the offensive died down in late September and ended as Russian troops had to be transferred to help Romania, which was being overrun by Austro-Hungarian, German and Bulgarian forces. Brusilov's operation achieved its original goal of forcing Germany to halt its attack on Verdun and to transfer considerable forces to the east. It also broke the back of the Austro-Hungarian Army, which suffered the majority of the casualties. The Austrians lost a staggering 1.5 million men (including 400,000 taken prisoner) and ceded almost 10,000 square miles of ground. With the launch of the Brusilov Offensive, all hopes of Austrian victory in the east were virtually ended. Austrian attacks in Italy were halted, and Romania finally entered the war with the Allies. Yet again the Eastern Front sucked German resources away from the Western Front.

THE BATTLE OF THE SOMME, 1 July–18 November 1916
Along a 25-mile front that extended across both banks of the River Somme – the British attacked along 15 miles, and the French along 10 miles.
The battle was the result of an Allied offensive, fought to relieve the incredible pressure on the French at Verdun. The opening artillery barrage was so heavy that it could be heard in southern England. However, so effective were the German defences that German troops survived the massive week-long preliminary bombardment almost unscathed. The Germans had deep trenches, effective bomb-proof shelters, and barbed wire as thick as a man's finger, up to 40 yards deep in places. As British infantry began to cross no man's land, German soldiers left their deep, well-protected bunkers and manned their machine-gun emplacements. Around 20,000 Britons were killed on the first day, while another 40,000 were either wounded or reported lost. During the four-and-a-half-month battle, the Allies managed to make a small advance of around 6 miles, at a cost of 146,000 lives. The German death toll was 164,000. Casualties were 420,000 British, 195,000 French and 650,000 German. After this battle, commentators began to speak of the 'lost generation' of British men. Fifty-one VCs were won at the Somme, seventeen posthumously, all going to NCOs or officers. For a private to be awarded a VC was rare.

THE ROMANIAN CAMPAIGN, August 1916–December 1917
Fighting in the 'Balkan theatre' took place across most of what is now Moldavia, Romania, including Transylvania which was part of Austria-Hungary, and north-eastern Bulgaria.
Romania entered the war after Allied successes, to try and to seize

Transylvania, a province of Hungary with a majority-Romanian population. Despite initial successes, the combined Russo-Romanian forces suffered several setbacks, and by the end of 1916 only Moldavia remained under Allied control. In 1917, the Allied front collapsed when the Bolsheviks took Russia out of the war. Romania, left surrounded by the Central Powers, signed an armistice. On 10 November 1918, a day before the German armistice, Romania re-entered the war. By then, about 220,000 Romanian soldiers had been killed.

THE MONASTIR OFFENSIVE, 12 September–11 December 1916
Monastir is now known as Bitola, in southern Macedonia. It was on the Salonika Front (Thessaloniki) in the war in north-eastern Greece.
The Allies tried to break the stalemate on the Macedonian front by attacking Bulgaria and relieving Romania. After a three-month battle, Monastir was taken. It suffered almost total destruction in the war. The Bulgarians and then the Germans fought at Monastir six times and gave way five times, retreating about 35 miles. The Central Powers lost around 61,000 men. Allied casualties were 27,337 Serbs, 13,786 French, 4,580 British, 1,116 Russians and up to 1,000 Italians. However, 80,000 Allied troops died or were evacuated with sickness, giving around 130,000 casualties.

1917

THE HINDENBURG LINE, February 1917–1918
This stretched from Verdun along the Franco-Belgian border to the North Sea.
Because of the tremendous losses incurred at Verdun and during the Somme Offensive, German forces between Cambrai and St Quentin withdrew to a new defensive line during February and March 1917. This disrupted General Nivelle's planned French offensive, of which the German General Staff had discovered the main details. The Germans called their planned retreat Operation Alberich. The defences were known as the *Siegfriedstellung*, the Siegfried Line, and the complex system of defensive fieldworks and mutually supporting fortifications was named the Hindenburg Line by the Allies. The defences were thought to be virtually impregnable. The withdrawal straightened the German line, reducing its length by 25 miles and releasing thirteen divisions for service in the reserve. The retreat was accompanied by the systematic destruction of the newly abandoned areas, to deprive the Allies of any shelter, and the planting of mines and booby traps to render the advance as dangerous as possible. The defences embodied

German acceptance of the 'strategic defensive policy', whereby they would incur fewer losses than attacking forces. More of a series of fortified zones than a single line, Haig was determined that they should be overcome within the next few weeks as part of a general Allied offensive. Lloyd George, in a 1917 speech welcoming America's entry into the war, said, 'The most characteristic of Prussian institutions is the Hindenburg line. What is the Hindenburg line? The Hindenburg line is a line drawn in the territories of other people, with a warning that the inhabitants of those territories shall not cross it at the peril of their lives. That line has been drawn in Europe for fifty years.'

The Hindenburg Line comprised five operational zones, or *stellungen*, which were named after figures of German mythology (from north to south): Wotan, Siegfried, Alberich, Brunhild, and Kriemhild. The most powerful of these sections was the Siegfried Line, which stretched 100 miles from Lens to Reims. It was built in just five months thanks to a massive workforce of more than 500,000 labourers, including German civilians and Russian prisoners of war. The defensive works comprised deep trenches, up to 18 feet deep and 13 feet wide, and dugouts with bands of barbed wire entanglements at least 65 feet wide in front of the front trench. Pillboxes and shelters were protected by reinforced concrete and sheets of steel. A line of more lightly defended outposts was built about 2 miles in front of the main line to slow down any Allied attack. Massive banks of artillery and machine-gun nests were perfectly positioned to eliminate any advancing infantry. As the war progressed a series of anti-tank ditches were also dug in front of the front lines. Temporarily abandoned during the last German bid for victory in March–April 1918, its re-garrisoning in 1918 was a last-ditch attempt to prolong the fighting into 1919.

THE NIVELLE OFFENSIVE, 16 April–9 May 1917 – 'THE ASSAULT THAT WOULD END THE WAR WITHIN FORTY-EIGHT HOURS' – General Nivelle

Generals Nivelle and Haig believed that the Germans were on the run, and very mistakenly expected casualties of only around 10,000 men with their offensive against the Hindenburg Line. Germany had discovered the plans for a three-stage attack. There was to be a British attack at Arras and Vimy Ridge, to capture high ground and divert German reserves from the French front. Complementing this, the French would attack on the Chemin des Dames Ridge, in what came to be known as the Second Battle of the Aisne and the Third Battle of Champagne. Having broken through the German lines, the British and French armies would meet and march upon Germany. This paper exercise carried out at HQ went horribly wrong, as the generals underestimated the power of German defences and their improved supply lines. German defences of 480,000 men faced 1,200,000 Allies with 7,000 artillery pieces.

Of a total of 128, 118 French and British tanks were destroyed, mostly by artillery fire. German losses were 163,000 men, including up to 20,000 taken prisoner. French casualties during 16–25 April alone were estimated at 118,000, of which 28,000 were killed, 80,000 wounded, 5,000 died of wounds and 5,000 were taken prisoner. Of the 80,000 French soldiers wounded, only 20,000 were fit to return to their units by 30 April. In 1920 it was estimated that British casualties were 160,000 and Russian casualties were 5,183. In 2005 Doughty quoted figures of 134,000 French casualties on the Aisne for 16–25 April, of whom 30,000 were killed, 100,000 were wounded and 4,000 were taken prisoner. The rate of casualties was the worst since November 1914, and the French could take no more bloodshed.

FRENCH MUTINY, 3 May–9 May 1917

The bloody Nivelle offensive had advanced the front line in part, by around 4 miles. By 25 April most of the fighting had ended. With the generals expecting only 10,000 casualties, there had been little medical assistance for the dead and dying. French troops had been virtually promised that the war was won, and had suffered massive losses. On 3 May, the French 2nd Division refused to follow its orders to attack, and this mutiny soon spread throughout the army. Towards the end of the offensive, the 2nd Division arrived on the battlefield drunk and without weapons. From 16–17 May there were disturbances in the 127th, 18th, 166th, 3rd, 18th and 17th divisions. The 69th Division petitioned for an end of the offensive. By 28 May full mutinies broke out in the 9th, 158th, 5th divisions and 1st Cavalry Division. By the end of May more units of the 5th, 6th, 13th, 35th, 43rd, 62nd, 77th and 170th divisions mutinied, and revolts occurred in twenty-one divisions in May. Around 27,000 French soldiers deserted, and the Nivelle offensive was suspended on 9 May. On 16 May Nivelle was sacked and replaced by the considerably more cautious Pétain, with Foch as chief of the General Staff. The new commanders abandoned the strategy of offensive warfare to one of recuperation and defence, to avoid high casualties and to restore morale. Pétain had between forty and sixty-two mutineers shot as examples – a small amount – and introduced reforms to improve the welfare of French troops, which had a significant effect in restoring morale.

'THE WHITE WAR' – TENTH BATTLE OF THE ISONZO, 12 May–8 June 1917

The Isonzo (in Italian) or Soča (in Slovene) is an 86-mile-long river in the Alps, flowing for 59 miles through western Slovenia and 27 miles in north-eastern Italy. 'The White War' refers to the Alpine snow and freezing conditions. This engagement was fought near Trieste, and around Gorizia in the Soča Valley. With nine largely unsuccessful Isonzo battles conducted within eighteen months, the Italians feared German intervention to aid their weakening Austro-Hungarian ally on the Italian front. It had become a war of attrition, and with each renewed battle, casualties tended to be higher on the Italian side as it was the attacker. At the end of the inconclusive tenth battle the Italians had suffered 157,000 casualties, including 27,000 men taken prisoner, while the Austrians had suffered 75,700 casualties, including 23,400 prisoners.

BATTLE OF MESSINES RIDGE, 7 June 1917
Just south of Ypres, Belgium.

The hills around Messines had been controlled by the Germans since 1914, and to give the Allies a necessary morale boost, the Allied High Command ordered an attack on Messines Ridge. The Allies had spent time digging tunnels packed with explosives underneath the ridge. Nineteen huge mines were detonated. The stunned German troops on the ridge were easily taken by Australian and New Zealand troops that attacked the ridge after the explosions. More than 10,000 German soldiers died instantly. Those who survived were severely stunned and had no idea what had happened. Around them were craters of more than 400 feet in diameter. Around 7,300 Germans were taken prisoner, while the rest retreated in shock. Although a relatively small battle, it had considerable psychological impact for both sides. It also broke the Germans' hold on the ridge, forcing them to retreat eastward. It was the beginning of a slow but continuous loss of ground by German forces in the west.

PASSCHENDAELE, THIRD BATTLE OF YPRES, 20 September–6 November 1917
North-east of Ypres.

The 'Third Battle of Ypres' became bogged down in torrential rains and mud, but British forces continued to push the Germans back a few hundred yards at a time toward the high ridge at Passchendaele. Conditions for the troops were appalling. Trench foot was common on both sides. The Germans fought back with mustard gas, a slow-acting chemical agent that maimed or killed enemy soldiers via severe blisters on the skin, or internally if breathed. The fight for Passchendaele itself, and the extra height the area would give the Allies, started on 12 October. By 6 November the area had been captured for the Allies at terrible loss for both sides. For less than half a mile of land, the British suffered 310,000 casualties, while German casualties numbered 260,000. This proved to be the last great battle of attrition on the Western Front. Captain Edwin Vaughan of the BEF wrote on 27 August 1917, 'The cries of the wounded had much diminished now, and as we staggered down the road, the reason was only too apparent, for the water was right over the tops of the shell holes.'

CAPORETTO, also known as THE TWELFTH BATTLE OF THE ISONZO and the BATTLE OF KARFREIT, 24 October–19 November 1917
Near Kobarid, now in Slovenia.
The Italians and Austrians fought battle after battle along the Isonzo River, and although losses were huge, progress by either side was negligible. The situation continued largely unchanged, until the Italians were defeated in the disastrous Battle of Caporetto by combined German and Austrian forces. The Italians were forced to retreat from the area. The Italians lost 300,000 men, of whom about 270,000 were captured and held as prisoners. Nearly all artillery guns were lost. A combined total of 750,000 casualties were lost on both sides during two and a half years of fighting along the Isonzo, in which nothing substantial was accomplished.

THE BATTLE OF CAMBRAI, 20 November–7 December 1917
Cambrai is in the Nord-Pas-de-Calais, northern France.
This was a key supply point for the *Siegfriedstellung*, part of the Hindenburg Line. It was a ground-breaking battle, as the Allies used what was then a revolutionary method of attack, utilising massed tanks and aircraft. This method was intensively studied and evolved into the *blitzkrieg* methods of the German Army in the Second World War. The Germans were surprised by an intense artillery attack upon the Hindenburg Line. Over 350 British tanks advanced across the ground, supported by infantry and an artillery rolling barrage that gave them cover from a German counter-attack. The 62nd Division covered more than 5 miles in this attack from their starting point. However, the 2nd Cavalry Division had a problem crossing the vital St Quentin Canal when a tank went over its main bridge and it collapsed. This was the bridge that the cavalry were supposed to use to advance to Cambrai.

Elsewhere, British units hit heavy resistance. By 30 November, the Germans were ready to counter-attack and defend Cambrai. Many British Army units became isolated and their command structure broke down in places. The German counter-attack was so effective that on 3 December, Haig gave the order that British units still near Cambrai should withdraw. The failure to build on the initial success of the attack was blamed upon middle-ranking commanders. German losses were about 45,000, while the British lost 55,207 men. Of Britain's 378 combat tanks, 179 were lost. Twenty-eight Americans digging trenches behind the front lines were victims to shellfire, the first American casualties of the war.

1918

DER KAISERSCHLACHT, THE EMPEROR'S BATTLE, 21 March 1918

In 1918 the Hindenburg Line was the starting point of one last push by Germany, inspired by the Kaiser. Some 900,000 men had been freed from the Eastern Front, and Germany enjoyed superiority in numbers on the Western Front for the first time since the earliest days of the war. Nonetheless, all sides, including Germany, were exhausted. Soon to join the Allies were 300,000 new American troops, and Germany had to try and win the war before the Americans were deployed. The objective was to push across the River Somme and then take Paris, whereby France would collapse. Their unexpected attack began with a heavy artillery barrage, lasting only five hours, a lesson learned from the Brusilov Offensive, and including a heavy concentration of poison gas shells.

As the Germans surged forward, they brought with them the newest long-range artillery cannons developed by Krupp, which enabled them to fire accurately upon Paris from a range of over 70 miles. On 23 March, shells killed more than 250 unsuspecting Parisians. On 24 March, the Germans raced across the River Somme, capturing the bridges before the French could destroy them. On 25 March, the Allied front broke precisely between the French and British troop lines. Only the appointment of Marshall Foch, as overall Allied commander-in-chief on the Western Front, prevented a wedge being driven between the armies.

MOREUIL WOOD, 30 March–5 April 1918

12 miles south of Amiens. (See Animals at War, Horses.)
German momentum continued for another five days, but the British still held the crucially important Vimy Ridge, and Ludendorff threw

his troops against the town of Amiens. Although they came within 11 miles, the Germans had great difficulty capturing Amiens and its railway junction, which the British and French were told to hold at all costs. Lacking sufficient horses, the Germans also had problems delivering artillery and supplies to their front-line troops. By the morning of 30 March, Germans had occupied Moreuil Wood. An Allied force including British and Canadian horses and air brigades launched a counter-offensive, and by the end of the day, the Allies had managed to halt the German advance there, despite suffering heavy casualties. Moreuil Wood broke the momentum of the German attacks. The German offensive had been successful up to this point, with a gain of almost 40 miles of territory and inflicting heavy losses on the Allies. Some 177,739 British troops died or were taken prisoner during the offensive, at a daily rate of 11,000 men. The French lost nearly 80,000 men. However, German troops had also lost over a quarter of a million men to injury or death. Ludendorff called off the attacks on 5 April, but the next stage of the offensive would begin just four days later.

THE BATTLE OF LYS, THE LYS OFFENSIVE, THE THIRD BATTLE OF FLANDERS, THE FOURTH BATTLE OF YPRES, 9–29 April 1918

Ludendorff was desperate to win the war before the ever-increasing number of American troops in France could enter the fighting. The German aim was now to capture Ypres and the surrounding high ground around Messines. The Germans planned to attack the 1st Army south of the River Lys before moving north-west. At Neuve Chapelle 50,000 German troops attacked 20,000 Portuguese soldiers who were due to be relieved that day. The Germans broke through and the 1st Army was forced to pull back to cover the gap created in the Allied line. Another German attack on 10 April took the Messines Ridge. Another advance retook Passchendaele. The Australian 1st Division famously halted the German advance 5 miles from the Allied logistics centre at Hazebrouk.

Between 10 and 14 April, British troops were so embattled that Haig, from a safe distance, issued his famous statement, 'With our backs to the wall, and believing in the justice of our cause, each of us must fight on to the end', and asked Foch for reinforcements. The Germans continued to advance and took several key targets but the attack had started to stall by 29 April with the arrival of French reinforcements. Ludendorff called a halt to the attack. The gains at the Battle of Lys were the last the Germans made in the war. The Germans lost 120,000 killed, wounded or missing, while British and French losses had been on the same scale. While the initial territorial gains in the battle may have boosted German confidence in their High Command, they could not keep coping with such losses.

SECOND BATTLE OF THE MARNE, 15 July–16 September 1918 – THE BEGINNING OF THE END

East and West of Reims.

Von Ludendorff was still convinced that an attack in Flanders was the best route to a German victory, and decided to launch a great diversionary attack further south in order to lure Allied troops away. This attack at the Marne, launched after the German capture of the strategically important Chemin des Dames ridge near the Aisne River on 27 May, was the latest stage of the 'Kaiser's battle'. Forty German divisions attacked the French east and west of Reims. It was an attempt to divide and conquer the French forces, which were joined by 85,000 US troops as well as a portion of the British Expeditionary Force (BEF), most of which was still located in Flanders. When the Germans began their advance after an initial artillery bombardment, however, they found that the French had set up a line of false trenches, manned by only a few defenders. The real front line of trenches lay further on, and had scarcely been touched by the bombardment. This deceptive strategy had been put in place by the new French commander-in-chief, Philippe Pétain.

As a German officer, Rudolf Binding, wrote in his diary of the 15 July attack, the French 'put up no resistance in front … they had neither infantry nor artillery in this forward battle-zone … Our guns bombarded empty trenches; our gas-shells gassed empty artillery positions … The barrage, which was to have preceded and protected [the attacking German troops] went right on somewhere over the enemy's rear positions, while in front the first real line of resistance was not yet carried.'

As the Germans approached the 'real' Allied front lines, they were met with a fierce barrage of French and American fire. Trapped and surrounded, the Germans suffered heavy casualties, setting the Allies up for the major counter-attack they would launch on 18 July. After suffering massive casualties, Ludendorff was forced to call off a major German offensive further north, in the Flanders region, which he had envisioned as Germany's best hope of victory. The Second Battle of the Marne turned the tide of war decisively towards the Allies, who were able to regain much of France and Belgium in the months that followed. Germany lost 139,000 dead or wounded, with

29,367 captured and 793 guns lost. Dead or wounded among the Allies were 95,165 French, 16,552 British, 12,000 Americans and 9,000 Italians.

MEGIDDO, 19–25 September 1918 – ARMAGEDDON
On the Plain of Sharon in the Judaean Hills, in Ottoman Syria, 60 miles north of Jerusalem.
Following the British success in capturing Jerusalem in December 1917, further progress north was halted in the face of strengthened German forces. In part this was because troops had been quickly transferred to the Western Front in March 1918 to assist in the Allies' defence against the German Spring Offensive. On 18 September Sir Edmund Allenby launched the Battle of Megiddo at Rafat. Of 35,000 Ottoman troops, only 6,000 escaped death or capture. This started a series of victories including battles at Damascus and Beirut. Because of these overwhelming victories Turkey sued for an armistice of surrender, which was agreed on 30 October 1918 in Mudros. British forces subsequently took possession of Constantinople (Istanbul) on 10 November 1918. Megiddo is the site of the Biblical Armageddon.

THE END
Towards Autumn 1918, the Central Powers were failing on all fronts. The reinvigorated Allies launched a massive attack on the German lines. In September 1918 the Allies used a huge number of tanks to break through the Hindenburg Line and by 10 October it had been completely overwhelmed. In just a few weeks the German Army had collapsed and the Kaiser abdicated. The blame was put on weak politicians rather than on military exhaustion. The Allied advance to victory was fast. Despite the Turkish victory at Gallipoli, later defeats by invading forces and an Arab revolt destroyed the Ottoman Empire's economy, and the Turks signed a peace treaty with the Allies on 30 October 1918. The Austro-Hungarian Empire, dissolving from within due to growing nationalist movements among its diverse populations, signed an armistice on 4 November.

   Food shortages in Germany itself had pushed many civilians to the brink of starvation. Farmers were short of labourers to bring in the harvest as young men had been drafted into the military. By the 'Turnip Winter' of 1916–17, the supply of potatoes had run out and the only real alternative was turnips. By 1918, Germany was producing only 50 per cent of the milk it had before the war. Lack of food had seriously weakened the ability of people to fight off disease. Influenza had a terrible impact on Germany as its people had little strength to fight the illness. It is thought that nearly 750,000 died of a combination of flu and starvation.

In October 1918, Germany's naval command at Kiel decided at last to take on the British Navy which was blockading Germany's northern ports and starving the nation. British submarines patrolled constantly off the north German coast and such a mission would have been suicidal, so the sailors of Kiel mutinied rather than go on such a mission. Officers were killed and ships were taken over. The army was not sent to crush this mutiny as the Kaiser and his government could not trust that they would not join the sailors. Demonstrations and strikes took place all over Germany and soldiers joined the protests. By early November 1918, many German cities had been taken over by workers' and soldiers' councils, and politicians were fearful of a communist takeover. The leading party in Germany's Reichstag was the Social Democrat Party, led by Friedrich Ebert, and he pleaded with the Kaiser to abdicate to save Germany from revolution. Despite dwindling resources on the battlefield, the threat of mutinies, discontent on the home front and the surrender of his allies, the Kaiser refused.

Upon 9 November the Social Democrats announced that the Kaiser had abdicated, although he had not. However, there was a general strike in Berlin at that time and the Social Democrats feared that extremists would take over and anarchy would occur. The Social Democrats thus announced that Germany was now a republic and that the country would be run by the Reichstag. The following day the Kaiser fled to Holland, and on 11 November 1918 an armistice was declared. Over 9 million soldiers had died in the war, and 21 million were wounded, many with life-changing injuries or illnesses. Civilian casualties caused indirectly by the war numbered close to 10 million. The nations most affected were Serbia, Germany and France, each of which sent 80 percent of their male populations between the ages of fifteen and forty-nine into battle. Mainly a war on land, it marked the fall of four imperial dynasties: those of Germany, Austria-Hungary, Russia and Turkey.

3

The First World War at Sea: How 'Cowardly Weapons' Nearly Won the War

There was a famous music hall song of the day which summed up public feelings towards the beloved and powerful Royal Navy and Germany: 'It's the Navy, the Fighting Navy,/We will keep them in their place,/For they know they'll have to face/The gallant little lads, in Navy blue ....'

The range and power of naval fleets, along with their ambition to control the world's waterways, were major reasons that the First World War spread so quickly. However, new technologies made it unpredictable. Mines, torpedoes, and submarines introduced new threats that made the greatest warships suddenly vulnerable to far cheaper vessels. Both Britain and Germany were unsure how best to use these new naval forces, and both were reluctant to commit their main fleets to heavy battles. In the First World War, naval power was more often used to maintain control of trade routes than to capture new territory, but Germany had best developed the most effective weapon of all – the *unterseeboot* – the U-boat.

The Bravest Service

As in the Second World War, the men of the Merchant Navy were the bravest, supplying not only Britain with food and supplies, but also its forces fighting across the globe. The UK, as in the Second World War, suffered disproportionately compared to its Allies. If we include neutral shipping sunk by Central Powers, then Britain suffered two-thirds of all merchant tonnage lost. Of Allied merchant shipping, Britain lost 76 per cent of the tonnage. If we do not include American shipping lost before the US entered the war, the figure is higher still. Almost 15,000 British merchant sailors were lost at sea.

Allied and Neutral Country Ship Losses in WWI

Country	Tonnage
United Kingdom (65 per cent of all losses)	9,055,000
Norway (neutral)	1,172,000
Italy	862,000
France	531,000
United States	531,000
Greece	415,000
Japan	270.000
Sweden (neutral)	264,000
Denmark (neutral)	245,000
Spain (neutral)	238,000
Holland (neutral)	229,000
Belgium	105,000
TOTAL	13,917,000

The Seasick Visionary Who Oiled Our Ships and Gave Us OMG!

Admiral John Arbuthnot 'Jackie' Fisher (1841–1920) suffered from seasickness all his life. Fisher was probably the most important figure in British naval history, serving for over sixty years. He joined in 1854 as a thirteen-year-old, serving on *Calcutta*, an old ship of the line with eighty-four guns but with only sail for propulsion. On his first day, he was in tears on seeing eight men being flogged in front of the ship's company. He served in the Crimean War, became a midshipman and served in the Second Opium War, and in 1860 passed his lieutenant's examination with top grades, including the highest score ever for navigation. In 1863, Fisher was gunnery lieutenant on *Warrior* (now in Portsmouth Harbour), the first all-iron seagoing armoured battleship and the most powerful ship in the fleet. His expertise with torpedoes led to him preparing a paper on the design, construction and management of electrical torpedoes, the cutting-edge technology of the time. As Mackay says, 'at the early age of twenty-eight, Fisher was promoted to commander, and served on HMS *Ocean*, flagship on the China Station. Here he wrote on new naval tactics, and installed a system of electrical firing so that all guns could be fired simultaneously. *Ocean* was the first vessel to be so equipped.' He was later captain of HMS *Inflexible*, bombarding Alexandria in 1882, and was placed in charge of a landing party. Lacking any reconnaissance, Fisher armoured a train with iron plates, machine gun and cannon. He became celebrated as a hero and met Queen Victoria.

From 1886 to 1890, Fisher was responsible for the development of quick-firing guns, to be used against the growing threat from torpedo boats and submarines. His expertise forced shipyards to reduce the time they took to complete a ship, making savings in cost and allowing new designs to enter service more rapidly. As Third Sea Lord, Fisher decided to develop torpedo boat destroyers armed with quick-firing small-calibre guns, which he suggested should be called 'destroyers'. The first destroyers were a success and many more were ordered. Fisher conducted all manoeuvres at full speed while training the fleet, and expected the best from his crews. Unusually, he would socialise with junior officers so that they were not afraid to approach him with ideas.

When appointed First Sea Lord in 1904, Fisher controversially removed 154 ships from active service. He called them 'too weak to fight, and too slow to run away' and immediately began constructing a modern fleet, prepared to meet Germany's growing strength. Fisher saw the need to improve the range, accuracy and firing rate of naval gunnery, and was one of the earliest proponents of torpedoes, which he believed would supersede big guns for use against ships. Fisher was almost solely responsible for the construction of HMS *Dreadnought*, the first all-big-gun battleship, and the class of battleships which followed it. His new 'destroyer class' was added to the fleet, and he also produced a new type of cruiser in a similar style to *Dreadnought*. This new 'battlecruiser' could achieve a high speed at the expense of armour protection. He also believed that submarines would become increasingly important and urged their development amid strong opposition.

Fisher forced through the introduction of more powerful and efficient turbine engines to replace reciprocating designs, and the introduction of oil fuelling to replace coal. Replacing coal with oil allowed the construction of a smaller, more economical ship with the same performance, or a much more powerful ship of the same size. The problem for Britain was security of supply, as it had little oil. Its naval and mercantile might had been based upon huge reserves of excellent Welsh steam coal, which had been particularly suited for use by warships. Oil was superior to coal as a fuel for ships. The Royal Navy experimented until 1904, when it solved the technical problems, and from that time most of its destroyers were fuelled entirely by oil. The supply issue, however, meant that oil was used initially only as an auxiliary to coal in cruisers and battleships. By 1912, the case for oil had become so compelling that construction began of entirely oil-fuelled cruisers and battleships. The British were extremely fortunate to have a visionary, who, like his great supporter Winston Churchill, recognised the German threat before the First World War.

In 1908, Fisher predicted that war with Germany would break out in October 1914, following the anticipated completion date of work on the Kiel Canal to allow the passage of German battleships between the Baltic to the North Sea. However, the Kiel Canal was completed early, in July, and war commenced in August 1914. Fisher was forced to retire in 1911 upon reaching seventy years of age, but became First Sea Lord again in November 1914. He resigned seven months later in frustration over Churchill's Gallipoli Campaign. Fisher always believed that nations fought wars for material gain, and that maintaining a strong navy deterred other nations from engaging it in battle, thus decreasing the likelihood of war. He is credited by the *Oxford English Dictionary* with the earliest known use of the phrase 'OMG' as an abbreviation for 'Oh my God', but in Fisher's case it was 'Oh! My God!' in a letter to Churchill dated 9 September 1917.

'Castles Of Steel' – The Dreaded Dreadnoughts

From 1910, batteries of small surface guns were added to existing battleships and cruisers. The all-steel, armoured battleships had breech-loading artillery mounted on revolving turrets, but were rendered obsolete by the dreadnought class from 1906. The original *Dreadnought* was the most heavily armed ship in history, with ten 12 inch guns whereas the previous record was four 12 inch guns. The gun turrets were situated higher to allow more accurate long-distance fire. In addition to her 12 inch guns, the *Dreadnought* also had twenty-four 3 inch guns and five torpedo tubes below water. In the waterline section of her hull, the *Dreadnought* was armoured by steel plates 11 inches thick. She was the first major warship driven solely by steam turbines, and was faster than any other warship, reaching speeds of 21 knots (24 mph). The introduction of this new class of warship resulted in an arms race between Britain and Germany. By 1914 the Royal Navy had nineteen dreadnoughts (thirteen under construction), compared with Germany's thirteen (seven under construction). Other fleets with dreadnoughts at sea by 1914 were the United States with eight, France with eight, Japan with four, Austria-Hungary with two and Italy with one. In 1915 Britain produced the *Queen Elizabeth*, the first of the 'Super-Dreadnoughts'. It had eight 15 inch guns, each capable of firing a 1,920-pound projectile 35,000 yards. This was followed by four more ships of the same design.

The Royal Navy had built forty-two armoured cruisers between 1885 and 1907, but upon Admiral Fisher's orders they were gradually replaced by battlecruisers, with the speed of a cruiser and the power of a battleship. Torpedo boats were fast, light surface craft armed with torpedoes, and the Royal Navy had to develop strategies to deal with the expected swarms of torpedo boats attacking at high speed. Fisher developed small, fast 'destroyers' as defence for battle fleets against the new threat of torpedo boats. Armed with torpedoes, destroyers were generally deployed in flotillas of four to twenty ships, which accompanied battleships and battlecruisers. Britain's losses of 102 of its most expensive capital ships – thirteen battleships, twenty-five cruisers and sixty-four destroyers – were immense, at 40 per cent of the total losses upon both sides. For the dearest ships, battleships and cruisers, the rate is even higher, at 47 per cent. There was no real decisive clash between battle fleets in the First World War. Jutland was indecisive, and Germany never risked its huge capital ships again, with Germany realising that U-boats could win the war. Battleships were helpless against the cheaper weapons of submarines. This period has echoes in today's decision by Britain to buy aircraft carriers, now virtually helpless against attack by dozens of pilotless drones at once.

Warships Destroyed in the First World War

Nation	Battleship	Cruiser	Destroyer	Gunboat	Torpedo boat	Sub	Total
Allies							
Britain	13	25	64	7	11	54	174
France	4	5	11	2	8	12	42
Russia	4	2	14	1		14	35
Italy	3	3	8	1	6	8	29
Japan	1	4	2		1		8
USA		3	2	1			6
ALLIES	25	42	101	12	26	88	294
Central Powers							
Germany	1	7	68	8	55	200	339
Aus-Hung.		3	2	4	4	7	20
Turkey	1	2	3	4	5		15
CENTRAL POWERS	5	9	75	12	64	207	374
TOTAL	30	53	176	24	90	295	668

How the Ottoman Empire was Tricked into the War

Rear-Admiral Sir Ernest Troubridge (1862–1926) commanded a squadron of four old cruisers in the Mediterranean. Germany had two ships in the Mediterranean at the start of the war, the battlecruiser *Goeben* and the light cruiser *Breslau*. Troubridge was sent to prevent Rear-Admiral Wilhelm Souchon from entering the Adriatic and joining the Austro-Hungarian fleet. However, Troubridge had also received orders that, on the instructions of First Lord of the Admiralty Winston Churchill, the British force in the Mediterranean was not to engage superior forces. Churchill had intended this to mean the Austro-Hungarian and Italian fleets, but Troubridge took it to include the Germans. From his experiences in the Russo-Japanese War, Troubridge was aware that modern naval ordnance could devastate his squadron, and that the *Goeben*'s 11 inch guns considerably outranged his own, which consisted of 9.2 inch and 7.5 inch guns.

Troubridge attempted to catch the Germans in narrow waters to reduce the range, but his flag captain, Captain Wray, argued against seeking battle. The flag captain argued that it would be suicide for the squadron to fight the bigger and longer-ranging guns of the *Goeben*, and as Captain Wray had a particular reputation in the fleet as an expert on gunnery, Troubridge allowed himself to be persuaded. In tears, Troubridge ordered the chase to be abandoned, a decision that caused Wray to say, 'Sir, this is the bravest thing you have ever done.' This enabled the Germans to enter port at Constantinople (Istanbul). Troubridge was court-martialled, and acquitted, but his reputation had been permanently damaged and he was sidelined from command. The Ottoman Empire, centred on what is now Turkey, was neutral at this time. Germany was desperate for allies outside Central Europe, especially in the Mediterranean. High-placed Ottoman officials, such as Minister of War Enver Pasha, thought that an alliance with Germany could help bolster the faltering empire, then known as the 'Sick Man of Europe'.

In August 1914, Ottoman officials had signed a secret treaty promising to aid Germany if Russia attacked Austria-Hungary. Later in August the German warships *Goeben* and *Breslau* docked in Turkey, escaping Troubridge's fleet. The Ottomans promptly bought the ships, renamed them, and incorporated them into the Ottoman navy. German crews remained on board and in control of both vessels. On 27 October, the *Goeben* and *Breslau* sailed under Ottoman flags into the Black Sea, ostensibly to practice manoeuvres. On 29 October, under the command of Wilhelm Souchon, the two ships appeared unexpectedly off the Russian coast, fired on several Russian seaports, sank a Russian gunboat and six merchant ships, and set fire to a Russian oil depot.

It appears that the Germans were working in collaboration with Turkish Minister of War, Enver Pasha. Russia, believing that the attack had come from Turkey, invaded Turkey from the east. Britain and France also responded by attacking Turkish forts along the Dardanelles. Turkey then responded by declaring war on all three. Admiral Souchon, probably along with Enver Pasha, had helped manipulate the Turks into entering the war on the German side, leading to the fall of the Ottoman Empire.

The Baited Trap – The Battle of the Bight, 28 August 1914

The Heligoland Bight is a partly enclosed patch of water off the north coast of Germany, which sheltered several German naval bases. Two British commodores, Reginald Tyrwhitt and Roger Keyes, planned to lure German warships into the open sea, where they would be vulnerable. A small group of British ships sailed into the Bight, and when spotted by German patrols fled out to sea, where a larger British force was waiting. For the first couple of hours, the chasing German ships slipped in and out of a thick fogbank to fire on British ships, but in time they ventured into open waters. After a battle that lasted nearly eight hours, Germany lost three cruisers and 1,200 men, while Britain lost only thirty-five sailors and not a single ship. This defeat intimidated the Kaiser, who now insisted that the German navy should be kept off the open seas and used primarily as a defensive weapon.

The Expected Suicide – The Battle of Coronel, 1 November 1914

The German East Asia Squadron, a small defensive fleet under Vice-Admiral Maximilian von Spee, was based on the Caroline Islands in the western Pacific, near China. When war broke out, von Spee feared being defeated by the much larger Japanese navy, and sailed across the Pacific Ocean to Chile. There was a large German population here, and it would offer a safer base of operations to attack British shipping routes. His fleet soon encountered the British West Indian Squadron, which had been diverted from its patrol duties in South America and the Caribbean, specifically to destroy von Spee's forces and remove the threat to British shipping routes. The British squadron, led by Rear Admiral Sir Christopher Cradock, consisted of obsolete cruisers which were a hopeless match for von Spee's faster and more powerful ships. Cradock's fleet was significantly weaker than von Spee's, consisting of elderly vessels manned by largely inexperienced crews. Cradock's *Good Hope* and *Monmouth* were destroyed with the loss of all 1,600 sailors, including Cradock.

Departing from Port Stanley, Cradock had left behind a letter to be forwarded to Admiral Meux in the case of his death. In it he stated that he did not intend to suffer the fate of Rear-Admiral Ernest Troubridge, who in August had been court-martialled for failing to engage the enemy despite the odds being severely against him. The Governor of the Falklands and the governor's aide both reported that Cradock had not expected to survive.

Revenge for Coronel – The Battle of the Falkland Islands, 8 December 1914

A month after Coronel, the Royal Navy again came across von Spee, whose East Asia Squadron had rounded Cape Horn into the South Atlantic. Von Spee's mission was to disrupt British trade and supply routes as much as possible. However, he made a fateful decision to attack the British colony on the Falkland Islands off Argentina, which he believed would be undefended and an easy victory. He wished to destroy the coaling station and radio station, which was critical to British military communications. Unfortunately for von Spee, an entire British squadron was in port, taking on coal. The squadron was far better equipped than Cradock's had been, with two modern battlecruisers that were faster and better armed than von Spee's ships. The squadron chased the German ships for almost a day, and the ensuing battle ended with the destruction of the German East Asia Squadron. Von Spee went down with his ship, the *Scharnhorst*, and three other German ships and 2,100 German sailors were lost.

'There's Something Wrong with Our Bloody Ships Today, Chatfield' – The Greatest Naval Battle in History, 31 May 1916

The German High Seas fleet was bottled up in the North Sea. Only narrow channels led to the Atlantic Ocean and these were heavily guarded by the Royal Navy. Because of the greater number of British dreadnoughts, a full fleet engagement would probably result in a British victory. German admirals had to try to begin an engagement where they had a tactical advantage. They wished to fight only a part of the Grand Fleet. Failing this, they needed to fight near the German coastline, where their minefields, torpedo boats and submarines could level the odds.

When the more aggressive Admiral von Scheer was appointed to lead the German navy in 1916, he ordered Admiral von Hipper to begin a sweep along the Danish coast with forty ships. He wished to bring the British fleet out for battle on his terms. Behind von Hipper's faster battlecruisers, von Scheer led the rest of the fleet. Admiral Jellicoe ordered the Grand Fleet to put to sea. Vice-Admiral Beatty and fifty-two ships sailed at the same time from the Rosyth base to join Jellicoe's main fleet, which had left Scapa Flow in the Orkneys. Instead Beatty came into contact with von Hipper, who turned away to sail back to von Scheer's fleet. The two fleets opened fire at a range of 10 miles off Jutland, Denmark. Poor visibility created problems for both sides but the position of the sun gave a significant advantage to the German captains.

The first near-disaster of the battle occurred when a salvo from the *Lützow*'s 12 inch guns wrecked 'Q' turret of Beatty's flagship *Lion*. Dozens of crewmen were instantly killed, but catastrophe was averted when the mortally wounded turret commander immediately ordered the magazine doors shut and the magazine flooded. He prevented the propellant from setting off a massive magazine explosion. *Lion* had been hit several more times when it saw the *Indefatigable* blown up, followed by two other ships of the line, with no German losses. There were only two survivors of the 1,019 men on the *Indefatigable*. The next ship down, thirty minutes later, was the *Queen Mary*, with only nine of 1,275 crew surviving. She sank in just under thirty seconds. Seeing von Scheer's fleet sailing towards the battle zone, Beatty ordered the British fleet to head back towards Jellicoe's oncoming fleet. The *Princess Royal* was next reported lost to Beatty, as she was obscured in smoke and spray. She survived, but Beatty now made his famous remark to his flag captain, ordering him to turn more towards the German fleet: 'There seems to be something wrong with our bloody ships today, Chatfield.' The British armour-piercing shells tended to explode outside the German ships' defensive armour, whereas German shells actually penetrated and exploded within the body of British ships.

As Jellicoe's fleet neared, Beatty's *Invincible* was sunk. Twice Jellicoe's line of twenty-four battleships crossed in front of the enemy, when all British guns could fire but only the front guns of the German ships could reply. On the second crossing, the Germans had mounted a massive torpedo attack using their destroyers. As ordered to do in such an event, the British fleet turned away. Jellicoe did not make a serious attempt to intercept the enemy that night and the Germans escaped. Jellicoe had interpreted von Scheer's retreat as an attempt to lure the British fleet into either a submarine trap, a German minefield, or both. He had also received false information that Germany had developed a new torpedo which did not leave a trail of bubbles.

Jellicoe did not follow the retiring German fleet, but decided to sail his fleet south to cut off the Germans when they tried to sail back to port, and later the *Lützow* was sunk, and the *Seydlitz* and *Derfflinger* were badly damaged. The Germans claimed that Jutland was a victory for them as they had sunk more capital ships than the British. Jellicoe claimed that the victory belonged to the British as his fleet was still seaworthy, whereas the German High Seas fleet was not. The British lost more ships (fourteen ships and over 6,000 lives) than the Germans (eleven ships and over 2,500 casualties). However, the German fleet was never again to be in a position to put to sea and challenge the

British Navy in the North Sea. More than 250 warships and 100,000 men of the rival navies had been involved, and it is possibly the last 'line of battle' engagement, where the ships of a fleet form a line end to end. In reality this marked the end of the battleship's supremacy as a warship. The German fleet retired to its bases for the remainder of the First World War, and Germany then began unrestricted submarine warfare. The battle had forced the Germans to switch from using surface ships to U-boats. By November 1917, 2,932 Allied warships were being employed to combat just 170 U-boats.

Unlearned Lessons for the Second World War – How 'Cowardly Weapons' Nearly Won the War

Since the war could not be won on the land, both sides tried to win it at sea. The Royal Navy imposed a blockade around the ports of Central Europe. Even ships carrying food and raw cotton were turned away from Germany into British and French ports. Admiral Tirpitz urged a policy of unrestricted submarine warfare. At first, U-boats obeyed 'prize rules', surfacing before attacking merchant ships and allowing the crew and passengers to get away. However, this was dangerous for the U-boats, and on 4 February 1915, Germany declared a 'war zone' around Britain, within which merchant ships were sunk without warning. In the first six months of 1915, German U-boats sank almost 750,000 tons of British shipping. This 'unrestricted submarine warfare' angered neutral countries, especially the United States. The tactic was abandoned on 1 September 1915, following the loss of American lives on the torpedoed liners *Lusitania* and *Arabic*. The *Lusitania* was sunk off Ireland, with 1,198 deaths, including 128 Americans. Its loss helped to eventually sway public opinion to draw the USA into the conflict. Germany's U-boat campaign against shipping intensified over the course of the war, nearly bringing Britain to her knees in 1917. U-boats were responsible for destroying around half of all the food and supplies transported by the British, and 50 per cent of all British merchant shipping was sunk by U-boats. The strategy was to sink ships faster than they could be built, forcing Britain to have to buy ships, often useless, from all over the world at inflated prices. U-boats generally stayed on the surface, and submerged only to attack ships with torpedoes.

The war showed how vulnerable modern battleships were to cheaper forms of weaponry. When war began the Germans had twenty-nine U-boats at their disposal. In 1914 a single U-boat, *SM U-9*, sank three British armoured cruisers in less than hour. In the first ten weeks of the conflict they sank five British cruisers. British naval commanders therefore kept their fleet well clear of the waters of the North Sea. Although Britain did have a submarine fleet of its own, British naval leaders generally considered submarines to be 'cowardly weapons' and discouraged their use. After failing to seize control of the sea after Jutland in 1916, Germany resumed unrestricted submarine warfare on 1 February 1917. This, coupled with the *Zimmermann Telegram*, brought the United States into the war on 6 April, but the new U-boat blockade had nearly succeeded. Between February and April 1917, U-boats sank more than 500 merchant ships. A ship leaving Britain had a one-in-four chance of being sunk. Britain was dependent upon imports, and during the war, America alone shipped about 7.5 million tons of supplies to France to support the Allied effort. This included 70,000 horses or mules as well as nearly 50,000 trucks, 27,000 railway carriages, and 1,800 locomotives.

From 1914 to 1918, 274 German U-boats sank 6,596 ships. The five most successful U-boats were *U-35* (sank 224 ships), *U-39* (154 ships), *U-38* (137 ships), *U-34* (121 ships) and *U-33* (84 ships). Most of these were sunk near the coast, particularly in the English Channel. Between October 1916 and January 1917 a grand total of 1.4 million tons of Allied shipping was lost to U-boats. During the First World War Germany built 360 U-boats, 178 of which were lost, along with 5,000 submariners. In total they were responsible for the loss of more than 11 million tons of Allied shipping.

In 1915 Allied ships began using depth charges, waterproof bombs which exploded at a chosen depth. Fairly ineffective, between 1915 and the end of 1917 depth charges accounted for the destruction of just nine U-boats. However, they were improved in 1918 and in that year were responsible for destroying twenty-two U-boats. The most successful method of dealing with submarines was placing mines at various depths along busy sea routes. An estimated seventy-five U-boats were destroyed in this way. Minefields were also used to blockade hostile submarine bases. When the USA entered the war there was a stalemate on land and sea, with the odds turning against the Allies. By the time America had landed enough troops to play a significant role, the Russians had signed the Treaty of Brest-Litovsk with Germany, freeing all Germany's eastern forces for the war in the west. French offensives in the north had failed, and ten French divisions mutinied. German troops were being redeployed from the Russian front to Europe, and U-boat attacks were taking a growing toll on Allied shipping. In April 1917 alone, U-boats destroyed more than 800,000 tons.

However, the U-boat threat was eventually conquered by grouping together a large number of merchant vessels into defensive convoys from 1917, surrounded by warships for better protection. The Admiralty had previously resisted the convoy system, fearing losses to its ships. Advances in early sonar technology, and the increased use of aircraft to find and track German U-boats also helped. The extra naval presence brought by the entry of the United States into the war in April 1917 tilted the balance against Germany. In the Second World War, Churchill said that the only battle he was afraid of losing was the longest battle of the war, the War of the Atlantic. U-boats once again almost won the war before the Americans entered, first joining British forces in North Africa in November 1942.

Allied & Neutral Submarines Lost

Year	1914	1915	1916	1917	1918	Total
Lost to submarines	3	396	964	2,439	1,035	4,837
Lost to mines	42	97	161	170	27	497
Lost to surface craft	55	23	32	64	3	177
Lost to aircraft	0	0	0	3	1	4
TOTAL	100	516	1,157	2,676	1,066	5,515

'Motown Makes Mines'

Another 'cowardly weapon' played a major role. Under a treaty signed at The Hague in 1907, placing explosive mines at sea was limited to areas within 3 miles of an enemy's coastline, thereby not endangering neutral ships. Britain and Germany quickly ignored this agreement, and the North Sea was heavily mined, a major problem for the neutral countries of Norway and Sweden, which depended heavily on the North Sea for commerce. Compared to dreadnoughts, which took years to build and were manned by hundreds of men, submarines were cheap and generally used a crew of fewer than two dozen. Mines were cheaper still.

Mines were used extensively to defend coasts, coastal shipping, ports and naval bases around the globe. The Germans laid mines in shipping lanes to sink merchant and naval vessels serving Britain. The Allies targeted the German U-boats in the Strait of Dover and the Hebrides. In an attempt to seal up the northern exits of the North Sea, the Allies developed the North Sea Mine Barrage laid eastwards from the Orkneys to Norway. During a period of five months from June almost 70,000 mines were laid spanning the North Sea's northern exits. The total number of mines laid in the North Sea, the British East Coast, Straits of Dover, and Heligoland Bight is estimated at 190,000 and the total number during the whole of the First World War was 235,000 sea mines. The objective was to prevent U-boats from operating in the North Atlantic, preying on transatlantic shipping.

The US Navy tendered an order for Mk 6 mines in October 1917 together with 80 million feet of steel wire rope, required to moor the mines to the bed of the North Sea. All mine components other than wire rope, explosives, and detonating circuitry were manufactured by Detroit motor companies. A similar barrage had already been placed across the English Channel, forcing U-boats to divert north around Scotland. The new barrage would help close this route, and it also made it hard for U-boats to get supplies. The Mk 6 mine was a 34-inch-diameter steel sphere with a buoyancy chamber and 300 pounds of TNT. A sensor locked the cable reel so the falling anchor would pull the buoyant mine below the surface; and the float extended the pressure-sensitive antennae above the mine. The mine barrage was within a belt 230 miles long and 15–35 miles wide, and the final mines were laid only a matter of days before the end of the war.

The Genius of the Admiralty

In November 1916 the admirals present at the War Committee, including First Sea Lord Jellicoe, told Lloyd George that convoys presented too large a target for enemy ships, and that merchant ship masters lacked the discipline to 'keep station' in a convoy. Because of merchant losses, Britain was starving. In late April 1917 the War Cabinet discussed the 'convoy controversy'. Lloyd George had pressed for the introduction of convoys for merchant vessels but Lord Jellicoe resisted the measure and was asked to make another report to the War Cabinet. He made the report on the submarine menace at the next Cabinet, but there was no mention of convoys. It was therefore decided on 25 April 1917 that the exasperated Lloyd George would formally visit the Admiralty to conduct his own investigation. Between 26 April and the Prime Minister's visit on 30 April, the Admiralty hastily decided that convoys would be given a thorough trial and their structure reorganised.

Not until 24 May 1917 did the Admiralty finally gave in to demands to establish a system of convoys. Under the plan, British warships would provide heavily armed escorts for all ships coming to Britain from the United States, Canada, and other countries. The plan was especially important from the US perspective, as American soldiers would soon begin heading to Britain by ship in large numbers. More than half a dozen convoy gathering points were soon established along the North American coast. The convoys had an immediate and dramatic effect. The number of ships, supplies, and men lost to German submarines fell dramatically, virtually nullifying Germany's effort to force Britain's surrender. However, Britain now had far fewer ships available to protect its coast or to engage the German Navy at sea.

There was a loss of confidence in both Jellicoe and Sir Edward Carson, First Lord of the Admiralty. Carson was replaced in July and Jellicoe was dismissed in December, having declared that nothing could be done to defeat the U-boats. Lloyd George wanted to get rid of Jellicoe in July and again in October, but was prevented by having to appease the Conservatives, when he asked Churchill to return from the Western Front to serve as Minister of Munitions. Jutland had shown that the southern North Sea had been turned by mines and submarines into a maritime 'no-man's land' for battle fleets, but the Admiralty was genuinely clueless about progress. Jellicoe, a dinosaur among naval thinkers, was promoted to Admiral of the Fleet in 1919, having been deliberately sidelined while the war at sea was being won. A grandmaster freemason, he was created 1st Earl Jellicoe and showered with honours, being buried in St Paul's Cathedral. His biographer somehow claimed that Jellicoe was 'the conqueror of the U-boats'. Thus is history rewritten.

Naval Nicknames

Men used nicknames for camaraderie, and sometimes it could be useful. With so many men on board ship, it was easier to remember someone's nickname. Some of the reasons are obvious such as Happy Day, Timber Wood, Snip Taylor or Frosty Snow. Shiner Wright rhymes with Bright. Others owe their origins to entertainment or history, e.g. Rajah Brooke of Sarawak and Brigham Young of the Mormons, but the origins of many are unremembered. Some are: Daisy Bell, Windy Gale, Piggy May, Tommy Thomas, Wiggy Bennett, Dusty Miller, Topsy Turner, Charlie Beresford, Tosh Gilbert, Pony Moore, Guy Vaughan, Spud Murphy, Hookey Walker, Johnny Bone, Jimmy or Dodger or Shiner Green, Charlie Noble, Shiner Black, Nelly Wallace, Rajah Brookes, Bagsy Baker, Chats Harris, Nosey Parker, Sharkey Ward, Ginger Casey, Granny Henderson, Whacker Payne, Banjo West, Nobby Clarke, Nobby Hewitt, Jack Shepherd, Knocker or Snowy or Darky White, Tod Sloan, Tod Hunter, Chippy Carpenter, Doughy Baker, Shiner Wright, Jumper Collins, Cosher Hinds, Jumper Short, Tug Wilson, Happy Day, Gibley Howe, Frosty Snow, Timber Wood, Bandy Evans, Flapper Hughes, Rusty Steel, Slinger Woods, Nobby Ewart, Bogie Knight, Spike Sullivan, Florrie Ford, Dodger Long, Shoey or Smudger or Darky Smith, Buck Taylor, Brigham Young, Harry Freeman, Pedlar Palmer, Charlie Peace, Lottie Collins, Fanny Fields, Bandy Evans, Old Moore, Pincher Martin, Dolly Gray, Betsy Gay and

Snip Taylor. Of course, Welsh, Scottish and Irish crewmembers could also be referred to as Taff, Jock and Paddy/Mick.

Naval nicknames have been applied to many warships at one time or another. The following are just some that served in the war. Dates in brackets are launch dates: EGGSHELLS, *Achilles* (1905); AGGIE, *Agamemnon* (1906); GIN PALACE, *Agincourt* (1913); MAGGIE, *Magnificent* (1894); 'AM AND TRIPE, *Amphitrite* (1898); BILLY RUFFIAN, *Bellorophon* (1907); NORTHO, *Northumberland* (1865); CENTURY ONE, *Centurion* (1911); ONE-EYE, *Polyphemus* (1881); BIG LIZZIE, *Queen Elizabeth* (1914); REZZO, *Resolution* (1916); COCOA BOAT, *Curacoa* (1917); TIDDLY QUID, *Royal Sovereign* (1916); DREADO, *Dreadnought* (1906); TEA CHEST, *Thetis* (1817); TRAFFIE, *Trafalgar* (1887); HE-CAT, *Hecate* (1914); ARCHDEACON, *Venerable*, (1889); ANGRY CAT, *Henri IV* (French, 1899); THE LORD'S OWN, *Vengeance* (1889); NIFFY JANE, *Iphigenia* (1891); and TIN DUCK, *Iron Duke* (1913).

What Does 'Artificial Fog' Have to Do with the Shooting down of the First Zeppelin?

The sea bombardment and raid on Zeebrugge took place on St George's Day, 23 April 1918. German submarines were operating from a base 8 miles inland at Bruges and were inflicting heavy losses on Allied shipping. The U-boats were emerging at Zeebrugge, and the Admiralty decided that this dangerous exit must be closed. A fleet of 162 British and 11 French cruisers, monitors, destroyers, submarines and small craft assembled for the raid. The 4th Battalion Royal Marine Light Infantry and 200 naval ratings formed storming parties. Under cover of a smokescreen and against heavy odds, assault parties from the cruiser HMS *Vindictive* stormed ashore on the Harbour Mole. The smokescreen was the brainchild of Wing-Commander Frank Arthur Brock (1888–1918). He served with the Royal Naval Air Service, later the RFC and RAF, and was in charge of the Royal Navy Experimental Station. Among his inventions was the Dover Flare, used in anti-submarine warfare. His Brock Bullet (or Brock Incendiary Bullet or Brock Anti-Zeppelin Bullet) enabled the first Zeppelin to be shot down. On the Zeebrugge Raid, Brock brought on board a box marked 'Highly Explosive, Do Not Open' that actually contained bottles of vintage port, which were drunk by his men. For the attack, Brock was in charge of the massive smokescreens that were to cover the approach of the raiding party.

His new and improved smokescreen, or 'artificial fog' as he preferred to call it, was a chemical mixture. It was injected directly under pressure into the hot exhausts of the motor torpedo boats and other small craft, or onto the hot interior surface of the funnels of destroyers. At Zeebrugge, Brock was anxious to discover the secret of the German system of sound ranging. He begged permission to go ashore, not content to watch the action from an observation ship. Brock joined a storming party on the Mole and was killed in action. His body was never recovered.

As the storming parties drew the enemy fire, three block ships were sailed into the harbour and, just after midnight, there was a tremendous explosion. The submarine C3 had been blown up as planned, under the viaduct joining the Mole with the mainland. The block ships were sunk in the approaches to the canal entrance and, two and a half hours after the preliminary bombardment had begun, the signal to withdraw was given. Around 7,000 officers, ratings and other ranks were involved in the raid and casualties were 170 killed and 445 wounded or missing. The following honours were awarded: 11 VCs, 21 DSOs, 29 DSCs, 16 CGMs, 143 DSMs and 283 mentions in dispatches. The canal was blocked, which meant that twelve submarines and twenty-three torpedo craft were bottled up in Bruges. It was six months before the Germans were able to use the exit effectively again.

The Guided Missile

Admiral Sir Percy Scott, in *Fifty Years in the Royal Navy* (1919), recounted an incident when the Mediterranean fleet bombarded Alexandria in Egypt for nine hours. A naval brigade was then sent ashore to restore order, and Scott was serving as a lieutenant on the *Inconstant*:

> While gathering up unexploded naval projectiles in the town we found a gigantic 16-inch shell outside the door of a baker's shop, that had penetrated the roof, wrecked the inside but without caus-ing apparent external damage. A sailor remarked, 'I wonder how this ****ing thing came here; there is no hole anywhere.' His mate looked around and seeing one of the extremely narrow alleys of Alexandria behind him replied, 'I suppose it must have made it up this ****ing street.'

Scapa Flow and Hiroshima

After the armistice, seventy-four ships of the German High Seas Fleet were ordered into Scapa Flow, the great British naval base near the Orkneys. They arrived in November 1918, and became a tourist attraction, with boat trips to see them. By June 1919, Rear Admiral von Reuter, the German officer in command at Scapa Flow, knew that Germany would have to accept surrender terms. For months the peace talks had dragged on, with several extensions to the Armistice, and the Treaty of Versailles was not ready until May 1919. The treaty involved the surrender of the interned ships.

Reuter was concerned that the British would seize the ships without notice, and started active planning to scuttle the fleet. When the main part of the British fleet left for exercises on 21 June he gave the order for the German fleet to be scuttled. Reuter signalled the fleet 'Paragraph eleven. Confirm.' This was the code for the immediate scuttle. The only British warships present were the destroyers *Vespa* and *Vega*. They signalled the First Battle Squadron, which returned to base at full speed. The British managed to beach the *Baden* and the cruisers *Nürnberg, Emden* and *Frankfurt*, but all the other major ships sank. In the confusion nine Germans were shot dead, the last kills of the First World War. Over 400,000 tons of modern warships were sunk, the largest loss of shipping in a single day in history. Salvage continued until the advent of the Second World War, and only eight scuttled ships now remain in the Flow. Since Hiroshima, they remain an important source of quality radioactive-free metals, necessary for certain types of sensitive scientific instruments.

4

War in the Air:
The Beginnings of Modern Warfare

The first powered flight had been in December 1903, when the Wright brothers flew their aircraft up to 200 feet, only feet above the ground, at less than 7 mph. The first powered crossing of the English Channel was by Louis Blèriot in 1909, flying at 45 mph at an altitude of 250 feet. Airplanes had previously been rich men's toys, flimsy biplanes or triplanes with barely enough power to lift a single pilot and perhaps a passenger. Aerial warfare did not initially play a major role in the First World War, but technology was rapidly developed. The overall stability, power, speed, manoeuvrability and safety of flying improved tremendously. Aircraft were at first only used for reconnaissance but as the war progressed, planes transmogrified into fighters and bombers. *The Illustrated Encyclopaedia of Military Aircraft* tells us that 'for all practical purposes the warplane came into being at the end of 1914, with the adoption of the machine gun. In the early stages of the war reconnaissance planes, used for observation of enemy troop movements and of artillery fire, used to come into close confrontation with each other. Although these aircraft were unarmed, battle was joined using whatever weapons were to hand, such as pistols and rifles, many of which had been specially adapted for use by air crews; some also carried steel darts to throw at the enemy's fabric-covered planes, and even hooks suspended on cables, a device invented by Captain Alexandr Alexandrovich Kazakov, Russia's leading air ace of the war.'

Training and Survival
Royal Flying Corps pilot training was cursory both because of a shortage of pilots and of people who could train them. A sporting man who could ride a horse and drive a car, i.e. someone independently wealthy, was considered a good candidate for pilot training. Many

recruits had only two or three hours of flying instruction before being expected to fly solo, so ambulances were always on standby at training airfields. In 1914 aircraft were still crude, difficult to control, and a new recruit to the Royal Flying Corps had a great chance of being killed during training. In fact 8,000 young men died in Britain during flight training, more dying from accidents and equipment failures than from enemy action. Survivors were often sent to France having logged only fifteen hours in the air. Incidentally, a third of all RFC pilots were Canadian volunteers. When aircraft took off from England to fly to bases in France for the first time in the war, navigation was based on map reading while in the air and, if visibility allowed, looking out for landmarks on the ground.

Most newly recruited pilots usually flew with less than five hours training, and lasted only an average of about three weeks once they arrived at the Western Front. The poor state of pilot training meant that in 1916 and 1917, the average life expectancy of an RFC pilot dropped to little more than two weeks. The chances of an airman being killed in action were four times higher than in the infantry. The average age of a pilot or aircrew for most of the war was twenty. The average age for a dead pilot or aircrew was twenty-one. Inexperienced pilots not only fell victim to enemy aces but also suffered from bad weather, mechanical problems, anti-aircraft fire or loss of control due to pilot error. It was common for pilots simply to become lost and then run out of fuel over enemy lines. Many were shot from behind without ever having even been aware of their attackers. Although parachutes had been invented decades before, pilots from countries such as Britain were not allowed to carry them, because military leaders believed their use to be 'cowardly'. Towards the end of the war, German pilots were using parachutes.

Cecil Lewis, in his autobiography, *Sagittarius Rising*, mentions flying secretly from France to England for a weekend rendezvous in London. He recalled that the RFC attracted 'adventurous spirits, devil-may-care youth, fast livers, furious drivers, and risk-takers', which gave the infant air force a cachet of style and mystique. Many pilots lived extravagantly and wildly, knowing that their days were numbered. Pilots were allowed to fly for fun during their time off, possibly to give them more airtime and experience. Some Americans disagreed with the USA's initial refusal to join the war and so they formed the *Lafayette Escadrille*, which was part of the French air force and was one of the top fighting units on the Western Front. Planes used a mix of castor oil to fuel them and the pilots always had stomach troubles from breathing the exhausts.

Air Raids

British air-raid casualties totalled 1,414 killed and 3,416 injured.
American Lena Ford, who wrote the lyrics to the popular song 'Keep
the Home Fires Burning', was killed in an air raid on London, along
with her son. During air raids, London policemen rode about on
bicycles or in cars with placards announcing that people should take
cover. Boy Scouts bugled the 'All Clear' when the raids were over.

Types of Planes

At the start of the war, planes were thought to be of little combat use,
with one British general stating, 'The airplane is useless for the purposes
of war.' Thus they were initially mainly used for reconnaissance, feeding
back information for artillery strikes, recording troop movements, etc.
A pilot would fly the plane and take notes, or sometimes a photographer
or observer would ride along with the pilot. The use of aircraft for
reconnaissance grew rapidly during the first few months of the war
and played an increasingly vital role. These early planes were unarmed,
until pilots from opposing sides began to fly in the same airspace, and
see each other flying by. The earliest armaments were bricks, or heavy
objects to try and throw at passing enemy planes. Soon pilots carried
pistols, to try and shoot the other enemy pilot. From these early days,
two different types of plane developed: fighters and bombers.

A few planes were built with a propeller at the back, allowing a clear
view in front of the airplane. However, there were stability problems,
and any piece of the wooden frame or canvas skin that came off the
plane would get sucked into the propeller. The pilot needed a gun
that he could aim by steering the plane, but it couldn't obstruct his
view of the air ahead. Thus the machine gun was adapted for use with
airplanes. There was only room if it was placed above the propeller,
and then the pilot could not see. One design thus placed the gun in
the centre of the nosecone, firing through the centre of the propeller.
Another device was metal deflectors on the propeller blades to ricochet
any bullets that hit the propeller. The invention of 'interrupter gear'
enabled a machine gun to be mounted in the nose, timing its shots to
fire when a propeller blade was not in front of the gun.

There were about seventy different types of planes used during
the war. The Fokker DR. triplane was the finest fighter, used by
Manfred von Richtofen and his 'Flying Circus'. It possessed excellent
manoeuvrability and its rate of climb gave it a major advantage over
Allied planes. In 1916, the Germans controlled the skies over the
trenches, and the English had to develop fighters to regain control of

the air war. The most famous was the Sopwith Camel, which became the most common Allied plane design. Small and lightweight, the Camel shot down 1,294 enemy aircraft, more than any other Allied fighter. However, it was so difficult to fly that more men lost their lives while learning to fly it than by using it in combat. The pilot, engine, armament and controls were all crammed into a 7-foot space at the front of the airplane, which helped give the plane its phenomenal performance, but it also made the plane awkward to control. The Camel featured twin Vickers machine guns which were mounted side by side in front of the cockpit. Camels could also be fitted with up to eight air-to-air rockets, which even in their relatively primitive First World War state proved to be quite effective, and four bombs beneath the fuselage. Largely made out of fabric and wood, the planes were susceptible to fire. Unable to carry a parachute and fearing death by fire, the British ace Mick Mannock carried a pistol, which he claimed he would use on himself if his aircraft ever caught fire.

Bombers

Bomb aiming was initially crude. The pilot or co-pilot simply dropped a small bomb over the side of the aircraft in the general direction of a target. By the end of the war aircraft that could be recognised as long-range bombers had been developed. Much larger than fighters, and far less manoeuvrable, their task was to carry as many bombs as possible, and to drop them on the target with a degree of accuracy. Russia was the first to develop an airplane specifically as a bomber. The Murometz, a large, four-engine airplane that Igor Sikorsky had developed in 1913 as a passenger plane, was adapted for use in 1914 and was used successfully throughout the war. The Germans developed the Gotha while the British introduced the Handley Page bomber. While the deliberate targeting of civilians was not a new military tactic, bombers now made such an aerial attack possible. Now a nation's civilians, its means of war production and supplies, factories and ports, could be attacked from the air.

Fighter Planes

To enable machine guns to fire without shattering the propeller, a French pilot named Roland Garros covered propeller blades with sheets of steel, so bullets bounced off. For a few weeks the Germans could not respond to this new, deadly weapon, until they captured a crash-landed plane and began copying the invention. The main problem was that a bullet could bounce off the propeller in any direction, perhaps wrecking the engine. Even more seriously, it could ricochet backwards and kill the pilot. The Fokker Eindecker (monoplane), operational from July 1915, was the first fighter plane in history with an 'interrupter gear'.

The Fokker Eindecker was equipped first with one and eventually with two machine guns that could fire straight ahead through the aircraft's propellers. It had an immense impact on air combat and put the *Luftstreitkrafte*, the German Air Service, far ahead of the Allies during 1915. The British referred to the feared plane as the Fokker 'Menace' or the Fokker 'Scourge'. In August 1915, the first planes were shot down using machine guns coupled to Fokker's invention of 'interrupter gear'. Using a captured plane, French and British copies were in production within a year, negating Germany's advantage. The Germans began with monoplanes, moved on to biplanes and ended with triplanes. Only later in the war were planes made strong enough to carry guns on their wings. The Royal Flying Corps nicknamed April 1917 'Bloody April' because they lost 245 planes and more than 200 pilots and aircrew, and at least 100 more men were captured and taken as German prisoners of war.

Air Engine Development, 1914 Onwards

The Rolls-Royce Eagle and its successor the Falcon marked the beginning of a famous line of aviation engines that were later used in the Second World War. This liquid-cooled V-12 was developed in 1915, and built in several versions for many types of plane, including the Handley Page heavy bomber. It powered the Vimy plane that John Alcock and Arthur Whitten Brown flew across the Atlantic in June 1919. Mercedes engines powered some of the best-known German fighter planes in the last two years of the war, including the Albatros D.V., Fokker D VII, and Pfalz D XII.

Aces

The top German 'ace' was Manfred von Richthofen, the 'Red Baron' with eighty 'kills'. The other leading aces were René Fonck of France (seventy-five); Edward 'Mick' Mannock of Britain (seventy-three); William 'Billy' Bishop of Canada (seventy-two); Robert Little of Australia (forty-seven) and Eddie Rickenbacker of the United States (twenty-six). Canadian pilots had more kills, received more medals, and logged more flight time than any other country in the British Empire, including Britain.

The Unknown Russian Ace

Alexander Alexandrovich Kazakov DSO, MC, Légion d'Honneur (1889–1919) was the most successful Russian ace. Unofficially he shot down thirty-two German and Austro-Hungarian planes, although his official tally is twenty because only planes which crashed in Russian-held territory were counted. In 1915, Kazakov made the first successful aerial ramming attack. Aerial ramming is a last-ditch tactic, sometimes used when all else has failed. A ramming pilot could use his entire aircraft as a ram or he could try to destroy the enemy's controls, using the propeller or wing to chop into the enemy's tail or wing. Ramming took place when a pilot ran out of ammunition yet still wanted to destroy an enemy, or when his plane had already been damaged beyond saving. Most rammings occurred when the attacker's aircraft was economically, strategically or tactically less valuable than the enemy's, such as by pilots flying obsolescent aircraft against superior ones, or by single-engine aircraft against multiple-engine bombers. In January 1918, in the wake of the Revolution, Kazakov joined the Slavo-British Allied Legion to fight against the Bolshevik Red Army air force. In August 1918, Kazakov became a major in the new RAF (the old RFC), appointed as commanding officer of a squadron of the Slavo-British Allied Legion made up of Sopwith Camel planes. After the British withdrawal from Russia, which left the Russian White Army in desperate straits, Kazakov died in a plane crash during an air show in 1919, which was being performed to boost the morale of the Russian anti-Bolshevik troops. Most witnesses of the incident, including the British ace Ira 'Taffy' Jones, thought Kazakov committed suicide.

The Unknown Welsh Ace with the Fastest Kill Rate

James Ira Thomas 'Taffy' Jones DSO, MC, DFC and Bar, MM, Russian Order of the Cross of St George (1896–1960) was an illegitimate Welsh clerk with a bad stutter who enlisted in the TA in 1913. He transferred to the newly formed RFC, where he served as an air mechanic on ground duties. Jones was posted to France in July 1915, and by January 1916 was flying combat missions as an observer/gunner, winning his Observer's brevet in October 1916. 'Taffy' Jones was awarded the Military Medal in May 1916 for rescuing two wounded gunners under artillery fire when he was working at a wireless interception station in the front line. He was awarded the Russian Order of the Cross of St George in January 1917 after receiving several commendations for bravery. Jones was now sent to England for pilot training, and posted to 74 Squadron in France, where he became a great friend of 'Mick' Mannock (see Heroes). Like Mannock, he was regarded as one of the lower classes by some officers. Jones wrote, 'My habit of attacking Huns dangling from their parachutes led to many arguments in the mess. Some officers, of the Eton and Sandhurst type, thought it was "unsportsmanlike" to do it. Never having been to a public school, I was unhampered by such considerations of form. I just pointed out that there was a bloody war on, and that I intended to avenge my pals.'

Jones flew a Royal Aircraft Factory SE-5 biplane, which was not as agile as a Sopwith Camel in dogfights. In June 1918, Jones became a flight commander, and in July shot down a German plane while flying a badly damaged SE-5a, which collapsed on landing. Throughout his service, Jones had a reputation for crashing his aircraft when attempting to land, reportedly surviving twenty-eight flying accidents of varying severity. In August 1918, there was an announcement that he would be awarded the Distinguished Flying Cross: 'In eleven days this officer attacked and destroyed six enemy aeroplanes, displaying great courage, skill and initiative.' A month later Jones was awarded the Military Cross, his citation reading, 'For conspicuous gallantry and devotion to duty. This officer, one of an offensive patrol, engaged and shot down in flames a two-seater, which fell to earth. Ten days later, on offensive patrol, he shot down a Hannover two-seater, which crashed. The next day, when patrolling, he pursued, overtook and shot down an Albatross two-seater. During the same flight he met a Halberstadt two-seater and killed the observer, who either jumped or fell overboard, but had to break off as his ammunition was finished. The next day he shot a balloon down in flames. Three days later he got a good burst with both guns on a Pfalz Scout, both wings coming off. He has driven two others down out of control.'

Also in September 1918, Jones received a second DFC, being described as 'a gallant officer who in the last three months has destroyed twenty-one enemy'. In November 1918, Jones was awarded the Distinguished Service Order, his citation reading,

> Since joining his present Brigade in May last this officer has destroyed twenty-eight enemy machines. He combines skilful tactics and marksmanship with high courage. While engaged on wireless interception duty he followed a patrol of nine Fokker biplanes, and succeeded in joining their formation unobserved. After a while two Fokkers left the formation to attack one of our artillery observation machines. Following them, Captain Jones engaged the higher of the two, which fell on its companion, and both machines fell interlocked in flames.

Thus he gained a DSO, DFC and Bar in just three months, with a faster 'kill' rate than any other pilot in the war.

By the end of the war, Taffy Jones had scored thirty-seven victories in just three months with 74 Squadron in France. There were probably more 'kills', but those actually witnessed were one balloon destroyed, twenty-eight (and one shared) aircraft destroyed, and six (and one shared) 'down out of control'. Jones next volunteered to fight with the Whites in the Russian Civil War against the Bolsheviks. He retired from the RAF in 1936, but at the age of forty-five tried re-enlist for the Second World War. At Windsor Castle, George VI told him, 'You are too old, Taffy. It's a young man's game.' However, he was recommissioned. In July 1939 Jones was acting Wing Commander at the Bombing and Gunnery School, RAF Porthcawl. While flying an unarmed Hawker Henley, he attacked a Junkers Ju 88 bomber with the only weapon he had, a Very flare pistol. His actions were enough to stop the Junker from bombing Swansea docks. He also reportedly flew several unofficial operations in a Spitfire, taking part in several fighter sweeps over Europe. Among the books he wrote was a biography of his great friend Mick Mannock, *King of Air Fighters*.

Tethered Balloons

Sometimes air balloons, winched up and carrying an observation basket, would be used for reconnaissance. Tethered to the ground, they relayed positions via telegraph. They were easy to shoot down as hydrogen is extremely flammable. They were defended by fighter pilots and anti-aircraft guns. Both sides developed and fired anti-aircraft artillery rounds into the air that released smoke clouds and shrapnel on explosion. Both sides also used special incendiary bullets to exploit their flammability.

How to Shoot down a Zeppelin

Germany used lighter-than-air dirigibles (rigid airships), or Zeppelins, to drop bombs on targets as far away as London and Paris. The slow-moving Zeppelins, which had a long range and could carry a relatively large cargo of explosives, reached the peak of their success early in the war, during 1915. However, as the war continued, the giant airships became increasingly vulnerable to the rapidly improving capabilities of fighter planes. Because of their stealth, Zeppelins were favoured in night bombing raids, killing around 1,500 British citizens. They initially were almost impossible to shoot down, as 'if you shoot a bullet at a balloon of hydrogen, all you get is a small hole'. Not until an incendiary bullet was invented could they be shot down by machine gun fire, forcing the bombing raids to halt. When the raids ended in 1917, 77 of the 115 airships had been shot down.

When the Zeppelins first floated over London in 1915, dropping incendiary bombs from around 1,000 feet overhead, they were unopposed, as it was only ten years after planes had been invented. British planes did not have sufficient climb to reach them. As the British improved their planes, the Zeppelins flew higher, until the crew were passing out in the thin air of the unpressurised cabin. Hydrogen gave the Zeppelins their lift, and hydrogen, unlike helium, is explosively flammable. However, British planes and ground forces still found it difficult to shoot them down. When the British managed to get their improved planes to the height of the Zeppelins, their bullets passed harmlessly through the hull. Within the Zeppelin's rigid canvas shell, gas-impermeable sacs kept the hydrogen carefully segregated from the air. Hydrogen has to have access to air to burn. Puncturing these sacs was not enough, as a bullet hole compared to the scale of the Zeppelin was 'like a pinprick hole in a child's balloon – it takes a long time for the gas to seep out'.

The British needed to rupture the sacs on a great enough scale so that hydrogen and oxygen would mix into a pyrotechnic cocktail. The breakthrough came in the pairing of two revolutionary bullets: one to explode, the other to ignite. In order to rupture the gas bags they used James Pomeroy's exploding bullet, which was fitted with a nitroglycerine tip, primed to explode at the lightest touch. However, used alone these did not ignite the Zeppelins. The bullet's momentary explosion was over before the gases had a chance to mingle. The answer was the invention of the Buckingham incendiary bullet, which drew a trail of phosphorescent flame in its wake. Firing alternate rounds of Buckingham and Pomeroy meant the pilots could deliver flame after puncture. Using this technique, the Zeppelin threat was effectively neutered in 1917.

How Bratwurst Ban Kept the Kaiser's Zeppelins Flying

To a great extent Zeppelin production had been slow because of the lack of numbers of cattle in the war. Germany's 115 airships had required the intestines of around 30 million cattle in their construction. Zeppelin airships were the biggest flying machines and their manufacture placed a huge demand upon cow guts, used to make the cells to hold lighter-than-air gas to make them fly. It took the intestines of more than 250,000 cows to make a single airship. The sausage skins were made wet, then stretched and allowed to dry, when they could be bonded to make perfect containers for gas. Kaiser Wilhelm thus issued an edict that sausages were banned, as the skins were needed to encase gas containers for the Zeppelins. The ban was also imposed upon occupied Austria, Poland and northern France, and the intestines were so valuable that they became known as 'goldbeaters' skins'. Each butcher was required to deliver up the intestines of every animal he killed.

The Beginnings of Modern Warfare

The commander of the Zeppelin Corps, Peter Strasser, said that bombing civilians was necessary: 'There is no such thing as a non-combatant any more. Modern war is total war.' In September 1914, a Zeppelin dropped three 200-pound bombs on Antwerp, and in January 1915 bombs were dropped in Norfolk, before London came under attack from May 1915. Dr Hugh Hunt stated, 'For the first time, aeroplanes and airships, luxury toys, became instruments of war. And for the first time, a capital city was under attack when the battlefield was nowhere near it. The Zeppelin bombings were the beginning of modern warfare' (*Attack of the Zeppelins*, Channel 4, 26 August 2013).

5

Casualties of the First World War

Technically, casualties is the term for the total number of people who are killed, wounded, or captured in a battle. Use of this word varies, but historians generally follow this convention. The following list does not include the thousands of Merchant Navy seamen who lost their lives.

Military Casualties of the First World War

Nation	Mobilised	Killed/Died	Wounded	Prisoners	Total Casualties	%
Allies						
Russia	12,000,000	1,700,000	4,950,000	2,500,000	9,150,000	76.3
France	8,410,000	1,357,800	4,266,000	537,000	6,160,800	73.3
Brit. Emp.	8,904,467	908,371	2,090,212	191,652	3,190,235	35.8
Italy	5,615,000	650,000	947,000	600,000	2,197,000	39.1
Romania	750,000	335,706	120,000	80,000	535,706	71.4
Serbia	707,343	45,000	133,148	152,958	331,106	46.8
USA	4,355,000	116,516	204,002	4,500	323,018	7.1
Belgium	267,000	13,716	44,686	34,659	93,061	34.9
Portugal	100,000	7,222	13,751	12,318	33,291	33.3
Mtngro	50,000	3,000	10,000	7,000	20,000	40.0
Greece	230,000	5,000	21,000	1,000	17,000	11.7
Japan	800,00	300	907	3	1,210	0.2
TOTAL	42,1888,810	5,152,115	12,831,004	4,121,090	22,104,209	52.3
Central Powers						
Germany	11,000,000	1,773,700	4,216,058	1,152,800	7,142,558	64.9
Aus.-Hung.	7,800,000	1,200,000	3,620,000	2,200,000	7,020,000	90.0
Turkey	2,850,000	325,000	400,000	250,000	975,000	34.2
Bulgaria	1,200,000	87,500	152,390	27,029	266,919	22.2
TOTAL	22,850,000	3,386,200	8,388,448	3,629,829	15,404,477	67.4
Military Total	65,038,810	8,538,315	21,219,452	7,750,919	37,508,686	57.6
Avg. per cent	100	13	33	12		57.6

Civilian casualty: 8,865,650 (est.)

1918 Flu deaths: 50–100 million (est.)

First World War trench warfare was so intense that 10 per cent of all soldiers who fought were killed, more than double the 4.5 per cent of soldiers who were killed in the Second World War. The country with the most military deaths was Germany, with 2.1 million, while Russia lost at least 3.8 million people including civilians. Russia's losses were never actually counted, so it may well be that over 6 million Russian soldiers were killed in the First World War. Serbia had the highest percentage of its population killed, with 16.1 per cent. Austria-Hungary had the highest percentage of casualties with 90 per cent, followed by Russia (76.3 per cent), France (73.3 per cent) and Germany (64.9 per cent). During the summer and autumn of 1914, France lost as many men on the battlefield as the US Army would lose in all of the twentieth century. During the course of the First World War 11 per cent of France's entire population was killed or wounded. On 22 August 1916, the French lost a staggering 27,000 men in battle. For each hour of the four and a quarter years of war, 230 soldiers perished. The US was in the war in actual combat for only seven and a half months. During this time 116,000 Americans were killed and 204,000 were wounded.

The Central Statistical Office in the 1920s gave total British Army casualties:

Total killed in action, plus died of wounds, disease or injury, plus missing presumed dead: 956,703
Of which Royal Navy and RFC/RAF casualties: 39,527
British Isles dead: 704,803
Canada, Australia, India and other places dead: 251,900
Total British Army deaths in France and Flanders: 564,715
Of which died of disease or injury: 32,098
Total British Army deaths on the Gallipoli front: 26,213
Total British Army deaths on all other fronts: 365,375

In March 2009, the totals of those buried from the Commonwealth War Graves Commission for the First World War figures include all three services. 587,989 First World War dead are buried in named graves. Some 526,816 men have no known grave, but are listed on a memorial to the missing. Of these, 187,861 were buried but are not identifiable by name. The remains of the other 338,955 men could not be found, and they were not buried. This last figure includes those lost at sea. Thus about half of those who served are buried as known soldiers, with the rest either buried but unidentifiable or lost. The figures are similar for Germany, France, etc.

According to figures produced in the 1920s in the *Official History of the Medical Services*, total British Army wounded were as follows:

Total British Army wounded in action, plus other casualties (if a man was wounded twice he appears here twice): 2,272,998
Royal Navy and RFC/RAF casualties: 16,862
Proportion returned to duty: 64 per cent
Proportion returned to duty but only for lines of communication, garrison or sedentary work: 18 per cent
Proportion discharged as invalids: 8 per cent (i.e. approximately 182,000)
Proportion died of wounds received: 7 per cent

More than 65 million men from thirty countries fought in the First World War, with the Allies (the Entente Powers) losing almost 2 million more soldiers than the Central Powers. Nearly two-thirds of military deaths in the First World War were in battle, whereas in previous conflicts most deaths were due to disease. Losses were horrific: for example, *The Times* of 24 July 1916, during the Battle of the Somme, listed 608 British officer casualties with 156 dead, and 5,500 other ranks. Men were killed and wounded even on 'quiet' days in the trenches. The concussion from shell blasts could stop a man's heart or rupture internal organs, so that he died with no obvious external trauma.

There were 80,000 recorded cases of shell shock in the British Army, approximately 2 per cent of the men who were called up for active service. 250,000 British soldiers suffered a partial or full amputation as a result of the war, around 6 per cent of combatants.

It could take up to six hours for stretcher bearers to carry a man off the battlefields to where a wheeled ambulance was available. If one of the troops fell ill while his company was marching, the medical officer would put a tag on him with a diagnosis, and leave the man by the side of the road to be picked up by a passing ambulance. Without the signed note, the man could have been considered a deserter and could be shot. Blood transfusion was in its infancy and not used reliably until the last couple of years of the war. Those who donated blood were kept in bed for one to two days and then given three weeks' special leave to recuperate.

The winters of 1916–17 and 1917–18 were among the coldest in living memory, so it was miserable as well as difficult for staff and patients alike in field hospitals. The tents were occasionally blown down in storms. Some of these tented and hutted hospitals had 2,000 or more beds, and with all the accommodations and facilities required for medical and support staff, they were like small towns. With the huge numbers of casualties that often streamed into hospitals, orderlies, nurses, and even padres were sometimes required to administer anaesthetics. Morphine was given sparingly and only in extreme cases in hospital, so men had to suffer through the painful cleaning and irrigation of wounds. However, brandy, champagne, and port were dispensed regularly to the sick and wounded.

Although well behind the front lines, the base hospitals were sometimes hit in bombing raids. During one on 19 May 1918, over sixty staff and patients were killed and eighty wounded at the 1st Canadian General. Contrary to the Geneva Convention, some of these hospitals had been placed next to vital military installations that were legitimate targets for the German bombers.

The Trenches and 'the Greatest Medical Holocaust in History'

During the summer of 1918, an unusually severe strain of influenza spread rapidly around the world. Although influenza was not normally associated with high mortality rates, this strain was especially virulent, and it would eventually kill millions of people. The cause of the outbreak is unknown, but the war was most certainly a contributing factor. The war encouraged large-scale movements of people back and forth around the globe, which accelerated the spread of the virus. Also, it is thought that the numerous war-ravaged regions of the world experienced poorer nutrition and less sanitary conditions, leaving their populations especially susceptible.

At the same time, the spread of the disease directly affected the war itself. All sides lost soldiers to the flu outbreak, but Germany and Austria-Hungary were hit especially hard, with the armies of both countries severely weakened just as the Allies were beginning to take the offensive. The epidemic continued well into 1919, when it suddenly died out just as quickly as it had started. The Great Influenza Pandemic (Spanish Flu) of 1918–1919 is thought to have killed from 50 to 100 million people worldwide. This virulent Spanish Flu killed a disproportionate number of people in their twenties and thirties. Pregnant women had the highest death rates – from 23 per cent to 71 per cent.

The second wave of the 1918–1919 Spanish Flu pandemic was much deadlier than the first. The first wave was much like a typical flu epidemic, with those most at risk being the sick and elderly. However, in August, when the second wave began in France, Sierra Leone and the United States, the virus had mutated into a much deadlier form. This has been attributed to the circumstances of the First World War. Soldiers with a mild strain stayed where they were, while the severely ill were sent on crowded trains to crowded field hospitals, spreading the deadlier virus. The second wave began and the flu quickly spread around the world again. Most of those who recovered from first-wave infections were now immune so it must have been the same strain of flu. Now the most vulnerable people were those like the soldiers in the trenches, young and healthy adults. An estimated 10 per cent to 20 per cent of those who were infected died. With about a third of the world population infected, this means 3 per cent to 6 per cent of the entire global population died.

As many as 17 million died in India, about 5 per cent of the population. In Japan, 23 million people were affected, and 390,000 died. In Samoa, in November and December 1918, 20 per cent of the population of 38,000 died. In the USA, about 28 per cent of the population suffered, and 500,000 to 675,000 died. In Britain, as many as 250,000 died, and in France, more than 400,000. Every continent suffered. The majority of deaths were from bacterial pneumonia, a secondary infection caused by influenza, but the virus also killed people directly, by causing massive haemorrhages and oedema in the lungs. Many of those who survived had lifelong health problems.

Civilian Casualties

Some 9 to 10 million combatants on both sides are estimated to have died, along with an estimated 6.6 million civilians. Most of the civilian fatalities were due to famine or illness rather than military action. The relatively low rate of civilian casualties in this war is due to the fact that the front lines on the main battlefront, the Western Front, were static for most of the war, so that civilians were able to avoid the combat zones. Civilian casualties for the Western allies were relatively slight. Germany, on the other hand, suffered 750,000 civilian dead during and after the war due to famine caused by the Allied blockade. Russia lost millions of civilians in the Russian Civil War, and Turkey suffered civilian losses with the invasion of Anatolia and deportation of Ottomans from the Balkan region. It is virtually impossible to give a reasonable estimate of war dead, for instance 150,000 civilians are said to have died in the Belgian Congo, but they are not noted in the above estimate.

6

The Weapons of War

The First World War pioneered the multinational business of weapons and arms technology. Most of today's military weapons were either built for this war, or developed using concepts derived from the blueprints of those weapons. Flamethrowers, tanks, submarines, fighter planes, bombers, poison gas, great guns, machine guns and small arms were either invented or developed using new mass production methods.

Great Guns

Only the artillery never entirely ceased any day or night. Every shell had a personality of its own and could be identified with fair accuracy by old-timers. Most cannon were light horse-drawn field pieces which fired small shells, usually shrapnel, about three miles. The British 18-pounder, the famed French 75, and the German 'whiz-bang' 77 were all in this category. They were not too difficult to detect en route and gave the men several seconds to dive into cover. On the other hand, high-velocity pieces were hated because their projectile was thrown at terrific speed in a nearly straight line and gave almost no warning. And except for the great railway guns the howitzers were the largest of all: gaping monsters that tossed their fat shells almost straight up and down. The men called them 'crumps'. The German 5.9 was also polite and gave the recipient some small time for acquiring shelter. The last part of its passage was a deep roar; one was safe if the roar lasted, but if one was in its path it descended fast and the best that could be hoped for was an extreme case of shell shock. These were called 'coal boxes'.

The sounds of the projectiles created a bizarre symphony. Field-gun shells buzzed in a crescendo and burst with a clattery bang.

The heavies flung their black bodies like great loaves of bread (they could be seen in flight) across vast reaches of the infinite sky and approached with the roar of an oncoming express train. Over valleys they all echoed distractingly and defied prediction. Those that fell in hollows burst with terrible suddenness and a double crash. Fabulous indeed was the blast of the 30.5 Australian trench-mortar. And there were shells that screamed, shells that hissed, gas shells that exploded with a simpering pop, shells that whistled, and shells that wobbled across heaven rattling like a snare drum. Finally there was drumfire, reserved for special occasions, when all the instruments blended into one homogeneous mass of sound of such intensity as cannot be described, all bursting into jagged fragments of hot metal that slammed into the bodies of men and mules with familiar results.

The troops hated artillery more than machine guns, more than snipers, or bayonets, or even gas; for there was no fighting it, nor could much really be done to elude it.

In Flanders Fields: The 1917 Campaign,
Leon Wolff (1958)

Artillery consists of large guns which fire explosive shells great distances. It can be relatively stationary, movable (field artillery), or mounted on a large vehicle such as a ship or train. The largest guns in the First World War could have a range of 70 miles. Many thousands of men were blown apart or atomised by falling shells, their body parts being lost forever in the earth. Nearly 8 million shells of 75, 155 and 220 mm were used on a total front line of 30 miles in two months in the Champagne and Artois offensive in 1915. In the Chemin des Dames offensive in 1917, French artillery shot nearly 19 million shells in two months, on a front line of less than 25 miles.

The great majority of military deaths were caused by artillery. Appearing in the French Army in 1897, the field gun of 75 mm became state of the art for several years. It was nicknamed the 'field hare' as it was so manoeuvrable. Such field artillery, or light artillery, could be used to support infantry in offensive operations, for which the mobility of the gun was essential, or in defensive operations where firepower was important. From 1914 it was rapidly improved by the French and copied by other armies, with single ammunition (joined shell and cartridge), a hydro-pneumatic recoil brake, and a fast-handling breech mechanism. The cannon was accurate up to 4 miles, at the rate of a shell every four seconds. The French armies had nearly 4,800 'field hares' in 1914, but by the end of the war had more than 17,300 such 75 mm guns. German soldiers called it the 'Devil Gun' and French military commanders claimed that it was 'the gun which won the war'. However, the French general staff, believing they had the best gun in the world, '*notre 75*', were extremely slow to invest in heavy artillery of a stronger calibre. From 1916 the Germans had an efficient field gun of 77 mm, with a lengthened tube for a greater range, but numerous other calibres were also used in their field artillery, including the famous 100 and 105 mm guns.

In 1914, heavy artillery was considered to be useful only for siege warfare. The French believed that the new war would be fast and fluid, with no real need for such guns. However, the war soon became a war of position, with opposing troops grounded in deep shelters or fortresses which needed to be destroyed. Germany, on the other hand, knew that the execution of their Schlieffen Plan necessitated quickly destroying French fortified positions. They began equipping their armies with large-calibre guns well before 1914. Such guns maximised the 'rupture effects', and need very long barrels for very long ranges, so weighed tens of tons. Railroads were needed to transport and use them. In 1914, the Germans and Austrians had very large-calibre artillery of 305 mm and 420 mm, ready to be transported in several parts by road, intended to crush Belgian and French fortresses. 'Big Bertha' was the nickname given by the Germans themselves to the M-Gerät 420 mm Kurze MarineKanone. Big Bertha was a 48-ton howitzer, named after the wife of its designer Gustav Krupp. It took a crew of 200 men six hours or more to assemble, but could fire a 2,050-lb shell over 9 miles. Germany had thirteen of these huge guns or 'wonder weapons'. Even more enormous guns of 480 and 520 mm were designed, but did not take part in the conflict.

The Germans put increasingly heavy calibres of between 150 and 390 mm on railway wagons from 1916. The 'Lange Max' shelled Paris from a distance of more than 67 miles with projectiles of 210 mm. These guns weighed between 24 and 65 tons, their shells weighed more than a ton and could exceed the size of a man. England learned from its experience with naval guns, and brought into service mounted guns from 3 to 9.2 inches, and railway weapons from 9.2 to 18 inches. In 1914 France only had 104 obsolete heavy guns, but had to catch up, having 6,722 great guns by 1918.

The First World War saw a massive advance in precision firing of artillery. In 1916, 'the Russians conducted their first registration point shoot: the adjustment of fire onto one target to identify inaccuracy, then switching to another while applying the known correction to achieve accuracy and surprise.' Artillery began shifting away from massed firing to a greater emphasis on precision firing. 'From the middle of the eighteenth century to the middle of the nineteenth, artillery is judged to have accounted for perhaps 50 per cent of battlefield casualties. In the sixty years preceding 1914, this figure was probably as low as 10 percent. The remaining 90 percent fell to small arms, whose range and accuracy had come to rival those of artillery … [By the First World War] the British Royal Artillery, at over one million men, grew to be larger than the Royal Navy … the percentage of casualties caused by artillery in various theatres since 1914 [was] in the First World War, 45 percent of Russian casualties and 58 percent of British casualties on the Western Front; in the Second World War, 75 percent of British casualties in North Africa and 51 percent of Soviet casualties (61 percent in 1945) and 70 percent of German casualties on the Eastern Front; and in the Korean War, 60 percent of US casualties, including those inflicted by mortars.' An estimated 75,000 French soldiers were casualties of 'friendly' artillery in the four years of the First World War.

Moaning Minnies and Plops

The vertical walls of trenches generally protected troops from direct hits of light artillery, so the old principle of mortars was readopted. Mortars sent their shells from an almost vertical direction, and explosive loads now began to pour into the trenches instead of passing over like normal artillery shells. Germany was first to invent a heavy weapon able to carry out curved trajectories, at very short distance with very large loads of explosive. They developed differing categories of mine throwers, *minenwerfers*, from 77 to 340 mm. They were known to the British as 'moaning Minnies' from their sound. Germany also used small bomb launchers, *ladungswerfer* to hurl at the first line of trenches.

The English also designed trench artillery, the most famous being the 'Stokes' mortar. Invented in 1915, it is the prototype for every mortar since designed. It consisted of a smooth-bore barrel with a closed end, resting on a base plate and held up at an angle of 45 degrees by a bipod. A screw mechanism allowed the barrel to be adjusted for angles of elevation. It fired a simple cylindrical bomb with a perforated tube at the rear end, into which a shotgun cartridge filled with gunpowder was fitted. The bomb was simply dropped down the barrel, to strike a firing pin fixed at the base. This ignited the shotgun cartridge and the explosion of the powder ejected the bomb. The Stokes mortar could fire as many as twenty-two bombs per minute and had a maximum range of 1,200 yards. The 3-inch cast-iron mortar bomb itself weighed around 10 pounds. In addition to the light Stokes mortar, the British also produced a 2-inch medium mortar and a 9.45-inch heavy mortar, nicknamed a 'Flying Pig'. By 1918 each British division possessed twenty-four light Stokes mortars, twelve medium and several heavy models. Mortars were very effective in trench warfare. Soldiers would often strain their ears to catch the 'plop!' sound that indicated the firing of an enemy mortar, and hurry into the nearest cover. Over 16 million acres of France had to be cordoned off at the end of the war because of unexploded ordnance. Approximately 13 million explosive and chemical shells, 'duds', were left in place. Shells are even now uncovered when farmers plough their fields, called the 'iron harvest', and are also found when construction work is carried out.

'Long Lee', 1888–1957

The basic British infantry soldier, like the French and German, was issued with a uniform, webbing and a rifle with bayonet. The main weapon used by British soldiers on the front line was the bolt-action Lee-Enfield 0.303 rifle. The first version had been produced in 1888, and a later version was called 'Long Lee' because of its barrel length. It could kill a person over 1,500 yards away. The rifle had a ten-bullet magazine and its rate of fire in the hands of well-trained men was about twelve well-aimed bullets in a minute. Because of this rate of fire, at Mons the advancing Germans believed that they were under fire from machine guns. However, its firing mechanisms were susceptible to dirt and grit. With further developments, the rifle was renamed by the British Army 'Rifle No. 1' and used throughout the Second World War until being replaced in 1957. The French had problems with the Lebel rifle which was replaced by the Berthier in 1916. However, the Berthier's magazine could only take six rounds, so its overall rate of fire was not high, as reloading the magazine was a constant issue in combat. German infantry were issued with the Mauser rifle. It was popular because of its reliability but its magazine only took five bullets. Like the Berthier, reloading was a constant problem in battle.

Big Game Hunters

Sniping had not been developed as a professional arm of the infantry in 1914. It soon became obvious that snipers were ideally suited to the static conditions of trench warfare, and big-game hunters such as Hesketh Hesketh-Prichard were called upon to transform the quality and practice of sniping within different armies. Standard army rifles were modified to suit the requirements of sniping, with innovations in optics. The Germans had telescopes attached to their G98 service rifle. 'Hyposcopes' were developed which enabled rifles to be fired from below the parapet of the trenches. Turkish sniping proved an especial problem for Allied troops based in Gallipoli. In static trench conditions, the danger of snipers meant that many new recruits were lost just peeping over the parapet into no man's land for a fraction of a second. Snipers were reluctant to fire unnecessarily at anything but a certain target. This was because once the enemy was able to detect the locale from which a sniper operated, artillery would be immediately signalled to wipe out the sniper's post. Captured snipers could be badly treated by the enemy, particularly because snipers would often be expected to shoot men involved in entirely peaceful tasks behind the enemy line, or even tending the wounded. Snipers operated in pairs, the sniper usually being accompanied by an observer who would often make use of a periscope ('sniperscope') to scour the surrounding countryside. Their most valued targets were inevitably officers and specialist servicemen. Each army also trained 'sniper hunters', to snipe at snipers, including the English poet Julian Grenfell, who died in action in 1915. The 2001 film *Enemy at the Gates* depicts the ultimate shooting competition – a duel between sniper hunters at Stalingrad in the Second World War.

'The Assassin' and 'Abdul the Terrible'

William Edward 'Billy' Sing DCM (1886–1943) was a part-Chinese Australian soldier, best known as a sniper in the Gallipoli Campaign. He made at least 150 confirmed kills, and may have had over 200 kills in total, with one estimate putting his tally at close to 300 kills. There was considerable anti-Chinese sentiment in Australia, but Sing became well known for his marksmanship, both as a kangaroo shooter and as a competitive target shooter, winning prizes. On 24 October 1914, Sing enlisted as a trooper on the Australian 5th Light Horse Regiment. He was accepted into the army only after a recruitment officer chose to disregard the fact that Sing was part-Chinese. At this time, only those of European ancestry were generally considered suitable for Australian military service. Sing became a sniper.

Biographer John Hamilton described the Turkish landscape thus: 'It is a country made for snipers. The Anzac and Turkish positions often overlooked each other. Each side sent out marksmen to hunt and stalk and snipe, to wait and shoot and kill, creeping with stealth through the green and brown shrubbery ...' An account by Private Frank Reed, a fellow Australian soldier, states that Sing was so close to the Turkish lines that enemy artillery rarely troubled him. According to Reed, 'Every time Billy Sing felt sorry for the poor Turks, he remembered how their snipers picked off the Australian officers in the early days of the landing, and he hardened his heart. But he never fired at a stretcher-bearer or any of the soldiers who were trying to rescue wounded Turks.'

Sing's reputation resulted in a champion Turkish sniper, nicknamed 'Abdul the Terrible' by the Allies, being assigned to deal with him. The Turks were largely able to distinguish Sing's sniping from that of other ANZAC soldiers, and only the reports of incidents believed to be Sing's work were passed on to Abdul. Through analysis of the victims' actions, place of death and wounds, Abdul discovered Sing's hidden firing position. Abdul spent several days quietly setting up his own position to give him an excellent sighting of Sing's 'possie', then settled down to await an opportunity. After another few days, Sing's spotter alerted him to a potential target, and he took aim, only to find the target, Abdul, aiming a rifle in his direction. Sing fired first and killed Abdul. Very quickly, Turkish artillery fired on Sing's position, and he and his spotter barely managed to evacuate alive. In August 1915, Sing was hospitalised for four days with influenza, and then injured by a bullet that ricocheted off his spotter's telescope. Sing used a standard Lee-Enfield .303 rifle.

Sing's marksmanship at Gallipoli saw him nicknamed 'The Assassin' or 'The Murderer' by his comrades. By early September 1915, he had taken 119 kills, according to the commanding officer of the 2nd Australian Light Horse Brigade. Regimental records list Sing as having taken 150 confirmed kills, but on 23 October 1915, General Birdwood, commander of ANZAC forces, issued an order complimenting Sing on his 201 unconfirmed kills. An official kill was recorded only if the spotter saw the target fall. If the first shot missed the target, it was very risky to take a second shot, as this could give away the sniper team's position. Major Stephen Midgely estimated Sing's tally at close to 300 kills. General Birdwood told Kitchener that 'if his troops could match the capacity of the Queensland sniper the Allied forces would soon be in Constantinople'. Sing was Mentioned in Dispatches and awarded the DCM. He transferred to the 31st Infantry Battalion after illnesses, and then served on the Western Front from January 1917. He was wounded in action several times, and commended many times in reports by Allied commanders. For leading a counter-sniper unit he was awarded the Belgian Croix de Guerre and was recommended for the Military Medal. He was by now in very poor health, owing to at least three gunshot battle wounds and the effects of gas poisoning. It was recommended that he was discharged as permanently unfit for service. Following work in sheep farming and gold mining, he died in relative poverty and obscurity in Brisbane in 1945. A biography by John Hamilton, *Gallipoli Sniper: The Life of Billy Sing*, was published in 2008.

'The Broomhandle' and *Star Wars*

All British officers were issued with pistols, usually the Webley Mark IV 11.6 mm. However, it was also issued to the military police, machine gunners and personnel in tanks, airplanes and armoured cars, as carrying a rifle was impossible for these servicemen. Around 300,000 Webleys were made during the war. Much practice was required to use it accurately, since it jumped on firing. British officers generally preferred the use of a captured Luger when the opportunity arose, possibly on account of its longer range. In 1908, the German Army had adopted the Luger 9mm P08 as a pistol. Like the Webley, it was reliable and such was its popularity that it became the world's most used pistol. The Luger semi-automatic possessed a seven-round magazine loaded via the pistol butt. Recoil-operated, the Luger had a long service life and was accurate but was never available in sufficient supplies to meet the ever-increasing demand. A variant of the Luger, the Parabellum M17, was issued in 1917. Possessing a longer barrel, it resembled a machine carbine, with a magazine capable of holding thirty rounds. About 2 million Lugers were produced by Germany in the war, and it was such a reliable weapon that it was used by the German Army until 1945.

The Mauser C96 was probably as popular and widespread as the Luger in the German Army. Although bulky and somewhat awkward, the Mauser pistol could fire a powerful 7.63 mm or 9 mm round. The Mauser also had a wooden holster which, when fitted, effectively turned it into a shoulder-fired carbine. A carbine is a shorter rifle. This Mauser C96 semi-automatic pistol was produced from 1896 to 1937. Its distinctive characteristics are the integral box magazine in front of the trigger, the long barrel, and the wooden shoulder stock which can double as a holster or carrying case. The grip earned the gun the nickname 'broomhandle' from Allied troops because of its round wooden handle. With its shoulder stock, long barrel and high-velocity cartridge, it had superior range and better penetration than most other pistols. Indeed, the Mauser 7.63 x 25 mm cartridge was the highest-velocity commercially manufactured pistol cartridge until the .357 Magnum cartridge in 1935. Mauser manufactured around a million C96 pistols. Churchill used the C96 at Omdurman and in the Second Boer War, and Lawrence of Arabia had one in the First World War. A C96 was modified to form Han Solo's 'blaster pistol' for the Star Wars movies. The US Army and Navy essentially used three pistol models. The Colt 0.45 automatic was introduced in 1911 and was also used by the Royal Navy in modified format. A total of 150,000 each of Colt 0.45 revolvers and Smith and Wesson 0.45 revolvers were manufactured. British officers often bought Colt revolvers and automatics for their own use.

Forks, Toothpicks, Corkscrews and Kitchen Spits

Blades affixed to rifle muzzles were common to all armies, being necessary for hand-to-hand fighting, and killing the wounded rather than wasting bullets. The French preferred a long 'needle bayonet', whereas the Germans adopted a 'pioneer bayonet' with the rear edge formed into a saw. The British used the standard 'sword bayonet'. Apart from killing in hand-to-hand fighting, it was used to toast bread, open cans, scrape mud off uniforms, poke a trench brazier or even to help prepare communal latrines. One advantage of using a bayonet in close combat, as opposed to a rifle or pistol, was to avoid injuring one's fellow soldiers. A bullet fired at close range into an enemy could easily pass through his body and enter a friend. Soldiers were instructed to direct the bayonet at the vulnerable points of the enemy's body: the throat, left or right breast and left or right groin. Aiming the bayonet blade at the breast ran the risk of driving into the breastbone, making removal of the blade difficult. Similarly, aiming the blade at the groin inevitably resulted in excruciating pain to the victim, such that they would often grab the bayonet in an attempt to pull the blade out. In some cases soldiers often had to remove the blade from the rifle simply in order to continue with the attack. The bayonet was known to the French as *la fourchette*, the fork, and *le cure-dents*, the toothpick. It was also known as a *tire-Boche*. *Boche*, the general slang term for the Germans, was substituted into *tire-bouchon*, a corkscrew. Soldiers were taught to twist the bayonet on entry and pull it straight out. Equally, another nickname for a bayonet, *tourne-Boche*, was formed from *tournebroche*, a kitchen spit for roasting meat and fowl in the fireplace. So you could turn a German on a spit …

Emma-Gee, Belgian Rattlesnakes, Flesh Grinders, Sewing Machines and Typewriters

The machine gun was a heavy, virtually unusable weapon in attack. However, it was essential equipment when mounted in a defensive trench or bunker, firing hundreds of bullets per minute. In later wars, planes and tanks would make movement and attack possible, but the First World War belonged to the machine gun. Its use resulted in the terrible war of attrition. Often generals such as Haig, far removed from the realities of the front line, decided upon offensive actions, probably to let the politicians know that they were doing something to try and end the war. Haig said, 'The idea that a war can be won by standing on the defensive and waiting for the enemy to attack is a dangerous fallacy, which owes its inception to the desire to evade the price of victory.'

The results of any attack were usually horrifying, which accounts for greater losses by the French and British than the Germans. In February 1916, the Germans themselves attempted to negate the machine gun by simply pouring men against the French and British lines at Verdun. The battled lasted for six months and 700,000 men lost their lives on both sides. Most generals at last realised that neither side could advance and alter the war's course. However, Haig then tried to take the offensive at the Somme. In July 1916, a million shells were fired at German trenches, and then 100,000 men tried to storm them. Some 20,000 British soldiers were killed on the first day alone, with another 40,000 wounded, and not a single British soldier reached the German lines. They were under orders to walk towards the machine guns, not to run, dodge or dive. After four months and the loss of another 1.1 million men it was yet again realised that the machine gun reigned supreme.

Machine guns were fairly primitive and heavy at the start of the war, when troops were trying to advance rapidly. Each weighed from 65–130 pounds, plus much more again with their mountings, carriages and supplies. The early machine gun was usually positioned on a flat tripod, and would require a gun crew of four to six men. They could fire 400–600 small-calibre rounds per minute, a figure that was to more than double by the war's end, with rounds fed via a fabric belt or a metal strip.

However the guns quickly overheated, and became inoperative without cooling mechanisms, so were fired in short rather than sustained bursts. Cooling was originally by water jackets and later they were air-cooled. Water-cooled machine guns could overheat within two minutes, so large supplies of water needed to be quickly accessible. In times of shortage, a machine gun crew would be forced to urinate into the water jacket. They still often jammed, so would frequently be grouped together to maintain a constant defensive fire. Each machine gun was said to be worth around eighty rifles, but the British Army had pathetically dismissed its potential.

Rapid-firing weapons, such as the 0.50-inch-calibre Gatling gun, invented in 1862, all required some form of manual intervention, e.g. hand cranking. However, the American Hiram Maxim invented the automatic machine gun in 1884, and offered it to Britain in 1885. Despite its proven value in the Matabele War of 1893–94, generals saw no real value in it. However, unlike the British, the German Army quickly produced a version of Maxim's gun, the Machinengewehr 08. At the war's outbreak, Germany had 12,000 machine guns, and 100,000 in 1918. The British and French had access to just a few hundred machine guns when war began. The German Army had created separate machine gun companies before the war to support infantry battalions, but the British did not create the Machine Gun Corps until October 1915. Only two guns had been allocated to each infantry battalion in 1914. General Haig especially had dismissed their usefulness.

The British Vickers was a water-cooled machine gun that used the same ammunition as the Lee-Enfield rifle, 0.303-inch bullets, and could fire at a rate of 450 bullets a minute. The Vickers weighed about 45 pounds and thus had to be used on a tripod with a gun team of up to six men. By the end of 1915, it was replaced by the Lewis gun on the Western Front. Because Germany used guns copied from Maxim's design, they were known to Allied troops as Maxims, whereas British machine guns were known as Lewis guns. Frustrated in his aim of persuading the US Army to adopt his new design of machine gun, Colonel Isaac Lewis had retired from the army and set sail for Belgium, arriving in January 1913. The Belgian Army ordered that his gun was manufactured at Liege, using common British 0.303-inch-calibre bullets. Shortly afterwards the Birmingham Small Arms Company also bought a licence to manufacture Lewis's weapon. Weighing just 25 pounds, the air-cooled 1914 model Lewis gun featured a forty-seven-cartridge circular magazine. The gun's firing rate could be regulated, ranging from 500–600 rounds per minute, although shorter bursts were more usual. With its adjustable sights and bipod support the Lewis gun proved effective to some 700 yards, but was still considered too heavy and bulky for rapidly advancing infantry. It was said to be nicknamed 'the Belgian rattlesnake' by German forces. By 1916 approximately 50,000 had been produced. Although in 1915 each British battalion on the Western Front had just four Lewis guns, by 1917 each infantry section boasted its own Lewis gunner and backup, with battalions deploying forty-six Lewis Guns. When used in the air, the air cooling jacket and fins on the Lewis were dispensed with, and it was used for anti-aircraft fire, mounted on armoured cars, tanks and even motorcycles.

'Emma-Gee' was its British nickname, from the military phonetic alphabet of the time. The Germans menacingly callers their machine gun the *fleischhackmaschine*, flesh grinder. Equally the French named theirs *la machine B decoudre*, the machine to rip open seams, formed from their *machine B coudre* or sewing machine. The verb *decoudre* also denotes the action of a horned animal ripping open its attackers. ANZAC forces more prosaically referred to them as 'typewriters', from their chattering noise.

Jam Bombs, Pineapples, Sticks, Cricket Balls, Eggs, Toffee Apples and Parties

Hand grenades are small missiles, usually containing an explosive charge, and generally thrown by hand. At the start of war, Germany had 70,000 hand grenades, and 106,000 rifle grenades. As with the machine gun, Haig and the British high command did not foresee a use for the hand grenade. Because there were severe shortages, British and ANZAC soldiers improvised them using tin cans and jars. For example, 'jam bombs' were made out of empty jam cans, gunpowder (or guncotton or dynamite), stones or scrap metal, and cord. Soldiers were encouraged to improvise, and this led to the development of similar 'jam tin grenades' being manufactured in vast quantities before safer designs were available. British forces outside the Western Front, which was given first call on grenade supplies, were lacking grenades until well into 1916. Consequently many British soldiers such as those based in Gallipoli carried on making home-made, or 'jam-tin' bombs.

When Britain entered the war on 4 August it did so with small quantities of just one type of grenade, the unpopular Mark I. It was liable to explode prematurely if it came into contact with an object while in the act of being thrown. However, within a year Britain was producing an average of 250,000 hand grenades each week, with peak production of 500,000. Grenades, either hand or rifle-driven, were detonated upon impact (percussion) or via a timed fuse. The three most common types were the British 'Mills Bomb', the French 'pineapple grenade', and the German 'stick grenade'. A trained soldier could throw a grenade up to 50 yards. They were generally fitted with a four-second fuse, sufficient time for the grenade to reach the enemy, but not enough time for it to be thrown back. A modified version of the Mills Bomb was fitted with a steel rod at the base so it could be fired from a rifle. In addition to explosive grenades, smoke and gas grenades were also used, being extremely effective in enclosed areas such as trenches, buildings, and underground tunnel networks.

Referred to officially as 'No. 5', the Mills bomb became the dominant British grenade from mid-1915. Weighing 1.25 pounds, its exterior was serrated so that when it detonated it broke into many fragments, acting as a fragmentation bomb. Soldiers were instructed to lob the Mills bomb using a throwing action similar to bowling in cricket. During the course of the war around 70 million Mills bombs were thrown by the Allies, with perhaps 35 million other types. The Allies also improved the range of cup grenades from an average 200 yards to over 400 yards using rifle-driven fin grenades. The German Army, having popularised the use of the grenade from the start of the war, developed numerous models, including the *stielhandgranate* (stick bomb), *diskushandgranate* (disc grenade), *eierhandgranate* (hand grenade) and *kugelhandgranate* (ball grenade). These were respectively referred to by the British as 'toffee apples', 'eggs', 'cricket balls' and 'pineapples'.

'Bombing parties' grew in frequency as the war progressed, becoming a major component of any infantry attack. A British bombing team usually consisted of an NCO, two throwers, two carriers, two bayonet-men to defend the team and two 'spare' men for use when casualties were incurred. As an attack reached an enemy trench the grenadiers would be responsible for racing down the trench and throwing grenades into each dugout they passed. The greatest grenade battle of the war occurred on the Pozières Heights on the night of 26 July 1916. It lasted for twelve and a half hours as Australians, with British support, exchanged grenades with Germans. The Allied contingent alone threw some 15,000 Mills bombs during the night. Many grenadiers were killed, while others fell down owing to complete exhaustion.

The New 'Greek Fire'

As early as the ninth century BCE, the Assyrians used combustible substances as weapons, and Thucydides mentions the use of tubed flamethrowers at the Siege of Delium in 424 BCE. 'Greek Fire' was developed around 672 BCE and was used to defend the Byzantine Empire against Islamic attacks. Specialised ships were able to hurl flames against the enemy. The German Army had tested two models of *flammenwerfer*, flamethrower, in the early 1900s, one large and one small. The smaller, lighter *kleinflammenwerfer* was designed to be carried by a single man. Using pressurised air and carbon dioxide or nitrogen it spewed a stream of burning oil for up to 20 yards. The larger model, the *grossflammenwerfer*, was too heavy for a single person, but its maximum range was 40 yards, and it could also sustain flames for 40 seconds. The German Army deployed it for use in three specialist battalions from 1911 onwards, and used it against the Allies from October 1914.

With the success of portable flamethrowers in the Hooge attack on 30 July 1915 against the British in Flanders, the German Army adopted the device across all fronts of battle. The *flammenwerfers* tended to be used in groups of six during battle, each machine worked by two men.

They were used mostly to clear forward defenders during the start of a German attack, preceding their infantry colleagues. British and French poured rifle fire against the operators, who could expect little mercy if they were taken prisoner. During the war the Germans launched in excess of 650 flamethrower attacks. The British found them of limited use, and no numbers exist for British or French attacks. Germany also made extensive use of flamethrowers in the Second World War.

'Green Cross', 'Yellow Cross', 'White Star', 'Hun Stuff', 'the Comical Chemical Corporals' and Scotsmen in Tights

> Gas! GAS! Quick, boys! – An ecstasy of fumbling,
> Fitting the clumsy helmets just in time;
> But someone still was yelling out and stumbling,
> And flound'ring like a man in fire or lime …
> Dim, through the misty panes and thick green light,
> As under a green sea, I saw him drowning.
> In all my dreams, before my helpless sight,
> He plunges at me, guttering, choking, drowning.
> Wilfred Owen, 'Dulce et Decorum est', 1917

'The Comical Chemical Corporals' was the name given by the troops to men in the distinctive uniform of Special Brigade, Royal Engineers, responsible for poison gas and flame attacks. Chemical warfare was necessitated by the need to find new ways of overcoming the stalemate of trench warfare. The first use seems to have been in August 1914, when the French fired tear-gas grenades (xylyl bromide) against the Germans. In October 1914 at the capture of Neuve Chapelle, the Germans fired shells at the French which contained a chemical irritant to induce a violent fit of sneezing. The first instance of large-scale use of gas as a weapon was on 31 January 1915, when Germany fired 18,000 artillery shells containing liquid xylyl bromide tear gas at Russians near Warsaw at the Battle of Bolimov. However, instead of vaporising, the chemical froze and failed to have the desired effect.

The first real 'poison gas', chlorine, was used on 22 April 1915, at the start of the Second Battle of Ypres. Sentries posted among the French and Algerian troops noticed a strange yellow-green cloud drifting slowly towards their line. Within seconds of inhaling its vapour it harmed the victim's respiratory organs, bringing on choking attacks. Defending troops fled in disorder, creating a 4-mile gap in the Allied line, but the Germans were too slow to follow and make a decisive breakthrough. Respiratory disease and failing eyesight were common post-war afflictions. Of the Canadians who, without any effective protection, had withstood the first chlorine attacks during the Second Battle of Ypres, 60 per cent of the casualties had to be repatriated and half of these were still unfit by the end of the war, over three years later. The use of different types of poison gas escalated.

Britain trained 1,400 men as Special Gas operatives and instructions were given to prepare for a gas attack at Loos in 1915. Around 400 chlorine gas emplacements were established among the British front line. Gas was released by turning a cock on each cylinder, just before dawn on 25 September. A mixture of smoke and chlorine gas was released intermittently over a period of about forty minutes before the infantry assault began. However, in parts of the British line the wind shifted and quantities of the smoke and gas were blown back into the British trenches. A more reliable delivery mechanism was needed by Britain, France and Germany, so they began to deliver gas using artillery shells, over a longer range.

German phosgene gas was next used, called by the Allies 'green cross', from the marking painted on the delivery shell casing. While chlorine was potentially deadly, it caused the victim to violently cough and choke, but probably survive. Phosgene caused much less coughing so more was inhaled, and it often had a delayed effect. Apparently healthy soldiers could succumb to phosgene gas poisoning up to forty-eight hours after inhalation. It was adopted by both sides. A 'white star' mixture of phosgene and chlorine was commonly used on the Somme, with the chlorine content supplying the necessary vapour with which to carry the phosgene.

Germany always led the gas war, with the Allies trying desperately to catch up, and it next developed mustard gas, in artillery shells against the Russians at Riga in 1917. An almost odourless chemical, it caused serious internal and external blisters several hours after exposure. Protection against mustard gas proved more difficult than against either chlorine or phosgene gas. The chemical remained potent in soil for weeks after release, making dangerous the capture of infected trenches. A positive correlation has been proven between exposure to mustard agents and skin cancers, other respiratory and skin conditions, leukaemia, several eye conditions, bone marrow depression and subsequent immunosuppression, psychological disorders and sexual dysfunction. Chemicals used in the production of chemical weapons have also left residues in the soil where the weapons were used. The chemicals that have been detected can cause cancer and can have an impact on a person's brain, blood, liver, kidneys and skin. The Germans marked their shells yellow for mustard gas and green for chlorine and phosgene, so the Allies called the new gas 'yellow cross'. It was known to the British as HS (Hun Stuff), while the French called it Yperite.

Nurse Vera Brittain wrote, 'I wish those people who talk about going on with this war whatever it costs could see the soldiers suffering from mustard gas poisoning. Great mustard-coloured blisters, blind eyes, all sticky and stuck together, always fighting for breath, with voices a mere whisper, saying that their throats are closing and they know they will choke.' Another British nurse treating mustard gas cases wrote, 'They cannot be bandaged or touched. We cover them with a tent of propped-up sheets. Gas burns must be agonizing because usually the other cases do not complain even with the worst wounds, but gas cases are invariably beyond endurance and they cannot help crying out.' Scots regiments wearing kilts were especially vulnerable to mustard gas injuries due to their bare legs. At Nieuwpoort in Flanders, some Scots battalions wore women's tights beneath their kilts as a form of protection.

Many other types of gases included bromine and chloropicrin, and the French Army occasionally made use of a nerve gas obtained from prussic acid. Deaths from gas after about May 1915 were relatively rare. It has been estimated that among British forces the number of gas casualties from May 1915 amounted to some 9 per cent of the total, but only around 3 per cent were fatal. However, gas victims often led highly debilitating lives after the war, with many unable to seek employment. Gas never turned out to be the weapon that turned the tide of the war, as was often predicted. Innovations in its use were quickly combated and copied by opposing armies. This is one of the reasons why the First World War has been called 'The Chemists' War.' The types of protection initially handed out to the troops around Ypres following the first use of chlorine in April 1915 had been primitive. Some 100,000 wads of cotton pads were made available. These were dipped in a solution of bicarbonate of soda and held over the face. Soldiers were also advised that holding a urine-drenched cloth over their face would serve in an emergency to protect against the effects of chlorine. By 1918, soldiers on both sides were far better prepared to meet the ever-present threat of a gas attack. Filter respirators using charcoal or antidote chemicals proved highly effective, although working in a trench while wearing such respirators generally proved difficult and tiring.

Approximately thirty different poisonous gases were used during the First World War. It is estimated that Germany used 68,000 tons of poison gas, the French 36,000 tons and the British 25,000. By 1918 the use of use of poison gases had become widespread, particularly on the Western Front. If the war had continued into 1919, both sides had planned on inserting poison gases into 30–50 per cent of manufactured shells.

Country	Total Poison Gas Casualties	Deaths
Russia	419,340	56,000
Germany	200,000	9,000
France	190,000	8,000
British Empire	188,706	8,109
Austria-Hungary	100,000	3,000
USA	72,807	1,462
Italy	60,000	4,627
Others	10,000	1,000
TOTAL	1,240,853	91,198

The Inventor of Death, the Cost of Killing Germans and the Dishwasher

William Howard Livens DSO MC (1889–1964) enrolled as a second lieutenant in the Royal Engineers in September 1914. The German use of poison gas at the Second Battle of Ypres in April 1915 drove him to anger and he started experimental work. The commander of British II Corps, Lt Gen. Ferguson, had stated of gas: 'It is a cowardly form of warfare which does not commend itself to me or other English soldiers … We cannot win this war unless we kill or incapacitate more of our enemies than they do of us, and if this can only be done by our copying the enemy in his choice of weapons, we must not refuse to do so.' On his own initiative, Livens fitted out makeshift laboratories at his Chatham barracks. For a firing range he used vacant land which overlooked the Thames estuary, where he worked on developing flamethrowers and small mortars to throw oil and gas.

The Livens Gas and Oil Bomb Projector was known more simply as the Livens Projector. It was a large, simple mortar that could throw a projectile containing about 30 pounds of explosives, incendiary oil or, most commonly, poisonous phosgene gas. His projector combined the advantages of gas cylinders and shells, by firing a cylinder tank at the enemy. It consisted of a simple metal pipe that was half-buried in the ground at a 45-degree angle and which could throw large drums filled with inflammable or toxic chemicals.

The weapon was so simple and inexpensive that hundreds of projectors could be fired simultaneously, catching the enemy by surprise. On 31 March 1918, the British conducted their largest ever 'gas shoot', firing 3,728 cylinders. Livens had rapidly developed the projector, increasing its range from the original 200 yards, first to 350 yards and eventually 1,300 yards. Prior to the invention of the Livens Projector, chemical weapons had been delivered either by 'cloud attacks' or by chemical-filled shells fired from howitzers. Cloud attacks were made by burying gas-filled cylinder tanks just beyond the parapet of the attacker's trenches and then opening valves on the tanks when the wind was right. This allowed a useful amount of gas to be released but there was danger that the wind would change and the gas would drift back over the attacking troops. Chemical shells were much easier to direct at the enemy but could not deliver nearly as much gas as a cylinder tank.

The Livens Projector became the standard means of delivering gas attacks and it remained in use until the early years of the Second World War, in which Livens also contributed to such weapons. Gas warfare in the early years had been primitive. Heavy cylinders of poison gas were manhandled to the front trenches and their contents vented out through metal pipes, relying on wind to carry the toxic cloud over the enemy trenches. However, the wind could change direction, leading to the first British gas attack at Loos being a disaster. Livens had witnessed some of his test projector firings from an aircraft and in his report he estimated that 'if the projectors were used on a large scale the cost of killing Germans could be reduced to sixteen shillings each'. Livens Projector production was given a high priority, with the total for the Allies eventually exceeding 150,000 units. The Livens Projector was also used to fire other substances. At one time or another, its drums contained high explosive, oil and cotton-waste pellets, thermite, white phosphorous and 'stinks'. Stinks were foul-smelling but harmless substances used to simulate a poison gas attack, thereby compelling the enemy to put on their cumbersome masks, used on occasions when gas could not be safely employed.

Another invention, the Livens Large Gallery Flame Projector, was 56 feet long, weighed 2.5 tons, and took a carrying party of 300 men to bring the pieces to the front line and assemble it, where it was operated by a crew of eight. The weapon was designed to be used from a shallow tunnel dug under no man's land. The weapon consisted of a long chamber containing the fuel, a 14-inch-diameter pipe and a nozzle on the surface. Piston-driven compressed gas was pushed into the long fuel chamber, and fuel was forced out of the surface nozzle, ignited and directed to the target. The maximum range of the weapon was 100 to 130 feet. Livens had been put in charge of Z company, a special unit that was tasked with developing a British version of the German flamethrower recently deployed on the Western Front. Four of Livens' massive fixed flame projectors were used on 1 July 1916 at the start of the Battle of the Somme. Constructed in underground chambers, two were knocked out by German artillery before the offensive. The other two were effective in demoralising the German defenders. The weapon was only used once more in 1917. The remains of one of these projectors were discovered and excavated in 2010 in a *Time Team* television documentary. In 1924, Livens invented a small dishwasher suitable for domestic use, with all the features of a modern dishwasher, including a front door for loading, a wire rack to hold crockery and a rotating sprayer. According to family tradition, Livens built a prototype. When it was tried out by their maidservant, she was later found in tears with water flooding across the floor. At that point the experiment was abandoned.

Big Willie and Little Willie

In June 1915, a Killen-Strait tractor with caterpillar treads was demonstrated to an audience including Winston Churchill, First Lord of the Admiralty, and David Lloyd George, soon to become Prime Minister. The tractor successfully passed over a barbed wire entanglement, and impressed both men. Churchill sponsored the establishment of the Landships Committee to investigate the potential of constructing this new military weapon. The vehicle was seen an extension of armoured seagoing warships, so they were called landships. Its codename, given because the shape of the shell resembled water carriers, was 'tank'. Criteria for the finished design were that it must boast a minimum speed of 4 miles per hour, be able to climb a 5-foot-high obstacle, successfully span a 5-foot trench, and be immune to the effects of small arms fire. It was to be equipped with two machine guns, have a range of 20 miles and be maintained and operated by a crew of ten men.

This first prototype tank was given the nickname 'Little Willie', mocking the German Prince Wilhelm, and had a Daimler engine. It weighed 14 tons, had 12-foot-long track frames, and could carry three people in cramped conditions. However, its top speed was only 3 mph, and only 2 mph in battle conditions over poor terrain. It was initially unable to cross trenches, a fault that was rectified, and later tanks achieved 4 mph. 'Little Willie' never saw action and can still be seen in the Bovington Tank Museum. The second Mark I prototype, later known as 'His Majesty's Land Ship', HMLS *Centipede* or 'Mother' was a marked improvement. 'Mother' was also known as 'Big Willie' after Prince Wilhelm's father, Kaiser Wilhelm.

Tanks were relatively ineffective when they were first introduced, but by the end of the war they were armoured enough to protect their crews, and able to support an advance with their own gunfire. Once the problems were worked out with the innovative caterpillar tread, they could operate as real all-terrain vehicles. Initially the Royal Navy supplied the crews for tanks. On 15 September 1916, Captain H. W. Mortimore guided a tank into action at the terrible Battle of the Bois d'Elville, known as 'Devil's Wood'. In the Battle of the Somme, a subsidiary attack on Flers–Courcelette by the 41st Division was supported by forty-nine tanks. Such was their lack of reliability that seven failed to start, others broke down or were stuck in muddy ditches and only fifteen got to the battle zone and took part on 15 September 1916. A strong supporter of the tank, Churchill was annoyed that it was being used too early by Haig: 'My poor land battleships have been let off prematurely on a petty scale.' A RFC pilot corps saw one of the four remaining tanks out of ten scheduled to attack Flers going down the main road of the village. He radioed the following: 'A tank is walking down the High Street of Flers with the British Army cheering behind it.' The attacks on Flers–Courcelette temporarily undermined German morale, as rifle and machine gun fire had little impact on the tanks that got through. In the first three days of the Battle of Flers–Courcelette, the Allies advanced over a mile. These early tanks were still too unreliable and were susceptible to artillery fire.

Tanks were deployed into the swampy conditions of Passchendaele from June to November 1917, also known as the Third Battle of Ypres, and simply sank in the mire. However, in the first really successful British demonstration of the potential of the tank, the entire British Tank Corps of 474 tanks went into action at Cambrai on 20 November 1917. Twelve miles of the German front was breached, with the capture of 10,000 German prisoners, 123 guns and 281 machine guns. Nevertheless, Germany learnt to deal with First World War tanks very effectively. During the Battle of Amiens in 1918, 72 per cent of Allied tanks were destroyed in just four days, and six days before the end of war the Tank Corps had only eight tanks left fit for action. By the time the war drew to a close the British, the first to use them, had produced some 2,636 tanks. The French produced 3,870. The Germans produced only 20. The first successful display of German tanks came on 24 April 1918, when thirteen German tanks, some of which had been captured from the British, drove back British and Australian infantry at Villers Bretonneux. The battle was the site of the first tank-*versus*-tank engagement, as three British Mark IVs drove away three German A7Vs just south of the battle.

British tanks were initially categorised into males and females. Male tanks had cannons, while females had heavy machine guns. Conditions for tank crews were often dreadful. The heat generated inside the tank was tremendous and fumes often overcame the men inside. Good vision was difficult, but steering them was even worse. Steering was controlled by varying the speed of the two tracks by four of the crew. There were two drivers, one of whom also acted as commander and operated the brakes. The other driver operated the primary gearbox. Two 'gearsmen', one for the secondary gears of each track, were also needed to control direction and speed. As the noise was deafening, the driver, after setting the primary gear box, communicated with his gearsmen with hand signals, first getting their attention by hitting the engine block with a heavy spanner. For slight turns, the driver could use the 'steering tail'. This was an enormous contraption dragged behind the tank consisting of two large wheels, each of which could be blocked by pulling a steel cable. This caused the whole vehicle to slide in the same direction. If they broke down they were an easy target for German artillery. There was no wireless, so communication with command posts was by using two pigeons, which had their own small exit hatch. Because of the noise and vibration, early radios were impractical, so lamps, flags, semaphore, coloured discs and carrier pigeons were part of the standard equipment of tanks.

'The Pool of Peace' and the Unluckiest Cow in the World

Mining had been used in siege warfare of walled towns and castles, and now it saw a resurgence as a military tactic. Engineers tried to break the stalemate of the trenches by tunnelling under no man's land and laying large quantities of explosives beneath the enemy's trenches. When detonated, the explosion would destroy that section of the trench. The infantry would then advance towards the enemy front line, hoping to take advantage of the confusion that followed. It could take as long as a year to dig a tunnel and place a mine. As well as digging their own tunnels, the miners had to listen out for enemy tunnellers, which was the background for the Sebastian Faulks' recent novel *Birdsong*. On occasion miners accidentally dug into the opposing side's tunnel and an underground fight took place. When an enemy's tunnel was found it was usually destroyed by placing an explosive charge inside.

General Sir Herbert Plumer gave orders for twenty-one mines to be placed under German lines to try and take the heavily defended Messines Ridge at Ypres in Belgium. The mine at Spanbroekmolen was started by 171st Tunnelling Company, on 1 January 1917. In February 1917 the Germans dug a tunnel underneath the British gallery and set explosive charges, and the right-hand branch of the British gallery was damaged and it was abandoned. In March 1917 the Germans exploded about

900 feet of the main gallery. A new gallery had to be mined to bypass the damaged tunnel, and the detonator leads had to be rerouted through this new tunnel. There was serious difficulty with gas while the new tunnel was being dug. In a race against time, the new bypass gallery was completed and tamped. The detonating charge, consisting of 500 pounds of ammonal and 500 pounds of dynamite, was laid on 1 June. To celebrate the mine's completion, two officers made their way into the explosion chamber with four bottles of champagne and drinking glasses. The main charge for the mine was made up of 50-pound boxes of ammonal totalling 90,000 pounds. The mine was to be ready to blow only hours before the launch of the major attack on the German lines on the Messines Ridge.

The Messines offensive was preceded by a week-long offensive bombardment. Nine divisions of infantry then advanced upon a 9-mile front. Over six months, around 5 miles of tunnel had been dug and 600 tons of explosives were placed in twenty-one tunnels under the German defences. Nineteen of the mines were blown at 3.10 a.m. on 7 June 1917. The Spanbroekmolen mine actually went up fifteen seconds late, killing some infantry who had already begun to advance and who had been instructed to advance, whether the mine exploded or not. The sound of the nineteen mine explosions was heard in Dublin, London and in Downing Street itself, and was considered the loudest man-made sound until that point. The attack was a huge success, killing 10,000 Germans, and the Allies made significant gains during that first day. Following the war, in 1929, there was concern that all of the mine craters left by the offensive were being lost as each was being reclaimed by local villagers. This led to the purchase of Spanbroekmolen by Lord Wakefield and its renaming as 'the Pool of Peace'. It has been left ever since as a memorial. It measured 430 feet from rim to rim. Now filled with water as a result of the high water table and the clay soil in the area, it is 40 feet deep.

Of the twenty-one mines, two were outside the battlefield and not detonated. However, the British misplaced the documents containing their precise details and positions. One detonated on 17 June 1955 during a thunderstorm, the only casualty being was a cow. The second mine, containing 50,000 pounds of explosives, remains undetected. In the fighting between Austrians and Italians in the Alps, tunnelling played a major part, and sometimes mountain summits were detonated, deliberately causing avalanches.

'Like Fish Caught in a Net'

Joseph Glidden (1813–1906) was an American farmer who patented 'Barb Wire' in 1874. It radically changed ranching in the American

West, allowing for much larger areas to be enclosed and many more cattle to be run. Barbed wire across the great prairies, along with the 'Iron Horse', also sealed the fate of Native American civilisation. When he died in 1906, Glidden was one of the richest men in the USA. Lord Kitchener's remorseless use of barbed wire in the South African war, using it in concentration camps and hampering Boer horsemen's movements, was the next development in its use.

During the First World War, both sides laid barbed wire by the mile in front of trenches to slow enemy attacks. Much thicker than today's wire, the metal prongs were also made longer and stronger. The wire was so effective at stopping troops that it gave defenders a profound advantage in the war. In the early part of the war, nearly all large-scale attacks featured massive artillery bombardments meant to cut the wire, but owing to its open construction, the wire was almost never cut. Millions of miles of barbed wire were laid by both sides. In some cases, the barbed wire in front of a trench could be up to 150 feet in depth. The only time it was safe to lay the wire was at night. Work parties of soldiers would be organised to construct or repair barbed wire in front of the trench. They had to be quiet so that the enemy would not think that they were launching an attack and begin shooting at them. Special construction equipment was developed by the men to limit the noise that occurred during construction. Glidden's invention, like Alfred Nobel's invention of TNT, was meant for peaceful purposes, but was adapted to kill millions.

The next morning we gunners surveyed the dreadful scene in front of our trench. There was a pair of binoculars in the kit, and, under the brazen light of a hot midsummer's day, everything revealed itself stark and clear. The terrain was rather like the Sussex downland, with gentle swelling hills, folds and valleys, making it difficult at first to pinpoint all the enemy trenches as they curled and twisted on the slopes.

It eventually became clear that the German line followed points of eminence, always giving a commanding view of No Man's Land. Immediately in front, and spreading left and right until hidden from view, was clear evidence that the attack had been brutally repulsed. Hundreds of dead, many of the 37th Brigade, were strung out like wreckage washed up to a high-water mark. Quite as many died on the enemy wire as on the ground, like fish caught in the net. They hung there in grotesque postures. Some looked as though they were praying; they had died on their knees and the wire had prevented their fall. From the way the dead were equally spread out, whether on the wire or lying in front of it, it was clear that there were no gaps in the wire at the time of the attack.

Concentrated machine gun fire, from sufficient guns to command every inch of the wire, had done its terrible work. The Germans must have been reinforcing the wire for months. It was so dense that daylight could barely be seen through it. Through the glasses it looked a black mass. The German faith in massed wire had paid off.

How did our planners imagine that Tommies, having survived all other hazards – and there were plenty in crossing No Man's Land – would get through the German wire? Had they studied the black density of it through their powerful binoculars? Who told them that artillery fire would pound such wire to pieces, making it possible to get through? Any Tommy could have told them that shellfire lifts wire up and drops it down, often in a worse tangle than before.

Machine Gunner George Coppard after the
Battle of the Somme

'The Unproven Weapon' – The Self-Propelled Torpedo

The first truly self-propelled torpedo was invented by Robert Whitehead, a Scot, in the 1860s. The Whitehead torpedo was straight-running and propelled by compressed air, becoming the model for most later torpedoes. The first recorded launch of a self-propelled torpedo in battle by a submarine was on 9 December 1912, during the Balkan Wars, when a Greek submarine unsuccessfully fired on a Turkish cruiser. The loss of the British cruisers *Pathfinder*, *Aboutir*, *Cressy*, *Hogue*, *Hawke* and *Hermes* to U-boat torpedoes in the first three months of the war was a tremendous shock. Many at the Admiralty refused to believe it, attributing the losses to mines. Although still unreliable, torpedoes could run for up to 3.5 miles at 38 knots. The prevalent attitude among officers of the various surface fleets, including even the Germans, was to scoff at this 'unproven weapon'.

7

Structures:
Trenches and Tunnels

When all is said and done, the war was mainly a matter of holes and ditches.
Siegfried Sassoon, *Memoirs of an Infantry Officer* (1930)

Trenches

Trench warfare began after the Allied French and British forces halted the German advance on Paris at the First Battle of the Marne, 5–12 September 1914. The Western Front then saw the digging of deep trenches on both sides, across a rough front line of 400 miles. Trench networks crisscrossed approximately 25,000 miles from the English Channel to Switzerland. Over 200,000 men died in the trenches, but it is alleged that General Haig, leader of the British forces, never went to the front line or set foot in a trench. There is still a great network of trenches, tunnels and craters forming landscape features across France, Belgium and elsewhere.

In September 1914 the German commander, General von Falkenhayn, ordered his men to dig trenches that would provide them with protection from the advancing French and British troops. The Allies realised that they could not break through this defensive line, protected by barbed wire and machine guns, and also began to dig trenches. As the Germans had decided first where to defend, their engineers chose the best sites, on higher ground with better sight lines. Apart from this tactical advantage, it also forced Allied soldiers to live in worse conditions. Most of the area had a high water table, and as soldiers began to dig down they would invariably find water two or three feet below the surface. Mud was a constant problem, only partially solved by the addition of wooden 'duck-boards' at the bottom of trenches. As well as on the Western Front, trenches were used at Gallipoli, the Italian Front, the Eastern Front and other theatres of war.

The trench system generally consisted of front-line trenches, support trenches and reserve trenches. Connecting these trenches to one another were communication trenches, where soldiers from one trench could easily communicate with, or exchange with, troops within other trenches. They were deep enough to conceal the men from enemy fire. Millions of yards of barbed wire were twisted into dense barriers ahead of the trenches, to provide more protection from attacking troops. Each trench contained a fire step, from which a soldier could fire or very briefly observe enemy trenches. The trenches were built in a zigzag fashion, bending every 10 yards or so, to stop an attacking soldier firing down the trenches. The zigzag pattern also made difficult for enemy aircrafts to map the trenches. At night soldiers also dug out forward listening posts, or 'saps', where they would sit and quietly listen for enemy movement within underground tunnels, or for signs of a night offensive. These saps extended into no man's land, the varying distance of up to 800 yards or so between opposing forces.

Construction techniques evolved with the war. To make a 300-yard trench about 2,800 of man hours at night were required. Entrenching was the simultaneous digging of the trench by large group of diggers. Sapping involved two or three diggers extending the current trench by its sides. The side of the trench facing the enemy is called a parapet and the rear side is known as a parados. After capturing the trench, the attacking army used to alter the parados with a firestep to use as a parapet. The sides of the trench were protected with sandbags, wooden frames and wire mesh while the floor was covered by wooden duckboards. Sandbags helped muffle the effects of an explosion and absorbed bullets. Loopholes were made in the parapet for soldiers to fire without exposing their heads.

New recruits would often be overcome by the putrid stench, and some were physically sick even before they reached the front line. The smell of a dead body is remarkably memorable. There was rotting flesh from body parts scattered across no man's land, and the same decomposing bodies in nearby shallow graves or shell craters, and overflowing cesspits full of faeces and urine. Creosote and chlorine was used to cover up the cesspits and to try and stave off infections or disease, but many thought this made the odours even worse. Adding to the smell there were also millions of sandbags rotting through dampness from the effects of constant rain, and stagnant mud. Also, many of the men in the trenches were stinking from not having a reasonable wash in weeks. Additionally there were acrid cordite smells from almost continuous heavy shellfire, the gunpowder smell from rifles and machine guns and sometimes the lingering odour of poison gases. This was all apart from the rodents and lice which infested the trenches and their occupants.

At least 10 per cent of fighting soldiers were killed in trench warfare and around 50 per cent were wounded. While British and French trenches were poorly equipped, as their generals believed that they were only very temporary accommodation, German trenches were in stark contrast. Their generals knew that they were in a holding campaign until Russia was defeated. German trenches were built to last and some included bunk beds, furniture, cupboards, water tanks with taps, electric lights and even doorbells. They also were dug deeper, with safer underground tunnels and properly reinforced shelters.

The Unknown Chinese Contribution to Winning the War

The Chinese Labour Corps (CLC) was used to free troops for front-line duty by performing support work and manual labour. Around 140,000 men served in the CLC before it was disbanded and most of the men were repatriated to China between 1918 and 1920. In 1916, Field Marshall Haig had asked for 21,000 labourers to fill the manpower shortage caused by casualties. China was not involved in the war, and its citizens were not allowed by their government to participate in the fighting. The scheme to recruit Chinese to serve as non-military personnel was pioneered by the French government with a contract to supply 50,000 labourers, who began arriving in France in July 1916. The British government also signed an agreement with the Chinese authorities to supply labourers, and their journey to the Western Front in France took three months.

Around 100,000 men served in the British Chinese Labour Corps, about 40,000 served with the French forces, and hundreds of Chinese students served as translators. In March 1917, the Admiralty was no longer able to supply ships for transporting them, and the British government was obliged to bring recruitment to an end. The workers served as labour in the rear, helped build munitions depots, unloaded ships, built dugouts and trenches, repaired roads and railways and filled sandbags. Some worked in armaments factories, others in naval shipyards, for a pittance of one to three francs a day. At the time they were seen as cheap labour, and not even allowed out of camp to fraternise locally. Throughout the war, trade union pressure prevented the introduction of Chinese labourers to the British Isles. When the war ended some Chinese were used to clear mines, or to recover the bodies of soldiers and fill in miles of trenches. After the Armistice, the Chinese, each identified only by an impersonal reference number, were shipped home. Only about 5,000 to 7,000 stayed in France, forming the nucleus of the later Chinese community in Paris.

As well as Chinese workers, there were labour corps serving in France from Egypt, India, Fiji, Malta, Mauritius, Seychelles and the British West Indies, and a Native Labour Corps from South Africa. It was estimated that at the end of the war over 300,000 workers from the colonies had aided the front-line troops. There were 100,000 Egyptians, 21,000 Indians and 20,000 South Africans working throughout France and the Middle East by the end of the war in 1918. Some historians and academics say China's role even prevented a German victory, such was the Allies' manpower shortage toward the end of the war. Some 10,000 never returned home. Their remains lie in thirty French graveyards, each headstone marked in Chinese characters. Their contribution went forgotten for decades until military ceremonies resumed in 2002 at the Chinese cemetery of Noyelles-sur-Mer.

Tunnels

Le Touquet consisted of a number of huge mine craters, roughly between the German front line and our own. In some cases the edge of one crater overlapped that of another. Companies of Royal Engineers, composed of specially selected British coal miners, worked in shifts around the clock digging tunnels towards the German line. When a tunnel was completed after several days of sweating labour, tons of explosive charges were stacked at the end and primed ready for firing. Careful calculations were made to ensure that the centre of the explosion would be bang under the target area.

This was an underground battle against time, with both sides competing against each other to blast great holes through the earth above. With listening apparatus the rival gangs could judge each other's progress, and draw conclusions. A continual contest went on. As soon as a mine was blasted, preparations for a new tunnel were started. On at least one occasion British and German miners clashed and fought underground, when the final partition of earth between them suddenly collapsed.

On the completion of one of the mines, the troops in the danger area withdrew when zero time for detonation was imminent. If the resultant crater had to be captured, an infantry storming party would be ready to rush forward and beat Jerry to it. Some of the craters measured over a hundred feet across the top, descending funnel-wise to a depth of at least thirty feet. At the moment of explosion the ground trembled violently in a miniature earthquake. Then, like an enormous pie crust rising up, slowly at first, the bulging mass of earth crackled in thousands of fissures as it erupted. When the vast sticky mass could no longer contain the pressure beneath, the centre burst open, and the energy released carried all before it. Hundreds of tons of earth hurled skywards to a height of three hundred feet or more, many of the lumps of great size. A state of acute alarm prevailed as the deadly weight commenced to drop, scattered over a huge radial area from the centre of the blast.

George Coppard, *With a Machine Gun to Cambrai* (1969)

Like sapping, tunnelling involved extending the trench, but keeping the roof intact. At times of heavy enemy bombardments, troops would take cover in underground tunnels. The German tunnels were about 45 feet below ground, much deeper than French or British tunnels. Specialist miners were used to dig tunnels under no man's land in order to place mines under enemy positions. Explosives would be packed at the end, the tunnels then sealed, and the explosives detonated. Sealing the tunnels forced the explosion upwards. If the men in the listening saps detected a tunnel being dug, they would have to stop the enemy from setting their mines. To stop the explosives from being placed and triggered, they would send a counter-mining team, which would dig its way into the tunnel and they would try and prevent the mines from being placed. When successfully detonated, the explosion would destroy that section of the trench and the infantry would then advance towards it. Soldiers in the trenches developed different strategies to discover enemy tunnelling. One method was to drive a stick into the ground and hold the other end between the teeth and feel any underground vibrations. Another involved sinking a water-filled oil drum into the floor of the trench. The soldiers then took it in turns to lower an ear into the water to listen for any noise being made by miners.

It could take as long as a year to dig a tunnel and place a mine. As well as digging their own tunnels, the miners had to listen out for enemy tunnellers. When an enemy's tunnel was found it was usually destroyed by placing an explosive charge inside. Mines became larger and larger. At the beginning of the Somme Offensive, the British detonated two mines that contained 24 tons of explosives. In January 1917, General Plumer gave orders for twenty-one mines to be placed under German lines at Messines Ridge. Over the next five months more than 600 tons of explosives were placed in position. On 7 June the blast killed an estimated 10,000 soldiers and could be heard in London.

8

Inventions that Changed Warfare: Land, Sea and Air

In 1915, British Admiral Jacky Fisher wrote, 'The war is going to be won by inventions.' New weapons, such as tanks, the Zeppelin, poison gas, the airplane, the submarine and the machine gun increased casualties and brought the war to civilian populations. For instance, the Germans shelled Paris from 70 miles away with long-range guns, and London was bombed from the air for the first time by Zeppelins. None of these weapons alone proved decisive, as any development was quickly copied, but all of them managed to increase the death toll to unheard-of levels. From the onset, those involved in the war were aware that technology would make a critical impact on the outcome.

Land War Inventions

Artillery (see Weapons)
Larger and larger powerful artillery guns were developed, such as the German 'Big Bertha', which had to be moved on railroads. It could fire an explosive shell the size of a Volkswagen Beetle over 70 miles.

Explosives
Guncotton, the first high explosive, was invented in 1846, and the world's first factory to make it under licence was established in Faversham in Kent in 1847. After the introduction of other high explosives, like cordite and TNT, two huge new factories were built near Faversham. Together these occupied 500 acres, about the same size as the City of London. On 2 April 1916, one of them was the scene of the Great Explosion, the worst in the history of the UK explosives industry, when 100 people died. TNT, or trinitrotoluene, is the most important military explosive, discovered in 1863 as a dye

agent. It was not used as an explosive until 1904. It became popular as a military explosive during the First World War and it became the standard military explosive by the Second World War. The power of other explosives is frequently expressed as an equivalent amount of TNT. It can be cast easily by melting the material and then it can be poured into shells. It is very stable and can be stored for long periods. It is extremely moisture resistant and is not likely to be detonated by physical shock.

Thermite
It was first used as a military incendiary in the war, dropped from German Zeppelins, and was the forerunner of much later napalm bombs. The German formulation was of magnesium powder and magnesium oxide, and the French introduced aluminium iron oxide. Allied troops also introduced thermite destruction grenades, which raiding units used to destroy German equipment.

Machine Guns (see Weapons)
Hand-cranked Gatling guns were still used, but by 1914 gas-driven, water-cooled machine guns had been perfected, and a two-man team could fire hundreds of rounds per minute. Combined with barbed wire to slow or stop attacking troops, machine guns ruled the battlefield. The inventor Hiram Maxim's automatic machine gun was devised after he visited the Paris Electrical Exhibition in 1881. At the exhibition he met a man who told him, 'If you want to make a lot of money, invent something that will enable these Europeans to cut each other's throats with greater facility.' In 1885 Maxim demonstrated the world's first automatic portable machine gun to the British Army. The energy of each bullet's recoil force was used to eject the spent cartridge and insert the next bullet. The gun would therefore fire until the entire belt of bullets was used up. Its success led to an almost direct copy by the German Army – the *maschineengewehr*. It fired 7.92 mm ammunition from a 250-round fabric belt. The German Army deployed over 12,000 machine guns on the Western Front during August 1914, but the British Army had decried Maxim's invention and had hardly any machine guns. The German version had a practical range of 2,200 yards and an extreme range of 4,000 yards. The Russian Pulemyot Maxima was also based on Maxim's invention. In 1910, John Browning produced a new 0.30 inch 'light' machine gun, but the gun was not ordered by the US Army until 1917. Over the next eighteen months, 57,000 of these Browning machine guns were produced for soldiers fighting in Europe.

Rifles

In 1897 the Mauser Gewehr magazine rifle was invented, the German answer to the French Lebel M1888, and it was acclaimed as the most successful bolt-action rifle ever designed. The light machine gun inventor John Browning also produced an automatic rifle which fired a twenty-round magazine. Over 52,000 of these were purchased by the US Army in the war and deployed as support weapons for his light machine gun. The Lee-Enfield bolt-action, magazine-fed, repeating rifle was the main firearm of the Empire and Commonwealth forces, and used by the British from 1895 until 1957. Its fast-operating bolt-action and large magazine capacity enabled a well-trained rifleman to perform the 'mad minute', firing twenty to thirty aimed rounds in sixty seconds, making the Lee-Enfield the fastest military bolt-action rifle of the day. The current world record for aimed bolt-action fire was set in 1914 by a rifle instructor in the British Army, who placed thirty-eight rounds into a 12-inch-wide target at 300 yards in one minute.

Cordite/Poudre B

There had always been great difficulty in giving orders on a battlefield that was swathed in thick smoke from the gunpowder used by guns. In 1886 a smokeless gunpowder called Poudre B was invented in France, and adopted by the French Army. Other countries copied the formula, and the powder revolutionised the effectiveness of small guns and rifles. It was much more powerful than gunpowder, giving an accurate rifle range of up to 1,000 yards. In 1887, Alfred Nobel also developed a smokeless gunpowder, 'ballistite'. This eventually became known as cordite, a powder easier to handle and more powerful than Poudre B. In 1866, Nobel had produced what he believed was a safe and manageable form of nitroglycerine called dynamite. He established his own factory to produce it but in 1864 an explosion at the plant killed Nobel's younger brother and four other workers. Nobel then worked on a safer explosive and in 1875 also invented gelignite.

Tracer Bullets

Fighting at night was unproductive because there was no way to see where you were shooting. The British invented tracer bullets, rounds which emitted small amounts of flammable material that left a phosphorescent trail. The first attempt, in 1915, only left an 'erratic' trail and was limited to 100 yards or so, but the second tracer model, developed in 1916, emitted a regular bright green-white trail. There was an unexpected side benefit: the flammable agent could ignite hydrogen, which enabled it to be used for 'balloon-busting' the German Zeppelins then terrorising England.

Flare Guns

A flare gun is a firearm which launches coloured flares for signalling, generally used in emergencies for people at sea or from the ground to an aircraft. The most common type of flare gun is a Very, which was named after an American naval officer who developed a single-shot, breech-loading, snub-nosed pistol that fired what we call Very flares. They were used to provide illumination in trench warfare at night in the form of brilliant white flares. They were not used to help one's own side, but rather to see if the enemy were out in no man's land, either working (wiring, digging, etc.), patrolling or on a raid. When the Germans or British had their own patrols or working parties out, they did not use Very lights anywhere near them. The lights did not burn for very long, unlike German 'parachute flares'. The best defence was to stand stock still until the flare went out, hoping it did not fall at your feet. Movement while the flare burned was easily spotted, and immediately attracted enemy rifle or machine gun fire. A trench song used the tune of 'When Irish Eyes are Smiling':

> When Very lights are shining,
> Sure they're like the morning light
> And when the guns begin to thunder
> You can hear the angels shite.
> Then the Maxims start to chatter
> And trench mortars send a few,
> And when Very lights are shining
> 'tis time for a rum issue.
>
> When Very lights are shining
> Sure 'tis like the morning dew,
> And when shells begin a bursting
> It makes you think your times come too.
> And when you start advancing
> Five-nines* and gas comes through,
> Sure when Very lights are shining
> 'tis rum or lead for you.
> *German 5.9-inch artillery shells.

Flamethrowers (see Weapons)

These were used by the Byzantines and Chinese two millennia earlier, hurling flaming materials at ships and defensive positions. However, the first design for a modern flamethrower was submitted to the German Army by Richard Fiedler in 1901, and the devices were tested by the Germans through an experimental detachment in 1911. Their true potential was realised during trench warfare. After a massed assault on enemy lines, it was not uncommon for enemy soldiers to 'hole up' in bunkers and dugouts hollowed into the sides of the trenches. Unlike grenades, flamethrowers could neutralise (burn alive) enemy soldiers in these confined spaces without inflicting structural damage. The bunkers could then be used by new occupants of the trenches.

Chemical Weapons (see Weapons)

Germany had the most advanced chemical industry in the world, making 80 per cent of the world's dyes, so using chemicals as weapons happened quickly. Germany pioneered the large-scale use of chemical weapons with a gas attack on Russians on 31 January 1915, during the Battle of Bolimov. The first successful use of chemical weapons occurred on 22 April 1915, near Ypres. Germans sprayed 5,730 cylinders containing 168 tons of chlorine gas towards trenches held by the Allies. The troops fled, but the Germans were slow to follow up with infantry attacks, the gas dissipated and the Allied defences were restored.

The Allies began using poison gas too, and over the course of the war both sides resorted to increasingly insidious compounds to beat gas masks, another new invention. The Germans used around thirty different gas compounds, including phosgene and mustard gas. Phosgene was first used in December 1915, being eighteen times stronger than the green gas cloud of chlorine and much harder to detect. The most effective gas was mustard gas, which was very hard to detect and lingered on the ground. Chlorine caused the lungs to break down and choke a victim to death; mustard gas blinded its victims, and other forms of gas caused the skin to burn and nerves to seize. Chemical warfare caused over a million causalities.

Gas Masks

Wilfred Owen's poem 'Dulce et Decorum est' speaks of the horror of watching a friend fail to get his gas mask on in time. Initially, the only protection from gas attacks was to take a cloth and wet it with water or your urine. The inventor of the gas mask was a Canadian doctor who used a helmet taken from a German prisoner, a canvas hood with eyepieces and a breathing tube. The helmet was treated with chemicals that would absorb chlorine gas. Dr MacPearson's gas mask was improved and first used by the British. This invention was noted as the most important protective device of the First World War.

'The Father of Chemical Warfare' and the Nobel Prize

The German Jew Fritz Haber carried out research in developing chemical fertilisers. Chris Bowlby noted, 'Crops needed better supplies of nitrogen to produce more food. Previously this had been supplied in a limited and laborious way by ships full of bird droppings or nitrates mined in South America. But in 1909 Haber found a way of synthesising ammonia for fertiliser from nitrogen and hydrogen ... The fertiliser went on to be used on a large scale, bringing about a huge increase in crop yields, and practically banishing the fear of famine in large parts of the world.' One scientist has claimed that Haber's was 'the most important technological invention of the twentieth century', for which he was awarded the Nobel Prize in Chemistry in 1918.

At the beginning of the war, Haber offered his services to the German Army and began experimenting with chlorine gas to be used in trench warfare, against the wishes of his wife. Its first use was against the French at Ypres in April 1915. The chlorine gas destroyed the respiratory organs of its victims and this led to a slow death by asphyxiation. Haber was promoted to the rank of captain but when his wife heard about the use of chlorine on soldiers she picked up Haber's military pistol and shot herself in the chest. She died in her son's arms. Later Haber's son also committed suicide in protest against his father's work in the war. Haber became known as the 'father of chemical warfare' and after the war feared arrest as a war criminal, instead receiving a Nobel Prize. The story gets worse. In the 1920s Haber and his team successfully developed cyanide gas. After Hitler gained power in the 30s, Haber was refused entry to his research laboratory because he was a Jew, and went into exile in Switzerland. Haber's research into pesticide gases including cyanide was developed by other German scientists to develop Zyklon B, used by the Nazis to murder millions in concentration camps. Haber died in 1934 but several members of his own extended family were gassed.

Sanitary Napkins

A cotton shortage made the bandaging of dying and wounded soldiers a major problem. Kimberly-Clark was an American paper mill company that realised it could do more with wood pulp besides just make paper. With the right combination of pulp, they developed a material that was five times more absorbent than cotton, yet significantly cheaper to produce. Kimberly-Clark named the new material 'cellucotton' and the Allied Forces began using it for bandages. Women had traditionally improvised all kinds of disposable or washable undergarments to deal with their monthly period. The modern sanitary napkin was made possible by the introduction of Kimberly-Clark's new cellulose bandage material during the war. French nurses began using these clean, absorbent cellulose bandages, followed by British and American nurses. Manufacturers in America began experiments, and in 1920 Kimberly-Clark introduced the first commercial sanitary napkin, Kotex ('cotton' + 'texture'). No publications would carry advertisements for such a product, and it was not until 1926 that Montgomery Ward broke that particular barrier, carrying Kotex napkins in its catalogue. Only since 1988 have sanitary protection products, used by half the British population, been allowed upon British television, and only now in restricted time slots.

Barbed Wire (see Weapons)
The most destructive weapon of the First World War was invented in Illinois in 1874 to help cattle farmers keep control of their herds. Initially used to fence off large sections of the American West, barbed wire was strung by the mile in front of the opposing trenches. Soldiers would become tangled in the wire, easily killed by machine gunners in the defending trench.

Bangalore Torpedo
Designed by Captain McClintock of the Bengal, Bombay and Madras Sappers and Miners in 1912, these were used as a means of exploding booby traps and barricades left over from the Boer and Russo-Japanese Wars. In the First World War, they were put to use as a way of destroying thick enemy barbed wire entanglements, being placed underneath and then detonated. Bangalore torpedoes remained in widespread use into the Second World War and beyond, notably as a means of clearing the beaches during the D-Day landings.

'Armoured Forts' – The Enemy of Barbed Wire
Lieutenant-Colonel Edward Swinton saw the Americans using tractors with caterpillar tracks to transport artillery in 1914. He wrote that 'petrol tractors on the caterpillar principle and armoured with hardened steel plates' would be able to counteract the machine-gunner. Swinton's proposal that the British should build such a machine was summarily rejected by General Sir John French and his scientific advisers. However, the Navy Minister Winston Churchill was impressed by Swinton's views and in February 1915 he set up

a Landships Committee to look in more detail at the proposal to develop a new war machine. In 1914, the 'war of movement' expected by most European generals settled down into a seemingly unwinnable war of trenches. With machine guns reinforcing massed rifle fire from the defending trenches, attackers were mowed down by the thousands before they could even get to the other side of no man's land. A heavily armoured vehicle could advance even in the face of overwhelming small arms fire. With guns, and wheels replaced by armoured treads to handle rough terrain, the tank was born. The first tank, the British Mark I, was designed in 1915 and first saw combat at the Somme in September 1916. Early First World War tanks were equipped with Lewis guns, but were unreliable and often broke down. The French soon followed with the Renault FT, which established the classic tank design with the turret on top. There were some successes and many failures and the tank was not the decisive weapon its backers thought it would be. However, during the Allied summer offensive of 1918, which eventually won the war, the tank played an increasingly large role and was instrumental in taking out barbed wire and allowing infantry to breach German lines.

Armoured Cars

The first fully armoured car was the 'Motow War Car' designed by Vickers in 1902. A great variety of armoured cars appeared on both sides during the war, used in various ways. The cars were primarily armed with light machine guns. As air power became a factor, armoured cars offered a mobile platform for anti-aircraft guns. The first effective use of an armoured vehicle in combat was by the Belgians in August–September 1914. They placed armour plating and a Hotchkiss machine gun on Minerva armoured cars. In Britain, 'fighting cars' were based on either Rolls-Royce, Talbot or Wolseley chassis. Rolls-Royce armoured cars arrived on the Western Front in December 1914, but the mobile period on the Western Front was already over. The Rolls-Royce had been developed by the Duke of Westminster, who took a squadron of the cars to France in time to for the Second Battle of Ypres. They then were sent to the Middle East to play a part in the British campaign in Palestine and elsewhere. The Canadian Automobile Machine Gun Brigade was the first fully mechanised unit in the British Army, established in September 1914. The brigade was originally equipped with eight 'Armoured Autocars', each mounting two machine guns. By 1918 it consisted of two Motor Machine Gun Brigades, each of five gun batteries containing eight weapons apiece. The brigade, and its armoured cars, provided real service in many battles, notably at Amiens.

Mobile X-Ray Machines

With millions of soldiers suffering life-threatening injuries, there was a huge need for the latest medical diagnostic device, the X-ray machine. However, these were very large machines, both too bulky and too delicate to move. Marie Curie began developing mobile X-ray stations for the French military immediately after the outbreak of war. By October 1914, she had installed X-ray machines in several cars and small trucks which toured smaller surgical stations at the front. By the end of the war there were eighteen of these 'radiologic cars' or 'Little Curies' in operation.

Sea War Inventions

Submarines

The German U-boat campaign against Allied shipping sank millions of tons of cargo and killed tens of thousands of sailors and civilians, forcing the Allies to find a way to combat the menace. At the start of the war, Germany had twenty-nine U-boats, and in the first ten weeks they sank five British cruisers. On 5 September 1914, the Royal Navy's *Pathfinder* was sunk by a U-boat, the first ship to be sunk by a submarine using a self-propelled torpedo. Around 55 of 274 crew survived. On 22 September, another U-boat sank three obsolete British warships of the 'Live Bait Squadron' in a single hour. At Gallipoli, U-boats prevented eighteen cruisers and battleships from supporting Allied troops by sinking two of them.

Depth Charges

The solution to the U-boat threat was the depth charge, basically an underwater bomb that could be lobbed from the deck of a ship using a catapult or chute. So that they would not damage surface vessels, depth charges were set to go off at a certain depth by a hydrostatic device that measured water pressure. The first practical depth charge, the Type D, was produced by the Royal Navy's Torpedo and Mine School in January 1916. The first German U-boat sunk by depth charge was the *U–68*, destroyed on 22 March 1916.

Q-Boats

Britain developed Q-boats, attack ships disguised as merchant ships, to meet the U-boat menace. U-boats initially surfaced to threaten unarmed merchant ships and allow their crews to escape. With the realisation that Q-boats existed, they reverted to using torpedoes and giving no warning.

Torpedo

Robert Whitehead in the 1850s was working for the Austrian government, having been asked to develop a new weapon for warships. With the help of his son, he produced a floating torpedo, but it lacked speed and range. By 1870 he had managed to increase its speed to 7 knots and it could now hit a target 700 yards away. In 1871, the Royal Navy purchased Whitehead's invention. Although a 'spar torpedo', a charge attached to a long pole and carried by a small boat, had been used during the American Civil War, Whitehead was the first to produce a self-propelling torpedo. It was propelled by a compressed-air engine and carried 18 pounds of dynamite. Its most important feature was a self-regulating device which kept the torpedo at a constant preset depth. Whitehead's torpedo became very popular and by 1881 his customers included Britain, Russia, France, Germany, Denmark, Italy, Greece, Portugal, Argentina and Belgium. The German Navy was the first to fire an automotive torpedo in the war when, on 8 August 1914, a German U-boat unsuccessfully attacked the British battleship *Monarch*. Torpedoes in 1914 carried a contact-triggered explosive warhead, had a range of 11,000 yards and could travel at 41 knots. However, their ideal range was about less than a mile because they tended to be inaccurate over longer distances. Most large ships were not risked at sea because of torpedoes, and they were mainly used against ships transporting troops and supplies.

Hydrophones

These are microphones that can work underwater, first invented in 1914 by Reginald Fessenden, a Canadian. He had started working on the idea as a way to locate icebergs following the *Titanic* disaster, but his hydrophones were of limited use because they could only give the distance of an underwater object, not the direction. The hydrophone was further improved by the Frenchman Paul Langevin and the Russian Constantin Chilowsky. They invented an ultrasound transducer relying on piezoelectricity, or the electric charge held in certain minerals. A thin layer of quartz held between two metal plates responds to the tiny changes in water pressure resulting from sound waves, allowing the user to determine both the distance and direction of an underwater object. Researchers developed the idea that Allied ships and submarines should be outfitted with sensitive microphones which could detect engine noise from enemy submarines. The Allies also developed ASDIC, what the Americans call 'sonar', but it came too close to the end of the war to be of much help. The hydrophone is said to have claimed its first U-boat victim in April 1916.

Aircraft Carriers

In May 1912, a Short S.27 pontoon biplane was launched from a moving ship, from a ramp on the deck of the HMS *Hibernia* in Weymouth Bay. However, the *Hibernia* was not a true aircraft carrier, as planes could not land on its deck. Seaplanes had to land on the water and then be winched aboard. The first real aircraft carrier was HMS *Furious*, which began life as a 786-foot-long battle cruiser equipped with two massive 18-inch guns. However, naval designers found out that these guns were so large that they might shake the ship to pieces. Looking for other uses for the warship, they built a long platform capable of both launching and landing airplanes. To make more room for take-offs and landings, the airplanes were stored in hangars under the runway, as they still are in modern aircraft carriers. Squadron Commander Edward Dunning became the first person to land a plane on a moving ship when he landed a Sopwith Pup on the *Furious* on 2 August 1917.

Naval Improvements

The naval arms race between Britain and Germany was one of the main causes of the war. In 1906, Britain launched *Dreadnought*, the largest battleship ever, which revolutionised naval ship building. Electricity also began to have a huge impact upon the war. Battleships could have electric signalling lamps, an electric helm indicator, electric fire alarms, remote control from the bridge of bulkhead doors, electrically controlled whistles, and remote reading of water level in the boilers. Electric power turned guns and turrets and raised ammunition from the magazines up to the guns. Incandescent and carbon-arc searchlights became vital for night navigation, for long-range daytime signalling, and for illuminating enemy ships in night engagements.

Air War Inventions

Bombers and Fighter Planes

Airplanes were used for the first time in battle. The First World War started only eleven years after the Wright brothers had flown just 40 yards at less than 7 mph. Airplanes were initially used only for reconnaissance, replacing hot-air balloons. Quickly each side sent their own planes to deny the enemy any advantage through the air. Hugo Junkers in 1915 designed the world's first all-metal plane, the Junkers D-1, but his ideas were too advanced for his time, and it did not begin production until 1918. He also produced the Junkers CL-1, the best German ground-attack plane of the war. Larger airplanes were developed to drop bombs.

The Balloon's Going Up!

Observation balloons were employed as aerial platforms for intelligence gathering on enemy movements and for artillery spotting. From 1914 to 1918, both the Allies and Germany employed balloons, generally a few miles behind the front lines. They were fabric envelopes filled with hydrogen gas, and their flammable nature led to the destruction of hundreds of balloons on both sides. Observers manning these observation balloons frequently had to use a parachute. Typically, the balloons were tethered to a steel cable attached to a winch. This reeled the gasbag to its desired height, often above 3,000 feet, and retrieved it at the end of an observation session. Artillery had been developed to the point where it was capable of engaging targets beyond the visual range of a ground-based observer. Positioning artillery observers at altitude on balloons allowed them to see targets at greater range than they could on the ground. This allowed the artillery to take advantage of its increased range. The balloons were also deployed at sea for use in locating submarines. The idiom 'The balloon's going up!', as an expression for impending battle or major problems, is derived from the fact that a balloon's ascent often signalled a preparatory bombardment for an offensive. Because of their importance as observation platforms, balloons were heavily defended by anti-aircraft guns and patrolling fighter planes. The most successful pilots who attacked the balloons were known as 'balloon-busters'. On 6 October 1918, a single balloon was attacked four different times, and the two men inside, 1st Lt J. A. McDevitt and 2nd Lt G. D. Armstrong, had to parachute jump twice, bringing McDevitt to three jumps within twenty-four hours.

Zeppelins

Gottlieb Daimler and Wilhelm Maybach developed the internal combustion engine for propelling road vehicles. They concentrated on producing the first light-weight, high-speed engine to run on gasoline. In 1889, Daimler and Maybach placed their engine into a horse carriage and drove the car at speeds of 11 miles per hour. They had therefore produced the first four-wheeled automobile. After the men had devised a four-speed gearbox and a belt-drive mechanism to turn the wheels, they decided to sell their cars. In the first road race, held between Paris and Rouen in 1894, only 15 of the 102 cars completed the course. All 15 cars were powered by Daimler engines. This impressed Count Ferdinand Graf von Zeppelin, who decided to use Daimler engines in the airships he was building. They were also used in the armoured cars that were being developed during this period. Gottlieb Daimler died in 1900 but Wilhelm Maybach continued to develop the Mercedes car and the Zeppelin airship.

Interrupter Gear

Propeller blades got in the way of using machine guns in planes. After a Swiss engineer patented his idea for an interrupter gear in 1913, a finished version was developed by Dutch designer Anthony Fokker, whose 'synchroniser', centred on a cam attached to the propeller shaft, allowed a machine gun to fire between the blades of a spinning propeller. The Germans adopted Fokker's invention in May 1915, and the Allies soon produced their own versions.

Drone Bombs

The first pilotless drone was developed for the US Navy in 1916 and 1917 by two inventors, Elmer Sperry and Peter Hewitt, who originally designed it as an unmanned aerial bomb. This was essentially a prototype 'cruise missile'. Measuring under 19 feet across, with a 12-horsepower motor, the Hewitt-Sperry Automatic Aircraft weighed 175 pounds and was stabilised and directed with gyroscopes and a barometer to determine altitude. The first unmanned flight in history occurred on Long Island on 6 March 1918. In the end, its targeting technique, 'point and fly', was too imprecise for it to be useful against ships during the war.

Air Traffic Control

In the first days of flight, once a plane left the ground the pilot was isolated from the terrestrial world, unable to receive any information apart from signals using flags or lamps. The US Army installed the first operational two-way radios in planes during the First World War, but prior to US involvement. Development began in 1915 at San Diego, and by 1916 technicians could send a radio telegraph over a distance of 140 miles. Radio telegraph messages were also exchanged between planes in flight. In 1917, for the first time, a human voice was transmitted by radio from a plane in flight to an operator on the ground.

Land, Air and Sea Inventions

Wireless Telegraphy

Invented by Italian Guglielmo Marconi in 1910, wireless telegraphy allowed communication with ships at sea and overland. The apparatus he used was based on the ideas of the German physicist Heinrich Hertz. Marconi improved Hertz's design by earthing the transmitter and receiver, and found that an insulated aerial enabled him to increase the distance of transmission. Marconi's system was adopted by the Royal Navy, and by wartime ground forces.

Radio

The First World War was the first major war able to draw upon new electrical technologies: radio, for example, became essential for communications. The most important advance in radio was the transmission of voice rather than code, something the electron tube, as oscillator and amplifier, made possible. Large naval vessels were fitted with radios, although when they were used, it did make it easier for enemy submarines to discover where they were. Reconnaissance aircraft with enough power to carry heavy wireless sets of up to 100 pounds were quickly able to communicate positions of enemy artillery.

Synthetic Rubber

During the war, Germany was forced to develop the industrialised version of this synthetic product. A pilot plant of methyl rubber from dimethylbutadiene had been developed in 1911, but not until 1915, during the First World War, did commercial production take place in Germany. Mark Michalovic noted that 'war was usually the catalyst for sparking interest in synthetic rubber ... mechanised warfare requires lots of rubber hoses, belts, gaskets, tires, etc., for tanks, airplanes and such. In the First World War, British naval blockades, however, kept Germany from getting natural rubber from Southeast Asia.' Over 24,000 tonnes of methyl rubber were produced by Germany between 1914 and 1918. This research, paired with a rise in natural rubber prices, was the springboard for the massive development of the synthetic rubber industry all over the world, eventually producing elastomers.

9

Animals at War:
Heroes and Villains

We must remember the role played especially by horses, as evidenced in the recent film *War Horse*, but also mules, dogs, camels and pigeons, which were also used in war. Even cats, white mice, canaries, glow-worms and slugs served a purpose. However, there were also the horrors of disease-carrying lice, fleas, nits, rats and frogs, especially in the trenches.

Animal Heroes

War Horses and Mules

The thriller writer Dennis Wheatley served as a lieutenant in the Royal Field Artillery and took to wearing a monocle. Wheatley said that he wore it not for affectation but because it helped him look brave in action as it stopped him from ducking – the monocle would have fallen out. Serving with the Divisional Ammunition Column, he was based behind the front line but occasionally came under fire from German artillery. Wheatley later described a 1917 attack where horses and mules were killed: 'There were dead ones lying all over the place and score of others were floundering and screaming with broken legs, terrible neck wounds or their entrails hanging out. We went back for our pistols and spent the next hour putting the poor, seriously injured brutes out of their misery by shooting them through the head. To do this we had to wade ankle deep through blood and guts. That night we lost over 100 horses.'

At the start of war, the British Army owned only eighty motor vehicles but over 25,000 horses, and during the next two weeks a further 165,000 horses were compulsorily requisitioned from Britain. Horses were also purchased from the USA, New Zealand, South Africa,

India, Spain and Portugal. Horses aged three to twelve were trained as rapidly as possible by British soldiers called 'roughriders'. When they were ready, the horses were formed into squadrons and taken to action. The best horses were taken by the cavalry. They had to be strong, as the average cavalryman's weight was 12 stone and equipment, saddle, ammunition, etc. could weigh another 9 stone. Men in the cavalry were told to take the weight off their horses as much as they could, so they dismounted and walked with their horses, unsaddling them at every opportunity. We must remember that most horses were large working animals, not like racehorses or today's 'pet' horses. They were used for working the farms, pulling carriages and carts, etc. All armies were extremely dependent on horses for transporting goods and supplies, especially on the Western Front, where muddy conditions made it very difficult to use motorised transport. Gas masks were made for horses on both sides to protect their eyes in the 'death zones'.

The British Army also purchased a large number of mules from the USA. These had terrific stamina, and endured the terrible conditions on the front lines better than the horse. By 1917, the British Army alone was employing around 530,000 horses and 230,000 mules. Large numbers of horses were killed, wounded, became lame, sick or simply dropped dead from exhaustion or fear. The Army had to buy about 15,000 horses a month just to maintain the number they needed, and up to half a million British Army horses were killed during the war. Horses served with the BEF from the very start until the end of the war, serving at the front, in the rear and in the support lines. Horses and mules followed every forward push or retreat across no man's land, supplying food (including their own), water and ammunition. They were worked to the point of death, and died in their thousands from starvation, overwork and injuries. Without the light draught horse and mule, it was impossible to fight on the Western Front. They were taken, sometimes forcibly, from families, farms, factories and coal pits across the world, to be shipped to war zones. Horses designated as 'light draught' formed the backbone of the Army's logistic support. Measuring from 15 hands and 2 inches to 16 hands, and weighing up to 1,200 pounds, they were desperately needed to pull light artillery carriages, supply carts, food, munitions wagons and ambulances,

The larger Shire horses were classed as 'heavy draught', and were teamed together to pull larger artillery pieces. However, over the years they were replaced, as bigger and bigger guns needed tractors, motor vehicles and sometimes locomotives to pull them. The light draught horse and mule, however, were needed constantly. Indeed, their numbers with the BEF in France rose from 25,000 to over 475,000 by the autumn of 1918. On all fronts and theatres a staggering 1 million-plus horses and mules were listed in service with British and Commonwealth forces by the close of war. By the end of the War, the British alone had used 870,000 horses.

At the rearguard action at Le Cateau, 26 August 1914, Artillery Sergeant Albert George, remembered, 'We could see ammunition wagons trying to replenish, getting about half-way to the gun, then a couple of shells would burst, blowing the drivers and horses to smithereens, it was a terrible sight but the last two days had made us used to it.' In the same retreat, Gunner J. W. Palmer recorded the difficulties in keeping horses fed and watered during the retreat:

The position over the rations for both men and horses was rather precarious. These were the days when we went without rations of any kind or water. The horses were more or less starved of water. On the retreat we went to various streams with our buckets, but no sooner had we got the water halfway back to them, than we moved again. We had strong feelings towards our horses. We went into the fields and beat the corn and oats out of the ears and brought them back, but that didn't save them. As the days went on, the horse's belly got more up into the middle of its back, and the cry was frequently down the line, 'Saddler – a plate and a punch!' This meant that the saddler had to come along and punch some more holes in the horse's leather girth to keep the saddles on.

Supplying the fodder for horses and mules was a permanent problem. The average ration for the light draught horse during a 'normal' spell in France was 12 lbs of oats, 10 lbs of hay and some bran for a bran mash at least once a week. They actually were given around 25 per cent grain below what a horse would be fed in Britain, so horses were constantly hungry and were even seen trying to eat wagon wheels. When grain was in short supply, these hard-working, exhausted horses and mules would be fed on sawdust cake.

A shaggy coat keeps horses warm and protects them from the elements but also aggravates skin disorders and parasitical activity, all of which can become seriously debilitating. The decision to clip horses meant that many were lost to exposure or pneumonia in the first winter. Those in charge of horses and mules then ignored orders and left most of the winter coat unshorn. Some dead horses were rendered down for fat and eaten. A horse produces around 15 kg of droppings a day, which was used as fertilizer, burnt, or heated to give off a gas which could light lamps and burners.

In just one day during the 1916 Battle of Verdun in France, for instance, some 7,000 horses were killed, including nearly 100 animals that died after being struck by a French naval gun blast. One of the last cavalry charges of the war came at the Battle of the Somme in 1916. The attack was on 14 July on High Wood, a German strongpoint that was holding up the British advance. Men from the 20th Deccan Horse, an Indian cavalry unit, attacked the German positions. Armed with lances and going uphill, which slowed down the charging horses, some of the men did reach the woods. Some Germans surrendered when confronted by cavalry in woodland, something they could not have expected. However, the attack, while brave, was very costly, with 102 men killed along with 130 horses. 'Horses were easier targets than men, and you could do more damage to the enemy's supply lines if you hit the horses.'

At the end of the great Arras offensives in April 1917, gunners were short of 3,500 draught horses. The Royal Regiment of Artillery's 167th Brigade noted in its diary that 'many horses died of sheer fatigue'. Gunner Philip Sylvester remembered the stark horror of this time: 'We moved forward, but the conditions were terrible. The ammunition that had been prepared by our leaders for this great spring offensive had to be brought up with the supplies, over roads which were sometimes up to one's knees in slimy, yellow-brown mud. The horses were up to their bellies in mud. We'd put them on a picket line between the wagon wheels at night and they'd be sunk in over their fetlocks the next day. We had to shoot quite a number.' It was not only on the Western Front that horses were vital. In the Iraqi city of Kut in April 1916, the surrounded British garrison was forced to shoot its horses. A young British officer, Edward Mousley, watched sadly as an NCO walked through the stables, placing a revolver shot in the head of each victim in turn. When the man approached Mousley's beloved mount, Don Juan, the lieutenant could no longer bear to look. He kissed the horse, then turned away. However, that night he ate Don Juan's heart and kidneys, as custom decreed that each horse's organs were allotted to its owner. Mousley wrote in his diary, 'I am sure he would have preferred that I, rather than another, should do so.' He kept its black tail for the rest of his life. In March 1918, the British launched a cavalry charge at the Germans. Out of 150 horses used in the charge, only four survived. The rest were cut down by German machine gun fire.

At the war's end, 'standard' and 'poor quality' animals were either auctioned off at rock-bottom prices or sold to French butchers. Of the 1 million horses which left for the Western Front, just 60,000 returned. And even those animals might never have made it home had it not been for a vigorous campaign by Churchill, charities and the press to save them from Continental abattoirs. A nation which had depended on domestic horsepower up until 1914 suddenly lost its workhorses to the front lines and quickly had to find mechanised alternatives.

The Real 'War Horse' – 'The Horse the Germans Couldn't Kill'

John Edward Bernard Seely, 1st Baron Mottistone (1868–1947), was a great friend of Winston Churchill and was the only cabinet minister to go to the front in 1914 and still be there four years later. Known as 'General Jack', Seely was famed for his heroics at the battle at Moreuil Wood, where he led the charge on the back of Warrior. He said of his horse, 'He had to endure everything most hateful to him – violent noise, the bursting of great shells and bright flashes at night, when the white light of bursting shells must have caused violent pain to such sensitive eyes as horses possess. Above all, the smell of blood, terrifying to every horse.'

The first time General Seely rode Warrior through shellfire, it was at the Battle of Mons on the French border, and he was amazed to discover that Warrior did not try to run away and instead the thoroughbred 'was pretending to be brave and succeeding in his task'. From February 1915, Seely commanded the assorted ranchers, clerks, expats, Mounties and Native Americans who made up the three regiments of the Canadian Cavalry. Over countless battles Seely and Warrior fought together, and they gained a mascot status among the troops. General Seely recounted, 'Men would say not "Here comes the general" but "Here's old Warrior".' Once, when Warrior went lame and Seely rode another horse, a shell killed his mount. He wrote, 'I had three ribs broken myself … but my first thought was "What luck it was not Warrior".' Warrior was almost killed when a sniper missed him by inches and hit a horse he was touching noses with. In September 1914, his groom, Jack Thompson, had to gallop him 10 miles across country to escape encirclement by the advancing enemy. In 1915, a shell cut the horse beside Warrior clean in half. Warrior survived the disaster of the advance of tanks and 27,500 horses on Cambrai, when Seely and Warrior had trotted behind the leading tank, only to see it crash through the bridge into the canal at Masnières, destroying the chance of any quick victory. A few days later, the cottage he was stabled in was bombed, and Warrior somehow emerged from the rubble. In 1917, only frantic digging extricated him from mud in Passchendaele. In 1918, a direct hit on the ruined villa in which he was housed left him trapped beneath a shattered beam. Three days later he was ready for one of the last great cavalry charges.

This took place on 30 March 1918 at Moreuil Wood, on the banks of the River Avre near Amiens. Victory would not only secure the riverbank, it would also help stem the great German Spring Offensive of 1918. Behind Warrior were the 1,000 horses of the Canadian Cavalry. The Germans had disbanded their cavalry at the end of 1917, and Lloyd George had argued for the Allies to do the same, as horses were easy targets. In the ten days since the German breakthrough against the Fifth Army at St Quentin, the Canadian Cavalry had trekked a 120-mile loop south from Peronne to cross the Oise, and then worked back north to get around the spearhead of the enemy advance. The Germans had smashed the British line, advancing 40 miles and taking more than 100,000 prisoners. Churchill wrote, 'Actual defeat seemed to stare the Allies in the face.'

Churchill had been urgently sent as a special envoy from Lloyd George to be briefed. He met with Marshal Foch of France and then General Rawlinson, the commander of the beleaguered British Fifth Army, at his headquarters 10 miles south of Amiens. Rawlinson told Churchill, 'The men are just crawling slowly backwards ... They are completely worn out.' Churchill asked Rawlinson if he would still be in position the next day, and wrote, 'He made a grimace, the dominant effect of which was not encouraging to my mind.'

A few miles away, Seely made an independent decision that was crucial to halting the Germans and restoring the Fifth Army's morale. He knew that at full gallop he could shift hundreds of men half a mile in a couple of minutes. The general led the charge. In fact, he could not hold Warrior. After they had crossed a bridge and come up out of the hollow, according to Seely, 'he was determined to go forward, and with a great leap started off. All sensation of fear had vanished from him as he galloped on at racing speed. There was a hail of bullets from the enemy as we crossed the intervening space and mounted the hill, but Warrior cared for nothing.' Seely, Prince Antoine and six others in his squadron made it to the German lines, but five cavalrymen were killed. Seely believed that it was riding Warrior at the enemy which made them retreat, believing there were 'thousands' of soldiers following, although in truth, half of his group had been hit. The cavalry's pennant was planted. Squadron after squadron came thundering up the hill, taking many casualties but also causing them. They were supported by the Royal Flying Corps, which dropped 190 bombs and fired 17,000 rounds into the melee. The German official history records that one bomb knocked out an entire battalion staff: 'Moreuil Wood is hell.' A sad Easter Service was held next morning. Although Moreuil Wood had been taken and the German advance had been checked, a quarter of the men and half of the horses had been lost.

Another summons came that afternoon. Seely and Warrior were to report 6 miles north to Gentelles at 2 a.m. to plan an attack in the morning. On the way, Warrior lamed himself in the dark and was out of action. Next day, Seely was gassed and both his replacement horses were killed. Warrior was still a survivor. General Jack Seely was aged fifty-one in the Moreuil Wood attack, and legend has it that he later recommended Warrior for the Victoria Cross with the simple citation, 'He went everywhere I went.' After the his injury in 1918, Warrior had recovered sufficiently to join the victory parade in Hyde Park and three years later won the race at the Isle of Wight point-to-point that his sire won in 1909. Warrior lived until 1941, when Seely felt that the extra corn rations needed to keep the thirty-three-year-old hero going could not be justified in wartime, and he was put to sleep.

Horses and the German Failure to Take Paris

Germany could have overrun France in 1914, but were halted at the River Marne because of a shortage of hay for their horses. Horses were a logistical necessity for transporting their supplies, ammunition, food, hauling artillery and machine guns and the like. When the Germans advanced quickly beyond the railheads that supplied their fresh fodder, horses began to suffer, being fed green corn and other unsuitable feeds. The German Army had 84,000 horses in the battlefield, which required 2 million pounds of good fodder per day, and their horses were weak and collapsing. There were also shortages of horseshoes and nails. Because of this the German attack was halted, and eventually reversed, not only because the horses were starving but also because the troops were also famished. This lack of horse feed led to the stabilisation of the front and to trench warfare.

Simpson and His Donkey

While a mule is the offspring of a male donkey and a female horse, the donkey is a separate animal, also known as an ass, and they were widely used at Gallipoli for hauling supplies around cliff paths. John 'Jack' Simpson Kirkpatrick (1892–1915) was an ANZAC stretcher bearer at Gallipoli. This role was generally only given to physically strong men. After deserting from the Merchant Navy and travelling around Australia prior to the war, Simpson apparently enlisted as a means to return to England. One account alleges that he dropped Kirkpatrick from his name and enlisted as John Simpson to avoid being identified as a deserter. He landed at Anzac Cove on 25 April 1915, and in the early hours of the following day, as he was bearing a wounded comrade on his shoulders, he spotted a donkey. He quickly began making use of it to bear his fellow soldiers. From South Shields, as a youth he had worked with donkeys on local beaches during summer holidays. The donkey came to be named Duffy. Simpson would sing and whistle, seeming to ignore the deadly bullets flying through the air, while he tended to his comrades. Colonel (later General) John Monash wrote, 'Private Simpson and his little beast earned the admiration of everyone at the upper end of the valley. They worked all day and night throughout the whole period since the landing, and the help rendered to the wounded was invaluable. Simpson knew no fear and moved unconcernedly amid shrapnel and rifle fire, steadily carrying out his self-imposed task day by day, and he frequently earned the applause of the personnel for his many fearless rescues of wounded men from areas subject to rifle and shrapnel fire.' On 19 May 1915, Simpson was struck by machine gun fire and died, just three weeks after his first action. A whole mythology grew up around 'Simpson and his Donkey'.

Dogs are Horses in the British Army

In the war, dogs were classified as horses by the British Army, as were oxen and camels, for the purposes of simplifying bookkeeping. Dogs had a vital part to play as the complexes of trenches spread throughout the Western Front. Two dogs in particular were used because of their superior strength, agility, territorial nature and trainability: Doberman Pinschers and German Shepherds. Dobermans were used because they are highly intelligent, easily trainable, and possess excellent guarding abilities. Being of slight frame and extremely agile, their dark coat allowed them to slip undetected through no man's land without alerting the enemy. German Shepherds were used also because of their strength, intelligence and trainability. Other dogs used were smaller breeds such as terriers, who were most often employed as 'ratters', trained to hunt and kill rats in the trenches.

Sentry dogs were patrolled using a short leash and a firm hand. They were usually trained to accompany one specific guard and were taught to give a warning signal such as a growl, bark or snarl to indicate when an unknown or suspect presence was in the secure area, be it a camp or military base. Scout dogs were highly trained and had to be of a quiet, disciplined nature. Their role was to work with soldiers on foot, patrolling the terrain ahead of them. These dogs were useful to the military because they could detect enemy scent up to 1,000 yards away, sooner than any man could. Instead of barking and thus drawing attention to the squad, the dog would stiffen, raise its hackles and point its tail, which indicated that the enemy was encroaching upon the terrain. Scout dogs were widely used because they were highly efficient in avoiding detection of the squad. Casualty, or 'Mercy', dogs were trained to find the wounded and dying on battlefields, and were equipped with medical supplies to aid those suffering. Those soldiers who could help themselves to supplies would tend to their own wounds, while other more gravely wounded soldiers would seek the company of a Mercy dog to wait with them while they died.

Messenger dogs proved to be as reliable as soldiers in the dangerous job of running messages. The complexities of trench warfare meant that communication was always a problem. Human runners were potentially large targets and weighed down by uniforms and there was a chance that they would not get through. A trained dog was faster than a soldier, presented less of a target to a sniper and could travel over any terrain. Over 40,000 war dogs were killed while serving with the Allied armies. Dogs were trained to be used as messengers, carrying orders to the front lines in capsules attached to their collars or bodies. Dogs were also used to lay down telegraph wires and telephone cables in dangerous areas, often being shot or blown to bits by mines. Some were harnessed to drag machine gun carriages across the mud, and the Italians used them to pull small supply carts in their mountain war in the Alps.

Rin Tin Tin, a German Shepherd war dog born in a trench in 1918, helped shape our image of dogs as problem solvers, paving the way for the films of Lassie. Rin Tin Tin was rescued by an American soldier and starred in more than forty films. In Britain, the word German was intensely disliked, and German Shepherd dogs were renamed Alsatians, after their origin in Alsace, a part of Europe disputed by Germany and France. Terriers, especially Jack Russells, were used in the trenches to try and clear rats and mice. One stray dog was adopted by a British regiment as a lucky mascot and they made a tin hat for it. Gas masks were adapted for dogs in the war.

In 1917, a bulldog terrier with a short, stubby tail wandered into the Connecticut National Armoury, was adopted by troops training on the Yale Campus and went to France with the 102nd Infantry Regiment. Private John Robert Conroy stowed 'Stubby' below decks when his regiment shipped off to France. Stubby first entered the trenches in February 1918 at the Battle of Chemin des Dames. He was wounded twice, once by shrapnel and once by gas, and took part in seventeen battles. His hearing allowed him to recognise incoming shells well before his comrades could, and he would run through the trenches barking to alert the troops. Trained to recognise English, Stubby also was keen to locate American wounded in no man's land. He would run around no man's land until he heard soldiers speaking English and stand near the wounded, barking until a medic arrived. One time he accosted a German soldier mapping out the American trenches. Stubby bit him and caused him to trip. American soldiers then took the German prisoner. For this act, Stubby was promoted to the rank of sergeant, outranking his owner Corporal Conroy and becoming the first animal ever to be given a rank in the US military. After the war, Stubby was introduced to Presidents Wilson, Harding and Coolidge and attended parades wearing his medals and stripes. When his owner enrolled at Georgetown University, Stubby became the school's mascot for a few years. He died in Conroy's arms in 1926, the most renowned animal war hero in American history.

In Germany, the first guide dog training schools were established during the war, to enhance the mobility of returning veterans who were blinded in combat. The guide dog movement did not take hold in America until Morris Frank returned from Switzerland after being trained with a female German Shepherd named Buddy, the offspring of a German Shepherd war dog. Buddy became America's first guide dog. In 1929, the Seeing Eye Dog Organisation was founded. The first guide dogs in Britain were also German Shepherds. Three of these first were Judy, Meta, and Folly, who were handed over to their new owners, veterans blinded in the First World War, on 6 October 1931. In 1934 the Guide Dogs for the Blind Association was founded in Britain.

Camels

The Imperial Camel Corps Brigade (ICCB) was a camel-mounted infantry brigade that was raised in 1916 and served in the Middle East. It was part of the Egyptian Expeditionary Force, and fought across the Sinai and Palestine and in the Arab Revolt. Unlike the campaigns in Europe, which were bogged down in trench warfare, fighting in the Middle East was more fluid, with both man and animal subjected to extreme climatic conditions. Camels were initially used as beasts of burden to transport equipment and supplies. However, the camel became an effective means of transport for the troops, covering an average distance of 3 miles an hour, or 6 miles an hour trotting, while carrying a soldier, his equipment and supplies. Two companies helped Lawrence of Arabia, and in July 1918 carried out operations sabotaging the Hejaz railway line. Over two years of service there were 246 deaths: 106 British, 84 Australians, 41 New Zealanders, and 9 men from India. A memorial on the Thames Embankment names the soldiers, with the inscription, 'To the Glorious and Immortal Memory of the Officers, NCOs and Men of the Imperial Camel Corps – British, Australian, New Zealand, Indian – who fell in action or died of wounds and disease in Egypt, Sinai, and Palestine, 1916, 1917, 1918.' The German colony of German South West Africa (modern Namibia) used a Camel Corps (*Schutztruppe*) throughout the war to tie down Allied troops in Africa.

Oxen
These were used extensively by the Russian and Serbian armies to transport artillery and supplies.

The Carrier Pigeon with the Croix du Guerre
In 1914, Germany formed the Ostend Carrier Pigeon Detachment. This was a disguise for a Zeppelin unit intended to bomb English port cities. However, pigeons were of immense value to all sides in the war. Each British army was equipped with a motorised mobile pigeon loft, fourteen horse-drawn pigeon lofts and three fixed pigeon lofts. Pigeon lofts were equipped with gas-protection filters. More than 500,000 pigeons carried messages between headquarters and the front lines. Groups of pigeons trained to return to the front lines were also dropped into occupied areas by parachutes, and kept there until soldiers had messages to send back. They were an extremely reliable way of sending messages, with an astonishing success rate of 95 per cent getting through to a destination with their message. Wire-based communications systems were easily cut in two, blown up or tapped into by enemy forces.

In 1914, at the First Battle of the Marne, the French just managed to halt the German attack upon Paris. They began to push back the Germans who had out-advanced their supplies. As the French advanced, they took their seventy-two mobile pigeon lofts with them. However, many of the French Army's pigeons were 'on duty' carrying messages back and forth to HQ. Incredibly, all the pigeons at the Marne returned to their lofts, despite the fact that they would have flown 'blind', not knowing where their loft had moved to. A pigeon's great strength was not only this extraordinary homing instinct but also the speed at which it flew. Shooting one down was very difficult. The only natural way to counter them was to bring birds of prey to the front line as a falcon could bring down a pigeon. However, a bird of prey might also bring down one's own messenger pigeons, so raptors were only mainly used by German forces to try and stop cross-Channel messages.

When pigeons landed back in their home loft, wires in the coop would sound a bell or buzzer, and a soldier of the Signal Corps would know a message had arrived. He would go to the coop, remove the message from the canister, and send it to its destination by telegraph, field phone, or personal messenger. Nearby enemy soldiers often tried to shoot down pigeons, knowing that released birds were carrying important messages. One pigeon, 'The Mocker', flew fifty-two missions before he was wounded. In the Somme advance of 1 July 1916 a soldier was given the job of taking a messenger pigeon in a basket to the front. He was told that an officer would use it to send a message when the first target was reached. Back at headquarters they waited for hours for the pigeon and finally it appeared. The commander cried, 'Give me the message!' and it was handed to him. He opened it and read, 'I am absolutely fed up with carrying this bloody bird around France.'

In October 1918, as the war neared its end, the 194 surviving American soldiers of the 77th Infantry Division found themselves trapped by German soldiers. Of their number, 197 men had been killed in action and approximately 150 were missing or had been taken prisoner. They were cut off from other Allied soldiers and had no working radios. Their position was also being attacked by 'friendly fire', as the Americans were shelling an area they thought was now German. The only chance they had of alerting anybody about their desperate situation was to send a pigeon, with their co-ordinates attached to its leg. The pigeon's name was Cher Ami, and she had already delivered twelve important messages within the American sector at Verdun. When released, she flew 25 miles from behind German lines to the American HQ. Armed with the 'Lost Battalion's' co-ordinates, the Americans launched a rescue mission and the 194 men were saved. Cher Ami was awarded the Croix de Guerre with Palm for her astonishing flight. She would not have known where the Americans' nearest headquarters was, but her natural homing instincts took over. Cher Ami lost her foot and one eye. The crucial message was found in the capsule hanging from a ligament of her shattered leg. She died in 1919 as a result of her battle wounds, and is on display at the National Museum of American History, next to Sergeant Stubby.

Canaries and White Mice
Miners took canaries and white mice into the underground tunnels with them to test for bad air. Only yellow canaries were considered proper; any other colours were returned. There is a memorial to these canaries and white mice entitled *The Tunnellers' Friends*, in the Scottish National War Memorial in Edinburgh Castle.

Goats and Regimental Mascots

The earliest record is that of a goat belonging to the Royal Welsh Fusiliers in the 1775 American War of Independence. Some mascots in the British Army are indicative of the recruiting area of a regiment, such as the Derbyshire Ram, Staffordshire Bull Terrier, Irish Wolfhounds and Welsh Goats. British Army mascots are classified as either regimental pets or regimental mascots. The former are unofficial mascots since they are not recognised by the Army, while the latter are official mascots, having been recognised by the Army. The following were known mascots during the war.

The Royal Welsh Fusiliers, now the 1st Battalion of the Royal Welsh, has a Kashmir goat, always called William (the anglicised version of Gwilym) or Billy for short. In 1775 a wild goat wandered onto a battlefield in Boston, and ended up leading the Welsh regimental colours off the battlefield at the end of the Battle of Bunker Hill. Since then, a goat has always served with the battalion. The goat is a full member of the battalion and, back when it was a 1,000-strong unit, it was in fact comprised of 999 men plus the goat. If the goat is well behaved and does well on parades, quite often it is promoted to lance corporal. It is accorded the full status and privileges of the rank, including membership in the corporals' mess and the right to be saluted by its subordinates. Billy gets a two-a-day cigarette ration. He eats them, as traditionally the tobacco is thought to be good for the coat. He is given Guinness to drink when he is older, 'to keep the iron up'.

During the Crimean War in 1855, it is said that on one particularly cold night, a Private Gwilym Jenkins was on sentry duty. To keep himself warm, he placed a kid goat inside his greatcoat, but he fell asleep. Fortunately, the kid goat bleated when it heard movements of the enemy, and woke up Pte Jenkins, who spotted an advancing Russian patrol. He was able to warn the forward picket and the enemy was driven off. From then on, every time the 41st (Welsh) Regiment of Foot, a predecessor of the Royal Regiment of Wales, went into battle, a goat led the way as good luck. The goat is officially recorded on the battalion ration roll as Gwilym Jenkins, but he is known by his nickname, Taffy. The Royal Regiment of Wales, now the 2nd Battalion of the Royal Welsh, still has a goat named Taffy, officially known as 'Her Majesty's Goat'. The 3rd Battalion (formerly the Royal Welsh Regiment) has a goat named Shenkin, a direct descendant of the original mascot given to the 3rd Royal Welsh Regiment by Queen Victoria after the Crimean War.

Each of the Queen's Royal Hussars and the Royal Scots Dragoon Guards have a great 'drum horse', powerful enough to carry large silver drums. The Royal Irish Regiment has had an Irish Wolfhound since 1902. It was presented by the members of the Irish Wolfhound Club, who hoped the publicity would increase the breed's popularity with the public. The Worcestershire and Sherwood Foresters Regiment has been subsumed into the Mercian Regiment, and has a Private Derby, a Swaledale ram, as the official mascot. It was originally with the defunct 95th Derbyshire Regiment. The first Private Derby was adopted as a mascot in 1858 at the siege and capture of Kotah during the Indian Mutiny. The Royal Regiment of Fusiliers has an Indian blackbuck antelope named Bobby, formerly the mascot of the Royal Warwickshires when they were stationed in India in 1871. The 3rd Battalion The Mercian Regiment has a Staffordshire bull terrier named Watchman, dating back to the Siege of Khartoum and the South Staffordshire Regiment in 1882. The American 27th Infantry Regiment has a Russian Wolfhound, dating from the Russian Civil War when the American Expeditionary Force was sent to Siberia in 1918. The tenacious pursuit tactics of the regiment won the respect of the Bolsheviks, who gave them the name 'Wolfhounds'. This emblem continues to serve as the symbol of the 27th Infantry Regiment. The Australian regiments in Egypt in the First World War had kangaroos as mascots in Egypt, and some went to Gallipoli.

The Cat Detectors
During the First World War, cats were used in the trenches by both sides in an attempt to keep the rat population down. Some cats were used as poison gas 'detectors'. Troops noted that cats became restless and agitated before a gas attack, possibly because they could sense the poison gas in very low concentrations before the appearance of the main cloud.

Dick the Chick
In 1918 a driver named David Spink found a starving hen near St Quentin, and his colleagues called it 'Dick the Chick'. The chicken dived for cover when German planes approached, but wandered around normally if they were Allied planes, and Spink's company followed Dick's example. Spink brought it home to Blighty in his haversack.

Bertha and Bella
The Scots Guards found two cows near Ypres in late 1914, the only remaining animals in a herd wiped out by shellfire. A battalion adopted them as mascots, calling them Bertha and Bella, and they provided fresh milk. They returned to Scotland after the war, and accompanied the Scots Guards on the Victory Parade in London.

Seagulls and Periscopes

After the failure early in the war of the 'Channel boom' defence against U-boats, reliance was placed on mines and on an auxiliary motorboat patrol. Only one in ten of these vessels were armed, one in eighty-five had wireless, and there were too few to patrol vast areas. To deal with a submarine on encounter, 'teams of two swimmers were organised in each motor launch. One man carried a black bag, the other a hammer. The plan was that if a periscope was sighted, the launch would cruise as near to it as possible, then the swimmers would dive in, seize the periscope, and after one man had placed the black bag over it, the other would attempt to shatter the glass with the hammer. Inglefield's other brainchild was to attempt to train seagulls to defecate on periscopes, and for a short while a remote corner of Poole harbour in Dorset was littered with dummy periscopes and hopefully incontinent seagulls.' Between 1915 and 1917, the Admiralty Board of Invention and Research (BIR) considered the use of gulls, pigeons and other birds to indicate the presence of U-boats. The BIR commissioned trials in summer 1917, but then decided to abandon the possibility. The BIR had received suggestions to train gulls to detect periscopes in 1915 and in late 1916 it was proposed that merchant ships should tow a dummy periscope 'from which at intervals food would be discharged like sausage-meat from a machine' to teach the birds to associate periscopes near ships with food, leading them to swoop on the periscopes of real submarines. By August 1917, when the BIR was ending its seagull trials with submarine B3, Admiral Starten asked the scientists how seagulls would be able to distinguish between friendly submarines and U-boats. The scientists responded that British submarines should therefore not go to sea.

Let Slip the Sea Lions of War

In April 1917, fewer than one in four merchant ships was returning to England because of the U-boat menace. 'Captain' Joseph Woodward was commissioned to work with his music-hall animals under the supervision of Admiralty Board of Invention and Research scientists at Lake Bala, Wales, between March and July 1917. He was asked to train his sea lions to indicate the presence of submarines. Curious gulls circled above the sea lion as it surfaced for air for less than a second after remaining submerged for up to a minute at a time, so sometimes helped as intermediate observers: 'We were often greatly helped in following the track of the animals, and in finding them when they were lost by watching the action of the gulls. These birds were always disturbed when one of the sea lions came near them, and they often followed the animals for considerable distances, circling round above them, and swooping down when the sea lion put his head out of the water to breathe' (E. J. Allen, 'Report upon experiments on the hearing powers of sea-lions under water, and on the possibility of training these animals as submarine trackers', BIR 30051/17, Admiralty Board of Invention and Research, London, 1917).

Goldfish and Gas Helmets
After a gas attack, gas helmets were rinsed with water and a goldfish was dropped into the rinsing water. If it died, the mask was still poisoned and needed washing again.

Glow-Worms and Map-Reading
One of the most unlikely nonhuman contributions to the First World War was made by *Lampyris noctiluca*, more commonly known as the European glow-worm, which emits light through bioluminescence. Huddled in dank, dark trenches, enlisted men and officers turned to the incandescent insects for help, collecting them in jars by the thousands. These instant lanterns allowed soldiers in the unlit trenches to examine intelligence reports, study battle maps or simply read letters from home. According to a 2010 study, just ten glow-worms can provide the same amount of illumination as a modern-day street lamp.

Slugs
The common garden slug, *Limax maximus*, was deployed by the American Army in the trenches as an early warning system for the presence of mustard gas. Slugs can detect one particle per 10 million–12 million particles of air, three times better than humans. They would indicate their discomfort to the presence of gas in enough time for the soldiers to put on their gas masks. The chemical warfare unit of the US Army researched the best creature to detect the presence of oncoming gas in time for the soldiers to don their masks. Cows, rats, mice, guinea pigs, cats, flies and fleas were all tested. By the slug's reaction it was also possible to determine the actual proportion of gas in the air. Since one part of mustard gas in 4 million parts of air marked the danger point in man, the slugs gave enough time to sound a signal for putting on masks. Strangely, every creature that had been tested by the Army for gas detection purposes developed pneumonia, except for the slug. The slug was made available for duty in the trenches starting in June 1918.

Winnie the Pooh
Winnipeg, or Winnie (1914–1934), was the name given to a female black bear bought for $20 in Canada from the hunter who shot her mother. Her owner, Lt Harry Colebourn of the Fort Garry Horse, a

Canadian cavalry regiment, smuggled her into Britain as his regiment's unofficial mascot. He was the regiment's veterinarian, and named her after his home city. He had bought the cub en route to the Western Front, and before leaving for France left her at London Zoo. He was going to take her to Winnipeg Zoo after the war, but she was much loved by her keepers and visitors, and stayed in London until her death in 1934. One of her greatest fans was Christopher Robin Milne, the son of A. A. Milne, who altered the name of his own teddy from 'Edward Bear' to 'Winnie the Pooh'. A. A. Milne consequently wrote *Winnie-the-Pooh* in 1926 and *The House at Pooh Corner* in 1928.

Animal Villains

Rats and the Unknown Soldier
The front-line soldier lived with rotting corpses. No man's land in the Ypres Salient at any one time had 10,000 dismembered, fetid corpses rotting on the ground, thus the shrine for the Unknown Soldier was placed there. When shellfire hit these decomposing bodies, parts would be flung into the trenches, hitting the occupants. Often, during a battle, bombardment would destroy the trenches and they would have to be re-dug. It was common practice during combat to hastily bury dozens of bodies in shell holes. When trenches were re-dug, they would regularly have to dig through these mass graves, which involved hacking off green, maggot-ridden limbs. Huge rats fed on the corpses, growing so large and fearless that they often killed badly wounded soldiers. A French soldier wrote of Germans, killed by machine guns, who lay in front of his trench for over a month: 'lined up as on a manoeuvre. The rain falls on them inexorably and bullets shatter their bleached bones. One evening on patrol, we saw enormous rats fleeing from under their faded coats. They were fat from animal meat. A friend of mine, his heart pounding, crawled towards a dead man with a grimacing face, no flesh, skull bare, eyes eaten. Out of his gaping mouth a foul animal jumped.'

Rats were a nightmare in the trenches, spreading diseases and scurrying over sleeping and wounded men. There were millions upon millions of black and brown rats, with the brown being particularly hated. Rats would gorge themselves on human remains, disfiguring them by eating their eyes and liver. They would eat the dying. A single rat couple could produce up to 900 offspring in a year, spreading infection and contaminating food, and they could grow to the size of a small cat. Veteran soldiers used to say that rats sensed impending heavy enemy shellfire and would run away before it began. The biggest rats, so-called 'corpse rats' would fight and possibly chase off cats and dogs.

Rats thrived in their millions among trenches in most fronts of the war – Eastern, Italian, Gallipoli – but primarily on the Western Front. Conditions were ideal for rats, with empty food cans piled in their millions throughout no man's land, thrown out of the trenches on a daily basis. Aside from feeding on rotting food, rats would invade dugouts in search of food and shelter. Rats would also crawl across the faces of sleeping men. Rats openly fed on the decaying remains of comrades killed while advancing across no man's land. Attacking and eating the eyes first, rats would steadily work their way through the remainder of the body in a short space of time. In *Goodbye to All That*, Robert Graves recalled, 'Rats came up from the canal, fed on the plentiful corpses, and multiplied exceedingly. While I stayed here with the Welch [Regiment], a new officer joined the company and, in token of welcome, was given a dugout containing a spring-bed. When he turned in that night he heard a scuffling, shone his torch on the bed, and found two rats on his blanket tussling for the possession of a severed hand.' Shooting at rats was strictly prohibited as a pointless waste of ammunition, but many soldiers took pot shots at nearby rats or attacked them with bayonets.

Lice *(see Diseases)*
Body lice were a never-ending problem, breeding in the seams of filthy clothing and causing men to itch unceasingly. They were impossible to get rid of even when clothes were periodically washed and deloused. Lice eggs invariably remained hidden in the seams, and within a few hours of the clothes being re-worn the body heat generated would cause the eggs to hatch. Allied soldiers described lice as a pale fawn colour, and they left itchy and blotchy red marks all over the body. They created a sour, stale smell on people. One way the soldiers tried to get rid of them was to run a candle over their trousers and shirts. If they put the candle where the lice were thickest, they would pop like popcorn. Lice caused trench fever, a particularly painful disease that began suddenly with severe pain followed by high fever. Recovery, away from the trenches, took up to twelve weeks, but many died from it, especially on the Eastern Front.

Nits
Many men chose to shave their heads entirely to avoid another prevalent scourge, head lice, *Pediculus humans capitis*, and their unhatched eggs, or 'nits'. Hair lice were different to body lice.

Frogs

Frogs were found by the thousands in shell holes covered in water and in the bases of trenches. Slugs and horned beetles crowded the sides of trenches.

Flies and Insects

The ANZAC and British forces in Gallipoli in summer 1915 suffered terribly with swarms of flies, some of which bit, because of the thousands of unburied corpses of humans and animals. They spread disease, and a British soldier wrote that 'in order to eat your food, you had to move your hand over it and then bite suddenly, otherwise a fly came with it. Any bit of food uncovered was blotted out of sight by flies in a couple of seconds.' With so much rotting flesh and food around, flies and maggots were a constant problem for the soldiers. Most soldiers wrapped scarves or towels around their mouths to avoid swallowing them, and flies were responsible for the spread of many infections and diseases in the trenches. Rupert Brooke wrote, 'If I should die, think only this of me: that there's some corner of a foreign field that is forever England.' On his way to fight in Gallipoli he was bitten on the lip by an insect and died on the Greek island of Skyros. Mosquitoes were also a major problem in some war sectors.

The Battle of the Bees

A British force of 8,000 men landed at the port of Tanga to recapture German East Africa upon 5 November 1914, but the gunfire upset several nests of vicious African bees, which forced the invading troops back to their ships. A naval bombardment from the British fleet also hit the British troops. A British soldier was awarded the MC because he kept sending his signal while being stung by 300 bees, the first time in history that a medal was given for bravery under aerial attack. *The Times* claimed that the Germans had deliberately and 'unsportingly' used the bees as biological warfare. The battle claimed eighty-five Germans and Europeans and fifty-four German Askaris (local soldiers) dead or wounded, while the British lost 800 dead, and another 800 wounded or missing in the mangrove swamps. The British had landed all their supplies and weapons, and armed with these, German resistance was enabled. With a force of only 155 German soldiers, 1,200 African Askaris and 3,000 porters, the Germans tied up 120,000 Allied soldiers in Africa until the Armistice was signed.

10

The Strangest Spies and Espionage

We must remember that this was truly a global war. Agents operated across the world for all sides, seeking military intelligence and spreading disinformation. In the latter stages of the war Central Asia was the big prize, where Frederick Bailey and his agents were intent upon uncovering Comintern plots and blunting Soviet efforts to make common cause with Muslim radicals. This particular 'Great Game' did not end until 1921 when the starving Russians withdrew, under threat of exposure, all its backing for anti-British and anti-Western guerrilla wars. In this way, MI6 proved its worth and became an important asset for British governments until it was itself infiltrated.

'M' and the Secret Invisible Ink
Sir George Mansfield Smith-Cumming KCMG CB (1859–1923) was the first director of what would become the Secret Intelligence Service (SIS), also known as MI6. A Royal Navy captain, he increasingly suffered from severe seasickness, and in 1885 was placed on the retired list as unfit for service. He was recalled to duty into the foreign section of Naval Intelligence in 1898, and travelled through eastern Germany and the Balkans pretending to be a highly successful German businessman, despite having absolutely no German language skills. He was oddly successful, and so was recruited to the Secret Service Bureau (SSB) as the director of the foreign section. When the SSB discovered that semen made a good invisible ink, his agents adopted the motto 'Every man his own stylo [fountain pen]'. In 1911, the various security organisations were reorganised, with Smith-Cumming heading the new Foreign Section, responsible for all operations outside Britain. Over the next few years he became known as 'C', after his habit of initialling papers he had read with a C in green ink. This habit became a custom for later

directors, although the C now stands for 'Chief'. Ian Fleming took his habit for James Bond's chief, 'M', Sir Miles Messervy, using Cumming's other name, Mansfield. Budgets were severely limited prior to the war, and Smith-Cumming had come to rely heavily on Sidney Reilly, the 'Ace of Spies', based in St Petersburg. At the outbreak of war Smith-Cumming was thus was able to arrest twenty-two German spies in England. Eleven were executed, as was Sir Roger Casement. Smith-Cumming's Foreign Section became the Secret Intelligence Service, or MI6.

The Man Who Wrote the Thirty-Nine Steps

John Buchan, 1st Baron Tweedsmuir PC GCMG GCVO CH (1875–1940) was a novelist, historian and politician who served as Governor-General of Canada. At the outbreak of war, he wrote for the War Propaganda Bureau and reported from France for *The Times*. He continued to write fiction, and in 1915 published his most famous work, *The Thirty-Nine Steps*, a spy thriller set just prior to the First World War. Buchan then was commissioned in the Intelligence Corps, where he wrote speeches and communiqués for General Haig. Buchan was appointed Director of Information in 1917.

The Spy Who Was Offered a Republic

Sir Compton Mackenzie OBE (1883–1972) was a prolific and popular writer and one of the co-founders of the Scottish Nationalist Party. He served with British Intelligence in the Eastern Mediterranean. His ill health made front-line duties impractical, so he was assigned counter-espionage work during the Gallipoli Campaign, and in 1916 built up a counter-intelligence network in Athens, Greece then being neutral. In 1917, he founded the Aegean Intelligence Service and enjoyed considerable autonomy for some months as its director. He was offered the Presidency of the Republic of Cerigo (the Greek island of Cythera), which was briefly independent while Greece was split between Royalists and the Venizelists (anti-monarchists), but declined the office. Mackenzie was recalled in September 1917. Smith-Cumming considered appointing him as his deputy, but withdrew the suggestion after opposition from within his own service. After the publication of his *Greek Memories* in 1932, he was prosecuted at the Old Bailey under the Official Secrets Act for quoting from supposedly secret documents.

The Highest-Paid Author

William Somerset Maugham (1874–1965), the famous British playwright, novelist and short story writer, was reputedly the highest-paid author during the 1930s.

Maugham trained and qualified as a doctor, but the first run of his first novel, *Liza of Lambeth* (1897), sold out so rapidly that Maugham gave up medicine to write full time. In the First World War, he served with the Red Cross and in the ambulance corps before being recruited in 1916 into the British Secret Intelligence Service, for which he worked in Switzerland and Russia before the Bolshevik Revolution of 1917. He became a conduit for Western cash to try and keep Bolshevism at bay. During and after the war, he travelled in India and Southeast Asia, and many of his experiences were reflected in his short stories and novels.

The Polymath

Conrad Fulke Thomond O'Brien-ffrench, 2nd Marqess of Castle Thomond (1893–1986), was an intelligence officer, captain in the Tipperary Rangers and 16th Queen's Lancers and a Mountie. His regimental nickname was 'Eagle', and he was an accomplished artist, linguist, mountaineer, skier and author. His elder brother was the even more exotically named Rollo Adrien Vladimir Thursby Marie Altieri O'Brien-ffrench. On the first day of the Battle of Mons he was severely wounded, captured and taken prisoner. After many failed escape attempts, he was transferred to what was considered an escape-proof camp at Augustabad. Here, through the use of invisible ink, in letters home he transmitted valuable details of troop movements and other strategic information gathered from incoming prisoners. From 1918 he was working for MI6 and, having learnt fluent Russian in prison camp, gathered information from Russian refugees fleeing the aftermath of the 1917 revolution. Later, he was persuaded to re-join the Secret Intelligence Service, and in Austria was friendly with another agent, Ian Fleming. Upon Friday 11 March 1938, he sent the first report that German troops were about to cross the Austrian border, which they did on 13 March as the prelude to the Second World War.

The Woman Who Created Modern Iraq and Jordan

Gertrude Margaret Lowthian Bell (1868–1926) was a famous writer, traveller, political officer, administrator, archaeologist and spy. She explored, mapped and became highly influential to British imperial policy making due to her contacts in what are now Iraq, Jordan, Syria and other parts of Asia Minor and Arabia. With T. E. Lawrence, she helped establish the Hashemite dynasties of today's Jordan and Iraq. Bell was trusted by tribal leaders throughout the Middle East. She was called to Basra to enable the British Army to reach Baghdad in safety, and was the field controller of another great agent, Harry St

John Philby, the father of the double agent and traitor 'Kim' Philby. T. E. Lawrence (1888–1935), also known as Lawrence of Arabia, worked for Allied intelligence in the Middle East. He also led an Arab revolt against the Turks and wrote about it in *The Seven Pillars of Wisdom*.

The Man Who Took the Rap for His Wife

Major Cecil Aylmer Cameron CBE DSO (1883–1924) was the son of a VC, serving in the Royal Artillery from 1901. In 1911 he and his wife Ruby were convicted of fraud in Edinburgh and sentenced to three years' imprisonment. It was claimed that they had attempted to defraud Lloyd's by claiming £6,500 for the theft of Mrs Cameron's pearl necklace, which had not actually been stolen. He refused to give evidence in his defence and served the full sentence. Following his release, a petition for a pardon was signed by, among others, five dukes, twenty Privy Councillors, and no less than 126 generals. During her imprisonment, his wife had confessed that she alone was the guilty party and Cameron had only been protecting her. He received a full pardon, and was Mentioned in Dispatches four times and awarded the DSO in the war. Cameron, under the codename EVELYN, was responsible for running spies in German-occupied France and Belgium from stations at Folkestone, Rotterdam and Montreuil. He served in Siberia after the war, receiving a CBE, but in 1924 was found shot dead in Hillsborough Barracks, Sheffield. The coroner recorded suicide while temporarily insane. Six other intelligence officers who served under 'O', Ormonde Winter, the monocled Chief of British Army Intelligence, committed suicide.

Marjoribanks, Pronounced Marshbanks

Lieutenant Colonel Sir Claude Edward Marjoribanks Dansey (1876–1947) was the assistant chief of the Secret Intelligence Service known as ACSS, commonly known as MI6. He was also known as Colonel Z, Haywood, Uncle Claude, and codenamed Z. He began his career in intelligence in 1900, and remained active until his death. A former lieutenant in the British North Borneo Company, he was recruited by MI5 and put in charge of 'port intelligence' and the surveillance of civilian passengers during the war. Later he joined MI5, the forerunner to MI6. 'On at least two occasions, assets he developed within the Irish Nationalist Movement were able to warn British Intelligence about plans to dynamite Buckingham Palace.' He worked in Switzerland and the Balkans until 1919. When stationed in Rome in the 1930s, he said that MI6 had no information upon Europe, which was about to erupt into the Second World War. Dansey called the head of MI6 'a half-mad paranoid who preferred to communicate with his people exclusively via messages left in a locked box – to which only his equally half-mad sister had the combination'. He later saved the compromised MI6 by building up a parallel structure, the Z Organisation, which effectively took over from MI6 at the start of the Second World War.

The 'British Agent'

Sir Robert Hamilton Bruce Lockhart KCMG (1887–1970) was a journalist, author and secret agent whose 1932 book *Memoirs of a Secret Agent* became an international bestseller. Aged twenty-one, he worked on a rubber plantation in Malaya where 'there were no other white men' and 'caused a minor sensation by carrying off Amai, the beautiful ward of the Dato' Klana, the local Malay prince ... my first romance'. He suspected he was being poisoned there, and next joined the British Foreign Service as its vice-consul in Moscow. Lockhart was the acting British Consul-General when the first Russian Revolution broke out and was asked by Lloyd George to become the first envoy to the Bolsheviks in January 1918, in order to try and counteract German influence, but he also worked for the Secret Intelligence Service. Lockhart was given £648 worth of diamonds to fund the creation of an agent network in Russia. Lockhart was involved in numerous espionage plots against the Bolshevik government, including a plan to snatch Tsar Nicholas II from them. In 1918, Lockhart and fellow British agent Sidney Riley were implicated in a plot to assassinate Lenin. Lockhart was imprisoned in the Kremlin, and feared being condemned to death, but in an exchange of secret agents was swapped for the Russian diplomat Litvinov. He later spoke in Arthur Ransome's favour, stating he had been a valuable intelligence asset.

The Author of *Swallows and Amazons* Who Married Trotsky's Secretary

Arthur Mitchell Ransome (1884–1967) was a journalist and author. Like many later intelligence officers, he was sometimes out of touch with reality. He dismissed the assassination which started the war as 'a characteristic bit of Balkans savagery'. His amazing triple life in Moscow was as a foreign correspondent, a confidant of Lenin and a British intelligence agent. In 1913 he had left his wife and daughter and went to Russia to study Russian folklore. After the start of the war, he became a foreign correspondent and covered the war on the Eastern Front for the radical newspaper *Daily News*. He also covered the 1917 Russian revolution, developing sympathy for the Bolsheviks and forming friendships with Lenin and Trotsky. Ransome provided some information to British officials and the Secret Intelligence Service (then known as MI1c), which gave him the code name S76 in their files. The British Security Service, MI5, now kept watch on Ransome because of his opposition to Allied intervention against the Russian Revolution. On one of his visits to the United Kingdom, he was searched and threatened with arrest. In 1919 he crossed battle lines twice to deliver a secret Estonian peace proposal to the Bolsheviks, accompanied by his mistress, Trotsky's secretary. As the chaos worsened in Russia and purges took hold among the Bolshevik leaders, Bruce Lockhart recommended official assistance to bring Trotsky's secretary, Evgenia Shelepina, to England. She later married Ransome. By 1937, MI5 were satisfied of Ransome's loyalty, although later evidence uncovered in KGB files suggests that Evgenia Ransome, at least, was involved in smuggling diamonds from the Soviet Union to Paris to help fund the Comintern. It may well be that Ransome was a double agent working for the Bolsheviks against the interests of MI6.

'The Ace of Spies' and the Model for James Bond

Lieutenant Sidney George Reilly MC (1873–1925) was a Russian-born Jewish secret agent employed by Scotland Yard's Special Branch, the British Secret Service Bureau and later the SIS, and is alleged to have spied for at least four nations. His real name may have been Salomon Rosenblum. In the 1920s, his friend, the diplomat and journalist Sir Robert Bruce Lockhart, publicised their thwarted operation to overthrow the Bolsheviks in 1918. Reilly famously became known as the 'Ace of Spies'. After his death, the *London Evening Standard* published in May 1931 a *Master Spy* serial detailing his exploits. Later, Ian Fleming used Reilly as a model for *James Bond*. Historians consider Reilly to be the first 20th-century super-spy. In 1904, working for the British and Japanese, he stole Russian plans for the defence of Port Arthur in the Russo-Japanese War. In 1914, he seems to have arranged munitions sales to both Russia and Germany, before joining the Royal Canadian Flying Corps. Britain's strategic interest had been to keep the Tsar in the war, but after his overthrow it switched to supporting the 'Whites' and overthrowing the Bolsheviks. SIS dispatched Reilly on counter-Bolshevik operations in Germany and Russia. His life is a whirlwind of intrigue, latterly working as a Russian double-agent on behalf of the British. A megalomaniac polyglot Jew, he thrived upon reckless plotting, including the assassination of the Bolshevik leadership, running a network of female couriers and often escaping Dzerzhinsky's ruthless Cheka (the KGB's forerunner) by a hair's breadth.

'The Man of 100 Faces' and 'The Greatest of All Soldiers'

Sir Paul Henry Dukes KBE (1889–1967) was a British author and MI6 officer. As a language teacher in St Petersburg, he acted as a secret agent. He also worked at the Petrograd Conservatoire as a concert pianist and deputy conductor. Dukes set up elaborate plans to help prominent 'White Russians' escape from Soviet prisons and smuggled hundreds of them into Finland. Known as the 'Man of a Hundred Faces', Dukes used a number of disguises, which aided him in assuming a number of identities and allowed him to infiltrate the Communist Party, the Comintern and the dreaded Cheka, or political police. Dukes also learned of the inner workings of the Politburo, and passed the information to British intelligence. He returned to Britain a distinguished hero, and was knighted in 1920 by George V, who called Dukes the 'greatest of all soldiers'. Dukes is the only person knighted based entirely on his exploits in espionage.

The Spy Who Found a Poppy and Looked For Himself

Lt Col Frederick Marshman Bailey CIE (1882–1967) was a British intelligence officer and one of the last protagonists of 'The Great Game', the fight for supremacy between the Russians and the British Empire along the Himalayas. Born in Lahore, he served with the 17th Bengal Lancers and the 32nd Sikh Pioneers, acquired the Tibetan language and explored unknown parts of China and Tibet. A noted geographer, he first discovered the Himalayan blue poppy for the West, the *Meconopsis baileyi*. Bailey served on the Western Front with the Sikh Pioneers, being shot in the arm. A fluent Urdu speaker, he was later wounded twice at Gallipoli, serving with the 5th Gurkhas. He became Political Officer on the North-West Frontier, and was instrumental in organising support for the Basmachi Revolt, an uprising against Russian Imperial and then Soviet rule, by the Muslim peoples of Central Asia. In 1918, he travelled to Tashkent in Central Asia to discover the Bolshevik government's intentions towards India. Here he shadowed Pratap, the nationalist leader of the Provisional Government of India, which was based in Kabul. Pratap was liaising with Germany and Bolshevik authorities for a joint Soviet-German assault into India. The 'Kalmyk Project' was the name given to Soviet plans to launch a surprise attack on the north-west frontier of India via Tibet, Afghanistan and other Himalayan buffer states in 1919–1920. It was a part of Soviet plans for destabilising Britain and the Western European powers through unrest in the Colonial empire. Bailey eventually had to flee for his life from Tashkent, only escaping after pretending to be an Austrian POW. He was then asked to join the secret police, the CHEKA, and his first assignment was to find a British agent called 'Bailey'. Managing to return to England, he was a national hero, and he recorded his exploits in his book *Mission to Tashkent*.

The Man Who Killed Rasputin?

Oswald Rayner (1888/1889–1961) was highly proficient in French, German and Russian, and was recruited to MI6 as an intelligence officer. He is believed to have been involved in the final murder plot against Rasputin and might be the person who fired the shot that actually killed him. Later he compiled an English translation of Yusupov's book *Rasputin: His Malignant Influence and His Assassination*.

The Spy Who Saved Lord Kitchener, and Churchill's Desire to Use Poison Gas

Sir Robert Nathan KCSI CIE (1868–1921) worked against Indian revolutionaries in Bengal, Britain and North America. In 1908, he uncovered the revolutionary organisation of the Anushilan Samiti, an armed anti-British revolutionary group. He began his work for British intelligence against Indian revolutionaries in October 1914, and was closely involved in the interrogation of Indians who worked with the Germans during the war. Nathan identified plans of the Punjabi Ghadar Party and the Berlin Committee to assassinate Lord Kitchener in 1915. Lenin was plotting Islamic revolution in India and the overthrow of the British Empire. Winston Churchill wanted to use poison gas on a massive scale to exterminate the Bolsheviks and sent out enough canisters to gas thousands. British gunboats were despatched to the Baltic and speedboats were launched to skim over mines and rescue spies trapped in Russia. In America, Nathan successfully brought the Ghadarites and staff at the German consulate to trial following the Annie Larsen Arms Plot. He organised the Hindu–German Conspiracy trial, which at the time was the longest in American legal history.

Agent 'X'

Vincent Kraft (1888–1914?) was a German double agent in Southeast Asia, involved in British counter-intelligence in the Hindu–German Conspiracy. He had been sent by the German high command as a part of the larger Indo-German conspiracy, and turned double agent for the British in Singapore in 1915. The conspiracy involved Irish republicans and Indian nationalists in India, Germany and America, and its aim was to overthrow the British Raj. Kraft was supposed to organise secret shipments from Germany for the Indian revolutionary underground, the Ghadar Party. The intelligence passed on by Kraft was instrumental in uncovering parts of the plot, especially the plans to ship arms to India on board two ships in June 1915. He also leaked details of the plans of the German consul at Shanghai to raid the penal colony of Andaman Islands, and raise an expeditionary force to raid towns on the Indian coast including Madras and Calcutta. He passed on detailed information of the Berlin Committee's activities in Washington DC, Siam and Persia. He was forced to flee through Mexico to Japan, his last known location at the end of the war, and he was only known by his codename until the 1950s, when secret Indian government archives were declassified.

'The Heroine of Nili'

Sarah Aaronsohn (1890–1917) was a member of Nili, a ring of Jewish spies working for the British. Israel at this time was a province of the Turkish-ruled Ottoman Empire. She had left Istanbul to escape an unhappy marriage, and, on her way home to Haifa, personally witnessed the Armenian Genocide. In her testimony, she describes seeing hundreds of bodies of men, women and babies, sickened Armenians being loaded onto trains, and a massacre of up to 5,000 Armenians by setting them alight on bonfires. Sickened, she decided to help the British overthrow the Ottoman Empire. With her brothers, sister and friends, she formed Nili, a spy organisation. Aaronsohn oversaw the operations of the spy ring and passed information to British agents offshore. When her brother was away, she headed the spy operations in Palestine. Sometimes she travelled widely throughout Ottoman territory, collecting information useful to the British, and brought it directly to them in Egypt. In 1917 her brother urged her to remain in British-controlled Egypt, expecting Ottoman reprisals, but she returned home. In September 1917, the Ottomans caught her carrier pigeon with a message to the British and decrypted the Nili code. In October, the Nili base was surrounded and she was captured. After four days of torture, she managed to shoot and kill herself with a pistol concealed under a tile in the bathroom. By avoiding further torture she knew she could protect her colleagues. In her last letter, she revealed her hopes for an Ottoman-free Jewish homeland. Because of Jewish attitudes to suicide, Aaronsohn was forbidden from being traditionally buried in a Jewish cemetery.

A State Funeral for a Heroine

Gabrielle Alina Eugenia Maria Petit (1893–1916) was a Belgian woman, who in 1914 helped her wounded soldier fiancé cross the border into the Netherlands, to be reunited with his regiment. She passed along to British Intelligence information about the German army acquired during the trip. They hired her, gave her brief training, sent her to spy on the German army, and she collected collect information about enemy troop movements using a number of false identities. She was also an active distributor of the clandestine newspaper *La Libre Belgique* and assisted the underground mail service. She helped several young men across the Dutch border, but was betrayed by a German who presented himself as Dutch. In 1916, Petit was tried and convicted for espionage, and given the death sentence. During her trial, Petit refused to reveal the identities of her fellow agents, despite offers of full amnesty. She was executed by firing squad and buried on the execution field. Her story was unknown until after the war, when she began to be seen as a martyr for the nation. In 1919 her state funeral and burial with military honours was attended by the Belgian queen, prime minister and the cardinal of Brussels.

The Arms Dealer in the Spy Swap

Maxim Maximovich Litvinov (1876–1951) was an exiled political activist who returned to Russia in 1903. After the 1905 Revolution he became editor of the SDLP's first legal newspaper. When the Russian government began arresting Bolsheviks in 1906, Litvinov left the country and spent the next ten as an arms dealer for the Bolsheviks, based in Paris. Deported from France in 1908, he moved to London where he was active in the International Socialist Bureau. After the October Revolution, Litvinov was appointed by Lenin as the Soviet government's representative in Britain. However, in 1918, Litvinov was arrested and held until exchanged for Bruce Lockhart, the British diplomat who had been imprisoned in Russia. Litvinov noted in his autobiography, 'After the October Revolution I was appointed the first ambassador to England. Ten months later I was arrested as a hostage for Lockhart and we were later exchanged. I travelled to Sweden and Denmark for negotiations with the bourgeois governments and concluded a series of agreements on the exchange of prisoners of war. I achieved the removal of the British blockade, made the first trade deals in Europe and dispatched the first cargoes after the blockade had been lifted.' Dying in Moscow, his last words to his wife were, 'Englishwoman, go home.'

The Exotic Dancer

Margaretha Geertruida Zelle (1876–1917) was asked to leave school in 1893 after being pursued by the headmaster, and went to live with her uncle in The Hague. In 1895, she married Rudolph MacLeod, after answering a personal ad in a newspaper. MacLeod was a thirty-eight-year-old officer on home leave from the Dutch East Indies. They spent much of their married life living in the tropics of Indonesia and MacLeod's coarseness and Margaretha's youth caused serious friction. In 1902, they moved back to Holland and were soon separated. The penniless Margaretha decided to go to Paris for a new start. She used her experiences in Indonesia to create a new persona, one that donned jewels, smelled of exotic perfume, spoke occasionally in Malay, danced seductively, and often wore very little clothing. She made her dancing debut in a salon and became an instant success. To sound more exotic, she took the stage name Mata Hari, Malayan for 'eye of the day'. She danced at both private salons and later at large theatres. She travelled extensively and took a large number of rich lovers.

During the First World War, her frequent travelling across international borders, her linguistic abilities and her varied companions caused intelligence forces to wonder if she was a spy or even a double agent. The French were confident that she was a spy and arrested her. After a short trial in front of a military court, conducted in private, she was sentenced to death by firing squad. On 15 October 1917, Mata Hari was shot and killed, aged forty-one years, with not a scrap of real evidence against her.

'The Black Panther' – 'The Man Who Killed Kitchener'

The most interesting and exotic of all spies was Frederick 'Fritz' Joubert Duquesne (1877–1956), a South African Boer soldier, prisoner of war, big game hunter, journalist, confidence trickster, war correspondent, stockbroker, adventurer and saboteur. He graduated from London University and then the Royal Military Academy in Brussels before joining the British Army in South Africa. He passed with troops through his parents' farm, finding it to have been destroyed under Kitchener's scorched earth policy. He learned that his sister had been killed and his mother was dying in a British concentration camp. Duquesne decided to take revenge on Kitchener and the British for the rest of his life. When the Second Boer War broke out in 1899, he joined the Boer commandos, and became known as 'the black panther' for his stealth and expertise. He was described by Frederick Burnham as 'the greatest scout the Boers produced ... He was one of the craftiest men I ever met. He had something of a genius of the Apache for avoiding a combat except in his own terms; yet he would be the last man I should choose to meet in a dark room for a fight to the finish, armed only with knives.'

Duquesne was wounded at the Siege of Ladysmith, captured at the Battle of Colenso, but escaped to fight at Bergendal. He was captured in Mozambique by the Portuguese and interned near Lisbon. A daughter of one of the guards helped him escape to Paris, and he then rejoined the British Army and was posted to South Africa in 1901 as an officer. Duquesne went to Cape Town with plans to sabotage strategic British installations and kill Kitchener. He recruited twenty men, but was betrayed by the wife of one. Duquesne escaped the death penalty by volunteering to give Boer codes to the British, which he falsified, but was sentenced to life in prison. The other twenty members of his team were executed by firing squad. He was injured attempting to escape, and then sent to Burt's Island, Bermuda, where he assumed the identity of an American before escaping to New York City. Here he became a journalist for the *New York Herald*, and became known as a travelling war correspondent and big game hunter. Duquesne was Theodore Roosevelt's shooting instructor and hunting companion. The Second Boer War ended and, with his family dead, Duquesne never returned to South Africa, becoming an American citizen in 1913.

For many years, starting in the Second Boer War, Duquesne had been under orders to assassinate Frederick Russell Burnham, a highly decorated American who was Chief of Scouts for the British Army. In 1910 the two men met in Washington DC while separately lobbying Congress to pass a Bill in favour of the importation of African game animals into the United States. After returning to the United States, Burnham had remained active in counterespionage for Britain and was trying to keep track of the elusive Duquesne. Around 1914, Duquesne became a German spy, being sent to Brazil as 'Frederick Fredericks' under the pretence of carrying out scientific research on rubber plants. From his base in Rio de Janeiro, he planted time bombs disguised as cases of mineral samples on British ships, and was credited with sinking twenty-two vessels. In 1916, Duquesne placed an article in a newspaper, reporting his own death in Bolivia at the hands of Amazonian natives.

In this year, when he disappeared from view, he claimed to have sunk the HMS *Hampshire,* killing Lord Kitchener. Details appear in his 1932 biography by Clement Wood, *The Man Who Killed Kitchener: The Life of Fritz Joubert Duquense.* Duquesne reported to Wood that he posed as the Russian duke Boris Zakrevsky and joined Kitchener in Scotland. While on board HMS *Hampshire* with Kitchener, Duquesne supposedly signalled the German submarine that sank the cruiser, and Duquesne claimed that he made his own escape using a life raft before the ship was torpedoed, and was rescued by the submarine. He was apparently awarded the Iron Cross for this act and he appears in several pictures in German uniform wearing an Iron Cross in addition to other medals. The story appears improbable, as there was a Force 8–9 gale around the ship at the time, and single-handedly winching and launching a heavy wooden lifeboat would have been virtually impossible. Apart from this physical task, sailors would have been on watch. Under the alias of Captain Claude Stoughton of the fictitious Western Australian Light Horse regiment, he also gave lectures to US audiences on the First World War. In this uniform, his picture was incredibly printed on US War Bonds.

Dusquesne was arrested in New York in November 1917 on charges of fraud for insurance claims. He had claimed for the 'mineral samples that were lost' with the ships he sank off the coast of Brazil. Duquesne had in his possession a large file of news clippings related to the bomb explosions on ships, as well as a letter from the assistant German vice-consul at Managua, Nicaragua, indicating that 'Captain Duquesne' had rendered considerable service to the German cause.

The British authorities and Burnham wanted Duquesne as the agent responsible for 'murder on the high seas, arson, faking Admiralty documents and conspiring against the Crown'. American authorities agreed to extradite Duquesne to Britain. While awaiting extradition to Britain, Duquesne pretended to be paralysed, and was sent to a hospital prison ward. After nearly two years of feigning paralysis, he disguised himself as a woman and escaped by cutting the bars of his cell and climbing over prison walls. Around a year later, Duquesne was in Boston, using the pseudonym 'retired British Major Frederick Craven'. In 1932, Duquesne was betrayed by a woman who revealed his true identity to the FBI. British authorities requested that he be extradited, but the statute of limitations had expired.

In June 1941, following a two-year investigation, the FBI arrested Duquesne, now calling himself Harry Sawyer, along with two associates on charges of relaying secret information on Allied weaponry and shipping movements to Germany. As a German spy, he went by the code name DUNN. He was found guilty in what was the largest espionage ring conviction in the history of the United States. In January 1942, the thirty-three members of the Duquesne Spy Ring were sentenced to serve a total of more than 300 years in prison. One German spymaster later commented that the ring's roundup delivered 'the death blow' to their espionage efforts in the United States. During the trial, Duquesne claimed that his actions were aimed at the UK as revenge for the crimes done to his people and his country during the Second Anglo-Boer War. The sixty-four-year-old then served twelve years, being mistreated and beaten by inmates, before being released on the grounds of ill health and dying a penniless tramp in hospital two years later.

The Most Important Telegram in History

The United States resolutely remained neutral, and in 1916 Woodrow Wilson was elected President for a second term, largely because of the slogan 'He kept us out of war'. Frustrated by the effective British naval blockade, in February Germany broke its pledge to limit submarine warfare, and in response the United States severed diplomatic relations with Germany. In January 1917, British cryptographers deciphered a telegram from German Foreign Minister Arthur Zimmermann to the German Minister to Mexico, von Eckhardt, offering United States territory to Mexico in return for joining the German cause. This message helped draw the United States into the war and thus changed the course of history. The telegram had such an impact on American opinion that, according to David Kahn, author of *The Codebreakers*, 'No other single cryptanalysis has had such enormous consequences.' It is his opinion that 'never before or since has so much turned upon the solution of a secret message'. In an effort to protect their intelligence from detection and to capitalise on growing anti-German sentiment in the United States, the British waited until 24 February 1917 to present the telegram to Woodrow Wilson. The American press published news of the telegram on 1 March. On 6 April 1917, the United States Congress formally declared war on Germany and its allies.

The Choctaw Code Talkers

The Germans were skilled at intercepting and solving Allied codes. With the tapping of the American Army's phone line, the Germans were able to learn the location of the American Forces as well as where their supplies were kept. Pushmataha, a Choctaw chief who died in 1827, had prophesised that the Choctaw 'War Cry' would be heard in many foreign lands. Among the Choctaw 'Doughboys' were sixteen members of the 142nd Infantry Regiment and two members of the 143rd Infantry Regiment who earned immortality as 'Code Talkers'.

In October 1918, the 36th Division was engaged in its first major battle. Attacking the Germans in the trenches, the Americans were unprotected while crossing a wide stretch of land, except for covering heavy artillery fire from the 142nd Infantry. Artillery fire kept the Germans pinned down, allowing the Americans to kill and capture Germans in their own trenches. Noticing German communications lines lying in the open on the ground, the Americans felt that they had been left behind so that they would be used and the messages could be intercepted. Messengers had normally been sent out from one company to another, but one in four of these messengers or runners were captured by the German troops. The Germans had decoded all transmitted messages up to this point in the war.

However, when a US commander used Choctaw tribe members to form the Oklahoma National Guard unit, they used an extremely complex language that the Germans could not translate. Using telephones, they became known as the Choctaw Code Talkers. Eighteen men were recruited to transmit messages and devise a system of communications for the Code Talkers. Within twenty-four hours after the Code Talkers began their work, the tides of the battle had turned, and in less than seventy-two hours the Germans were retreating and the Allies were on full attack.

After the withdrawal of the regiment it had been found that the Choctaw vocabulary of military terms was insufficient. The Indian for 'Big Gun' was thus used to indicate artillery; 'Little gun shoot fast' was substituted for machine gun; and the battalions were indicated by one, two and three grains of corn. Native Americans were not made US citizens until 1924, and the Choctaw hold dual nationality. Hitler knew about the successful use of the Code Talkers during the First World War. He sent a team of thirty anthropologists to learn Native American languages before the outbreak of the Second World War. Native American languages were used again in the Second World War, with the British using Welsh to a minor extent.

11

Heroes, Heroines and Villains

There are too many heroes – virtually everyone who participated had some heroic qualities – but following are some of the more notable or unknown. Again, it is tempting to treat the 'enemy' as all villains, but this is obviously not the case. The front-line soldier, sailor or seaman shared a common, horrifying experience, and as a rule it is not people who begin wars, but their political rulers. The will to fight is then fortified by propaganda.

Heroes

Sergeant York

Alvin Cullum York (1887–1964), known also by his nickname, Sergeant York, was one of the most decorated American soldiers in the First World War. He led an attack on a German machine gun nest, taking thirty-two machine guns, killing twenty-eight German soldiers and capturing 132 others. This action occurred during the US-led portion of the Meuse–Argonne Offensive in France, which was part of a broader Allied offensive masterminded by Marshal Ferdinand Foch to breach the Hindenburg Line. York returned home with a Medal of Honour, a promotion to sergeant, the French Croix de Guerre, and a gift of 400 acres of good farmland.

Boy Cornwell VC (1900–1916)

His father and brother joined the Army in 1914, and in 1915 Cornwell joined the Royal Navy as a boy sailor. 'Jack' Travers Cornwell, Boy first class, is the youngest recipient of the Victoria Cross, awarded for remaining at his post as sight-setter on the forward 5.5 inch gun in HMS *Chester* at the Battle of Jutland on 31 May 1916. He stayed at his station, although mortally wounded, with dead and wounded lying all round him, because 'he thought he might be needed'. During the exchange of fire he remained there until *Chester* retired from the action, with only one main gun still working. According to one report, 'Cornwell was found to be sole survivor at his gun, shards of steel penetrating his chest, looking at the gun sights and still waiting for orders'. In September 1916, Admiral David Beatty recommended Cornwall for a posthumous VC and George V endorsed it. The recommendation for citation included the following: 'John Travers Cornwell, who was mortally wounded early in the action, but nevertheless remained standing alone at a most exposed post, quietly awaiting orders till the end of the action, with the gun's crew dead and wounded around him. He was under 16½ years old. I regret that he has since died, but I recommend his case for special recognition in justice to his memory and as an acknowledgement of the high example set by him.'

The Harlem Hellfighters and the Battle of Henry Johnson

In 1917, President Wilson ordered the enlistment of all able-bodied men, black or white. The first all-black fighting unit to arrive in France was New York's 369th Infantry. The Commander of the American Expeditionary Forces, General John 'Black Jack' Pershing, bowed to political pressure back home and refused to use the men in combat. He assigned the 369th to the French High Command, who called them '*Les Enfants Perdus*' (the Lost Children.) The unit's white commander, Colonel William Hayward, praised them:

> The 369th Infantry would come to be known as the Harlem Hellfighters. Their motto was 'God damn, let's go.' Years later, a soldier, whose name has been lost to history, recounted his march to the front … 'There were a whole lot of blind men, and one-legged men, and one-armed men, and sick men, all coming this way. I asked a white man where all these wounded men come from? And he says, "Nigger, they're coming from right where you're going the day after tomorrow."'

In Minacourt, France, the officers and men of the 369th came face to face with the horrors of war, described by Major Warner Ross: 'Stones, dirt, shrapnel, limbs and whole trees filled the air. The noise and concussion alone were enough to kill you. Flashes of fire, the metallic crack of high explosives, the awful explosions that dug holes 15 and 20 feet in diameter. The utter and complete pandemonium and the stench of hell, your friends blown to bits, the pieces dropping near you.'

The Harlem Hellfighters were one of the few African American units that saw the front lines. For their extraordinary acts of heroism, the soldiers received the French Croix de Guerre, a medal awarded to soldiers from Allied countries for bravery in combat. However, in the USA their deeds were largely ignored. On the night of 14 May 1918, Privates Henry Johnson and Needham Roberts were standing watch when a grenade landed in their trench. Needham was badly wounded and Henry Johnson was left to face a German patrol on his own. One of the unit's white officers, Major Arthur Little, recounted, 'The little soldier from Albany came down like a wild cat upon the shoulders of the German. As Johnson sprang, he unsheathed his bolo knife, and as his knife landed upon the shoulders of that ill-fated Boche, the blade of the knife was buried to the hilt through the crown of the German's head.' In fierce hand-to-hand combat, the former porter from the New York Central Railroad singlehandedly wounded or killed twenty-four enemy soldiers. Back in America the press called the incident 'The Battle of Henry Johnson': 'Having shot one of his foes down and clubbed another with the butt of his rifle, he sprang to the aid of Roberts with his bolo-knife. As the enemy fell into disorderly retreat, Johnson, three times wounded, sank to the ground, seized a grenade alongside his prostrate body, and literally blew one of the fleeing Germans to fragments.'

Two days later, the men were presented with the Croix de Guerre, the first American soldiers, black or white, to be so honoured in the war. When asked about the event, Henry Johnson said, 'There isn't so much to tell. Just fought for my life. A rabbit would've done that.' The Harlem Hellfighters spent 191 days in front line trenches, more than any other American unit. There was often nothing between the German Army and Paris except these black volunteers from New York. They never had any men captured nor any ground taken. At the Battle of Belleau Wood, a French general ordered the Harlem Hellfighters to retreat. Their commanding officer refused. Colonel Hayward shouted, 'Turn back? I should say not! My men never retire. They go forward or they die!'

At the same Battle of Belleau Wood, Gunnery Sergeant Dan Daily of 6th Marine Regiment shouted at his men to attack: 'Come on you sons of bitches! Do you wanna live forever?' In the war, Daily was awarded the Medal of Honour twice in addition to the Navy Cross, the highest award for valour awarded by the Navy/Marine Corps.

Australia's Most Decorated Hero

Alfred John Shout was a New Zealander who had served in South Africa with the Border Horse between 1900 and 1902, where he was twice wounded. Shout was Mentioned in Dispatches and made

Queen's Sergeant, earning the Queen's South Africa Medal. He served with the Australian Imperial Forces in the First World War. 'On 27 April 1915 Lieutenant Shout showed conspicuous courage by continually exposing himself to the enemy at Anzac Cove, Gallipoli while organising, planning and leading a successful bayonet charge against the Turks. Following their charge, in the course of which their newly acquired position was secured, Shout and a corporal left the trench which was being continually swept with machine-gun fire, and advanced further into no-man's land, where they dug in before proceeding to snipe at the Turks. In the words of Private Charles Huntley Thompson of the 13th Battalion, "That was the bravest thing I ever saw"; for these actions Shout was awarded the Military Cross and Mentioned in Dispatches.' The 1st Division suffered 366 casualties between 25 and 29 April, including Lieutenant Shout, who was wounded when a bullet passed through his arm and entered his chest. On 29 July Shout was promoted to captain and given a special Mention in Dispatches. In the attack on Lone Pine the Australians lost 80 officers and 2,197 other ranks in five days. Seven members of the Australian contingent were to be awarded the Victoria Cross for their actions at Lone Pine. One, a posthumous award, was to Captain Shout MC. After days of gallantry, he set off down the trench, lighting three bombs, and had hurled two before the third went off prematurely. It blew off his hand and severely injured his face and body. Shout continued to direct the attack, then murmured, 'Good old First Brigade, well done!' before he lost consciousness through loss of blood, and died from his wounds at sea on 11 August 1915. Shout's VC citation reads, 'For most conspicuous bravery at Lone Pine Trenches, in the Gallipoli Peninsula. On the morning of 9 August, 1915, with a small party, Captain Shout charged down trenches strongly occupied by the enemy and personally threw four bombs among them, killing eight and routing the remainder. In the afternoon of the same day, from the position gained in the morning, he captured a further length of trench under similar conditions and continued personally to bomb the enemy at close range, under very heavy fire, until he was severely wounded, losing his right hand and left eye. This most gallant officer has since succumbed to his injuries.'

Bimbashi Garland of Arabia OBE MC FCS

Major Herbert Garland (1880–1921), a maverick explosives expert, was a mentor to Lawrence of Arabia and played a pivotal role in the Arab insurgency against the Ottoman Empire. Admired by Lawrence for his daring and cleverness, Garland died forgotten and almost penniless in Gravesend aged just thirty-eight. He was researching metals in Egypt at the outbreak of war, and joined the Arab Bureau along with Lawrence. He was initially given the nominal rank of sergeant, before he was later promoted to captain. However, he was always referred to as *Bimbashi* or major. The Arab Bureau was a group of intellectuals, spies and businessmen whose 'mission was to collect every possible bit of information about Turkish and German influence in the Middle East and act on it in the field'. Despite once blowing himself up with explosives and suffering severe shock, he joined Lawrence and Arab rebels to attack the Hejaz railway, one of the main supply lines of the Ottoman Empire. Garland developed new types of mines and taught Lawrence and the rebels how to use them in their guerrilla campaign. Their efforts acted as a great diversion, allowing the British to take Damascus and bring down the Ottoman Empire.

Lawrence writes that Garland 'had years of practical knowledge of explosives' and 'his own devices for mining trains and felling telegraphs and cutting metals'. 'His knowledge of Arabic' allowed Garland 'to teach the art of demolition to unlettered Bedouin in a quick and ready way. His pupils admired a man who was never at a loss ... Incidentally, he taught me how to be familiar with high explosive ... Sappers handled it like a sacrament, but Garland would shove a handful of detonators into his pocket with a string of primers, fuse, and fusées and jump gaily on his camel for a week's ride to the Hejaz railway.' In a letter, Lawrence wrote to a diplomat, 'Garland is much more use than I could be. For one thing he is senior to me and he is an expert on explosives and machinery. He digs their trenches, teaches them musketry, machine gun work, signalling, gets on with them exceedingly well and always makes the best of things and they all like him too.'

Garland was the Arab Bureau's explosives expert. He developed grenades and improvised a mortar system to launch them, which was used extensively at Gallipoli. Garland also designed a range of improvised explosive devices (IEDs) used by Lawrence and Garland himself in the Arab Revolt against Ottoman rule. Garland invented and planted the IED that was the first to derail a moving train in 1917, using an improvised pressure switch mechanism. He built and emplaced his IEDs so that they would not be spotted by Turkish troops employed to check the line before a train ran. His descriptions of Bedouin medical practices and beliefs act as a fascinating record of a lost world: 'The Bedouin have their own forms of treatment for disease, the chief of which are bloodletting and branding. I saw a sheikh who had burnt huge patches on the soles of his feet as a cure for dysentery.' His final act in the war was being sent to Medina, the last place to be surrendered by the Turks, in late 1918. He was responsible for overseeing the surrender of this key town to the Allies.

Downton Abbey and the Kingdom of Albania

Aubrey Nigel Henry Molyneux Herbert (1880–1923) was the half-brother of the 5th Earl of Carnarvon, who had funded the crucial excavations in Egypt led by Howard Carter. His home was Highclere, where *Downton Abbey* is filmed. An MP, Aubrey Herbert took up the Albanian cause in the Balkans and supported their independence claims against the Ottoman Empire. He had been an honorary attaché in Constantinople, and an Albanian delegation attending the Balkan Conference in London in May 1913 put to him the question of whether he would accept their throne. Lack of funds prevented him from accepting, but seven years later the Albanians offered him the throne once more, though again he had to refuse, for very different reasons.

He had terribly defective eyesight, which ruled him out of active service. To join the Army, Aubrey had walked into a military tailor's and asked to be fitted out in the uniform of an officer of the Irish Guards. Then he simply joined the departing regiment as it marched out of Wellington Barracks and joined their train to Southampton. He lost himself among the scuffle of soldiers as they embarked on a troop ship bound for France. On board, he somehow bluffed his way into the regiment with the rank of lieutenant as the ship steamed out of harbour with the BEF. On 1 September 1914, Aubrey Herbert was shot and wounded as he rode his horse Moonshine, delivering orders to a division of the Coldstream Guards south-west of Compiègne, France. Later that afternoon Herbert became a prisoner of the Germans when they overran the woods where he lay injured on a stretcher. He was moved to a makeshift hospital, which was in turn retaken ten days later by the French, and Herbert underwent a second operation to extract the fragmented bullet that was still causing him considerable pain.

Convalescing in England, Herbert tried to rejoin the Western Front, but his sight disability was now known. He managed to join the Arab Bureau in Cairo. Fluent in several languages, Herbert had many adventures during the war. He went on a secret mission in 1916 with Lawrence of Arabia in an attempt to secure the release of the besieged British-Indian garrison at Kut-Al-Amara, 100 miles south of Baghdad. Khalil Pasha, the military governor of the region, refused their bribe of £2 million. Surrender became the only option for General Townshend after about 1,750 of his men had died from wounds or disease during a siege that had lasted 147 days. Some 2,600 British and 9,300 Indian other ranks were rounded up and marched away, and 70 per cent of the British and 50 per cent of the Indian troops died of disease or at the hands of the Ottoman guards during the death marches or in captivity. General Townshend sat out the war in comfort on a small island in the Sea of Marmara, close to Istanbul, and was knighted while in captivity. The First World War is littered with instances of the higher officer classes being rewarded for failure.

Lawrence of Arabia

Thomas Edward Lawrence (1888–1935) was born in Tremadog, Wales, the second illegitimate son of Sir Thomas Chapman, 7th Baron of Westmeath. Lawrence came to consider himself Welsh enough to apply for and gain a Welsh scholarship to the 'Welsh College', Jesus College, Oxford. Joining Oxford University's Officer Training Corps, in January 1914, eight months before the war began, he was co-opted by the Army to carry out a military survey of the Negev desert. In 1916, he transferred to the Arab Bureau, but took a break to sail south and meet Emir Faisal of Arabia. In him Lawrence saw the leader of the Arab Revolt, and for the next two years he lived and fought alongside Faisal and other tribal leaders. A dangerous crossing of enemy territory, dynamiting enemy railways on the way, culminated in the taking of the port of Aqaba on the Red Sea from the Turks. Other successes followed, but Lawrence became worried that the British were playing a double game with the Arabs, and that Faisal would be let down by the Allies after the war. Lawrence played an important part in the Sinai/Palestine campaign, in particular the Arab Revolt against their Ottoman overlords from 1917 to 1918.

Lawrence resigned his commission in the Army and, to try and escape fame, enlisted in the RAF as aircraftsman John Hume Ross. At first Lawrence was rejected by the RAF recruiting officer, W. E. Johns, the creator of the Biggles stories, who thought that there was something 'fishy' about his application. Lawrence returned later in the day with a letter signed by someone in high authority, ordering Johns to enrol 'Mr Ross'. After a few years, when Lawrence's deception leaked out to the press, he resigned from the RAF. He then enrolled in the Tank Corps as T .E. Shaw, a role and name he retained until shortly before his death. Lawrence was killed in 1935, having been involved in an accident when, riding his motorbike to post a number of letters, he swerved to avoid two boys on bicycles in a dip in the road.

Major 'Mick' Mannock

Edward 'Mick' Mannock (1887–1918) was partially sighted in one eye from an infection picked up in India. In 1914, the National

Telephone Company sent him to work in Turkey. When war was declared he tried to return but was arrested and placed in a concentration camp. After several attempts at escape, which resulted in long periods of solitary confinement in a 6-foot cage, Mannock was eventually allowed to leave for England in April 1915, where he joined the Army. He was soon promoted to the rank of sergeant major, but his health was poor and the Army considered him unfit for military duties. In March 1916, he managed to obtain a transfer to the Royal Engineers as an officer cadet. Although he had very little formal schooling, it was not long before he achieved the rank of second lieutenant. In the summer of 1916, Mannock began reading in the newspapers about the exploits of Albert Ball, Britain's leading flying ace. Not yet twenty years old, Ball had already shot down eleven German aircraft. Mannock asked for a transfer to the RFC in August 1916, and displayed a natural aptitude for flying. Captain Chapman, one of the men responsible for training Mick, later reported that 'he made his first solo flight with but a few hours' instruction, for he seemed to master the rudiments of flying with his first hour in the air and from then on threw the machine about how he pleased'.

In April 1917, Mannock arrived at St Omer in France. At first his working-class mannerisms and political opinions upset the other pilots. Lieutenant Lionel Blaxland later recalled, 'He was different. His manner, speech and familiarity were not liked. New men usually took their time and listened to the more experienced hands; Mannock was the complete opposite. He offered ideas about everything: how the war was going, how it should be fought, the role of scout pilots, what was wrong or right with our machines. Most men in his position, by that I mean a man with his background, would have shut up.' Mannock in June 1917 made his first confirmed 'kill', but then was wounded in the head in a dogfight with two German pilots. He now developed a reputation as one of the most talented pilots in the RFC. In his first two weeks back at the Western Front he won four dogfights in his SE-5a, and on 16 August he shot down four aircraft in a day. The following morning he added two more victories, and on 17 September won the Military Cross for driving off several enemy aircraft while destroying three German observation balloons. The following month he was awarded a bar on his Military Cross. For this, the official citation read, 'He attacked a formation of five enemy machines single-handed and shot one down out of control; while engaged with an enemy machine, he was attacked by two others, one of which he forced down to the ground.'

However, Mannock was affected by the amount of men he was killing. In his diary, he recorded visiting the site where one of his victims had crashed near the front line: 'The journey to the trenches was rather nauseating – dead men's legs sticking through the sides with puttees and boots still on – bits of bones and skulls with the hair peeling off, and tons of equipment and clothing lying about. This sort of thing, together with the strong graveyard stench and the dead and mangled body of the pilot combined to upset me for a few days.' Mannock was especially upset when he saw one of his victims' planes catch fire on its way to the ground. From that experience, Mannock always carried a revolver with him in his cockpit: 'The other fellows all laugh at me for carrying a revolver. They think I'm going to shoot down a machine with it, but they're wrong. The reason I bought it was to finish myself as soon as I see the first signs of flames.'

His fear of fire was worsened by the British decision not to allow pilots in the RFC to carry parachutes, when German pilots had been using them successfully for several months. He was especially angry about the main reason given for this decision: 'It is the opinion of the board that the presence of such an apparatus might impair the fighting spirit of pilots and cause them to abandon machines which might otherwise be capable of returning to base for repair.' In 1917, Mannock was promoted to captain, and as flight commander was able to introduce a new approach to combat flying. Mannock believed that the 'days of the lone fighter was past and air fighting was now a matter for co-ordinated and planned fighting units which could inflict maximum damage and minimum losses'. In February 1918, Mannock became flight commander of 74 Squadron. The next three months saw thirty-six more victories, leading Mannock overtake Albert Ball's total of forty-four kills, and on 20 July he shot down an Albatros that brought him to fifty-eight victories, one more than the British record held by James McCudden. In June he was promoted to the rank of major and the following month became commander of 85 Squadron.

On 26 July, Major Mannock offered to help a new arrival, Donald Inglis, obtain his first victory. After shooting down an Albatros behind the German front line, the two men headed for home. While crossing the trenches, the fighters were met with a massive volley of ground fire. The engine of Mannock's aircraft was hit and immediately caught fire and crashed behind German lines. Mannock's body was found 250 yards from the wreck of his machine. He did not fire his revolver but it is believed he might have jumped from his blazing plane just before it crashed.

After his death, Mick Mannock was awarded the VC for 'an outstanding example of fearless courage, remarkable skill, devotion to duty and self-sacrifice which has never been surpassed'.

The Dead School Caretaker

Sidney Godley (1889–1957) began work aged fourteen in an ironmonger's shop, but six years later joined the Royal Fusiliers. By the time the Fusiliers reached Nimy on 22 August 1914, the French were having great difficulty in holding off the Germans. It was decided to try and retreat to the River Marne, where they hoped they would be able to stop the German advance towards Paris. The Royal Fusiliers were ordered to hold two bridges over the Mons–Condé Canal while the rest of the British Army retreated to the Marne. The Royal Fusiliers only had two machine guns against six divisions of the German Army. The Germans directed their fire at the two machine-gunners, as they knew these men had to be killed before they could advance over the bridges. As soon as one machine gunner was killed, another soldier moved forward to carry out the task.

Eventually, the commanding officer, Lt Steele, decided that his men would have to retreat. Before they left, Steele asked for two volunteers to man the machine-guns to cover the retreat. Godley and Maurice Dease volunteered and Godley had to remove three bodies before he could get to his machine gun. Within a few minutes of taking over the other gun, Dease was killed. A shell exploded by the side of Godley and a piece of shrapnel entered his back. Although in terrible pain, he continued firing at the Germans trying to cross the bridge. A bullet hit him in the head and lodged in his skull. Godley's single-handed defence of the bridge for two hours gave the Fusiliers enough time to retreat.

Godley was eventually captured by Germans soldiers and taken to a German field hospital where surgeons removed bullets from his head and back. News of Godley's bravery soon reached Britain and George V decided to award him the VC posthumously as it was thought that he had died. However, it was eventually discovered that Godley was alive and recovering in a German prisoner of war camp. Godley remained in the camp until the Armistice. After the war Godley became a school caretaker, dying in 1957.

The Iniquity of Charles Jarvis

Charles Alfred Jarvis (1881–1948), the son of a Scottish coastguard, was in the Army until 1907, and rejoined on the outbreak of war. Jarvis joined the Royal Engineers and arrived at Mons on 22 August 1914. The following day, Lance-Corporal Jarvis was one of the men sent to destroy eight of the bridges over the Mons–Condé Canal. Although coming under heavy German fire, Jarvis managed to blow up the bridge at Jemappes. He was awarded the VC, but in January 1917 Jarvis was dismissed from the Army after over seventeen years of service. He claimed in an interview with the *London Star* that the authorities had done this to avoid paying him the pension granted to men with eighteen years' service. The generals received earldoms and pensions and the heroes like Godley and Jarvis received nothing. After leaving the Army, Jarvis found work as a labourer.

The Orphaned Grandson of a Slave and the First Black Officer

Walter Tull, the son of joiner, was born in Folkestone in April 1888. Walter's father, the son of a slave, had arrived from Barbados in 1876. In 1895, when Walter was seven, his mother died. His father remarried but died two years later. Walter's stepmother was unable to cope with all six children and Walter and his brother Edward were sent to an orphanage in Bethnal Green. Tull served an apprenticeship as a printer, and also, by the beginning of the 1908/09 season, was playing for Clapton football team. They won the Amateur Cup, the London Senior Cup and the London County Amateur Cup and Tull was immediately signed by Tottenham Hotspur, probably becoming only the second black man to play professional football in Britain. He later became Northampton Town's most popular player. Glasgow Rangers wanted to buy Tull in 1914, but he abandoned football to join the 'Football Battalion' at the start of the war, where he was quickly promoted to sergeant.

Tull took part in the Somme Offensive in July 1916, and in December 1916 he developed trench fever and was sent home to England to recover. Tull had impressed his senior officers and they recommended that he should be considered for further promotion. When he recovered, instead of being sent back to France, he went to the officer training school at Gailes in Scotland. Despite military regulations forbidding 'any negro or person of colour' being an officer, Walter Tull received his commission in May, 1917.

Tull thus became the first black combat officer in the British Army, despite the fact that 'according to the *Manual of Military Law*, black soldiers of any rank were not desirable. During the First World War, military chiefs of staff, with government approval, argued that white soldiers would not accept orders issued by men of colour and on no account should black soldiers serve on the front line'. Lieutenant Walter Tull was sent to the Italian front as the first ever black officer in the British Army. He led his men at the Battle of Piave and was

Mentioned in Dispatches for his 'gallantry and coolness' under fire. Tull stayed in Italy until 1918, when he was transferred to the Western Front. On 25 March 1918, 2nd Lieutenant Tull was ordered to lead his men in an attack on the German trenches at Favreuil, where he was hit by a German bullet. Tull was such a popular officer that several of his men made valiant efforts under heavy fire from machine guns to bring him back to the British trenches. These efforts were in vain and Tull's body was never found.

The Eton Twins

Francis Octavius Grenfell (1880–1915) and his twin brother Riversdale 'Rivy' Grenfell (1880–1914) were Etonians, and keen sportsmen. In 1899, Francis joined Seaforth Highlanders in Egypt. He was commissioned in the King's Royal Rifle Corps. In 1901, he went to South Africa and fought in the Boer War before joining the crack cavalry regiment, the 9th Lancers, in India. In 1914, Captain Francis Grenfell and the 9th Lancers were sent to France, as was his twin, Rivy Grenfell, who had joined the Bucks Hussars.

On 16 August 1914, Francis Grenfell and his men were sent to carry out reconnaissance in the Harmignies area of Belgium before taking part in the Battle of Mons, where the 9th Lancers were ordered to charge the German gun positions. Hit by a hail of machine gun fire, shelling and rifle fire, casualties were heavy. When they reassembled, they discovered that they had suffered over eighty casualties. Later that day Grenfell and a small group of his men volunteered to try and rescue the men of the 119 Field Battery, who were in danger of being captured by the Germans. The operation was successful but Grenfell was badly wounded. He was taken by his friend the Duke of Westminster, in the duke's Rolls-Royce, to the nearby convent hospital, where he was treated by French nuns.

Grenfell recovered from his wounds and was awarded the VC for saving the 119 Field Battery. While Francis was in hospital he heard that his twin brother, Rivy Grenfell, had been killed on the Western Front. In October 1914, he became squadron commander of the 9th Lancers. He was again seriously wounded a few weeks later and was shipped back to England for treatment. By the spring of 1915 Grenfell had recovered, and on 7 April he had a farewell dinner with his close friends Winston Churchill and John Buchan (see Spies). Grenfell was sent to Ypres and on 24 May endured the first German chlorine gas attack. The following day Grenfell was shot and killed on the Ypres–Menin road. Grenfell was one of 208 casualties out of the 350 men in the 9th Lancers who had taken part in the action that day.

Winston in the Trenches

Less than a year after its outbreak, the First World War produced a bloody stalemate on the Western Front and serious setbacks for the Russians on the Eastern Front. Allied military officials needed solutions to this dual problem. Churchill asked if there were any alternatives to 'sending our armies to chew barbed wire in Flanders'. His advisors at the Admiralty wanted to invade the Gallipoli Peninsula via the Dardanelles Strait, reinforcing Russia and thus knocking Turkey out of the war. Churchill initially preferred, like Admiral Fisher, a more direct attack upon northern Germany from the Baltic Sea, which would relieve Russia and threaten the rear of the German Western Front. However, he succumbed to his advisers and eventually embraced the Dardanelles Campaign and became its champion. British forces had massive naval superiority, and troops from Australia and New Zealand (ANZACs) had not yet been committed in France. The operation failed due to a combination of the lack of proper coordination between the Army and Navy, the Navy's fear of U-boats and hesitancy on the part of commanders.

Churchill later wrote, 'The campaign of the Dardanelles had been starved and crippled at every stage by the continued opposition of the French and British High Commands in France to the withdrawal of troops and munitions from the main theatre of the war.' The Dardanelles failure was a major crisis and Churchill took the blame. Asquith remained Prime Minister only by entering into a coalition with the Conservatives. The price the Conservatives demanded was for Churchill to be forced out of the Admiralty and for the debacle to be pinned on him. Churchill bitterly remarked, 'I am the victim of a political intrigue. I am finished.'

Forced to leave the Admiralty, he was given a token position as Chancellor of the Duchy of Lancaster and hoped he could still influence policy. This not being the case, the heartbroken Churchill resigned from government and joined the Army, asking to be posted to the fighting in France. Here he was given the relatively junior post of lieutenant-colonel, commanding the 6th Battalion, Royal Scots Fusiliers on the Western Front. Prime Minister Asquith had vetoed any high command. His soldiers had reservations about being led by a politician, but he led by example, often venturing into no man's land on night patrol. One companion noted, 'He never fell when a shell went off; he never ducked when a bullet went past with its loud crack. He used to say, after watching me duck, "It's no damn use ducking; the bullet has gone a long way past you by now."' Churchill wrote, 'Amid these surroundings, aided by wet and cold, and every minor discomfort, I have found happiness and content such as I have not known for many months.'

Churchill grew extremely frustrated at the consequences of military policies he opposed on the Western Front. After six months, when his depleted battalion was merged with another unit, Churchill returned to the fray in Parliament. Lloyd George's new coalition government appointed Churchill head of the Munitions Office, despite massive opposition. Churchill envisioned the wider application of the airplane and the tank and was an early and consistent champion of both. Beginning with his days at the Admiralty, Winston promoted the development and use of aircraft. which saw tremendous technical advances during four years of war. The tank was conceived to break through barbed wire and trench fortifications and to support advancing troops with machine gun fire. Winston had endorsed its development while at the Admiralty in a memo to Prime Minister Asquith on 5 January 1915. The Munitions Office under Churchill became so effective that, in April 1918, Churchill was able to deliver twice as many guns and airplanes as had been lost in the recent German offensive and replace every tank with a newer, better model.

Since the revolution in 1917 and the separate peace with Germany in 1918, the British had no consistent policy on the Russian Civil War, although they had initially supported the Anti-Bolshevik (White) army. Churchill's views were widely known, and he stated, 'Of all the tyrannies in history, the Bolshevik tyranny is the worst, the most destructive, the most degrading.' Churchill, rising above the disaster of Dardanelles, continually showed the steel necessary to lead Britain through the next world war.

'The Man Who Won the War'

David Lloyd George (1863–1945) was one of the greatest statesmen of the twentieth century and was called 'the greatest prime minister since Pitt'. In the 1906 election, the Liberal Henry Campbell-Bannerman became the new Prime Minister, appointing the capable Lloyd George as president of the Board of Trade. Lloyd George impressed him so much that in 1908 he was promoted to become Chancellor of the Exchequer. He introduced Old Age Pensions (1908) and National Health Insurance (1911) when Chancellor of the Exchequer from 1908 to 1915. A fierce opponent of the Poor Law, the Chancellor wanted to 'lift the shadow of the workhouse from the homes of the poor'. A radical Welsh nationalist and a pacifist, Lloyd George had compared the Boers, in their fight against the Empire, to the Welsh. He only reluctantly moved from pacifism with the invasion of Belgium by Germany in 1914. Even so, with three other senior members of the government, he had written to the Prime Minister, Herbert Asquith, that he intended to resign rather than be party to a war declaration. The other three resigned, but Asquith managed to convince Lloyd George to stay on, as the country needed him.

In August 1914, the South Wales Miners' Federation proposed an international miners' strike to stop the outbreak of war, and there continued to be an anti-war movement in the South Wales mining areas. A massive increase in food prices, coupled with record profits for coal owners, caused a demand for a new wage agreement in 1915, which was refused. The South Wales miners went on strike. They were opposed by the government, coal owners, the Great Britain Miners' Federation and the national newspapers, and the government threatened to imprison any strikers. However, the strike was solid. By then Minister of Munitions, Lloyd George personally intervened and settled the strike, acceding to most of the demands of the South Wales Miners' Federation.

As Minister of War from 1915 to 1916, Lloyd George was put in charge of the total war effort, and found it difficult to control the poor and wasteful tactics of his generals on the Western Front. Lloyd George argued strongly with the dinosaur Douglas Haig, commander in chief of the BEF, and with General Robertson, chief of the Imperial General Staff, about their use of men as cannon fodder. He eventually managed to get Churchill back into government and to dismiss Haig. With great difficulty, he persuaded the Royal Navy to use the convoy system to ensure adequate imports of food and military supplies. The Coalition Government was impressed by Lloyd George's capabilities and began to question Asquith's leadership in these days of crisis. In December 1916, Lloyd George agreed to collaborate with the Conservatives to remove Asquith, becoming Prime Minister, a decision which split the Liberal Party. When at last Lloyd George's proposal was accepted, that the French and British forces fight under one joint commander, Marshall Foch, the war turned decisively the Allies' way. By his forceful policy he was, as Adolf Hitler later said, 'the man who won the war'.

One of the 'Big Three' at the peace negotiations, he was shown to be a brilliant diplomat. Lloyd George mediated a settlement with Germany that marked a compromise between the wishes of Woodrow Wilson and the more punitive actions desired by Clemenceau as France had lost so much in the war. His defeat in 1922 was mainly due to his ceding of 'the Irish Free State' – the modern-day Eire was given its independence by him against strong opposition from the Conservatives in his government. Lloyd George is also notable in world history for approving the Balfour Declaration, promising the Jews a national state in Palestine. Upon Lloyd George's death in 1945, Churchill told the Commons, 'He was the greatest Welshman which that unconquerable race has produced since the age of the Tudors. Much of his work abides, some of it will grow greatly in the future, and those who come after us will find the pillars of his life's toil upstanding, massive and indestructible.'

Heroines

A Woman But 'Not a Mother'

After entering Brussels on 20 August 1914, the German occupying forces allowed the British nurse Edith Louisa Cavell (1865–1915) to remain as matron of a teaching school, which was then converted into a Red Cross Hospital. However, the Germans began to supervise her work, as she began to treat an increasing number of injured German soldiers alongside the Allied injured. During this time she helped around 200 Allied soldiers escape from Belgium into neutral Holland. After a year, her activities were discovered and she was tried for treason by a German court martial in Brussels. Although not involved in espionage, she was condemned to face a firing squad. Her case was skilfully used by the British authorities of the day to boost the recruitment of soldiers at a time when there was no conscription.

The Revd Gahan gave us her final words: 'She then added that she wished all her friends to know that she willingly gave her life for her country, and said: "I have no fear nor shrinking; I have seen death so often that it is not strange or fearful to me." She further said: "I thank God for this ten weeks' quiet before the end. Life has always been hurried and full of difficulty. This time of rest has been a great mercy. They have all been very kind to me here. But this I would say, standing as I do in view of God and eternity, I realise that patriotism is not enough. I must have no hatred or bitterness towards any one."' Pastor le Seur attended her execution: 'The military judge told me that before I arrived with Miss Cavell he addressed the soldiers, saying it was hard for them to fire at a woman, but he wished to impress upon them that she was not a mother.'

The Lady Sapper

In 1914, aged nineteen, Dorothy Lawrence (1896–1964) was living in Paris and wished to be a war reporter on the Western Front. It was nearly impossible for even male reporters to get to the front line at that time. In her autobiography she later wrote, 'I'll see what an ordinary English girl, without credentials or money, can accomplish.' She befriended two English soldiers who taught her to drill and march. She persuaded two Scottish military policemen to cut her hair military style, and then dyed her skin using diluted furniture polish to give it a bronzed colour. With forged identity papers as Private Denis Smith of the 1st Battalion, Leicestershire Regiment, Lawrence headed for the front lines, arriving at the Somme by bicycle. A Lancashire coalminer found her work as a sapper with a tunnelling company, laying mines within 400 yards of the front line, where she was constantly under fire. He found her an abandoned cottage in a nearby forest to sleep in, and she returned to it each night after laying mines by day. The toll of the job, and of hiding her true identity, soon gave her a case of constant chills and rheumatism. She was concerned that if she was killed her true gender would be discovered and the men who had befriended her would be in danger. After ten days of service she presented herself to the commanding sergeant, who promptly placed her under military arrest.

Lawrence was taken to the BEF HQ, interrogated as a spy and made a prisoner of war. From there she was taken across country by horse to Calais, where her interrogation occupied the time of six generals and approximately twenty other officers. She was ignorant of the term camp follower (or prostitute) and she later recalled, 'We talked steadily at cross purposes. On my side I had not been informed what the term meant, and on their side they continued unaware that I remained ignorant! So I often appeared to be telling lies.' From Calais she was taken to St Omer for more interrogation. The Army was embarrassed that a woman had breached security and was fearful of more women taking on male roles during the war if her story got out. She was then taken to a convent where she swore not to write about her experiences and signed an affidavit to that effect, or she would be sent to jail. She was then sent back to London, where she was unable to write of her experiences, which had been her original intent. She later said, 'In making that promise I sacrificed the chance of earning by newspaper articles written on this escapade, as a girl compelled to earn her livelihood.' After the war ended she wrote of her experiences, but her work was censored by the War Office and not fully published until many years later when discovered by a historian in the archives. In 1919, the twenty-four-year-old Lawrence moved to Islington, but after claiming she had been raped by her church guardian, she was institutionalised as insane in 1925. She died at Friern Hospital, formerly Colney Hatch Lunatic Asylum, in 1964. She was possibly quite sane, but rotted for almost forty years. Until very recently, people could be locked up for life, with no chance of release, upon grounds which would be laughable today.

The 'Russian Joan of Arc' Who Founded 'the Women's Battalion of Death'

Maria Leontievna Bochkareva, née Frolkova, nicknamed 'Yashka' (1889–1920), was a Russian soldier. After two disastrous marriages to abusive men, in November 1914 she managed to join the 25th Tomsk Reserve Battalion of the Imperial Russian Army by securing the personal permission of Tsar Nicholas II. Men of the regiment treated her with ridicule or sexually harassed her until she proved her worth in battle. She bayoneted at least one German soldier to death. Bochkareva was twice wounded and decorated three times for bravery. In 1917, Bochkareva convinced the revolutionary leader Alexander Kerensky that a battalion formed exclusively of women would shame more men into fighting in the war. Bochkareva's 1st Russian Women's Battalion of Death initially attracted around 2,000 women volunteers, but her strict discipline drove all but around 300 dedicated women soldiers out of the unit.

The unit disbanded after facing increasing hostility from the male troops remaining at the front. She was detained by the Bolsheviks but released, then rearrested after taking a message to the White Army in the Caucasus. Bochkareva was scheduled to be executed, but rescued by a soldier who had served with her in the Imperial Army in 1915, who convinced the Bolsheviks to stay her execution. She was allowed to leave the country and left for America. In April 1919, she returned and attempted to form a women's medical detachment under White Army Admiral Kolchak. She operated around Omsk and became known as 'the Russian Joan of Arc', but before long she was again captured by the Bolsheviks. She was interrogated for four months and sentenced to execution, found guilty of being an enemy of the people. There was no evidence of any counter-revolutionary activity against the Red Army. The Cheka carried out her execution by firing squad on 16 May 1920.

The 'Sworn Virgin' Serbian Captain from Yorkshire

Flora Sandes (1876–1956) was the only British woman to officially serve as a soldier in the war. She volunteered to be a St John Ambulance driver and left for Serbia on 12 August 1914 with a group of thirty-six women to try and aid the humanitarian crises there. While there, Sandes joined the Serbian Red Cross and worked in an ambulance for the Second Infantry Regiment of the Serbian Army. During the retreat into Albania, Sandes was separated from her unit and, for her own safety, enrolled as a soldier with a Serbian regiment. Following the Balkan tradition of 'sworn virgins', it was not unknown for women to serve in the Serbian Army, but Sandes was the only British woman to do so. She was promoted to corporal, and in 1916, during the Serbian advance on Monastir, she was seriously wounded by a grenade in hand-to-hand combat. She subsequently received the highest decoration of the Serbian military, and was promoted to the rank of sergeant major. In 1916, Sandes published her autobiography, *An English Woman-Sergeant in the Serbian Army*, based on her letters and diaries. She used this account to help her raise funds for the Serbian Army. Unable to continue fighting due to her injury, she had spent the remainder of the war running a hospital. At the end of the war she was commissioned as a captain, and was finally demobilised in October 1922. She later drove Belgrade's first taxi. Sandes subsequently returned to England, spending spent the last years of her life in Suffolk.

The Romanian Lieutenant

Ecaterina Teodoroiu, born Cătălina Toderoiu (1894–1917), was a teacher when the Romanian kingdom entered the war on the Allied side in 1916. In October 1916, Ecaterina joined the Romanian Army during the first battle at Jiu, when its 1st Army threw back the Germans. She had initially worked as a nurse but she subsequently decided to become a front-line soldier, being deeply impressed by the patriotism of the wounded and by the death of her brother Nicolae. She was sent to the front rather reluctantly, but soon proved her worth. She was then taken prisoner but managed to escape by killing at least two German soldiers. She was wounded and hospitalised in November but returned to the front, where she was soon decorated, advanced in rank to second lieutenant and given the command of a twenty-five-man platoon. For her bravery she was awarded the Military Virtue Medal, 1st Class. The Russians and Romanians faced the Germans at the great Battle of Mărășești, where she was hit in the chest by German machine gun fire while leading her platoon. According to some accounts, her last words before dying were, 'Forward, men, I'm still with you!' A film was made of her life in 1930.

The Most Decorated Female Combatant in the History of Warfare

Milunka Savić (1888–1973) was a Serbian who fought in the Balkan Wars and the First World War. In 1913, her brother received call-up papers to serve in the Second Balkan War but she chose to go in his place. She cut her hair and donned men's clothes and quickly saw action. In the centre of the Serbian lines during the Battle of Bregalnica (13 June–8 July 1913), Savić and the Serbian 'Iron Regiment' bore the brunt of the Bulgarian attack, and then launched a desperate series of counter-attacks aimed at breaking their onslaught. On her tenth combat charge, leading a squad of men over barbed wire towards Bulgarian trenches, Savić was hit by an enemy grenade and blown off her feet, with shrapnel wounds throughout her body. The badly wounded Savic was carried to the field hospital, where the doctor discovered her true sex. Her commander offered a transfer to the nursing corps, but she told him she would not accept any position that did not allow her to carry a gun and fight the enemies of her people. He promoted her to junior sergeant. Romania now joined the Allies in the First World War. Sergeant Milunka Savić, now commander of the Iron Regiment's Assault Bomber Squad, charged into the Battle of the Kolubara River (3–9 December 1914) armed with her Mosin–Nagant rifle and three bandoliers of hand grenades, one across each shoulder and one worn across her waist like a belt. She single-handedly assaulted an Austrian trench, rushing across no man's land hurling grenades before diving feet-first into an Austrian bunker with her bayonet at the ready. Inside, she found twenty men, all of whom threw their weapons down and surrendered to her. Once these prisoners were secured, she continued into battle, hurling grenades at enemy machine gun nests from distances so impressive that she became known as 'the Bomber of Kolubara'. She was halted only when an artillery shell landed next to her and she was wounded by shrapnel in her head. Savić received the Karadjordje Star with Swords, the highest award for bravery offered by the Kingdom of Serbia, and the battle was such a success that the Serbs pushed the Austrians out of Serbia completely.

Sergeant Savić was back in action a few months later. At this point, Serbia was badly outnumbered, being attacked on all sides by Bulgaria, Austria, Germany, and the Ottoman Empire. She earned a second Karadjordje Star at the Battle of Crna Bend in 1916, when she attacked a Bulgarian trench, cleared it out with grenades, rifle fire and a bayonet, and single-handedly took twenty-three Bulgarian soldiers prisoner. However, the Serbs were forced to begin a long, brutal fighting withdrawal through the snowdrifts and snow-covered mountains of Montenegro, Albania and Kosovo as they headed for the coast. Milunka Savić was wounded seven more times during this fighting retreat as Serbia desperately attempted to evacuate tens of thousands of civilians and save the core of its army. When she reached the coast and was evacuated by French and British warships, she was one of just 125,000 soldiers left in the Serbian Army.

The Serbian Army withdrew to Corfu, then Greece, where they joined up with the French Army. Now serving in the Serbian Brigade of the French Army, Sergeant Savić continued commanding the Assault Bomber Squad, fought through the rest of the war and received the French Légion d'Honneur twice, the Russian Cross of St George, the British Medal of the Order of St Michael and the Serbian Milos Obilic Medal. She was the only woman from the First World War to receive the Croix de Guerre.

While stationed on a base in Salonika (Thessaloniki), a French officer heard that she was proficient with hand grenades. He laughed at the idea and took a bottle out of a case of extremely expensive 1880 cognac, and set it on a post 130 feet away. He said that she could have the rest of the case if she could hit it in one attempt with a grenade. She did so, and that night her unit drank nineteen bottles of the finest cognac. After the war ended and Serbia was liberated, Milunka Savić declined an offer from the French government to move her to Paris and give her a pension. She returned home, married, had a child, worked at a bank and adopted three children who had been orphaned by the war. When the Germans came through Belgrade during the Second World War in 1940, Savić refused an invitation to attend a banquet held in honour of them and was put for ten months in Banjica concentration camp.

The Double Nobel Winner

Maria Sklodowska was born in Warsaw, Poland, and went on to become the first woman to win a Nobel Prize, as Madame Marie Curie (1867–1934). She began studying at the Sorbonne in 1891, and was the first woman to teach there. She was also the first woman in France to earn a PhD, and married Pierre Curie, who taught physics at the University of Paris. They found that one uranium ore, pitchblende, contained much more radioactivity than could be explained solely by its uranium content. They then searched for the source of the radioactivity and discovered two highly radioactive elements, radium and polonium, which won them the 1903 Nobel Prize for Physics. Curie named polonium after her native country. In 1906, Pierre died when he was run over by a horse-drawn wagon. Madame Curie next won the 1911 Nobel Prize for Chemistry for isolating radium. She said, 'We must not forget that when radium was discovered no one knew that it would prove useful in hospitals. The work was one of pure science. And this is a proof that scientific work must not be considered from the point of view of the direct usefulness of it. It must be done for itself, for the beauty of science, and then there is always the chance that a scientific discovery may become like the radium a benefit for humanity.' When the First World War broke out, Curie knew that X-rays would help to locate bullets and facilitate surgery. It was important not to move the wounded, so she invented X-ray vans and trained 150 female attendants to use then. Curie died of leukaemia brought on by exposure to the high levels of radiation involved in her research.

Villains

The Architect of the Apocalypse

In 1906, Franz Conrad von Hötzendorf (1852–1925) was appointed chief of staff of the Austro-Hungarian Imperial-Royal Army and forcefully argued for a strategy of pre-emptive warfare. In 1907, he proposed a pre-emptive war against the Kingdom of Italy. Shortly after, the Kingdom of Serbia became his primary target, and von Hötzendorf formally proposed a pre-emptive attack on Serbia no less than twenty-five times prior to the First World War. He saw this as part of a great contest of survival between the German and Slavic peoples, and also distrusted the Hungarians in the Empire. His aggressive stance impressed the high command in Germany and he was called 'the most brilliant strategist in Central Europe'. According to Margaret MacMillan, Austria-Hungary, and above all von Hötzendorf, bore the main responsibility for the war because of their unremitting desire to attack Italy and crush Serbia. Another recent book suggests that from 1907 von Hötzendorf was driven by his desire to impress his young mistress, becoming addicted to face creams and refusing to wear glasses. Germany, paranoid about the interlocking treaties of the countries surrounding Central Europe, believed that war was inevitable, and had been preparing for years. It gave von Hötzendorf a 'blank cheque' of support if Austria-Hungary went to war. However, Russia mobilised far more quickly than Germany expected, and the German general staff refused to mobilise only against Russia. They stuck to the Schlieffen Plan to attack France through neutral Belgium. Thus Britain was drawn into the war.

The Man Who Gave You Hitler

In 1894, Erich Ludendorff (1865–1937) was appointed to the German general staff. Here he helped revise the Schlieffen Plan, Germany's strategy for quick victory over France, and campaigned for greater military expansion, in anticipation of war. When the Russians threatened to overrun the German 8th Army, Ludendorff was appointed chief of staff, serving under Paul von Hindenburg. They won great victories over the Russians at Tannenberg (1914) and at the Masurian Lakes (1915). In 1916, when Hindenburg was appointed chief of staff, he made Ludendorff his quartermaster general. Hindenburg and Ludendorff had worked together on the mobilisation of Germany to work towards 'total warfare', staking everything on the pursuit of a 'victorious peace' that would secure German gains. In 1917, Ludendorff supported unrestricted submarine warfare, which brought the United States into the war.

In March 1918, Ludendorff launched a massive, though doomed, offensive on the Western Front in an attempt to defeat the Allies before American troops arrived. In the autumn, in the face of the impending collapse of Germany's allies, he refused to accept the Armistice terms demanded by the Allies and insisted the war continued, resigning when he was overruled. After the war, Ludendorff claimed that he had been deprived of victory by influential forces operating behind the scenes. His claim that the German Army was undefeated in battle, rather being betrayed on the home front, helped prepare the country for Adolf Hitler's ascent.

Ludendorff participated in unsuccessful Nazi coups in 1920 and in 1923, and from 1924 to 1928 he was a Nazi member of the Reichstag. Fritz Thyssen recalled. 'I deplored the fact that there were not at that time men in Germany whom an energetic national spirit would inspire to improve the situation ... He [Ludendorff] recommended to me in particular the Overland League and, above all, the National Socialist party of Adolf Hitler ... He [told me that Hitler] is the only man who has any political sense. Go and listen.' Erich Ludendorff blamed Jews and Marxists for losing the war, originated the 'stab in the back' myth, undermined the Weimar Republic, and ended up too deranged even for Hitler to use him.

The Propaganda Villain – Kaiser Bill

Friedrich Wilhelm Viktor Albrecht von Preußen, Wilhelm II (1859–1941) was an ineffective war leader, with the war being overseen by von Hindenburg and Ludendorff. He was the son of Friedrich III, German Emperor and King of Prussia. Emperor Friedrich Wilhelm Nikolaus Karl was known informally as 'Fritz', giving the German soldiers that nickname. He was crowned Emperor but could not rule, owing to throat cancer, and died after a ninety-nine-day coma. Wilhelm II succeeded his father and was crowned Emperor in 1888, aged twenty-nine. He was the grandson of Queen Victoria, Edward VII was his uncle and George V was his cousin. Another first cousin was Czar Nicholas II of Russia.

Born with a withered left arm, he insisted that photographers would disguise the fact. His generals and court, when appearing with him, would also hide their left arms. He was pompous, even by the standards of European royalty, with a penchant for dressing in exotic military uniforms. During the course of a formal reception the Emperor often changed his uniform five or six times. When he met Winston Churchill in 1906, Churchill having been invited to watch the manoeuvres of the Imperial German Army, the Kaiser 'was resplendent in the uniform of the White Silesian Cuirassiers'.

John Röhl believes that the Kaiser was responsible for starting the world war. His analysis of the December 1912 War Council demonstrates that the people who made decisions were the Kaiser's naval and military friends, and that civilian leaders, such as the chancellor and foreign secretary, took second place. Resultantly, the 1913 Army Bill was pushed through, and naval plans for war against Britain were prepared. The stockpiling of gold, supplies and even horse fodder was approved. The Kaiser had already virtually single-handedly pushed through the acceptance of the 'Tirpitz Plan' to build a new fleet of very powerful battleships, a threat to British naval supremacy. The course was set for war in 1914 when the Kiel Canal would be ready, as the 'Tirpitz Plan' had demanded. In response, Britain came into the Continental Alliance system on the side of France and Russia.

Max Hastings refers to a remarkably homoerotic atmosphere at Wilhelm's court, where the Kaiser greeted male intimates with a full kiss on the lips. Wilhelm shot around a quarter of a million animals and birds in his lifetime. In 1908, the chief of his military cabinet died of a heart attack at a royal shooting lodge in the Black Forest. After dinner, the Kaiser had watched the man die. He was dancing a *pas seul*, dressed in a ballet tutu and a feather hat, as he collapsed. Courtiers, diplomats, civil servants and officers all became sycophants. Among the Kaiser's most intimate circle, one imperial count allowed himself to be led before the Kaiser imitating a poodle 'with a marked rectal opening'. His sense of humour included hitting, beating, stabbing or otherwise humiliating colleagues and servants. As far as his sex life was concerned, he had innumerable affairs with prostitutes before ascending the throne in 1888, after which time he seemed to become more interested in men, particularly soldiers. Through his closest friend Count Philipp zu Eulenburg and his circle, Wilhelm mixed mainly with homosexuals. Röhl comments, 'It is indeed disturbing to reflect that the generals who took Germany and Europe into the Armageddon of 1914 not infrequently owed their career to the Kaiser's admiration for their height and good looks in their splendid uniforms.'

It appears that the Kaiser suffered from painful growths and discharges in the inner ear near the brain, a condition which drove him almost mad. Lord Salisbury thought him 'not quite normal' and Sir Edward Grey thought him 'not quite sane', as did other European leaders. Bismarck explained that he had only wanted to remain in office after 1888 because he knew of Wilhelm's 'abnormal mental condition'. A German naval officer wrote in May 1914, 'He is vanity itself, sacrificing everything to his own moods and childish amusements, and nobody checks him in doing so. I wonder how people with blood rather than water in their veins can bear to be around him.' At his desk, Wilhelm sat in a saddle because it made him feel like a warrior.

Above all, the Kaiser wanted what he called 'a place in the sun' for the German people. 'I look upon the People and the Nation as handed on to me as a responsibility conferred upon me by God, and I believe, as it is written in the Bible, that it is my duty to increase this heritage for which one day I shall be called upon to give an account. Whoever tries to interfere with my task I shall crush.' The problem was that the British and French had huge colonial empires, and there were few territories left to conquer. However, the Kaiser forced through the growth of the German Army and built a naval fleet to threaten that of Great Britain.

The great historian Barbara Tuchman referred to the Kaiser as the 'possessor of the least inhibited tongue in Europe'. He said in 1913 that his cousin Tsar Nicholas II was 'only fit to live in a country house and grow turnips'. To Wilhelm, his English cousin George V, only six years his junior, was 'a very nice boy', but he said of his uncle King Edward VII, 'He is Satan, you cannot imagine what a Satan he is.' Born in Buckingham Palace, Wilhelm's mother Victoria, Princess Royal, was the eldest child of Queen Victoria. She wrote of her son, in 1879, 'I am afraid that he is turning into the archetypal Potsdam Lieutenant with that evil admixture of a very loud mouth and the chauvinist's hatred and ignorance of things foreign.' By the middle of 1880, she was complaining to her mother: 'Willy is chauvinistic and ultra Prussian to a degree & with a violence which is often very painful to me.'

In 1887, Wilhelm told two Austrian call-girls that in Austria 'the entire state was rotten' and about to collapse, its German provinces falling 'like ripe fruit' to Prussia, which alone was healthy and strong. Wilhelm likened Crown Prince Rudolf of Austria to his own father as being a spineless, characterless popularity seeker totally under Jewish influence. In 1888, when his father lay dying of throat cancer, Wilhelm came close to believing that there was an Anglo-Jewish plot, led by his mother, to take over Germany. In letters to his intimate friend Philipp Eulenburg, he described the doctors in attendance on his father as '*judenlümmel*', 'dogs', 'scoundrels' and *Satansknochen* filled with 'racial hatred' and 'anti-Germanism to the very edge of the grave'. He would never be able to forget, he wrote, that 'the family shield had been besmirched and the Reich brought to the edge of destruction by an English princess who is my mother'. In time he came to believe not only that Jewish and English doctors had killed his father, but also that an English doctor had been responsible for crippling his left arm.

From his accession in 1888 to the end of his life, he became obsessed with what he called the 'yellow peril'. In 1900, he ordered German troops on their way to China to behave like Huns, showing no mercy and taking no prisoners. Wilhelm informed the Tsar that a German agent had 'counted 10,000 Japanese men in the plantations in south Mexico, all in military jackets with brass buttons'. This secret Japanese army, he claimed, was intending to seize the Panama Canal. Wilhelm was the most anti-Semitic leader of his day: 'The Jews are the parasites of my empire. The Jewish question is one of the great problems I have to deal with, and yet nothing can be done to cope with it!' On his visit to England in 1907, he 'declaimed vehemently against the Jews', telling Sir Edward Grey, 'There are far too many of them in my country. They want stamping out.'

In September 1914, after the German victory at Tannenberg, the Kaiser proposed that the 80,000–90,000 Russian prisoners of war be driven onto a barren spit of land in the Baltic and kept there till they died of thirst and hunger. One of his generals politely pointed out that this would be 'genocide'. In conversations with the American ambassador, he made it clear that 'mere democracies like France and the United States' could never take part in a peace conference, since 'war was a royal sport, to be indulged in by hereditary monarchs and concluded at their will'. He said that 'he knew Germany was right, because God was on their side'. Woodrow Wilson's special envoy Colonel House, when he heard of these conversations, asked whether the Kaiser was 'crazy'.

In post-war exile, Wilhelm evolved conspiracy theories whereby the Jesuits, Freemasons and Jews were plotting to take over the world. In an article he wrote in 1928 for the American *Century Magazine* on 'the Sex of Nations', he declared the French to be a feminine race with an inbred love of parliamentary government, whereas the Germans were racially masculine, biologically in need of leadership because they were at home only in primitive, 'purely vertical masculine, monarchical' structures which were the 'opposite of parliamentarism'. In 1923, after hearing a lecture by an anthropologist, the Kaiser realised, he said, that the French and the English were not whites at all but blacks.

He called for a 'regular international all-worlds pogrom à la Russe' as 'the best cure'. Wilhelm stated that Jews and mosquitoes were 'a nuisance that humanity must get rid of in some way or other', and wrote that 'I believe the best would be gas'. In 1940, the Kaiser was thrilled as Hitler put into effect the policies which Wilhelm had pursued in his own reign, calling the war 'a succession of miracles'. Wilhelm died in June 1941, just three weeks before Hitler's attack on the Soviet Union. When we examine leaders throughout history – religious, royal, military or political – there is often a hint of madness somewhere in their make-up. Wilhelm had far more than a hint.

The Master of Genocide

Enver Pasha (1881–1922) was both War Minister and Ottoman Commander in Chief. He is strongly suspected of murdering the reforming Crown Prince Sehzade Efendi on 1 February 1916. From 1915 to 1918, he orchestrated a policy of genocide against the Ottoman Armenians. The death toll is argued to be around 800,000–1.5 million. Armenians were driven from their homes and forced on a subsequent death march across the Syrian Desert. The Turkish government somehow, unfortunately, still maintains that the 'allegation of genocide' is not valid, and maintains that it was a series of unfortunate killings on both sides. This crime is the 'first genocide of the twentieth century', however, and was acknowledged by Mehmet VI, the last Sultan of the Ottoman Empire, on 16 December 1918:

> My sorrow is profound at the mistreatment of my Armenian subjects by certain political committees acting under my government. Such misdeeds and the mutual slaughter of sons of the same fatherland have broken my heart. I ordered an inquiry as soon as I came to the throne so that the fomenters might be severely punished, but various factors prevented my orders from being promptly carried out. The matter is now being thoroughly investigated. Justice will soon be done and we will never have a repetition of these ugly events.

The Earl and the Order to Walk into Machine Gun Fire

There is not enough space to describe Haig's especial brand of idiocy during the war. Like some modern politicians and business leaders, he always shot the bearer of bad news and believed what he wanted to believe. The eleventh son of a whisky baron, it is tempting to think that his arrogant brain was riddled through from birth with alcohol fumes. Even as the war progressed through its first terrible months, he saw little value in machine guns and grenades. Field Marshal Douglas Haig (1861–1928) was a cavalry officer in India, Sudan and in the Boer War. On the outbreak of war in 1914, Haig was commanding the BEF's 1st Army Corps, whose overall commander was Sir John French. By the end of 1915, French had proved terribly unsuitable, and unfortunately Haig was appointed commander-in-chief in his place. To break the stalemate on the Western Front and relieve the pressure on the French at Verdun, Haig ordered the Somme Offensive, which began on 1 July 1916. He wrote that day, 'Very successful attack this morning ... All went like clockwork ... The battle is going very well for us and already the Germans are surrendering freely. The enemy is so short of men that he is collecting them from all along the front line. Our men are in wonderful spirits and full of confidence.'

On that first day, the British army suffered 60,000 casualties, just under 20,000 of whom were killed, the highest in its history. The Battle of the Somme lasted fifteen weeks, until 13 November, with the British alone suffering 420,000 casualties. Haig's plan was to attack on a 15-mile front north of the River Somme, while five French divisions would attack an 8-mile front south of the Somme. To ensure a rapid advance, Allied artillery pounded German lines for a week before the attack, firing 1.6 million shells. British commanders were so confident they ordered their troops to walk slowly towards the German lines. Once enemy positions had been seized, cavalry units were to pour through to pursue the fleeing Germans. However, preparations for the assault were clearly visible to balloons and spotter planes, and the week-long bombardment gave the Germans clear warning. German trenches were thus heavily fortified. When the bombardment began, the Germans simply moved to tunnels around 50 feet underground and waited. Many of the British shells failed to explode. Around 7.30 a.m. on 1 July, whistles blew to signal the start of the attack. With the shelling over, the Germans left their bunkers and set up their machine gun positions.

Commanded to walk towards the German lines, the eleven British divisions were mown down, with 60 per cent of all officers involved on the first day being killed. Many 'Pals' Battalions, comprising men from the same town, had enlisted together to serve together, but suffered catastrophic losses, with whole units being wiped out. No man's land, the land between enemy positions, averaged up to 300 yards in length, and was crisscrossed with continuous barbed-wire entanglements. The British were mowed down by German machine guns, which were able to continuously fire up to ten bullets a second. With his 'decisive breakthrough' an abysmal failure, upon 15 September Haig renewed the Somme Offensive, using tanks for the first time. However, it was too soon to use them. They were lightly armed, small in number and often subject to mechanical failure, making minimal impact. Torrential rains in October turned the battlegrounds into a muddy quagmire and in mid-November the battle ended, with the Allies having advanced only 5 miles. The British suffered around 420,000 casualties, the French 195,000 and the Germans around 650,000.

'The Battle of the Somme was a great triumph for the genius of British leadership and command,' according to Lieutenant-Colonel J. H. Boraston OBE, Field Marshall Haig's Private Secretary. Boraston obsequiously edited *Sir Douglas Haig's Despatches December 1915–April 1919*, from which we read the following in amazement:

> The three main objects with which we had commenced our offensive in July had already been achieved at the date when this account closes; in spite of the fact that the heavy autumn rains had prevented full advantage being taken of the favourable situation created by our advance, at a time when we had good grounds for hoping to achieve yet more important successes. Verdun had been relieved; the main German forces had been held on the Western front; and the enemy's strength had been very considerably worn down. Any one of these three results is in itself sufficient to justify the Somme battle. The attainment of all three of them affords ample compensation for the splendid efforts of our troops and for the sacrifices made by ourselves and our Allies. They have brought us a long step forward towards the final victory of the Allied cause. The desperate struggle for the possession of Verdun had invested that place with a moral and political importance out of all proportion to its military value. Its fall would undoubtedly have been proclaimed as a great victory for our enemies, and would have shaken the faith of many in our ultimate success. The failure of the enemy to capture it, despite great efforts and very heavy losses, was a severe blow to his prestige, especially in view of the confidence he had openly expressed as to the results of the struggle.

Thus Haig believed that 420,000 British casualties in 1914 were worth 'a severe blow' to German prestige. However, only in the sense of relieving the French at Verdun can the British have claimed any measure of success. Of real interest are the comments of survivors of the Somme. Private G. Morgan said, 'We formed a line and walked slowly forward. We had only gone a few yards when my mate was hit. Lines of men were just disappearing. The Germans' machine guns fired at us like it was target practice. It was all over in ten minutes. It was slaughter. The commanders, Haig and Rawlinson, didn't care about us. I don't think they cared about human life.' Private Frank Lindley remembered, 'We were told to walk over. Walk. Which, in itself, was stupid. And you had to go over in a line, walking. That was the stupid idea. But, still, we had to do what we were told.' Private Russell Bradshaw, talking about the order to walk across no man's land, stated: "Whether they did this on purpose to show how lucky we were and had nothing to fear, whether they did it to cheer us up or whether they really thought they were correct, I don't know. But they made a huge mistake, a wicked mistake. There's no doubt about that.' Lieutenant J. A. Raws remembered, 'We were smelly, unshaven and sleepless. My uniform was rotten with other men's blood and partly spattered with a friend's brains. It is horrible, but why should you people at home not know? I cannot describe the horror. I honestly believe these men were murdered through the stupidity of the men in charge.'

Haig's 'tactic' of 'walking' in straight lines was the infantry tactic left over from the nineteenth century, and many generals had belonged to the elite cavalry. Haig and other generals kept thinking that long artillery barrages would destroy barbed wire defences and silence the enemies' machine guns. They did neither. To break the stalemate, Germans came up with 'Storm Troopers' who would literally 'storm' forward as fast as possible, backed by flame throwers who would clear out the trenches. The French invented the simple tactic of having the most forward lines of troops 'drop their packs' so they could run, leaving following waves to bring the packs up. The British High Command came up with the order of walking at the speed of slow and cumbersome tanks.

Haig stayed away from the trenches, and would not listen to his better generals or intelligence that he did not agree with. The German surrender was prompted more by increasing mutiny because of lack of food and supplies than any other reason. Haig also lied several times about court-martialling and executing soldiers who had shell shock. Even at the end of the war Haig wrongly believed that horses would continue to be used in warfare: 'I believe that the value of the horse and the opportunity for the horse in the future are likely to be as great as ever. Aeroplanes and tanks are only accessories to the men and the horse, and I feel sure that as time goes on you will find just as much use for the horse – the well-bred horse – as you have ever done in the past.' For his conduct of the war, General Haig was awarded an earldom. Most of the surviving infantry on the Western Front despised him.

The Black Hand Gang Member

In 1876, Bismarck had been asked in the Reichstag about whether he would support Russia or Austria, in the face of Ottoman uprisings in the Balkans. He replied, 'I am opposed to the notion of any sort of active participation of Germany in these matters, so long as I can see no reason to suppose that German interests are involved, no interests on behalf of which it is worth our risking – excuse my plain speaking – the healthy bones of one of our Pomeranian musketeers.' In another speech in 1888, he altered 'musketeers' to 'grenadiers'. In 1878, Bismarck stated that 'Europe today is a powder keg and the leaders are like men smoking in an arsenal ... A single spark will set off an explosion that will consume us all ... I cannot tell you when that explosion will occur, but I can tell you where ... Some damned foolish thing in the Balkans will set it off.'

Gavrilo Princip (1895–1918) was a Serbian nationalist, a member of the 'Black Hand Gang' who became the catalyst for the First World War. He assassinated Austrian Archduke Franz Ferdinand in Sarajevo on 28 June 1914. The murder started a chain reaction that led to the beginning of the war only one month later. A member of a complicated plot against the Austrian heir to the throne, Princip seized his opportunity when a wrong turn forced Ferdinand's car to stall right in front of him. Princip then shot the Archduke and his wife, Sophie, killing them both. At only nineteen years old, he was too young to face the death penalty and was sentenced instead to the maximum penalty, twenty years in prison. As the war raged around him, Princip wasted away in jail, dying of disease and neglect in April 1918. Bismarck's prediction was correct. In 1912–13 there were two Balkan Wars, followed by the First World War sparked by Gavrilo Princip. In the twentieth century we have seen the 'Third Balkan War' from 1991 to 2001 across what was Yugoslavia, Serbia, Montenegro, Slovenia, Croatia, Bosnia, Kosovo and Macedonia.

The Draft Dodger and Liar

Adolf Hitler (1889–1945) was born in a small town, Braunau-am-Inn, near Austria's border with Bavaria. Interestingly, the pro-Nazi Austrian Vice-Chancellor Edmund Glaise-Horstenau, who committed suicide at the end of the Second World War, was also born there, seven years before Hitler. A cleric born in that same year of 1882 in the same village of Braunau-am-Inn, Franz Jetzinger, documented some of the lies told by Hitler in his book *Hitler's Youth*. Austria was then part of the Hapsburg Empire, but from an early age Hitler believed that Austria should pursue *Anschluss*, the unification of Germanic Austria with Germany proper. In *Mein Kampf* he wrote, 'My inner aversion to the Hapsburg State was increasing daily … This motley of Czechs, Poles, Hungarians, Ruthenians, Serbs and Croats, and always the bacillus which is the solvent of human society, the Jew.' It was this, Hitler declared, that drove him to travel to Munich, the capital of Bavaria: 'I came to love that city more than any other place known to me. A German city. How very different from Vienna.'

Hitler arrived in Munich as a draft dodger, being actively pursued by the Austrian police. He was meant to have presented himself to the army authorities as early as 1910. When found in Munich, Hitler was given the choice of either appearing voluntarily at a board of inspection or facing extradition and arrest. He returned to Austria. On 5 February 1914 he was turned down for military service by the Austrian Army due to a lack of fitness. He later joined the German Army. In Nazi propaganda, he was a gallant First World War corporal who frequently risked his life. However, Dr Thomas Weber, lecturer in modern history at Aberdeen University, unearthed previously unpublished letters from veterans of Hitler's regiment. They challenge the Nazi portrayal which suggested his extreme nationalism was prompted by his experience on the Western Front. Hitler's unit, the List Regiment, was itself shunned as being a joke regiment which was never needed anywhere near the front lines. Even its own soldiers regarded Hitler as an object of ridicule, a loner, joking about him starving in a canned food factory, being unable to open a can with a bayonet.

Weber noted, 'I found his role was to deliver messages between regimental HQ and, for instance, battalions or the HQs of other units. So he would have been between 3 and 5 kilometres behind the front. Far from being considered a hero, Hitler was regarded as a "rear area pig" by the soldiers … The story was that World War One created Hitler and radicalised him and led to the birth of the Nazi movement. But his life in the war really was his Achilles heel and the story could collapse like a house of cards. I've been trying to show that this is a totally made-up story. Hitler was untypical of the regiment and he was not really radicalised in the war.'

It was known that Hitler served as a runner but Dr Weber realises that historians have not distinguished between regimental runners, a relatively safe job, and battalion or company runners, who had to brave machine-gun fire between trenches. Hitler was a runner at regimental HQ several miles from the front, living in comfort. Speaking of Hitler's famous 1st Class Iron Cross, Dr Weber says this was largely due to the fact he knew officers who made recommendations. Hitler sustained two injuries during the war. The first occurred in October

1916 when he was wounded by a grenade splinter. The other was on 13 October 1918, when a gas attack caused Hitler to go temporarily blind. It was while Hitler was recovering from the gas attack that the armistice was announced. Hitler was furious that Germany had surrendered and felt strongly that Germany had been 'stabbed in the back' by its leaders. Hitler returned to Munich and was determined to enter politics. In 1919, he became the 55th member of the tiny anti-Semitic German Worker's Party. He soon became the party's leader, created a twenty-five-point platform for the party, and established a bold, red background with a white circle and swastika in the middle as the party's symbol. In 1920, the party's name was changed to National Socialist German Worker's Party, i.e. the Nazi Party. *Der Führer*, The Leader, was the unique name granted by Hitler to himself, as *Vorsitzender*, Chairman, of the Nazi Party. The despised failed artist and loner made up a glorious war for himself, and systematically destroyed records or killed people who knew otherwise.

The Italian Corporal

Benito Amilcare Andrea Mussolini (1883–1945), Italy's fascist dictator from 1922 to 1945, served for a time on the Italian Front during the First World War. He resigned from the Italian Socialist Party in 1915 over its declared opposition to war against Austria-Hungary. The party favoured neutrality while Mussolini thought that support for the Allies would boost Italy's claim to recover lost Austro-Hungarian territory. In the Italian Army he saw service on the Italian Front in Slovenia, before being wounded and returning home. A mortar bomb had exploded during a training exercise in February 1917, killing four of Mussolini's fellow soldiers. In Milan, he edited his own right-wing newspaper, *Il Popolo d'Italia*. Mussolini and a group of fellow war veterans founded the Fasci di Combattimento, a right-wing, strongly nationalistic, anti-Socialist movement named after *fasces*, the ancient Roman symbol for discipline. In 1922, Mussolini led his 'black-shirts' in a march upon Rome, which succeeded in destabilising the government with a series of riots. Asked to form an administration by Vittorio Emanuele III in October, the movement towards dictatorship was increasing, and Mussolini became *Il Duce*, The Leader, three years later. Once Mussolini had assumed dictatorial powers, a concerted effort was launched to mythologise his somewhat limited role in the First World War. Corporal Benito Mussolini, like Corporal Hitler, systematically lied about his war service and transformed his country into a single-party, totalitarian state.

The Pox-Scarred Theology Drop-Out

It seems that all three of the major enemy leaders of the Second World War had rather undistinguished roles in the First World War. Hitler was a weakly corporal in the German Army who was too unfit to join the Austrian Army and avoided combat; Mussolini was a corporal who was hurt in a training exercise; and Stalin was unfit for service. Such is the nature of people whose main fight is for war to be fought by others. Iosif Vissarionovich Dzhugashvili was born in 1879, the son of Georgian cobbler who had a habit of drunkenly beating up his wife and son. Born with a club foot, the boy contracted smallpox at the age of seven, leading to other children calling him 'pocky' because of his scarred face. Aged twelve, two horse-drawn carriage accidents led to his left arm being permanently damaged. He was educated at the local church school, where he was to be trained as a priest, and won a free scholarship to the Tbilisi Theological Seminary. He adopted the name Stalin from the Russian word for steel. Aged twenty, Stalin was expelled from the seminary, being suspected of reading forbidden books and converting students to Marxism. Following the writings of Lenin, Stalin now became a full-time revolutionary.

As a member of Communist Party committees, he conducted subversive activities in the Caucasus, inciting strikes, spreading propaganda and staging bank robberies, kidnappings and extortion. The Tsarist government often sent him into exile in Siberia, but Stalin kept escaping, returning to engage in more ransom kidnappings, counterfeiting and robberies. In April 1912, Stalin moved to Saint Petersburg and created *Pravda* newspaper. During his last exile, Stalin was conscripted by the Russian Army to fight in the First World War, but was unfit for service owing to his damaged left arm. After the revolution of March 1917, Stalin resumed the editorship of *Pravda*, but did not play any role in the October Revolution. When civil war then broke out between the Red Army and the anti-Bolshevik White Army in May 1918, Lenin sent Stalin to the city of Volgograd. There he ordered the killings of many former Tsarist officers, and burned villages in order to intimidate the peasantry into submission. Before his death, Lenin became increasingly worried about Stalin's personality and conduct. After Lenin's death, Stalin systematically eliminated his rivals and by his fiftieth birthday, in 1929, had succeeded in establishing himself as the sole leader of the Soviet Union.

Stalin, as head of the Politburo, consolidated near-absolute power in the 1930s with a Great Purge of the Party, which he justified as being necessary to expel 'opportunists'. Stalin's reign, until his possible murder in 1953, saw up to 60 million Russians being killed in his purges and in famines caused by his policies, plus at least another 20 million killed during the Second World War. Stalin's thirty-year rule as absolute ruler featured so many atrocities, including purges, expulsions, forced displacements, imprisonment in labour camps, manufactured famines, torture, mass murder and massacres, that the complete extent of the bloodshed will never be known. There are many parallels between the early lives of Stalin, Hitler and Mussolini. Most of those who had faced the true horrors of the First World War never wanted another war.

Hero and Villain

Major General Sir Henry Hugh Tudor (1871–1965) was a friend of Winston Churchill, badly wounded in the Boer War. He served on the Western Front for the duration of the First World War, rising from captain to general. He had been a moving force in the development and adoption of the artillery box barrage and smoke shell, and had greatly reduced infantry casualties in the attack by substituting a smoke and high explosive barrage for the then conventional barrage of shrapnel. Tudor was the first British general to use smoke shells to create screens, and one of the first advocates of predicted artillery fire. He suggested an attack with tanks in the Cambrai sector in July 1917, and his artillery ideas helped lay the foundation for the British breakthrough in the battle there in November. However, the much decorated and respected general spent the last four decades of his life in Newfoundland, shunning photographs and interviews, scrupulously avoiding publicity and living a carefully quiet life in the shadows, far from his country, wife and children. 'Black' Tudor lived in fear, carrying a Webley revolver at all times, and a set of brass knuckles in case of a surprise attack. Assassins were seeking him.

After his wartime exploits, Tudor became commander of the Royal Irish Constabulary, the Dublin Metropolitan Police and the re-enforcements or 'specials' to the RIC such as the notorious 'Black and Tans' and the 'Auxiliaries'. They were known as 'Tudor's Toughs'. British forces in Ireland at that time were under orders from Whitehall to 'fight fire with fire' against the IRA in Ireland in 1920. Under Tudor's command, the Black and Tans, along with the Auxiliaries, became notorious for reprisal killings, burning whole villages, setting fire to the city of Cork, and turning guns on the football crowd in Croke Park among other actions. After Irish independence in 1922, Tudor was considered to be a marked man, and he escaped across the Atlantic to a permanent lonely exile on the island of Newfoundland, then an independent nation.

12

Desertions, Executions, Shell Shock and Mutinies

Between 1914 and 1918, the British Army identified 80,000 men with what would now be defined as the symptoms of shell shock. Those suffering from severe shell shock could not stand the thought of being on the front line any longer, and deserted. Once caught, they received a court martial and, if sentenced to death, were shot by a twelve-man firing squad. Some 306 British and Commonwealth soldiers were executed for crimes such as desertion and cowardice. The executions included twenty-five Canadians, twenty-two Irishmen and five New Zealanders. In contrast, the Germans only executed twenty-five men and the Americans executed none of their soldiers. Senior military commanders would not accept a soldier's failure to return to the front line as anything other than desertion. They also believed that if such behaviour was not harshly punished, others would be encouraged to do the same and discipline in the British Army would collapse. Some men faced a court martial for other offences but the majority stood trial for desertion from their post, 'fleeing in the face of the enemy'. A court martial itself was usually carried out very quickly, and the execution followed shortly after.

Few soldiers wanted to be in a firing squad. Many were soldiers at a base camp recovering from wounds which stopped them from fighting at the front but did not prevent them from firing a rifle. Some of those in firing squads were aged around sixteen, as were some of those who were shot for 'cowardice'. The British bandleader Victor Sylvester had lied about his age to join the Army, and served in five execution squads, aged only sixteen. The sixteen-year-old James Crozier from Belfast was shot at dawn for deserting his post. Before his execution, Crozier was given so much rum that he passed out. He had to be carried, semi-conscious, to the place of execution. Officers at the execution later claimed that there was a very real fear that the men in the firing squad would disobey the order to shoot. Two weeks earlier, 2nd Lieutenant Annandale had been found guilty of the same offence but was not sentenced to death due to 'technicalities'. Corporal Alan Bray refused to join a firing squad: 'I think one reason why I felt so strongly about it was the fact that the week before a boy in our own battalion had been shot for desertion. I knew that boy, and I knew that he absolutely lost his nerve, he couldn't have gone back into the line. Anyway he was shot, and the tragedy of it was that a few weeks later, in our local paper, I saw that his father had joined up to avenge his son's death on the Germans.'

Over the duration of the war, fifteen officers were sentenced to death, but all received a royal pardon. In the summer of 1916, all officers of the rank of captain and above were given an order that all cases of cowardice should be punished by death, and that a medical excuse should not be tolerated. However, this was not the case if officers were found to be suffering from 'neurasthenia'. This was 'officer-speak' for shell shock, which was diagnosed as 'hysterics' in the 'other ranks'. Private Abe Bevistein, aged sixteen, was also shot by firing squad at Labourse, near Calais. As with so many other cases, he had been found guilty of deserting his post. Just before his court martial, Bevistein wrote home to his mother: 'We were in the trenches. I was so cold I went out (and took shelter in a farm house). They took me to prison so I will have to go in front of the court. I will try my best to get out of it, so don't worry.' Because of the 'crimes' committed by these men, their names were not put on war memorials after the war.

A French military observer witnessed one execution by the French Army:

> The two condemned were tied up from head to toe like sausages. A thick bandage hid their faces. And, a horrible thing, on their chests a square of fabric was placed over their hearts. The unfortunate duo could not move. They had to be carried like two dummies on the open-backed lorry, which bore them to the rifle range. It is impossible to articulate the sinister impression the sight of those two living parcels made on me.
>
> The padre mumbled some words and then went off to eat. Two six-strong platoons appeared, lined up with their backs to the firing posts. The guns lay on the ground. When the condemned had been attached, the men of the platoon, who had not been able to see events, responding to a silent gesture, picked up their guns, abruptly turned about, aimed and opened fire. Then they turned their backs

on the bodies and the sergeant ordered 'Quick march!' The men marched right passed them, without inspecting their weapons, without turning a head. No military compliments, no parade, no music, no march past; a hideous death without drums or trumpets.

Four times as many men deserted in the United Kingdom than in France/Belgium, but no one was ever executed for desertion in the UK. The actual legal status of courts martial has been questioned. The accused did not have access to a formal legal representative who could defend him. Some had a 'prisoner's friend' while many did not even have this. Legally, every court martial should have had a 'judge advocate' present but very few did. The night before an execution, a condemned man had the right to petition the king for clemency but none ever did, which suggests that none were aware that they had this right. On 13 January 1915, General Routine Order 585 was issued which basically reversed the belief of being innocent until found guilty. Under 585, a soldier was guilty until sufficient evidence could be provided to prove his innocence.

The passage of time, declared Defence Secretary John Reid in September 1998, means that grounds for a pardon on the basis of unsafe conviction 'just did not exist'. Thankfully, this dinosaur was no longer in position when a new law was passed in November 2006 as part of the Armed Forces Act. This at last pardoned men in the British and Commonwealth armies who were executed in First World War. However, although the law removes the stigma of dishonour with regards to executions on war records, it still does not cancel out sentences. The pretexts for execution for British soldiers had a common theme. Many were suffering shell shock, also called 'war neurosis' or 'combat stress' and now recognised as post-traumatic stress disorder (PTSD). Most were deliberately picked out and convicted 'as a lesson to others'. Charges included desertion or cowardice, which may have been walking around dazed and confused, suffering from PTSD. Some were simply obeying orders to carry information from one trench to another. Most of those shot were young, defenceless and vulnerable teenagers who had volunteered for duty. They were selected, charged, and subjected to a mock trial, convicted, then shot at dawn the following day. They were universally from the ranks or NCOs, never officers.

General Haig (see Villains), when questioned, declared that all men accused of cowardice and desertion were examined by a Medical Officer (MO), and that no soldier was sentenced to death if there was any suspicion of him suffering shell shock. He was mendacious, and, having never visited the front lines, he had no idea of his men's conditions. Also, the Under-Secretary of State for War repeatedly misled the House of Commons upon this matter. Most soldiers accused of cowardice and desertion were never examined by an MO, and in the few cases where a medical diagnosis of shell shock had been made, the medical evidence was ignored and the man was convicted and shot anyway. General Haig not only signed all the death warrants but when questioned later on this issue lied repeatedly.

Haig and his acolytes believed that anyone suffering shell shock was 'malingering'. Among the Western nations involved in First World War, the British Military were the furthest behind in understanding trauma. Commanders wanted sufferers to be returned to the front as soon as possible. Many hospitalised victims, after being told they were going back upon recovery, shot themselves. The families of the victims suffered shame, humiliation and embarrassment, compounded by the government's refusal to allow the families to mourn these men alongside their comrades.

Mutiny

The British, despite their experiences in the Boer Wars, were committed to the theory of the offensive, and the sudden switch to defensive entrenchments baffled the generals. They believed that the offensive had a massive positive effect upon soldiers' morale, utterly failing to understand that enormous technological advances in weaponry worked more to the benefit of defensive strategies. The Western Front was shaped by artillery, the machine gun, barbed wire, and the spade. As early as October of 1914, a prescient young German officer wrote to a friend that the 'brisk, merry war to which we have all looked forward for years has taken an unforeseen turn. Troops are murdered with machines, horses have almost become superfluous … The most important people are the engineers … the theories of decades are shown to be worthless.' Unfortunately for the miserable troops in the wet, muddy, cold and filthy trenches, the generals refused to accept the deadly efficacy of defensive weapons, and spent the first three years of the war mounting one costly frontal assault after another. This lasted until the abortive Nivelle Offensive of May 1917 precipitated the mutiny of the French Army, and ended what J. M. Winter calls 'the great slaughter.'

In June 1916, in the Austrian Army, mutinies of the Czech and Ruthene units began during the Brusilov Offensive, and spread to other ethnic minority units in 1917 and 1918. In March 1917, mutinies began spreading in the Russian Army after the March

Revolution in Petrograd and then the failed Kerensky Offensive in July. Upon 3 May 1917, in the French Army, the 21st Division refused to renew Nivelle's offensive on the Chemin des Dames, and its leaders were shot. The French had had over a million deaths at this point, and had just been decimated in another disastrous offensive. Next the 120th Regiment refused to fight, then the 128th. From the army 20,000 deserted outright, and mutineers advanced on Paris. The 199th Regiment put machine guns in trucks to destroy the Schneider-Creusot weapons factory. By June, fifty-four divisions (half the French Army) was in mutiny, or, as the official French history wrote, in 'collective indiscipline'. A general wrote, 'The operation must be postponed. We risk having the men refuse to leave the assault trenches.' According to Richard Watt, 'French soldiers cursed their commanders, drank openly in the trenches, singing ditties about war profiteers and wooden graveyard crosses. Their commanders were unable to stem the distribution of *papillons*, the pacifist leaflets that filled French barracks like white spring snow.' The French conducted 3,427 courts-martial and condemned 554 soldiers to death, with 49 executions carried out. Nivelle was replaced by Marshall Pétain, who visited 100 divisions in person and promised no more Nivelle-like offensives. He told them he was waiting for the Americans and their tanks, and allowed more leave. (Unfortunately, Petain later was to become the anti-Semitic Prime Minister of Vichy France in the Second World War.)

From 1914 to 1920, only 1,800 British servicemen were court-martialled for mutiny with the Western Front accounting for only forty-two such charges. Following the 1915 Singapore Garrison Mutiny by Muslim soldiers of the 5th Light Infantry against British rule in India, which was actively encouraged by Germany, British soldiers carried out the execution of the thirty-seven ring-leaders by shooting. A further eighteen indigenes involved in the plot were hanged in India. More than 50,000 soldiers at any one time, from many different units, were passing through the base training and transit camps such as that at Étaples. Upon 9 September 1917, the Étaples Mutiny began at the British training camp 15 miles south of Boulogne, initiated by New Zealand troops who defied military police and broke into the office of the base commandant. The arrival of a British machine gun squadron stopped the demonstrations without bloodshed, and British commanders changed the training methods at the camp.

The *Daily Telegraph*'s defence correspondent John Keegan criticised the BBC TV series *The Monocled Mutineer*, which was based on these events. He said, 'The Étaples "mutinies" amounted to no more than a few days of disorder, a little disrespect to officers and some loudly voiced demands for human treatment. The Army reacted briskly. It restored discipline by bringing in unaffected troops. It removed the cause of discontent by replacing the worst of the staff with wise men. That is about all there was to the British Army "mutinies" of the 1914–1918 war.' As a direct result of the mutiny, only a few individuals were punished. Corporal Jesse Robert Short of the Northumberland Fusiliers was condemned to death; three others soldiers were sentenced to ten years' penal servitude and others were jailed for up to a year, with hard labour into the bargain. In 1919, 15,000 Canadians mutinied at Kinmel Camp in North Wales, furious at the delays in being sent home.

In October 1917, masses of Italian soldiers voluntarily surrendered to the Germans after the Battle of Caporetto. In December 1917, in the Turkish Army, desertions and mutinies increased after the fall of Jerusalem. For the men of the Imperial Army reserve garrison at Dresden, the final straw came on 5 December 1917, when one of their platoon leaders was executed after making a comment to a senior garrison officer that the officer regarded as gross insubordination. An outstanding combat soldier, the executed man had won the Iron Cross for heroism on the Eastern Front in 1915. On 7 December, the eve of the Dresden Mutiny, a special military tribunal convicted a corporal named Stefan Panier on a dubious charge of insubordination. He had dared to correct his battalion commander when said commander stated that one of Corporal Panier's platoon comrades was AWOL; Panier pointed out that the man had been killed in action on the Eastern Front. The corporal was given life imprisonment and the Dresden garrison mutinied the next day. Some 500 people died, many of them civilians who joined the mutineers.

The German Navy mutinied at Kiel in 1918. Germany began to discuss a possible armistice with the Allies and at the time the German Navy was in a mutinous state. When the German High Seas Fleet was ordered to sail to the North Sea for a major battle against the British, the sailors in Kiel refused to go and took up arms. Their mutiny, lasting from 29 October to 3 November, started an open revolution throughout Germany. Only U-boat crews remained loyal to the Emperor. Major revolts occurred in Hamburg, Bremen, and Lubeck (4–5 November) and spread to Munich (7–8 November). Bavaria declared itself a democratic and socialist republic. The Emperor was forced to abdicate, and on 11 November 1918, the war ended.

13

Diseases of the War

In the British Army alone, over 1.65 million men were wounded, many of them several times. As a result, around 240,000 British soldiers suffered total or partial leg or arm amputations. Most of these men were fitted with fairly primitive artificial limbs. Medicine advanced rapidly in the war years. Doctors learned better wound management and improved in the setting of bones, and Harold Gillies pioneered skin graft surgery. Reconstructive surgery was used to repair facial damage, but masks were also used to cover the most horrific cases. The massive numbers of injured and diseased men led to new medical specialisations and professional management. Some soldiers stayed in nursing homes their entire lives. Others, disfigured and unable to work, were forced into begging on streets.

Treatment at the Front

Nurse May Sinclair wrote of the Number 1 Belgian Field Hospital that it was 'a world apart, a world of insufferable space and agonising time, ruled over by some inhuman mathematics and given over to pre-transcendent pain'. It could take up to six hours for stretcher-bearers to carry a man off the battlefields to where a wheeled ambulance was available. There were no antibiotics to fight bacterial infection, as they were not discovered until 1924. Because of the delay in treating wounds and the filthy conditions, many servicemen died in agony from gangrene. A third of injured soldiers died from infections.

If a soldier fell ill while his company was marching, the medical officer would put a tag on him with a diagnosis, and leave the man by the side of the road to be picked up by a passing ambulance. Without the signed note, the man could have been considered a deserter and possibly shot. Some woke up, lost, and were arrested. Hospitals and convalescent homes were set up in large manors, hotels and the like across France and England. However, many field hospitals housed the wounded in tents. The winters of 1916–17 and 1917–18 were among the coldest in the last two millennia, and tents were occasionally blown down in storms. Some of these tented and hutted hospitals had 2,000 or more beds, and with all the accommodations and facilities required for medical and support staff, they were like small towns. During an offensive a hospital could have 600 admissions a day, and orderlies, nurses and even padres were sometimes required to administer anaesthetics. These hospitals were sometimes hit in bombing raids. Morphine was given sparingly and only in extreme cases in hospital, so men had to suffer through the painful cleaning and irrigation of wounds. However, alcohol was given regularly to the sick and wounded.

The First Blood Banks

Blood transfusion was in its infancy and not used reliably until the last couple of years of the war. While the first transfusions had to be made directly from donor to receiver before the blood congealed, around 1913 it had been discovered that by adding an anticoagulant and refrigerating the blood it was possible to store it for some days. 'Blood banks' became possible, and the first non-direct transfusion was performed in March 1914 by a Belgian doctor with a diluted solution of blood. The First World War accelerated the development of blood banks and transfusion techniques.

The first blood transfusion using blood that had been stored and cooled was performed on 1 January 1916. The younger brother of the economist John Maynard Keynes, Geoffrey Keynes (1887–1982), was a lieutenant in the RAMC, acting as a consultant surgeon. His expertise in blood transfusion enabled him to create a portable blood transfusion device that could store blood, which was recognised as saving thousands of lives. Oswald Hope Robertson (1886–1966) was an English-born scientist who pioneered the idea of 'blood banks' in the 'blood depots' he established in 1917 during service in France with the US Army Medical Corps. In France he experimented with preserving human blood cells for use in transfusions, and is now recognised as the inventor of the blood bank.

Plastic Surgery Is Invented

Sir Harold Delf Gillies (1882–1960) was a New Zealand-born (and later London-based) surgeon, considered to be the 'father of plastic surgery'. He joined the RAMC at the war's beginning, and learned a skin graft technique in Paris. He then persuaded the Army's chief surgeon to establish a facial injury ward, which opened in 1917 with 1,000 beds. Gillies and his colleagues developed many techniques of plastic surgery, with more than 11,000 operations being performed on over 5,000 men. His first operation was in 1917, giving 'flap surgery' to a sailor horribly disfigured facially at Jutland. The artist Paddy Hartley said, 'The First World War was a war dominated by high explosives and heavy artillery. Casualties treated by Sir Harold Gillies included an unprecedented number with horrific facial injuries. Often unable to see, hear, speak, eat or drink, they struggled to re-assimilate back into civilian life. Gillies is credited with developing new, untried techniques to treat the injuries created by this new kind of war, taking grafts from undamaged areas of flesh. He used tubular "pedicles" from the forehead, scalp, chest, neck or shoulders but retained a connection to allow blood flow.' He was not knighted until 1930.

The Advance in Anaesthetics

Before the war, anaesthetics such as chloroform or ether were given by doctors and surgeons via basic facemasks, and specialists were rare. However, vast numbers of injured men demanded the introduction of casualty clearing stations, to help triage and treat the wounded quickly and efficiently. The workload of these 'mini hospitals' created specialist anaesthetist posts within the military. These anaesthetists were able to help develop the relatively new techniques of blood transfusion and resuscitation. These were now recognised to be vital in preventing shock. While at the casualty clearing stations, Geoffrey Marshall (1887–1982) studied the effects of different anaesthetic agents in varying amounts of shock. This work led to the popularity of nitrous oxide, ether and oxygen, which in turn stimulated interest in anaesthesia machines. His work at the Queen's Hospital, Sidcup, where he treated those with facial and jaw injuries, highlighted the possibility of endotracheal intubation, a technique that had a drastic effect on the administration of anaesthetics.

Although there were no new wonder anaesthetics, something which would not occur until the neuromuscular blocking drugs of the 1940s, many of these concepts moved into civilian anaesthesia and enabled British anaesthesia to be at the forefront of anaesthesia development for much of the twentieth century. Sir Geoffrey Marshall was the catalyst for development of anaesthesia and respiratory medicine, becoming doctor to both Winston Churchill and George VI. He had first worked on an ambulance barge and then in the casualty clearing stations researching the increasing problem of surgical shock. His objective was to reduce the terrible mortality rate from shock, a condition that seemed to worsen with anaesthesia. He experimented with various anaesthetic techniques and settled on gas and oxygen. The machine he developed gave continuous gas through a mask he designed himself. His drawings were taken up by a Dr Boyle, and the machine was marketed as Boyle's Gas Anaesthesia Machine. Incorporating a water sight-feed for nitrous oxide, the machine was manufactured for the British Army for the remainder of the war but Marshall did not publish his research until 1920. Marshall wrote that 'with gas-oxygen we cut down the mortality from about 90 per cent to something like 25 per cent'. While surgeons had prided themselves in their abilities to carry out procedures timed in seconds, the addition of oxygen permitted more complicated operations to be carried out, sometimes lasting hours. Nitrous oxide-oxygen mixtures became even more practical with the introduction of devices that accurately measured their concentrations. Other devices were focused on portability and convenience on the battlefield, such as the Flagg can, used for administering ether.

Orthopaedics and the Welsh Bonesetters

In the eighteenth century a Spanish-speaking boy was the only survivor of a ship which floundered off Llanfairynghornwy in Anglesey, and he was adopted by a childless farming couple named Thomas. The boy took their name, married a local girl and became the ancestor of a line of *meddygon esgryn*, bone doctors, or bonesetters. The reputation of Evan Thomas (1735–1814) across North Wales and the Borders was such that Viscount Bulkeley paid for his memorial tablet in the church. Evan's son Richard ap Evan of Llanfaethlu carried on this expertise, and his son Evan Thomas developed an extensive practice from Liverpool. Hugh Owen Thomas was Evan's son, the great-grandson of the shipwrecked boy, and handled more fractures than any other surgeon in Britain. Hugh's nephew Sir Robert Jones, whom he trained, carried on with his work, and his 'Thomas calliper' saved thousands of limbs in the First World War and is still used across the world.

Henry Gray developed acute orthopaedic services on the Western Front from 1914. The main orthopaedic problem was a compound fracture of the thigh bone, the femur. Gray established that the mortality rate for this wound in 1914 and 1915 was around 80 per cent. Robert Jones described this wound as 'the tragedy of the war'. Many deaths were preventable, because Britain went to war in 1914 with a series of inadequate splints based on the Liston splint, which is simply a pole tied down the side of the leg with the fracture. Bone end grinds against bone end, resulting in excessive blood loss. By the time these wounded soldiers arrived back at the casualty clearing stations, they were completely drained with hypovolemic shock, an emergency condition in which severe blood and fluid loss make the heart unable to pump enough blood to the body. The Thomas splint overcame the problems of the Liston splint, with cords tied round the bottom of the splint. Traction was maintained, so it effectively immobilised the fracture, diminishing the blood loss. Wounded soldiers treated in a Thomas splint reached casualty clearing stations in good clinical condition. Jones introduced the Thomas splint to the Western Front and it was Gray who ensured its use in clinical practice. The Battle of Arras in 1917 lasted about six weeks and Gray had 1,009 compound femurs admitted to his casualty clearing stations. Before that battle, using a variety of splints based on the Rifle or Liston splint, the majority of patients reached the casualty clearing stations in terrible shock due to blood loss. The mortality rate in the casualty clearing stations was 50 per cent. Many had died before they got there. Many surgeons immediately amputated the limb.

At Arras, all compound fractures were treated using the Thomas splint. Only 5 per cent reached casualty clearing stations in clinical shock and the mortality was only 15.6 per cent, a very significant reduction in mortality. Gray's amputation rate was only 17.2 per cent. All regimental medical officers were taught how to apply the Thomas splint. All the patients who were fit for surgery also now had immediate radical wound excision. Patients were kept in France for six weeks until the fracture was 'sticky', not completely solid but solid enough to transfer the patient back to the United Kingdom to one of the orthopaedic centres without losing the position of the fracture. Colonel Mount Stewart RAMC recently wrote, 'Through three and a half years of concentrated experience of war wounds on a scale hitherto unimaginable and in collaboration with many brilliant young surgeons, Gray was able to define the principles of treatment in modern war surgery.' The action of Robert Jones in establishing the principle of segregation, unity of control and continuity of treatment of certain categories of wounded soldiers on the Western Front was an act of outstanding vision.

Robert Jones' principal role was the development of orthopaedic services in the United Kingdom for late orthopaedic problems. By December 1914, Jones recognised that hospitals were full of crippled soldiers who had been treated badly initially, were not fit to go back to the Army and were not fit for discharge into civilian life. He opened an experimental orthopaedic unit in Alder Hey in Liverpool in 1915, for the very first time segregating orthopaedic patients, then opened what was called an 'orthopaedic centre' in London in March 1916, holding 800 patients. This provided surgery for late orthopaedic problems. By 1918, there were no fewer than twenty orthopaedic centres, with a total of 20,000 beds.

Shell Shock

Shell-shocked men often had uncontrollable diarrhoea, could not sleep, stopped speaking, had uncontrollable anxiety, whimpered for hours and twitched uncontrollably. Some soldiers recovered, but many others suffered for the rest of their lives. Around 2 per cent of British soldiers serving in the trenches were the victims of shell shock, around 80,000 of the men who fought in the war. The early symptoms included constant tiredness, irritability, dizziness, headaches and a lack of concentration. Eventually men would suffer from a full mental breakdown, making it impossible for them to remain on the front line. They were often considered cowards or malingerers, and one doctor said that shell shock was a 'manifestation of childishness and femininity'. Treatment included electro-shock therapy, hot and cold baths, massage, daily marches, athletic activities and sometimes hypnosis. Officers were sometimes given psychoanalysis as well, especially at the famous Craiglockhart War Hospital in Scotland, which treated poets Siegfried Sassoon and Wilfred Owen. Shell-shocked officers were medically diagnosed as having 'neurasthenia', while the 'lower-class' ranks were classified as 'hysterics'.

It was initially thought that the constant barrage of shellfire from both sides was to blame. An exploding shell created a vacuum in the head, and when the air rushed into that vacuum it disturbed the cerebrospinal fluid, upsetting the workings of the brain. Medical evidence showed that shell concussion could cause neurological damage, consisting of tiny haemorrhages in the brain and central nervous system. However, soldiers exhibited symptoms of shell shock even when they had not been exposed to shellfire. In 1917, the term shell shock was no longer allowed. Men were classified as 'Not Yet Diagnosed Nervous' (NYDN). The men called this 'Not Yet Dead Nearly'.

Soldiers who had bayoneted men in the face developed hysterical tics of their own facial muscles. Stomach cramps seized men who knifed their foes in the abdomen. Snipers lost their sight. Nightmares of being unable to withdraw bayonets from the enemy bodies persisted long after the battle. An infantry captain complained that visions could occur 'right in the middle of an ordinary conversation' when 'the face of a Boche that I have bayoneted, with its horrible gurgle and grimace, comes sharply into view'. An inability to eat or sleep was common. As early as 1917, it was recognised that war neuroses accounted for a seventh of all personnel discharged for disabilities from the British Army. Once wounds were excluded, emotional disorders were responsible for one-third of all discharges. Even more worrying was the fact that a higher proportion of officers were suffering in this way. According to one survey published in 1917, while the ratio of officers to men at the front was 1 to 30, among patients in hospitals specialising in war neuroses, the ratio of officers to men was 1 to 6. What some medical officers quickly realised was that everyone had a 'breaking point'.

The purpose of hospital treatment was to restore the maximum number of men to duty as quickly as possible. Around 80 per cent of men who had entered hospital suffering shell shock were never able to return to military duty, so it was imperative that these high levels of 'permanent ineffectives' were reduced. The patient 'must be induced to face his illness in a manly way'. There was little understanding or sympathy. Men arriving at a hospital for servicemen suffering shell shock were greeted with silence. Men were described as hanging their heads in 'inexplicable shame'. After the war, tens of thousands of ex-soldiers committed suicide, and an equal amount were locked away in mental asylums.

Consumption: The Wasting Disease

This was an infection causing a chronic cough with blood-tinged sputum, fever, night sweats and weight loss, giving it the name of consumption as one wasted away. Now known as tuberculosis, it was a major cause of death in soldiers. Before the war was over, more than 2,000 men had died of tuberculosis in the Army, and thousands more had been hospitalised. Throughout the First World War, tuberculosis was the leading cause of discharge for disability, accounting for 13.5 percent of all discharges. The BCG vaccine was not used until 1921.

'Dangle Parades' and the 'Battle of the Wazzir'

Venereal diseases were the cause of much debility and loss of manpower during the First World War as well as in the Second World War. Salvarsan had been discovered in 1906 and was available for treatment of syphilis, although the older methods of treatment with mercury were still prescribed. Gonorrhoea was mainly treated by urethral washouts using medicated fluids, a treatment that was much detested by the men but was continued until the introduction of penicillin during the Second World War. The rate of venereal disease among Canadian troops was almost six times higher than that of the British troops, and was one in every nine men. Troops who ended up in specialised VD hospitals were docked their pay, while officers had to pay two shillings and sixpence for every day they spent in a VD hospital and also lost their field allowance of 2s 6d. Soldiers with VD were not eligible for leave for twelve months. In *Goodbye to All That*, Robert Graves remembered the queues of British soldiers outside the licensed French brothels. Those adorned with a blue light were for officers, and those with a red one for the other ranks.

Venereal disease was a major problem during the First World War, and only the great influenza pandemic of 1918–19 accounted for more soldiers taken out of the front line. In the early years of the war, the Army warned soldiers about venereal disease and held regular 'dangle parades' to check their genitals for symptoms. Safer-sex measures like the use of condoms were not mentioned, as this was seen as encouraging immorality. Only from 1916 were there some early-treatment facilities, to which men reported within several hours of intercourse for urethral irrigation with disinfectants. A global pandemic of syphilis and gonorrhoea followed the return of troops to their own countries. For instance, in New Zealand, venereal disease clinics were set up in Auckland, Wellington, Christchurch and Dunedin in 1919 and were soon overcrowded. In 1917, General George Richardson told the defence minister that about 7,600 New Zealand soldiers were being infected annually. At the war's end 16,000 New Zealanders were treated for venereal disease before being allowed to go home. The VD rate had risen quickly after the New Zealand Expeditionary Force arrived in Egypt at Christmas 1914 and soldiers visited prostitutes in Cairo's brothel district, the Haret el Wasser, known as the Wazzir. Before leaving for Gallipoli in April 1915, Australian and New Zealand troops banded together to wage 'the Battle of the Wazzir', a riot believed to have been begun by New Zealanders, partly as payback for venereal infection.

The three main diseases were syphilis, gonorrhoea and chancroid. In the summer of 1917 there were 23,000 British soldiers in hospital with venereal diseases and the French had suffered more than a million cases of syphilis and gonorrhoea. General Pershing gave out several orders regarding venereal diseases, for example on 2 July 1917: 'A soldier who contracts a venereal disease not only suffers permanent injury, but renders himself inefficient as a soldier and becomes an incumbrance [sic] to the army. He fails in his duty to his country and to his comrades.' In the US Army, of 3,500,000 admissions to sick report on account of diseases only, venereal diseases were the direct causes in 357,969 admissions, or 10.2 per cent of the whole. For admission to hospital, solely on account of venereal disease, there was a loss of 6,804,818 days from duty. As a class, venereal diseases stood second only to influenza among diseases as a cause of admission to sick report for the US Army, and exceeded the total number of men killed and wounded in action by approximately 100,000.

Diarrhoea

Latrines were pits dug to a depth of 4–6 feet, usually approached by a short trench to the rear of the line. However, in the front trench, they were often placed in advance of the line, probably to discourage any inclination to linger. When they were full, within 1 foot of the surface, they were supposed to be filled in and soldiers had to dig new ones. Sometimes there was not time for this and men used a nearby shell hole. Latrines were not meant to be permanent. Battalions leaving the line had to fill in their own latrines and prepare fresh pits for the incoming relieving force. On many occasions however, buckets and even biscuit tins would be used in place of deep pits. These would be emptied on a daily basis. Each company assigned two men to sanitary duties, often as punishment for minor breaches of the Army code. They were jokingly known as 'rear admirals' or 'shit-wallahs'. Apart from the strong smell associated with faeces, the area of the latrine was heavily dosed with quicklime. The combined smell was memorable and repulsive. Enemy forces would often detect increased activity at latrine sites, e.g. in the early morning, and shell the area. Commanding officers were almost always strict in insisting that troops use designated latrines rather than communication trenches for fear of the possibility of disease, but the primitive conditions and lack of opportunities for washing meant that diarrhoea was extremely common.

Dysentery

Dysentery is a disease involving the inflammation of the lining of the large intestines. The inflammation causes stomach pains and diarrhoea, with some cases involving vomiting and fever. Bacteria enter the body through the mouth in food or water, and also by human faeces and contact with infected people. Associated diarrhoea causes people suffering from dysentery to lose important salts and fluids from the body, which can be fatal if the body dehydrates. The disease struck the men in the trenches as there was no proper sanitation. Dysentery caused by contaminated water was especially a problem in the early stages of the war, as it took some time before regular supplies of water to the trenches could be organised. Soldiers were supplied with water bottles, which could be refilled when they returned to reserve lines. However, the water bottle supply was rarely enough for their needs and soldiers in the trenches often depended upon impure water collected from shell holes or other cavities. Later, to purify it, chloride of lime was added to the water. This was not popular with the soldiers as they disliked the taste of the purified water.

Trench Foot

Trenches were nearly always waterlogged. Wet feet caused a major problem called trench foot, a fungal infection. Wooden 'duckboards' were quickly introduced into the trenches in 1915 and cases of trench foot saw a rapid decline, although there were still a few sufferers throughout the duration of the war. It was initially believed to be a symptom of poor morale. Its effects on armies, before trench conditions were much improved, could be severe. Some 20,000 casualties resulting from trench foot were suffered by the British Army alone towards the end of 1914. Patients sometimes had to have toes amputated following gangrene. Improved trench drainage and conditions in general led to a rapid reduction in cases. Local commanders were also held accountable for such outbreaks, which consequently encouraged the provision of better trench conditions, along with regular feet inspections, greasing of toes and changes of socks. Better waterproof footwear also greatly helped.

Trench Mouth

This is a severe and painful form of gingivitis, or gum swelling. The term originates from the First World War, when the disorder was common among soldiers. The mouth normally contains a balance of different bacteria, and the infection occurs when there are too many abnormal mouth bacteria. The gums become infected and develop painful ulcers, and viruses may be involved in allowing the bacteria to grow too much. It is caused by stress, poor oral hygiene (water was often filthy), poor nutrition, smoking, and throat, tooth or mouth infections. Now rare, it is most common in the 15–35 age group. The many sufferers had bad breath, crater-like ulcers between the teeth, fever and a foul taste in the mouth. Painful gums appeared reddened and swollen, with a greyish film over them, but also bled in response to any pressure or irritation. The disease can now be treated with antibiotics, and was once called Vincent's Infection, classified as an 'acute necrotising ulcerative gingivitis'.

Trench Fever and Lice

The sickness resembles typhoid, a fever caused by salmonella and influenza. Headaches, skin rashes, inflamed eyes and leg pains are all symptoms, and 'Trench Fever' was first reported in the trenches of the Western Front in December 1914. Unlike trench foot and trench mouth, it continued to grow throughout the war.

The condition was not itself particularly serious, with most patients recovering after some five or six days, hence its nickname of 'five-day fever'. However, prolonged hospitalisation of several weeks was common. Some officers, such as J. R. R. Tolkien, spent months convalescing. Trench fever, although not usually life-threatening, was often highly debilitating and resulted in a trench casualty rate of up to 15 per cent. It was one of the most significant causes of sickness and military authorities were anxious to determine the cause. It was not determined until 1918 that trench fever was caused by a bacterium carried by lice. Lice were a constant problem for men in the trenches, and difficult to get rid of. Soldiers had an average of twenty lice crawling around their bodies, but the record was a soldier with 10,428 lice in his shirt, with another 10,253 lice eggs waiting to hatch.

The bacterium *Bartonella quintana* (formerly *Rickettsia quintana*) is transmitted by the contamination of a skin abrasion or louse-bite wound with the faeces of an infected human body louse (*Pediculus humanus corporis*). It is estimated that up to 97 per cent of officers and men who worked and lived in the trenches were afflicted with lice. The conditions of trench warfare proved ideal for their rapid spread. Body lice were far more common than head or public lice. They could only thrive in warm conditions, provided by body heat and clothing. In spreading from person to person, lice required the close proximity of a new potential host, readily provided as men huddled together to preserve a degree of warmth. Lice which had sucked the blood of one infected person quickly succeeded in spreading the infection to each successive host. Men would gather in groups to de-louse themselves, called 'chatting'. One favoured method of eradicating lice was to quickly run a lit candle along the seams of clothing, where lice would typically converge. It only brought temporary relief, as lice eggs which remained undetected in clothing would hatch within a matter of hours. Each female could produce as many as a dozen fresh eggs per day, which would hatch within two to four weeks. Men would only be offered a full bath two or three times per month, so lice were always prevalent.

Typhus Fever

Epidemic typhus has also been known as camp fever, jail fever, hospital fever, ship fever, famine fever, putrid fever and petechial fever. The causative organism is the micro-organism *Rickettsia prowazekii*, transmitted by the body louse *Pediculus humanus corporis*. *R. prowazekii* grows in the louse's gut and is excreted in its faeces. The disease is then transmitted via lice from an infected to an uninfected human who scratches the louse bite and rubs the faeces into the wound. *R. prowazekii* can remain viable and virulent in the dried louse faeces for many days. Typhus will eventually kill the louse, though the disease will remain viable for many weeks in the dead louse. Apart from the 1918–19 pandemic of influenza, this was the most fatal illness, mainly associated with the Central Powers' campaigns in Eastern Europe. Typhus fever is not typhoid fever, nor is it related to it, despite their similarity in names. Typhoid fever is a separate disease of the gastrointestinal tract caused by a bacterium, *Salmonella typhi*. Man acquires typhoid fever by eating or drinking food or water contaminated with faeces from an infected person. Typhoid fever is a disease of poor sanitation and impure food and water supplies.

Typhus fever is instead carried by lice. The lice cling to the seams of clothing, in cuffs, hems and any other space that provides them with a hiding place. They move from one person to another more or less at random. The accidental brushing against a person with lice, a temporary loan of clothing or simple proximity, especially at night, can lead to a migration from one person to another. Lice will make a mass exodus from a person when death overtakes their host and the rapidly cooling body forces them to find a more hospitable environment. Lice feed by sucking blood from their hosts. They are incredibly prolific, laying eggs, called nits, which stick to the clothing and body hair of their hosts. *Rickettsia prowazekii* multiplies in the louse's gut and is excreted in large amounts when the louse defecates. When dry these faeces retain their infective power for a considerable time. Man is infected when the dry faeces are rubbed into the skin, or when he crushes the louse in scratching and rubs the content of the gut into his skin and into the puncture made by the insect. Once in the victim's bloodstream, *Rickettsia prowazekii* begins to multiply. About twelve days after infection, the clinical symptoms of the disease begin suddenly, with a high fever, headache, chills, numbness and body pains, sometimes leading to delirium, coma and cardiac failure. Before antibiotics the fatality rate varied from 10 to 80 per cent. Children, surprisingly, had a lower mortality rate than adults.

At the start of the First World War, Serbia comprised 3 million people. Within six months, 500,000 Serbians had developed typhus fever. Over 200,000, of whom 70,000 were troops, died from the disease. One half of their 60,000 Austrian prisoners also died from typhus. The few existing hospitals were soon full to overflowing and others had to be improvised. There were fewer than 400 doctors in the country, many of them in the Army, and almost all of them contracted the disease, 126 fatally. There were hardly enough grave diggers left as they too fell victim. For six months across 1914 and 1915 Serbia was helpless, but Austria would not attack again while the epidemic raged. The Central Powers lost six months during the most critical time of the war. It is reasonable to believe that a quick thrust through Serbia at the time, the closing of Salonika and the establishment of a south-western front against the Russians, could have tipped the balance in favour of the Central Powers.

Typhus quickly established itself along the entire Eastern Front, but was kept from reaching epidemic proportions in either the Austrian or German lines by strict delousing of their troops. It was largely absent from the Western Front, but raged unabated among the Russian Army on the Eastern Front and made its presence felt upon the eastern forces of the Central Powers. Serbia's epidemic was a prelude to the greatest typhus fever outbreak of the twentieth century. Famine swept the country, refugees swarmed throughout the land. Cholera, typhoid fever and dysentery swept Russia as essential services collapsed. Then, in the winter of 1918, typhus fever appeared in epidemic form. From 1914, the disease had spread slowly but steadily. In the first years there were 100,000 cases. After the retreat of 1916, the reported number rose to 154,000, though only a handful of these cases involved the army. The great epidemic that broke out at the end of 1918 invaded the country along three fronts: Petrograd, the Rumanian front and the Volga region. For four years, the epidemic raged amid the famine and dislocation of the Russian Revolution. Of 20 million cases, half died. For some years it looked as if the fate of the revolution was at the mercy of typhus fever. In 1919, Lenin stated, 'Either socialism will defeat the louse, or the louse will defeat socialism.'

'The Most Devastating Epidemic in Recorded World History'

The influenza pandemic of 1918–19 killed more people than the First World War, somewhere between 50 and 100 million people. More people died of this influenza in a single year than in four years of the 'Black Death' of 1347–51. It was known as 'Spanish Flu' or 'La Grippe'. On Armistice Day 1918, Britain was in the grip of Spanish Flu, which could kill its victims in less than a day. In the months that led up to the 11 November Armistice of 1918, the world's armies and navies had begun to disperse. On their way home, the demobilised took with them a serious virus. The trenches of rotting bodies provided ideal breeding grounds for the virus that would be responsible for more than five times as many deaths as the war itself. The virus was thought to have originated in chickens and mutated in pigs before emerging in humans in the spring of 1918. The huge crowds that attended the Armistice celebrations in Trafalgar Square in London and hundreds of communal spaces up and down the country intensified the chances of the disease spreading.

In the autumn of 1918, the nation was struggling to come to terms with the catastrophe of war. Nearly 750,000 British men were estimated to have died and more than 1.5 million had been severely wounded. Almost no surviving individual had escaped the grief of losing a relative or friend. But now, when things were supposed to get better, those afflicted were feeling shivery upon waking up. By lunch, their skin had turned a vivid purple. By the evening, death would have occurred, often caused by choking on a thick scarlet jelly that suddenly clogged the lungs. Those aged from fifteen to forty were the most susceptible. The death toll included those who had survived the war but had not lived long enough to develop the immunities acquired during previous flu epidemics by older people. At the beginning of the outbreak, in the summer of 1918, the Royal College of Physicians announced that this strain of flu was no more threatening than the still well-remembered virus of 1890. *The Times* even suggested that the swift spread of the epidemic might have been a direct result of 'the general weakness of nerve-power known as war-weariness'.

Most doctors were still out at the front treating war casualties, with the majority of nurses in attendance. Influenza victims took second priority to the 10,000 wounded and shell-shocked men who continued to occupy hospital beds for months after the ceasefire. In 1918, no medical antidote was available, nor any prospect of a mass vaccination. The General Medical Council was challenged to come up with practical remedies. A small gauze mask made from three layers of butter muslin and worn across the mouth and nose seemed to inhibit the virus. In Arizona shaking hands was outlawed, and in France spitting became a legal offence. Medical advice was varied. Huge numbers of the public relied on their own resources. Older people used trusted household remedies. Laudanum, opium, quinine, rhubarb, treacle and vinegar were all invested with special healing powers. In London, nearly 1,500 policemen, a third of the force, reported sick simultaneously. Council office workers took off their suits and ties to dig graves. Coffins that had been stockpiled during the war were suddenly in short supply. A wartime agreement had been made that no bodies would be brought back from the battle lines. Railway workshops turned to coffin manufacturing and Red Cross ambulances became hearses. Whole classes of children were kept away from school by their wary parents, instead filling the London playgrounds and singing a skipping rhyme: 'I had a little bird/Its name was Enza,/I opened the Window/And in-flew Enza.' In just two years, a fifth of the world's population was infected. It infected 28 per cent of all Americans. An estimated 675,000 Americans died of influenza during the pandemic, ten times as many as in the war. Of the US soldiers who died in Europe, half of them fell to the influenza virus and not to the enemy.

14

Women at War

The war gave women the freedom and wages only men had enjoyed so far. Women replaced absent servicemen between 1914 and 1918 in government departments, public transport, the Post Office, and as office clerks, land workers, drivers and factory workers. The dangerous and toxic munitions factories were employing 950,000 women by Armistice Day. In July 1914, before the war broke out, there were 3.2 million women in employment. This had risen to 5 million by January 1918. Women's job mobility also increased enormously, with a large number of women abandoning service for factory work. Many middle-class women were now left without home help, an enlightening experience for many. Britain, like the other combatants, could not have carried on the war without women taking over what were essentially thought of as 'men's jobs'. However, their entrance into the workforce was initially greeted with hostility because the remaining male workers were worried that women's willingness to work for lower wages would put them out of work. Many married women were forced into the workplace by the death of their husbands. Other women were drafted into industries that had been depleted by military conscription.

The First World War was undoubtedly the catalyst for women to be given the vote. The war caused the British suffrage movement to split. Emmeline Pankhurst, leader of the Women's Social and Political Union, called for a temporary ceasefire in their campaign so that the country could focus fully on the war effort. Sylvia Pankhurst and her Women's Suffrage Federation were more radical, and wanted the 'votes for women' struggle to continue in spite of the situation. When the war ended in November 1918, 8.4 million women were granted the right to vote. The Eligibility of Women Act was also passed in November 1918, which meant that some women could now be elected as MPs.

However, women would have to wait to be granted the vote on equal terms with British men. This was brought by the Representation of the People Act in 1928, which stated that all women over the age of twenty-one could vote.

Munitionettes and Canaries

Lloyd George nationalised the munitions factories and also suspended all trade union activities in them. The masses of women employed in them became known as 'munitionettes', and they produced 80 per cent of the weapons and shells used by the British forces. They daily risked their lives working with poisonous substances without adequate protective clothing or the required safety measures. They were also nicknamed 'canaries', for the yellow tinge that skin acquired when exposed to sulphur. The women only got half the men's wages.

The Women's Land Army

The government also invited women to join the ranks of the Women's Land Army, an organisation that offered cheap female labour to farmers. The 260,000 volunteers that made up the WLA were given little more than a uniform and orders to work hard. With so many young men called up for the armed services, there was a real shortfall in farm workers. The women in the WLA did all the jobs that were required to make a farm function normally: threshing, ploughing, tractor driving, reclaiming land, drainage, etc. There was an agreed maximum working week – fifty hours in the summer and forty-eight hours in the winter. A normal week would consist of five and a half days. Along with their weekly pay, all members of the WLA who were posted more than 20 miles from their home would receive a free rail warrant for a visit home every six months. During harvest time, many WLA members worked from dawn to dusk and easily exceeded their fifty-hour week.

FANY and VAD Go to War

The First Aid Nursing Yeomanry (FANY) was created in 1907 by Lord Kitchener, as a first aid link between front-line fighting units and the field hospitals. During the First World War, FANYs ran field hospitals, drove ambulances and set up soup kitchens and troop canteens, often under highly dangerous conditions. By the Armistice, they had been awarded many decorations for bravery, including seventeen Military Medals, a Légion d'Honneur and twenty-seven Croix de Guerre. The young women had to pay a fee to join the FANY, as well as contributing ten shillings a week for supplies. FANYs were used during the war for dangerous ambulance driving between the front line and field hospitals that they also ran, and also for cooking and keeping canteens. FANY units stationed in Calais had to endure, and often drive ambulances through, 198 bombing raids. Nurses had been part of the military since Kitchener's establishment of the Voluntary Aid Detachment (VAD) in 1909, which formalised the trend initiated by Florence Nightingale during the Crimean War (1853–54) and overlapped with work by the International Red Cross and FANYs in some cases. VADs worked as assistant nurses, drove ambulances, cooked, did clerical work, etc.

When endless rivers of casualties overwhelmed staff, there was little difference between what was expected of VADs and fully trained nurses. VADs were often left in charge of as many as 100 dangerously ill men, looking out for bleeding from amputations, sepsis and death. Between 1914 and 1918, about 38,000 VADs worked as auxiliary nurses, ambulance drivers and cooks both in the hospitals of the home front and the units of the Western Front. Besides France, they worked on the Eastern Front and in Mesopotamia, Gallipoli and Malta.

VAD and Agatha Christie

British Nursing Sisters and VADs abroad were under strict regulations, and were forbidden to fraternise with men, including their co-workers, when off duty. VADs had to be at least twenty-three years old to be posted outside Britain. Many of them lied about their age because they were eager to get to France and 'do their duty'. One of the most famous was Agatha Christie, who learned about poisons and dispensed drugs, knowledge she later used in writing her mysteries. In Vera Brittain's *Testament of Youth* (1933), she describes in detail the gruelling working conditions that naive middle-class girls like her were subjected to. Like Brittain, VADs were generally from genteel, sheltered and chaperoned backgrounds. Some were aristocrats, like Lady Diana Manners, reputedly the most beautiful woman in England and expected to marry the Prince of Wales. Diana's mother was against her becoming a VAD, as she stated in her memoir, *The Rainbow Comes and Goes*: 'She explained in words suitable to my innocent ears that wounded soldiers, so long starved of women, inflamed with wine and battle, ravish and leave half-dead the young nurses who wish only to tend them.'

The American Mary Borden, a wealthy woman living in England when the war broke out, was awarded a Croix de Guerre for setting up a mobile hospital unit that nursed men wounded at Ypres and the Somme. She did so out of frustration with the incompetence of the French Red Cross, for which she had originally volunteered. She published in 1929 an impressive novel, *The Forbidden Zone*, which reflects her experiences. One of the professional nurses she employed, Ellen La Motte, published in 1916 an appalling account of her front-line nursing in Belgium, *The Backwash of War: The Human Wreckage of the Battlefield as Witnessed by an American Hospital Nurse.*

Tiaras And Hospitals

For an informative and engaging account of nursing during the First World War, read Lyn Macdonald's book, *The Roses of No Man's Land*. She quotes one nurse describing the Duchess of Westminster's hospital, which the duchess had set up in her villa at Le Touquet in France. In the early days of the war, the duchess and her friends would dress in full evening regalia, including diamond tiaras, to greet the incoming wounded whatever time of day. 'It's the least we can do to cheer up the men,' the duchess would say, her wolfhound at her side. The duchess was probably one of those upper-class volunteers whose nurse's uniform was designed by the couturier Worth.

The Forces

In the First World War, approximately 80,000 women served in the three British women's forces as non-combatants. The Royal Navy set up in 1916 the Women's Royal Navy Service (WRNS), staffed by women running kitchens, postal and phone services, and administration. The Women's Army Auxiliary Corps (WAAC) followed in 1917 at the instigation of Lt Gen. Sir Henry Lawson, and was filled with volunteers who were without full military status, even though they were subjected to German enemy fire all through their activities in France. WAACs, commanded by the efficient Helen Gwynne-Vaughan, were victims of a sexist campaign claiming that a significant number of them had been made pregnant at the front. An official investigation proved this was generally false. The Women's Royal Airforce (WRAF) came last, in 1918, first under the command of Lady Crawford, who soon resigned, annoyed by the lack of actual power the military had granted her.

15

War Poems, Trench Songs and the Reality of War

Poets like Wilfred Owen, Edward Thomas and Rupert Brooke drew upon their experiences to produce inspired and moving poetry from the trenches. The Anglo-Welsh Wilfred Owen (1893–1918) was one of the most powerful war poets, who depicted the reality and horrors of the First World War. During his first period in the trenches, he was blown into the air by a trench mortar and later spent days trapped in an old German dugout. These events and the constant artillery barrage left him with shell shock, and he was invalided to hospital in Edinburgh in 1916. In hospital Owen met and became friendly with another war poet, Siegfried Sassoon. They shared a love of poetry and held a common view of the tragedy of trench warfare. Sassoon was to play a key role in developing Owen as a war poet, and also helped to publicise his work. Owen's poetry became symbolic of the futility of the First World War, and he hated its glorification by writers and politicians who had no knowledge of its stark reality. In his preface to his collection of war poetry, Owen writes this fitting analogy: 'My subject is war, and the pity of war. The poetry is in the pity.'

Owen's 'Anthem for Doomed Youth' is one of the best-known war poems of all time:

> What passing-bells for these who die as cattle?
> Only the monstrous anger of the guns.
> Only the stuttering rifles' rapid rattle
> Can patter out their hasty orisons.
> No mockeries now for them; no prayers, nor bells,
> Nor any voice of mourning save the choirs,
> The shrill demented choirs of wailing shells,
> And bugles calling for them from sad shires …

In 1918, against the wishes of Sassoon, Owen returned to the front line and took part in the final Allied push of the war. In October 1918, he led men in storming enemy strongholds in the village of Joncourt. For his bravery in action he was awarded a posthumous Military Cross. Owen had wanted to receive this honour, not for personal gain, but to help give greater credence to his role as a realistic anti-war poet. The citation on the award reads, 'On the company commander becoming a casualty, he assumed command and showed fine leadership and resisted a heavy counter-attack. He personally manipulated a captured enemy machine gun from an isolated position and inflicted considerable losses on the enemy. Throughout he behaved most gallantly.' Owen was killed in battle on 4 November 1918, a week before the war's end, and his parents received the terrible news by telegram on Armistice Day 1918.

Siegfried Sassoon (1886–1967) was hit hard by the death of his brother in Gallipoli. Fighting on the front line in France in 1915, he was shocked by the reality and ugliness of trench warfare, and was also influenced by fellow poet Robert Graves. Sassoon gained a reputation for fearless bravery in action. He frequently took on dangerous missions with little regard for his own life, and his men were inspired by his courage. On one occasion, he single-handedly took a heavily defended German trench in the Hindenburg Line, killing an estimated fifty Germans with hand grenades. However, his response on taking the German trench was to sit down and read a book of poetry, rather than signalling for reinforcements. When he returned to his lines he did not even report the incident. Sassoon's commander, Colonel Stockwell, raged at him for his failure to capitalise on the situation. Stockwell said to Sassoon, 'I'd have got you a DSO, if only you'd shown more sense.' It was said that Sassoon's depression at the state of war encouraged him to take almost suicidal risks, gaining him the nickname 'Mad Jack'. He was later awarded the Military Cross for bravery in action.

Sassoon decided to take a public stand against the war, writing a letter to *The Times*. Sassoon stated that the war was being unnecessarily prolonged by the decisions of generals and politicians, who had no regard for the lives of the men they were sending into battle. There was the danger of a court martial. However, the authorities, with the encouragement of his close friend Robert Graves, decided to invalid him out for shell shock and he was withdrawn from military service. Around this time, Sassoon threw the ribbon of his MC into a river. Despite the near court-martial, Sassoon returned to active service in 1918. This time he was shot in the head by 'friendly fire'. His wound encouraged Owen, without Sassoon's knowledge, to go back into front-line service, where he was killed.

Robert Graves (1895–1985) was a war poet, translator of classics and novelist. On the outbreak of war Graves enlisted in the Royal Welch Fusiliers, and was one of the first poets to publish 'realistic' war poetry. Lines from his 'Through the Periscope' of 1915 read, 'Trench stinks of shallow buried dead/Where Tom stands at the periscope,/ Tired out. After nine months he's shed/All fear, all faith, all hate, all hope.'

Graves suffered from shell shock and had a tremendous fear of gas attacks. He was affected by loud bangs or any unusual smell throughout the rest of his life. In 1916, he was so badly wounded by shrapnel in the Battle of the Somme that he was recorded as having died from his wounds. Graves was a close friend of Owen and Sassoon, and wrote a biography of another friend, called *Lawrence of Arabia*. In 1929 he published *Goodbye To All That*, a superb and harrowing account of trench warfare and the difficulties of adjusting to life after the war.

Vera Brittain (1893–1970) was a writer, feminist and pacifist who wrote the bestselling *Testament of Youth*, detailing her traumatic experiences during the First World War. In 1915, she went to work as a volunteer nurse on the Western Front. Her fiancé, two close friends and her brother Edward Brittain were all killed in the war. Brittain described how young nurses worked long hours, in poor conditions, but with great morale. However, she later recounts how her initial idealism faded as she became more aware of the realities of war. She remembered soldiers telling how the German and British soldiers negotiated an unofficial truce, where they avoided shooting each other in the middle of no man's land. However, when a jingoistic officer came to the line, he ordered the men to machine gun the Germans. Incidents like this made Brittain aware that war atrocities were not the preserve of the Germans. Brittain was shocked at the state of some of the wounded men, and found it very testing to help treat men who were very badly injured: 'The first dressing at which I assisted – a gangrenous leg wound, slimy and green and scarlet, with the bone laid bare – turned me sick and faint for a moment.'

Edward Thomas (1878–1917) was a Welsh writer of prose and poetry, commonly considered a war poet, although few of his poems dealt directly with his war experiences. Thomas turned to poetry only in 1914, enlisted in the Artists Rifles in 1915, and was killed in action during the Battle of Arras in 1917, soon after he arrived in France. Being a mature, married man, he could have avoided enlisting. His close friend W. H. Davies, the writer-poet, was devastated and wrote his commemorative poem 'Killed In Action (Edward Thomas)'.

Lawrence Binyon's 1914 poem 'For the Fallen' contains these well-known lines:

> They shall grow not old, as we that are left grow old:
> Age shall not weary them, nor the years contemn.
> At the going down of the sun and in the morning
> We will remember them.

Equally well known is 'The Soldier', by Rupert Brooke (1887–1915):

> If I should die, think this of me:
> That there's some corner of a foreign field
> That is for ever England. There shall be
> In that rich earth a richer dust concealed;
> A dust whom England bore, shaped, made aware,
> Gave, once, her flowers to love, her ways to roam,
> A body of England's, breathing English air,
> Washed by the rivers, blest by suns of home …

There is an incredible amount of wonderful poetry associated with the war, and we must include 'In Flanders Fields', written by Lieutenant Colonel John McCrae of the Canadian Army in May 1915. It still plays an important part in Remembrance Day services across the British Commonwealth.

> In Flanders fields the poppies blow
> Between the crosses, row on row,
> That mark our place; and in the sky
> The larks, still bravely singing, fly
> Scarce heard amid the guns below.
>
> We are the Dead. Short days ago
> We lived, felt dawn, saw sunset glow,
> Loved and were loved, and now we lie
> In Flanders fields.
>
> Take up our quarrel with the foe:
> To you from failing hands we throw
> The torch; be yours to hold it high.
> If ye break faith with us who die
> We shall not sleep, though poppies grow
> In Flanders fields.

There is so much post-First World War prose literature that it is outside the compass of this short book to describe it, but the greater works include T. S. Eliot's *The Waste Land* (1923), Ernest Hemingway's *A Farewell to Arms* (1929), Erich Maria Remarque's *All Quiet on the Western Front* (1928) and T. E. Lawrence's *Seven Pillars of Wisdom* (1922). Hemingway served as an ambulance driver with the American Red Cross in northern Italy, was wounded and decorated for heroism, and fell in love with a nurse while in hospital, recounting the experiences in his novel.

The Lord of the Rings and the Dark Riders

J. R. R. Tolkien had just graduated from Oxford with a first-class degree in Literature when he saw his first active service at the Somme. From July 1916 until he was invalided out with trench fever at the end of October, he experienced the full relentless horrors of trench warfare on the Western Front. He lost his two closest friends, and while convalescing he began writing his posthumously published *The Silmarillion*. Many scholars have shown how the ferocious battles and scenes of slaughter in Tolkien's three-part *Lord of the Rings*, or in 'The Fall of Gondolin', part of *The Silmarillion*, were stimulated by his experiences. Morgoth's monstrous iron dragons owe something to the tanks first used in the First World War, which terrified the horses of the cavalry. The Revd John Waddington-Feather relates that

> Tolkien's son said the Dark Riders were based on a real recurring nightmare from the war. Tolkien, riding a good cavalry horse, had somehow got lost behind the German lines, and, imagining he was behind his own trenches, rode towards a group of mounted cavalrymen standing in the shade of a coppice. It was only when he drew nearer he realised his mistake for they were German *Ulhans*, noted for their atrocities and taking no prisoners. When they saw him they set off in pursuit with their lances levelled at him. He swung his horse round and galloped off hotly pursued by the Germans. They had faster steeds but Tolkien's horse was a big-boned hunter. They got near enough for him to see their skull-and-crossbone helmet badges. Fortunately for Tolkien (and us, his readers) he raced towards some old trenches which his horse, used to hunting, took in its stride. The *Uhlans*' horses weren't up to it and they reined in, leaving Tolkien to get away to his own side. He was terrified and the cruel faces of those *Uhlans* and their badges haunted him in nightmares for a long time afterwards. Years later, when he was writing his novel, the Dark Riders were the result of that terrifying chase.

Tolkien describes the desolation of the battlefield, strewn with the mangled corpses at the end of combat, and describes the haunted, poisoned land left by ancient battles of Mordor and the Dead Marshes. Tolkien stated in one of his letters, 'The dead marshes and the approaches to the Morannon owe something to Northern France after the Battle of the Somme.' The parallels between the landscapes of no man's land and Tolkien's landscapes of nightmare are striking. Mordor is a dry, gasping land pocked by pits that are very much like shell craters. The natural world has been almost annihilated by Sauron's power, much as modern weaponry almost annihilated the natural world on the Western Front. The desolation before the gates of Mordor is another savage landscape inspired by the Western Front. It is full of pits and heaps of torn earth and ash, some with an oily sump at the bottom. The sickly white-and-grey mud mentioned in the Dead Marshes is very like the terrain of no man's land on the Somme, where the underlying chalk bedrock was churned up by artillery bombardment and turned the ground grey and white: 'Here nothing lived, not even the leprous growths that feed on rottenness. The gasping pools were choked with ash and crawling muds, sickly white and grey, as if the mountains had vomited the filth of their entrails on the lands about.' As Frodo, Sam and their guide Gollum cross the marshes, they see the ghostly, rotting forms of the dead soldiers of a war that had swept across the region thousands of years before. As Frodo tells Sam and Gollum, 'They lie in all the pools, pale faces, deep under the dark water. I saw them: grim faces and evil, noble faces and sad. Many faces proud and fair, with weeds in their silver hair. But all foul, all rotting, all dead.'

The clouds of ash and fumes that leave Frodo and Sam gasping for air on their journey through Mordor are reminiscent of the use of poison gas in trench warfare. British gas masks were effective but uncomfortable and difficult to fight in. Gas often lingered in low spots like trenches and shell holes, precisely where men would go to shelter from machine gun fire and bombardments. While most kinds of poison gas were intended to kill or injure, some types of gas were intended merely to make the enemy miserable. Tolkien often describes places where the Shadow has been at work, such as the Dead Marshes, as having a foul or bitter smell. This is another echo of the battlefields of the First World War, which stank of chemicals and death. Post-traumatic stress disorder is shown by the injured Frodo after he returns home. The stress of his journey to Mordor was multiplied by the trauma he suffered from bearing the One Ring. Frodo had intrusive memories of being wounded by the Witch King's knife, Shelob's stinger, and Gollum's teeth. He was often ill and eventually dropped out of the social life of the Shire.

Trench Songs

This is the real poetry of the war, which helped hold troops together in the worst of times. Always someone would lighten the grim horrors by beginning to sing, and others would join in along the trenches and behind the lines. 'Pack Up Your Troubles in Your Old Kit-Bag, and Smile, Smile, Smile' was published in 1915. It was written by the Welshman George Henry Powell under the pseudonym of 'George Asaf' (after the Welsh St Asaf), and set to music by his brother Felix. Some music hall stars rescued the song from their rejects pile to win a wartime competition for the best 'morale-building song' and it proved immensely popular. It was noted as 'perhaps the most optimistic song ever written': 'Pack up your troubles in your old kit-bag,/And smile, smile, smile,/While you've a Lucifer [match] to light your fag,/Smile, boys, that's the style./What's the use of worrying?/It never was worthwhile, so/Pack up your troubles in your old kit-bag,/And smile, smile, smile.' George Powell was a pacifist and a conscientious objector when conscription was imposed in 1916, but Felix served as a staff-sergeant.

'Bless 'Em All' was written by Fred Godfrey while serving in France in 1916, and he reminisced that 'furthermore, it wasn't "Bless"': 'Bless 'em all, Bless 'em all,/The long and the short and the tall,/Bless all those Sergeants and WO1s [warrant officers],/Bless all those Corporals and their bleedin' sons,/Cos we're saying goodbye to 'em all,/And back to their billets they crawl,/You'll get no promotion this side of the ocean,/So cheer up my lads bless 'em all.'

Many music hall songs were written to boost civilian and military spirits, for instance 'Belgium Put the Kibosh on the Kaiser', first recorded on 6 October 1914. It references the 1914 campaign in Belgium, when the tiny BEF and the Belgians managed to delay the much larger German Army. This wrecked the Schlieffen Plan, which depended on total victory against the French in a matter of weeks. It is fairly unknown today, so reprinted in full:

A silly German sausage/Dreamt Napoleon he'd be,/Then he went and broke his promise,/It was made in Germany.

He shook hands with Britannia/And eternal peace he swore,/Naughty boy, he talked of peace/While he prepared for war.

He stirred up little Serbia/To serve his dirty tricks/But naughty nights at Liege/Quite upset this Dirty Dick.

His luggage labelled 'England'/And his programme nicely set,/He shouted 'First stop Paris',/But he hasn't got there yet.

For Belgium put the kibosh on the Kaiser;/Europe took the stick and made him sore;/On his throne it hurts to sit,/And when John Bull starts to hit,/ He will never sit upon it any more.

His warships sailed upon the sea,/They looked a pretty sight/But when they heard the bulldog bark/They disappeared from sight.

The Kaiser said 'Be careful,/If by Jellicoe they're seen,/Then every man-of-war I've got/Will be a submarine'.

We chased his ship to Turkey,/And the Kaiser startled stood,/ Scratched his head and said 'Don't hurt,/You see I'm touching wood';

Then Turkey brought her warships/Just to aid the German plot,/Be careful, Mr Turkey,/Or you'll do the Turkey Trot.

Belgium put the kibosh on the Kaiser;/Europe took the stick and made him sore;/And if Turkey makes a stand/She'll get gurkha'd and japanned,/And it won't be Hoch the Kaiser any more.

He'll have to go to school again/And learn his geography,/He quite forgot Britannia/And the hands across the sea,

Australia and Canada,/the Russian and the Jap,/And England looked so small/He couldn't see her on the map.

Whilst Ireland seemed unsettled,/'Ah' said he 'I'll settle John',/But he didn't know the Irish/Like he knew them later on.

Though the Kaiser stirred the lion,/Please excuse him for the crime,/ His lunatic attendant/Wasn't with him at the time.

For Belgium put the kibosh on the Kaiser;/Europe took the stick and made him sore;/We shall shout with victory's joy,/Hold your hand out, naughty boy,/You must never play at soldiers any more.

For Belgium put the kibosh on the Kaiser;/Europe took the stick and made him sore;/On his throne it hurts to sit,/And when John Bull starts to hit,/He will never sit upon it any more.

'Hanging on the Old Barbed Wire' is a bittersweet and brilliant evocation of the feelings of the troops and junior officers in the front lines. This song was not popular with senior officers, who thought it bad for morale, but attempts to suppress it were thankfully unsuccessful. Again, this is such a brilliant song that it is repeated in full. There are several different versions of this song. One version is:

If you want to find the lance-jack, I know where he is, I know where he is, I know where he is/If you want to find the lance-jack, I know where he is/He's scrounging round the cookhouse door./I've seen him, I've seen him/Scrounging round the cookhouse door, I've seen him,/Scrounging round the cookhouse door.

If you want to find the Sergeant,/I know where he is, I know where he is, I know where he is./If you want to find the Sergeant, I know where he is,/He's lying on the canteen floor./I've seen him, I've seen him, lying on the canteen floor,/I've seen him, I've seen him, lying on the canteen floor.

If you want to find the Quarter-bloke/I know where he is, I know where he is, I know where he is./If you want to find the Quarter-bloke, I know where he is,/He's miles and miles behind the line./I've seen him, I've seen him, miles and miles and miles behind the line./I've seen him, I've seen him, miles and miles and miles behind the line.

If you want the Sergeant-major,/I know where he is, I know where he is, I know where he is./If you want the Sergeant-major, I know where he is./He's tossing off [or thieving] the privates' [or squaddies'] rum./I've seen him, I've seen him, tossing off the privates' rum./I've seen him, I've seen him, tossing off the privates' rum.

If you want the C.O.,/I know where he is, I know where he is, I know where he is./If you want the C.O., I know where he is/He is down in a deep dugout,/I've seen him, I've seen him, down in a deep dugout,/I've seen him, I've seen him, down in a deep dugout.

If you want to find the whole [or old] battalion,/I know where they are,
I know where they are, I know where they are/If you want to find the
whole battalion, I know where they are,/They're hanging on the old
barbed wire,/I've seen 'em, I've seen 'em, hanging on the old barbed
wire./I've seen 'em, I've seen 'em, hanging on the old barbed wire.

A variant last line is 'if you want to find the privates, I've seen 'em' etc.
Other verses have the brasshats drinking claret at Brigade HQ and the
politicians drinking brandy at the House of Commons bar.

'The Hearse Song' has many variants, and was sung to Gounod's
'Funeral March of a Marionette' by American and British soldiers:

Don't you ever laugh as the hearse goes by,/For you may be the next
one to die./They wrap you up in a big white sheet / From your head
down to your feet.

They put you in a big black box/And cover you up with dirt and rocks/
All goes well for about a week,/Then your coffin begins to leak.

The worms crawl in, the worms crawl out,/The worms play pinochle
in your snout,/They eat your eyes, they eat your nose,/They eat the
jelly between your toes.

A big green worm with rolling eyes/Crawls in your stomach and out
your eyes./Your stomach turns a slimy green, And pus pours out like
whipping cream.

You'll spread it on a slice of bread,/And this is what you eat when
you are dead.

'Hunting the Hun' was also popular, with the first verses being:

Over in France there's a game that's played/By all the soldier boys in
each brigade/It's called Hunting the Hun/This is how it is done!

First you go get a gun/Then you look for a Hun/Then you start on
the run for the son of a gun/You can capture them with ease/All you
need is just a little Limburger cheese.

Give 'em one little smell/They come out with a yell/Then your work
is done/When they start to advance/Shoot 'em in the pants/That's the
game called Hunting the Hun!

'It's a Long Way to Tipperary' was allegedly written for a five-shilling bet in 1912 and became popular after a *Daily Mail* reporter heard the Connaught Rangers singing it as they marched through Boulogne in August 1914. It was soon picked up by other regiments, and recorded by the great tenor John McCormack. It concentrates upon a longing for home:

Up to mighty London/Came an Irishman one day./As the streets are paved with gold/Sure, everyone was gay,/Singing songs of Picadilly,/ Strand and Leicester Square,/Till Paddy got excited,/Then he shouted to them there:

It's a long way to Tipperary,/It's a long way to go./It's a long way to Tipperary/To the sweetest girl I know!/Goodbye, Piccadilly,/ Farewell, Leicester Square!/It's a long, long way to Tipperary,/But my heart's right there.

There are more verses, including an alternative and bawdy concluding chorus:

That's the wrong way to tickle Mary,/That's the wrong way to kiss./ Don't you know that over here, lad/They like it best like this./Hooray pour Les Français/Farewell Angleterre/We didn't know how to tickle Mary,/But we learnt how over there.

The song is an unusual example of a partner song, a 'simultaneous quodlibet' in that the chorus of the song can be sung at the same time as another well-known music hall song, 'Pack up Your Troubles in an Old Kit-Bag'.

Like the previous song, 'Keep the Home Fires Burning (Till the Boys Come Home)' encourages soldiers to get through the war and return to something worth fighting for. It was composed in 1914 by the music hall star and actor Ivor Novello:

They were summoned from the hillside,/They were called in from the glen,/And the country found them ready/At the stirring call for men./Let no tears add to their hardships/As the soldiers pass along,/ And although your heart is breaking,/Make it sing this cheery song:

Keep the Home Fires Burning,/While your hearts are yearning./ Though your lads are far away/They dream of home./There's a silver lining/Through the dark clouds shining,/Turn the dark cloud inside out/Till the boys come home ...

Many rugby players know 'Mademoiselle from Armentières' in the form 'Three German Officers Crossed the Rhine' and in the First World War it was considered a risqué song, but was very popular among soldiers. The lyrics are far too explicit to be reproduced here, and different verses have been added over the years, but the first verse goes:

> Three German Officers crossed the Rhine, *parlez-vous*/Three German Officers crossed the Rhine, *parlez-vous*/Three German Officers crossed the Rhine/F***ing the women and drinking the wine,/(Chorus) Inky-dinky *parlez-vous* …

The 'cleanest' original First World War version is as follows:

> Mademoiselle from Armentières, *Parlez-vous*,
> Mademoiselle from Armentières, *Parlez-vous*,
> Mademoiselle from Armentières,
> She hasn't been kissed for forty years. Hinky-dinky *parlez-vous*.

> Our top kick [sergeant] in Armentières, *Parlez-vous*,
> Our top kick in Armentières, *Parlez-vous*,
> Our top kick in Armentières,
> Soon broke the spell of forty years. Hinky-dinky *parlez-vous*.

> Oh Mademoiselle from Armentières, *Parlez-vous*,
> Mademoiselle from Armentières, *Parlez-vous*,
> She got the Palm and the Croix de Guerre,
> For washin' soldiers' underwear. Hinky-dinky *parlez-vous*.

> From gay Paree we heard guns roar, *Parlez-vous*,
> From gay Paree we heard guns roar, *Parlez-vous*,
> From gay Paree we heard guns roar,
> But all we heard was '*Je t'adore*'. Hinky-dinky *parlez-vous*.

> The Colonel got the Croix de Guerre, *Parlez-vous*,
> The Colonel got the Croix de Guerre, *Parlez-vous*,
> The Colonel got the Croix de Guerre,
> The son-of-gun was never there! Hinky-dinky *parlez-vous*.

> Oh Mademoiselle from Armentières, *Parlez-vous*,
> Mademoiselle from Armentières, *Parlez-vous*,
> You didn't have to know her long,
> To know the reason men go wrong! Hinky-dinky *parlez-vous*

You might forget the gas and shell, *Parlez-vouz*,
You might forget the gas and shell, *Parlez-vouz*,
You might forget the gas and shell,
You'll never forget the mademoiselle. Hinky-dinky *parlez-vous*

Other songs used current tunes. For instance, 'What a Friend we have in Jesus' became 'When this Lousy War is Over':

When this lousy war is over no more soldiering for me,
When I get my civvy clothes on, oh how happy I shall be.
No more church parades on Sunday, no more begging for a pass.
You can tell the sergeant-major to stick his passes up his arse.
No more NCOs to curse me, no more rotten army stew.
You can tell the old cook-sergeant, to stick his stew right up his flue.
No more sergeants bawling, 'Pick it up' and 'Put it down'
If I meet the ugly bastard I'll kick his arse all over town.

Equally, 'I Wore a Tulip' became 'I Wore a Tunic':

I wore a tunic, a lousy khaki tunic,/And you wore your civvy clothes./
We fought and bled at Loos/While you were home on the booze/The
booze that no one here knows …

Oh you were with the wenches/While we were in the trenches/Facing
an angry foe./Oh you were a-slacking/While we were attacking/The
Jerry on the Menin Road.

The patriotic song 'On Sunday I Walk Out with a Soldier' was turned into 'I Don't Want to Join the Army', another well-known rugby song of today:

I don't want to join the army,/I don't want to go to war./I'd rather
hang around Piccadilly underground/Living off the earnings of a
lady typist [high-born lady]./I don't want a bayonet in my belly,/I
don't want my bollocks shot away./I'd rather stay in England, in
merry, merry England,/And fornicate my bleeding life away.

'Bombed Last Night' refers to a shortage of respirators in gas bomb attacks:

Bombed last night, and bombed the night before.
Going to get bombed tonight if we never get bombed anymore.

When we're bombed, we're scared as we can be.
Can't stop the bombing from old Higher Germany.
They're warning us, they're warning us.
One shell hole for just the four of us.
Thank your lucky stars there are no more of us.
So one of us can fill it all alone.
Gassed last night, and gassed the night before.
Going to get gassed tonight if we never get gassed anymore.
When we're gassed, we're sick as we can be.
For phosgene and mustard gas is much too much for me.
They're killing us, they're killing us.
One respirator for the four of us.
Thank your lucky stars that we can all run fast.
So one of us can take it all alone.

Reproduced below are the lyrics to the popular 1917 wartime song 'Lloyd George's Beer', composed by R. P. Weston and Bert Lee in 1915. The song itself was essentially a good-natured complaint against Lloyd George's decision to stamp down on alcohol consumption during wartime. He argued that it lessened the rate of industrial and munitions production, and acted in limiting licensing hours and weakening the actual alcohol content of beer. His actions, while unpopular, were nevertheless successful, as consumption of alcohol dipped by half.

We shall win the war, we shall win the war,
As I said before, we shall win the war.
The Kaiser's in a dreadful fury,
Now he knows we're making it at every brewery.
Have you read of it, seen what's said of it,
In the Mirror and the Mail.
It's a substitute, and a pubstitute,
And it's known as Government Ale.
Lloyd George's Beer, Lloyd George's Beer.
At the brewery, there's nothing doing,
All the water works are brewing,
Lloyd George's Beer, it isn't dear.
Oh they say it's a terrible war, oh law,
And there never was a war like this before,
But the worst thing that ever happened in this war
Is Lloyd George's Beer.
Buy a lot of it, all they've got of it.

Dip your bread in it, Shove your head in it
From January to October,
And I'll bet a penny that you'll still be sober.
Get your cloth in it, make some broth in it,
With a pair of mutton chops.
Drown your dogs in it, pop your clogs in it,
And you'll see some wonderful sights.
Lloyd George's Beer, Lloyd George's Beer.
At the brewery, there's nothing doing,
All the water works are brewing,
Lloyd George's Beer, it isn't dear.
With Haig and Joffre when affairs look black,
And you can't get at Jerry with his gas attack.
Just get your squirters out and we'll squirt the buggers back,
With Lloyd George's Beer.

The 'Last Fighting Tommy' and the Reality of War

Henry John 'Harry' Patch (1898–2009) was briefly the oldest man in
Europe and the last surviving soldier to have fought in the trenches on
the Western Front. At the time of his death, aged 111 years, 1 month, 1
week and 1 day, Patch was the verified third-oldest man in the world,
and the oldest man in Europe. In October 1916, he was conscripted
and served as an assistant gunner in a Lewis gun section of the Duke
of Cornwall's Light Infantry. He fought at Passchendaele on 22
September 1917, where he was injured by a shell exploding overhead,
which killed three comrades. He was removed from the front line
and returned to convalesce in England on 23 December 1917. He
was still convalescing when the Armistice was declared the following
November. Patch later said,

When the war ended, I don't know if I was more relieved that we'd
won or that I didn't have to go back. Passchendaele was a disastrous
battle – thousands and thousands of young lives were lost. It makes
me angry. Earlier this year, I went back to Ypres to shake the hand
of Herr Kuentz, Germany's only surviving veteran from the war. It
was emotional. He is 107. We've had eighty-seven years to think
what war is. To me, it's a licence to go out and murder. Why should
the British government call me up and take me out to a battlefield
to shoot a man I never knew, whose language I couldn't speak? All
those lives lost for a war finished over a table. Now what is the sense
in that?

Like most veterans, Patch had refused to discuss his war experiences, until approached in 1998 by the BBC, when he realised that there were very few men left to describe the horrors of the time. In the ensuing 2003 television series, he said, 'If any man tells you he went over the top and he wasn't scared, he's a damn liar.' In spring 2005, Patch was interviewed by the *Today* programme, in which he said, 'Too many died. War isn't worth one life.' In his 2007 autobiography, *The Last Fighting Tommy*, he wrote, 'We came across a lad from A company. He was ripped open from his shoulder to his waist by shrapnel and lying in a pool of blood. When we got to him, he said: "Shoot me." He was beyond human help and, before we could draw a revolver, he was dead. And the final word he uttered was "Mother." I remember that lad in particular. It's an image that has haunted me all my life, seared into my mind.' This is the reality of war. Britain is still losing men in wars. Politicians never learn. The people who vote for such politicians also seem never to learn.

Remembrance Day, the Two-Minute Silence and Poppies
The First World War ended on the eleventh hour of the eleventh day of the eleventh month. Wesley Tudor Pole, backed by Winston Churchill, began periods of remembrance for the dead and injured in 1917. The first two-minute silence in London, on 11 November 1919, was reported in the *Manchester Guardian*:

> The first stroke of eleven produced a magical effect. The tram cars glided into stillness, motors ceased to cough and fume, and stopped dead, and the mighty-limbed dray horses hunched back upon their loads and stopped also, seeming to do it of their own volition. Someone took off his hat, and with a nervous hesitancy the rest of the men bowed their heads also. Here and there an old soldier could be detected slipping unconsciously into the posture of 'attention'. An elderly woman, not far away, wiped her eyes, and the man beside her looked white and stern. Everyone stood very still … The hush deepened. It had spread over the whole city and become so pronounced as to impress one with a sense of audibility. It was a silence which was almost pain … And the spirit of memory brooded over it all.

The remembrance poppy has been used since 1920 to commemorate soldiers who have died in war, and in wars ever since. It is sold across Britain, America and Commonwealth countries to raise funds for ex-servicemen and their families. Its use was inspired by the poem 'In

Flanders Fields' by Lieutenant Colonel John McCrae. Its opening lines refer to the many poppies that were the first flowers to grow in the churned-up earth of soldiers' graves in Flanders. McCrae wrote it the day after witnessing a friend die in action, and it was published in *Punch* in December 1915.

Professor Moina Michael was inspired by the poem and wrote in response a poem called 'We Shall Keep the Faith', lines of which read,

> We cherish, too, the poppy red
> That grows on fields where valour led;
> It seems to signal to the skies
> That blood of heroes never dies,
> But lends a lustre to the red
> Of the flower that blooms above the dead...

She had the idea of using poppies as a symbol of remembrance, and vowed always to wear a red poppy. Teaching a class of disabled servicemen at the University of Georgia, she realised the need to provide financial and occupational support for them and pursued the idea of selling silk poppies as a means of raising funds to assist disabled veterans. In 1921, her efforts resulted in the poppy being adopted as a symbol of remembrance for war veterans by the American Legion and she became known as the 'Poppy Lady' for her humanitarian efforts. Michael received numerous awards during her lifetime. In Britain, around 40 million poppies are sold each year in November. In November 2011, the English Football Association wanted its football team to wear poppies on their shirts in a match against Spain. However, FIFA turned down the proposal, claiming it would 'open the door to similar initiatives' across the world, 'jeopardising the neutrality of football', a questionable stance given its frequent bribery scandals.

16

The War's Firsts, Lasts, Greatests and Factoids

First Global War

When London declared war, the entire Empire was involved. The British Empire covered a quarter of the world's landmass, including Canada, Australia, South Africa, India, New Zealand, Malaysia, Kenya, Egypt, Uganda, Rhodesia, Sudan, Malta, Cyprus, etc. France had the second-largest colonial empire: Algeria, Tunisia, Morocco, Chad, Vietnam, Cambodia, Laos, part of Cameroon, Senegal, Mali, Niger, Central African Republic and others. Belgium was tiny but its colony of the Congo (later Zaire and now Congo again) took up a huge part of central Africa. Portugal possessed Mozambique, Angola and many islands around Indonesia. Germany had Tanzania, Namibia and a part of Cameroon. Japan, Britain's ally at that time, had Korea and Taiwan. The Ottoman Empire contained Turkey, Macedonia, Syria, Iraq, Kuwait, Lebanon, Jordan, Israel, and the few habitable parts of Saudi Arabia.

The Russian Empire had no colonies, but was the largest single country on Earth. The USA was also a huge nation, with its colonies of the Philippines, Puerto Rico, Guam, etc. Austria-Hungary did not have any colonies, but it was a massive area of central Europe containing Austria, Hungary, nearly all of Czechoslovakia, parts of Romania, parts of Serbia, Bosnia and Croatia. Each major combatant had territories around the world that touched the territories of other major combatants. Britain had the world's largest navy. The Germans had the second, with the USA third, France fourth and Japan fifth. These navies spanned the world, protecting colonial possessions. The airplane and automobile were beginning to make travel faster, and travel to distant places quicker. Canning food made feeding troops easier, and the invention of radio made communicating with troops almost instant.

The First World War began in Europe but quickly spread throughout the world. Many countries became embroiled within the war's first month, and others joined in the ensuing four years. Honduras announced hostilities with Germany as late as 19 July 1918. Romania entered the war for the second time just one day before it finished, on 10 November 1918. All nations of the British Empire, including Australia, Canada and New Zealand, automatically entered the war with Britain's decision to fight on 4 August 1914. On numerous occasions hostilities were assumed without a formal declaration, for instance Russia with Germany and Austria-Hungary in August 1914.

Austria-Hungary declared war with Serbia in July 1914, Russia and Belgium in August 1914 and Portugal in 1916. Belgium was invaded by Germany in August 1914. Bolivia and Brazil severed relations with Germany in April 1917, with Brazil declaring war in October 1917. Bulgaria declared war with Serbia in October 1915, and with Romania in September 1916. China declared war with Germany and Austria-Hungary in August 1917. Costa Rica severed relations with Germany, and then declared war in May 1918. Cuba declared war on Germany in April 1917, and Ecuador did the same in December 1917. France was invaded by Germany in August 1914, and declared war on Austria-Hungary in that month, then Turkey in November, then Bulgaria in October 1915.

Germany declared war with Russia, France and Belgium in August 1914, then Portugal in March 1916. Greece declared war with Austria-Hungary, Bulgaria, Germany and Turkey in June 1917. Guatemala declared war with Germany in April 1918, while Haiti and Honduras both did the same in July 1918. Italy declared war with Austria-Hungary in May 1915, then Turkey and Germany in August 1915, and with Bulgaria in October 1915. Japan declared war with Germany and Austria-Hungary in August 1914. Liberia declared war with Germany in August 1914. Montenegro declared war with Austria-Hungary and Germany in August 1914, and Bulgaria in October 1915. Nicaragua declared war with Austria-Hungary and Germany in May 1918, while Panama had declared war with Germany in April 1917 and with Austria-Hungary in December 1917. Peru severed relations with Germany in October 1917.

Portugal entered the war against Germany and Austria-Hungary in March 1916. Romania declared war with Austria-Hungary in August 1916, exited war in May 1918, and re-entered the war in November 1918. Russia declared war with Turkey in November 1914, and Bulgaria in October 1915. San Marino declared war with Austria-Hungary in June 1915. Serbia declared war with Germany in August 1914, and with Turkey in November 1914. Siam, now Thailand, declared war with Austria-Hungary and Germany in July 1917. Turkey declared war with Romania in August 1916 and severed relations with United States in April 1917. Uruguay severed relations with Germany in October 1917. The United Kingdom declared war with Germany and Austria-Hungary in August 1914, with Turkey in November 1914 and Bulgaria in October 1915. The USA declared war with Germany in April 1917, and with Austria-Hungary in December 1917. Many of these nations have since subdivided into more nations. Most of the world was involved.

H. G. Wells: The Prophet of Modern Warfare: 1907

In 1907, H. G. Wells published a science fiction novel called *The War in the Air*, where the German Kaiser launched 'a huge herd of airships' in a surprise bombing raid against the United States. Their largest craft, the *Vaterland*, was imagined as a 2,000-foot Leviathan. Airships had never yet been used in combat, and Germany only had two military Zeppelins at this time. However, in 1915, the Germans launched a fleet of vastly improved 600-foot-long dirigibles against London. This was the first aerial bombing campaign in history.

First Machine Gun Fired from an Aeroplane: 7 June 1912

A prototype Lewis gun was fired by Captain Charles Chandler of the US Army, from the foot-bar of a Wright Model B Flyer. Machine guns began to be used for the first time in aerial warfare in the First World War.

First Modern Warship Commissioned: 12 March 1914

The USS *Texas* is a dreadnought that served in both world wars and now exists as a museum ship in Texas. It is notable in naval design in that it was the first ship fitted with anti-aircraft guns, the first battleship to launch an aircraft, the first ship to control gunfire with rangefinders, the first warship fitted with radar, and the first warship to entertain its crew with films. Considered the most powerful warship afloat because of its ten 14 inch guns in five twin turrets, in 1916 *Texas* became the first US battleship to mount anti-aircraft guns and the first to control gunfire with directors and range keepers, the analogue forerunners of today's computers. After the USA entered the First World War, she joined the 6th Battle Squadron of the British Grand Fleet early in 1918. Operating out of Scapa Flow and the Firth of Forth, *Texas* protected forces laying the great North Sea mine barrage, and helped prevent enemy naval forces from interrupting the supplies of Allied forces in Europe.

First War Between Three First Cousins: August 1914–18
Kaiser Wilhelm II was a first cousin of both Tsar Nicholas II of Russia and King George V of Britain. All were grandsons of Queen Victoria of England.

First British Fighting: 2 August 1914
This occurred two days before the war started, when Londoners clashed with peace marchers.

The First 'Industrial Warfare'
Large states and empires could use the mechanisation and mass production methods of the Industrial Revolution to develop, manufacture and equip large armies and navies with vast quantities of powerful and reliable weapons.

The First Mass-Conscripted Armies and the Concept of 'Total War'
The war saw mass conscription by all countries, rapid transportation of troops by railways, sea and road, telegraph and wireless communications and the concept of 'total war'. With better mass production technology, the war witnessed the development of better rifles capable of high rates of fire, machine guns, accurate and powerful breech-loading artillery, mines, shells, mechanised armoured warfare, aircraft, submarines, metal warships and chemical warfare. The term 'total war' was first used by von Ludendorff, and called for the complete mobilisation and subordination of all resources, including policy and social systems, to the war effort. It has come to mean waging warfare with absolute ruthlessness, propaganda and rationing, and the war saw civilians and civilian infrastructure as legitimate targets in destroying a country's ability to engage in war.

First War Where There Were More Deaths in Battle
In every previous war, military deaths from sickness far outstripped those from action. By 1914, medical advances and an increasingly well-organised medical chain of evacuation made sure this was not the case.

The Smallest Army at the Start of War
The Territorial Army had been formed in 1908, but in 1914 there were only 247,432 regular soldiers in the British Army. The addition of the 'Territorials' made up the numbers to fewer than 750,000 men. Because of the experiences of the Franco-Prussian War in 1870, France

had been building up its forces, and had 823,000 men in regular service in 1914, over three times as many as Britain. By the end of that year France had another 2,700,000 reservists joining up, giving an army of 3,523,300 men. The Russian and German forces were even bigger. In 1914, when Britain joined the Western Front, it had 6 infantry divisions. France had 62, Germany 87 and Russia 114.

Best Forecast of Result of War: 5 August 1914

C. P. Scott, owner and editor of the *Manchester Guardian*, wrote in the newspaper: 'By some hidden contract England has been technically committed behind her back to the ruinous madness of a share in the violent gamble of a war between two militaristic leagues. It will be a war in which we risk everything of which we are proud, and in which we stand to gain nothing. Some day we will regret it.' The war cost Britain most of its assets, and led to another great war which effectively bankrupted Britain for all time.

First Strategic Bombing in History: 6 August 1914

This was the first instance of bombs being dropped upon a city from the air, when a Zeppelin bombed Liège in Belgium. In Britain, the British public was gripped by 'zeppelinitis'. Within months of the war's start, Germany had formed the Ostend Carrier Pigeon Detachment, in reality an airship unit intended for the bombing of English port cities.

First U-Boat Sunk: 9 August 1914

U-15 was rammed by HMS *Birmingham* off Fair Isle, with all twenty-five hands drowning.

First British Soldier to Die on the Western Front: 21 August 1914

It is believed that L/14191'6 Private John Parr, 4th Battalion, the Middlesex Regiment, was the first British soldier to die on the Western Front, when he was killed while on patrol near Obourg. A reconnaissance cyclist, the seventeen-year-old had lied about his age to enlist when aged fourteen. His battalion was in the midst of the action at Mons two days later when two of their number won the Victoria Cross.

First Early Closing: August 1914

British pubs instituted shorter hours and afternoon closing 'to keep factory workers sober', especially munitions workers. With some modifications, these restrictions lasted until the late twentieth century.

First Shots Fired by the British Army on the Western Front: 22 August 1914

A Squadron of the 4th Royal Irish Dragoon Guards pushed out two patrols and met the Germans for the first time. Corporal E. Thomas of the 4th opened fire near the chateau of Ghislain near Mons, the first British soldier to do so, but was uncertain whether he killed or wounded the German soldier that he aimed at.

First Heavy Bomber and a Dog: 1914

The Russian Empire possessed the only heavy bomber in the first year of the war, which outdistanced all other planes. Designed for both reconnaissance and bombing, the Sikorsky Ilya Muromets could carry 1,100 pounds of bombs, and operate for up to five hours or 300 miles. It set a world record in 1914 by carrying sixteen personnel and a dog. Supply depots, troop concentrations and transportation networks, especially railway yards and stations, were main targets. By March 1918, around seventy Ilya Muromets had been constructed and they had flown over 350 bombing or reconnaissance missions along the entire Eastern Front.

First Use of Poison Gas: August 1914

Although it is popularly believed that the German Army was the first to use gas, it was initially deployed by the French. They fired small tear gas grenades against the Germans, but these were not even detected owing to the small amount of xylyl bromide encased. In October 1914, Germany used also tear gas ineffectively, at Neuve Chapelle against British troops. The German Army then began developing other chemical weapons.

Greatest Mistake: 25 August 1915

By the end of the initial offensive on 25 August, Germany's front was uncontested by any of the other powers. The Schlieffen Plan had stated that the German Army should have overcome France in forty days and by the thirty-second day the Germans were only 25 miles from Paris. Von Moltke saw that the Germans were doing well in France, and therefore decided to send many divisions from Europe to stabilise the Eastern Front, which had been compromised by a quick Russian mobilisation. This loss of troops is thought to be the mistake that would eventually lose the war for the Germans.

First Effective Use of an Armoured Vehicle in Combat: August 1914

The Belgian Army's use was rapidly followed by Britain and Germany.

First Decision to Set up a Propaganda Campaign: 2 September 1914

In August 1914, after discovering that Germany had a propaganda agency, Lloyd George set up the War Propaganda Bureau. Lloyd George appointed the writer and MP Charles Masterman to head the organisation, and he invited twenty-five leading British authors to discuss ways of promoting Britain's interests during the war. Those who attended included Arthur Conan Doyle, Arnold Bennett, Ford Madox Ford, John Masefield, G. K. Chesterton, John Galsworthy, Thomas Hardy, G. M. Trevelyan, H. G. Wells and Rudyard Kipling. The War Propaganda Bureau published over 1,160 pamphlets during the war, and it was not until 1935 that its activities became public knowledge. In 1915, one of its pamphlets documented actual and alleged atrocities committed by the German Army against Belgian civilians, with lurid drawings. John Buchan was appointed to the bureau as a lieutenant in the Intelligence Corps, and his close relationship with Britain's military leaders made it very difficult for him to include any criticism about the way the war was being conducted. In 1917, the WPB became the Department of Information, with responsibility for influencing books, pamphlets, photographs, war art, telegraph communications, radio, newspapers, magazines and cinema. Unfortunately, post-war suspicion about its atrocity stories meant a British reluctance to believe the realities of Nazi persecution from the 1930s onwards. In Germany, Ludendorff had suggested that British propaganda had been instrumental in the German defeat. Hitler echoed his view, and the Nazis used many propaganda techniques pioneered by Britain.

First Ship Sunk by a Submarine Using a Self-Propelled Torpedo: 5 September 1914

The scout cruiser HMS *Pathfinder* was sunk off St Abb's Head, Scotland, by the U-boat *SM U-21*, becoming the first ship to have been sunk by a self-propelled torpedo. *Pathfinder* sank in four minutes, with only 18 of her 268 crew surviving. In 1864, USS *Housatonic* had been sunk by a 'spar torpedo', but this was a simple charge attached to a pole. *SMU-21* also sank the British battleships *Triumph* and *Majestic* at Gallipoli and the French armoured cruiser *Admiral Charner* off Syria. It survived the war, being sunk while on tow in 1919.

First Realisation That There Would be a Long War: 7 September 1914

'Victory will come to the side that outlasts the other.' – General Ferdinand Foch, then a field commander but later Marshall of France.

First Bombs Dropped from a Plane on Civilians: 5–9 September 1914

During the First Battle of the Marne, a German pilot flying reconnaissance missions over Paris regularly dropped bombs from his Taube. The first drop consisted of five small, hand-lobbed bombs and a note demanding the immediate surrender of Paris and the French nation. Before the Western Front stabilised, German Taubes dropped fifty bombs on Paris, slightly damaging Notre Dame Cathedral.

First Entente Strategic Bombing: 22 September 1914

On this date and 8 October, the Royal Naval Air Service bombed the production line and hangars of Zeppelin facilities in Cologne and Brussels. The planes carried 20 lb bombs, and at least one airship was destroyed. On 21 November, the RNAS flew across Lake Constance to bomb two other Zeppelin factories.

First Shooting Down of a German Airplane by Anti-Aircraft Fire: 23 September 1914

The gun team of No. 2 AA Section of the Royal Garrison Artillery shot down an enemy aircraft in France after firing seventy-five rounds.

First Allied Plane to Shoot Down an Enemy Aircraft: 5 October 1914

The French pilot Louis Quenault opened fire on a German aircraft with a machine gun fitted to a Voisin III, and the era of air combat was underway, as more and more aircraft were fitted with machine guns. The Voisin became the standard Allied bomber in the early years of the war. Successive models were more powerful and over 800 were purchased by the French Army Air Service. The RFC and the Russian and Belgian air forces also used them in the war. The Voisin V first appeared in 1915, the first plane to be armed with a cannon instead of a machine gun.

First Mobile X-Ray Machines: October 1914

X-ray machines were desperately needed, but they were very large machines that were both too bulky and too delicate to move. Marie

Curie developed mobile X-ray stations for the French military immediately after the outbreak of war. Curie turned up at a field hospital in Belgium with a mobile X-ray lab in a Renault van. Here she fixed the hospital wiring and rigged up a telephone by the bed of a visiting Belgian general so that he could speak to the King of Belgium. She then installed X-ray machines in several cars and small trucks, which toured smaller surgical stations at the front. By the end of the war there were eighteen of these 'radiologic cars' or 'Little Curies' in operation.

First Organised Attack by the British Army on the Western Front: 13 October 1914

Divisions of Pulteney's III Corps attacked enemy positions on the Meterenbeek, near Hazebrouck.

The Royal Navy's First Defeat in 100 Years: 1 November 1914

The German East Asia Squadron, a small defensive fleet under Vice-Admiral Maximilian von Spee, was based on the Caroline Islands in the Western Pacific, near China. When war broke out, von Spee feared being defeated by the much larger Japanese Navy, and sailed across the Pacific Ocean to Chile. With a large German population, it offered a safer base of operations from which to attack British shipping routes. His fleet encountered the British West Indian Squadron. It had been diverted from its patrol duties in South America and the Caribbean specifically to destroy von Spee's forces and remove the threat to British shipping routes. The British squadron, led by Rear Admiral Sir Christopher Cradock, consisted of obsolete cruisers which were a hopeless match for von Spee's faster and more powerful ships. In the ensuing Battle of Coronel, Cradock's squadron was obliterated, and two ships were lost. Cradock died along with 1,600 British sailors.

First Entente Civilian Bombing of a City: 4 December 1914

French pilots dropped propeller-guided bombs on Freiburg in south-west Germany. However, in 1916 a French Nieuport flew over Berlin and dropped leaflets assuring the people that, while they could have been bombs, 'Paris did not make war on women and children'.

First Shelling of Great Britain by Ships: 16 December 1914

While the cruiser *Kolberg* was laying mines along the Yorkshire coast, two supporting German battle cruisers began shelling Scarborough and damaged or destroyed over 200 buildings. Scarborough, Hartlepool and Whitby suffered 137 fatalities and 592 casualties. The attack resulted in public outrage towards the German Navy for an attack against civilians. The German vendetta against Scarborough continued. U-boats began attacking British trawlers, and over 24 and 25 September 1916, nineteen trawlers were sunk. They included eleven Scarborough ships, five from Grimsby, and one each from Hull, Hartlepool and Whitby. They were fishing 20 miles north-east of Scarborough when a U-boat surfaced, forced the crews to abandon, and then sank them all by gunfire except for one with a bomb placed in the engine room. Scarborough was again shelled, this time by a U-boat on 4 September 1917.

First Night Bombing Mission: 21 December 1914
Two French planes, the Farman MF-7 and the Farman MF-II, were popular Allied reconnaissance planes during the early stages of war. The Royal Naval Air Service used the Farman MF-II for its first night bombing mission when it attacked a German artillery installation.

Fastest Desertion: 22 December 1914
The forty-one-year-old William Gilligan of Hull joined the West Yorkshire Regiment at Hull, on 21 December 1914. On 22 December 1914, he deserted at York.

First Female-Run Military Hospital: December 1914
When war broke out, the Scottish Women's Hospital founder, Dr Elsie Maud Inglis, approached the War Office with the idea of either women-doctors co-operating with the Royal Army Medical Corps, or women's medical units being allowed to serve on the Western Front. The authorities were less than helpful and it is reported that an official said to her, 'My good lady, go home and sit still.' However, the SWH opened its first 200-bed auxiliary hospital at the thirteenth-century Abbaye de Royaumont, France, under the French Red Cross. The SWH went on to arrange fourteen medical units to serve in Corsica, France, Malta, Romania, Russia, Salonika and Serbia. They provided nurses, doctors, ambulance drivers, cooks and orderlies. During 1915, several women were captured by the Austro-German Army while running a series of field hospitals, dressing stations, fever hospitals and clinics in Serbia on the Balkan Front.

What War Should Be About: 24–25 December 1914
On Christmas Eve, soldiers on both sides of the Western Front sang carols to each other. On Christmas Day, troops along two-thirds of the front declared an informal truce. In some places the truce

lasted a week. While front-line officers, who shared the horrors of the trenches, were generally relaxed about the affair, the generals at the back were absolutely furious. A year later, sentries on both sides were ordered to shoot anyone who attempted a repeat performance.

First Attack by Sea-Based Airplanes on a Strategic Target: 25 December 1914

Cuxhaven is a small port on the North Sea near Hamburg, and the *Weihnachtsangriff*; 'Christmas Raid', is also known as the Cuxhaven Raid. The Zeppelin sheds there were out of range of British aircraft, so three tenders carried seven seaplanes to be lowered into the sea to take off and bomb the sheds. The author Erskine Childers took part. Fog, low cloud and anti-aircraft fire prevented the raid from being a complete success, although several sites were attacked. The raid forced the German Admiralty to remove the greater part of its High Seas Fleet to the Kiel Canal.

First Approval of Strategic Civilian Bombing by the Kaiser: 7 January 1915

Wilhelm II initially forbade attacks on London, fearing that his close relatives, the British royal family, might be hurt.

First Zeppelin Airship Raid on Britain: 19 January 1915

The first Zeppelin flew on 2 July 1900, and by the start of the war the German Army had seven Zeppelins. Around 600 feet long, they could reach a maximum speed of 85 mph and reach a height of around 14,000 feet. Each Zeppelin had five machine guns and could carry 4,400 pounds of bombs. In January 1915, two Zeppelin naval airships flew over the east coast of England and bombed Great Yarmouth and King's Lynn.

First Shelling of Great Britain by U-Boat: 29 January 1915

SM U-21 (see above) shelled the airship sheds on Walney Island off Barrow-in-Furness after also becoming the first U-boat to operate in the Irish Sea. It was driven off by shore batteries.

First Large-Scale Use of Chemical Weapons: 31 January 1915

The Germans pioneered large-scale chemical weapon use with a gas attack on Russian positions during the Battle of Bolimov, but low temperatures froze the tear gas (xylyl bromide) in the shells.

Kaiser Urges Air War: 12 February 1915

Wilhelm II expressed a hope to his aides that 'the air war against England will be carried out with the greatest energy'.

First Underground Mine Fired by British: 17 February 1915

The first British mine was blown at Hill 60 by Royal Engineers troops and the 5th Division.

First Use of Flamethrower: 26 February 1915

The *flammenwerfer* could fire a jet of flame out to a distance of 20 yards, and was designed to be carried and operated by a single soldier. Invented by a German engineer in 1900, the flamethrower was accepted into service by the German Army in 1911 and was used by specialist assault engineer units. It made its combat debut when the German 3rd Guard Pioneer Regiment used them in a successful small-scale attack against French trenches near Verdun. Unlike grenades, flamethrowers could 'neutralise' enemy soldiers in the confined trenches and dugouts without inflicting structural damage.

First Use of Deflector Propeller Blades to Fire a Machine Gun: 1 April 1915

Roland Garros was the first Frenchman to cross the Mediterranean by air, and served as a pilot on the Western Front. Garros knew that he would have more success in dogfights if he could find a way of firing a machine gun through the propeller. He added deflector plates to the blades of the propeller of his Morane-Saunier, and these small wedges of toughened steel diverted the passage of those bullets which struck the blades. Garros approached a German Albatros reconnaissance aircraft, and the German pilot was surprised when Garros approached him head-on. Accepted air fighting strategy at the time was to take 'pot-shots' with a revolver or rifle, but Garros shot down the Albatros through his whirling propeller. In the next two weeks Garros shot down four more enemy aircraft. However, a rifle shot from the ground fractured his fuel line and he was forced to land behind the German front line. Before he could set fire to his machine it was captured, and the German Air Force copied and began using these deflector plates on their propellers until the interrupter gear was invented.

First Twentieth-Century Genocide: 20 April 1915–23

In 1915, under the cover of the war, the Ottoman government resolved to expel Turkey's Armenian population of about 1.75 million entirely. The plan included deportation to the deserts of Syria and Mesopotamia, now Iraq. Hundreds of thousands of Armenians were driven out of their homes and either massacred or force-marched into the desert until they died. The German ambassador to Turkey wrote home, 'The government is indeed pursuing its goal of exterminating the Armenian race in the Ottoman Empire.' Between 1915 and 1923, the western part of Armenia was emptied of Armenians, and deaths are reliably estimated to be over a million. Those who did not die fled to the Middle East, Russia or the USA. The genocide was conducted in a well-organised way, making use of new technology available. Orders to begin the operation were sent to every police station, to be carried out simultaneously at the same time on the same day, 20 April 1915.

First Large-Scale Use of Poison Gas: 22 April 1915

The use of gas in warfare had been specifically banned by the Hague Convention of 1907. The German Army released gas against French, British and Canadian troops near Langemarck. The Germans released 180 tonnes of chlorine gas, in a flow which lasted for five minutes. A bluish-white mist rolled toward the Allies, and the subsequent fighting, with both sides rushing reinforcements into the area, developed as the Second Battle of Ypres. Chlorine has a powerful irritant effect on the lungs and mucous membranes and prolonged exposure is fatal. Men who stayed in position, especially on the fire-step of the trenches, suffered least as the cloud rolled past them. Terrified men who ran with it, and the wounded lying on the ground or in trench bottoms, suffered the worst exposure. By mid-May 1915, after gas had been used again in the Ypres Salient on several more occasions, the Allies were beginning to use rudimentary protection. The first batch of gas helmets – flannel bags with talc eyepieces, only sixteen to each infantry battalion – were provided for the machine gunners. Men knew by then that a piece of gauze or cotton wadding, soaked in urine, provided a crude protection.

The British retaliated five months later at Loos on 25 September 1915, principally to overcome a shortage of artillery for their opening barrage. All ranks were issued with gas helmets, but the battle and weather conditions at Loos proved them to be a severe hindrance. The talc eyepieces restricted movement and vision, rain caused chemicals in the flannel fabric to run out and irritate the eyes, and breathing was difficult. It was a failure. Next, carbonyl chloride, also known as phosgene, was used by the Germans in an attack at Ypres on 19 December 1915. It was similar to chlorine yet could be inhaled for a considerable time without being noticed, only to produce serious or fatal inflammation of the lungs. The Allies now decided to employ a phosgene-chlorine mixture, codenaming it 'White Star'. In the Battle of the Somme in 1916, the British army released 1,120 tons of gas, mostly White Star, in ninety-eight separate attacks.

First Use of Observation Balloon: 11 May 1915
The 1st Kite Balloon Section was sent to Steenvoorde for work on reconnaissance with the Second Army in the Ypres sector.

Greatest British Train Crash: 22 May 1915
The Quintinshill rail disaster near Gretna Green involved five trains, killed a probable 226 and injured 246. Territorial soldiers of the Royal Scots were on a troop train, on their way to Gallipoli. It collided with a local passenger train and an express train.

First Zeppelin Raid on London and the Beginning of Civilian Bombing: 31 May 1915
The raid on London killed twenty-eight people and injured sixty more and was followed by over fifty bombing raids on Britain. The initial air raid on London was the result of a navigation error. However, in July 1915 the Kaiser specifically authorised bombing attacks on Great Britain. He specifically excluded any attacks on royal palaces and residential areas. Both Zeppelin and Schütte-Lanz rigid airships were used. Initially, the airships could fly at a higher altitude than could be reached by defending aircraft or anti-aircraft fire and could carry a significant bomb load. However, weather conditions and night flying conditions made navigation difficult and therefore reduced bombing accuracy. The airships made twenty raids in 1915, dropping 37 tons of bombs, killing 181 and injuring another 455 people. In 1916, improved defensive measures, including the introduction of incendiary bullets, made raids more dangerous, and several Zeppelins were destroyed. Newer classes of ships with improved ceilings restored the advantage, but led to further flying and navigation problems. Oxygen was needed to fly at high altitude, and provision for an observation car, for bombing through clouds, reduced the bomb load. In 1916, twenty-three raids dropped 125 tons of bombs, killing 293 and injuring 691 people. The last Zeppelin raid on Britain took place in August 1918, when four ships bombed targets in the Midlands and the north of England. In total, Zeppelin raids killed 557 and injured another 1,358 civilians. More than 5,000 bombs were dropped on towns across Britain. Eighty-four airships took part, and of these thirty were lost, either shot down by enemy action or lost in accidents.

The Biggest Naval Battle in History: 31 May 1916

More than 200 warships and 100,000 men of the rival navies were involved at Jutland. The British Grand Fleet lost fourteen ships, and the German High Seas Fleet lost eleven ships.

First Zeppelin to be Downed by a Plane: 7 June 1915

LZ 37 was an Imperial German Navy airship shot down while returning from raiding London with two other Zeppelins. Sub-lieutenant Reginald 'Rex' Warneford, in his Morane Parasol monoplane, intercepted her outside Ghent, Belgium. The twenty-three-year-old tried firing a carbine at it, his only armament, but he was driven off by the Zeppelin's defensive machine guns. The airship began climbing, leaving the little plane behind, but Warneford, unknown to the Zeppelin crew, continued the pursuit, climbing slowly over two hours to an altitude of 13,000 feet. At this stage the airship began to descend in the direction of Brussels, and, seizing his opportunity, Warneford, now above the Zeppelin, dived towards it and from about 200 feet above he dropped his six bombs on its roof. Eight of its nine crew were killed when it fell onto a convent, killing two nuns. The explosion caused by the airship overturned Warneford's fragile aircraft and stopped the engine. Warneford glided down behind enemy lines and managed to restart the engine after repairing it. Ten days later, a wing fell off a plane he was testing and he was thrown out of the aircraft and died. Warneford, of the Royal Naval Air Service, was awarded the VC and Légion d'Honneur. He was a national hero, but his name is being omitted from Britain's 2014 commemorative stone slabs of VC winners because he was born in India.

First Mass Use of Flamethrowers: 30–31 July 1915

Units of the German 126th Regiment launched an attack using *flammenwerfer* against the British 14th Light Division holding front-line positions at Hooge in the Ypres Salient. The attack was launched with great secrecy, causing large numbers of casualties to the British defenders, and pushed the enemy line forward. However, British infantry soon learned to focus their fire on the slow-moving men carrying their cumbersome flamethrowers, and the British Army did not adopt the weapon.

Most Surprising Bombing Target: 1915 Onwards

Austro-Hungarian pilots flew forty-two bombing missions from Pula, over Venice, after the Italian Front had been advanced to within a few miles. Churches and frescoes, including two by Tiepolo, were damaged. A particularly severe raid was carried out on 27 February 1918, hitting central Venice and forcing many Venetians to take refuge in the Lido and Giudecca. A letter written in September 1915 explains how the Venetians instituted a blackout during the bombings:

> The mosquitos from Pula come buzzing over nearly every fine night, and drop bombs for half an hour or so … Venice is like a lovely prima donna in deep mourning. All the gilded angels [are covered with] sack-cloth painted dirty grey. Anything that shines is covered. At night all is as black as in the dark ages. 'Serrenos' call out 'all is well' every half hour. But when danger is signalled the electric light is cut off, sirens blow, cannon firebombs explode and the whole city shakes on its piles. All the hotels but the Danieli's are hospitals.

First Tank Demonstrated to British Military Chiefs: 11 September 1915
Despite Winston Churchill's approval on this occasion, the first tanks were not used in action for over a year.

First to Be Left Formally 'Out of Battle': 25 September 1915
When ordered to take part in the first attack in the Battle of Loos, units of the 47th (London) Division left a portion of the officers, NCOs and men behind. The idea was that they would form a cadre on which the unit could be rebuilt if it suffered very heavy losses. This gradually became a standard practice for all divisions on the Western Front.

First 'Chinese Attacks': 25 September 1915
The 142nd Brigade of the 47th Division did not attack in the Battle of Loos, but stood their ground to form a defensive flank. In order to add to the enemy's confusion, alongside a gas and smoke barrage, they erected and moved many wooden dummy soldiers. At a distance and through poor visibility, the enemy were uncertain whether they were being attacked, and wasted much attention and ammunition on the dummies. Called a 'Chinese attack', this method of battlefield deception was widely adopted.

First UK Conscription: 25 January 1916
Desperate for more troops, the Military Service Act was passed and specified that single men aged eighteen to forty-one were liable to be called up for service unless they were widowed with children, or ministers of a religion. Tribunals adjudicated upon claims for exemption

upon the grounds of performing civilian work of national importance, domestic hardship, health, and conscientious objection. Married men were exempt in the original Act, although this was changed in June 1916, and the age limit was eventually raised to fifty-one.

First Use of Searchlights to Dazzle the Enemy: February 1916

The aged General Kuropatkin was told of the Tsar's disappointment with progress on the Eastern Front after his Grenadier Corps had been pushed back to the Dvina River. He thus planned a night attack that included setting up batteries of searchlights to blind the German defenders. He sent his men 'over the top', not realising that his advancing troops were silhouetted against the lights, and 8,000 Russians were machine gunned to death in the failed attack.

The Longest Battle: 21 February–18 December 1916

French and German casualties at Verdun reached up to 975,000, with over 250,000 killed or missing. It is thought to be the battle with the greatest density of deaths per square yard in history.

The First U-Boat Sunk by Depth Charge: 22 March 1916

U-68 was sunk off Kerry, Ireland, by the Q-ship *Farnborough*. However, Germany only became aware of the new invention of the depth charge following unsuccessful attacks on *U-67* and *U-69* in the following month.

First Air-Dropped Supplies: 27 March 1916

A 70-pound millstone was dropped to the besieged 6th (Poona) Division at Kut-al-Amara in Mesopotamia. A large grain store had been discovered there, but the retreating Turks had removed the millstones. A total of 140 aircraft sorties were flown, dropping in addition 16,000 pounds of flour, sugar, salt, mail and other supplies at Kut before it surrendered.

Greatest British Military Surrender: 29 April 1916

General Sir Charles Townshend was in command of the Sixth Indian Division, and led the British campaign in Mesopotamia from 1915. He surrendered all 10,000 of his starving men at Kut, after a siege of almost six months, the largest military surrender in British history.

First Use of UK 'Daylight Saving Time': 30 April 1916

Germany and Austria-Hungary were the first to use *sommerzeit*, DST, to conserve coal stocks. Britain, most of its allies, and many European neutrals soon followed suit. Russia and a few other countries waited until the next year and the United States adopted it in 1918. Unfortunately, it is still in existence for some reason.

First Commissioning of War Artists for Propaganda: May 1916

The BEF included artists whose work was exhibited at the Imperial War Museum after the end of the war. The artist Paul Nash later protested about the strict control maintained by the Propaganda Bureau over the official subject matter, saying, 'I am no longer an artist interested and curious, I am a messenger who will bring back word from the men who are fighting to those who want the war to go on for ever. Feeble, inarticulate, will be my message, but it will have a bitter truth, and may it burn their lousy souls.'

The Loudest Man-Made Sound in History: 1 July 1916

At the time, this was the loudest non-natural event ever. Some 27 tons of ammonal explosive was blown to start the Battle of the Somme, and the explosions constituted what was then the loudest human-made sound in history, heard even in London. The mine created 'Lochnagar Crater', 300 feet across and 90 feet deep, with a lip 15 feet high. The crater is known after the trench from where the main tunnel was started.

Unluckiest Prize Donor: 1 July 1916

On the first day of the Somme, twenty-one-year-old Captain W. P. 'Billie' Nevill of the East Surreys gave each of his four platoons a football, offering a prize to the man who first kicked one into a German trench. The combination of Nevill's initiative and his men's gallantry proved successful and they gained their objective. Nevill was killed just in front of the German barbed wire. Two of his footballs were later found nearby and are in museums. A poem in the *Daily Mail* recalled the event: 'On through the hail of slaughter,/Where gallant comrades fall,/Where blood is poured like water,/They drive the trickling ball./ The fear of death before them,/Is but an empty name;/True to the land that bore them,/The SURREYS played the game.' In 2011, a ball was found which had been used by the Manchester Regiment, the men following up the attack by the Surreys. Football today appears to be more a game of expectoration than excitation.

Bloodiest Day in the History of the British Army: 1 July 1916

On the first day of the Somme Campaign, the Army suffered over 58,000 casualties, with at least 19,000 killed. Many more died of their injuries later, in what Haig regarded as a successful start to the offensive. Total casualties on both sides at the Somme were over a million, with over 300,000 killed or missing.

First Use of Thermite Shells: 2 July 1916

Thermite is an incendiary and thermite shells were designed to set a target ablaze. They were first used by the gunners of 30th Division, firing on Bernafay Wood on the Somme.

The Greatest Grenade Battle: 26–27 July 1916

This lasted for twelve and a half hours without a break. The Australians, with British support, exchanged grenades with Germans on the Pozières Heights. The Allied contingent alone threw 15,000 Mills bombs during the night.

First American Sabotage: The Black Tom Explosion and the Closing of the Statue of Liberty Torch, 30 July 1916

This was an act of sabotage on American ammunition supplies in Jersey City, New Jersey, by German agents. American industries were free to sell their materials to any buyer, but from 1915 the Allies were the only possible customers because of their blockade of enemy ports, leading to German discontent. It was reported that on the night of the attack, 2 million pounds of ammunition were being stored at the munitions depot in railway carriages, including 100,000 pounds of TNT on a barge, all ready for shipment to Britain and France. A series of small fires led to several massive explosions. The explosions were the equivalent of an earthquake measuring between 5.0 and 5.5 on the Richter Scale, being felt as far away as Philadelphia. Windows broke as far as 25 miles away, including window panes in Times Square, New York. Property damage from the attack was estimated at $20 million, or $429 million in 2014 values. The damage to the Statue of Liberty was estimated to be $100,000, $2.1 million in 2013 values, and included the skirt and the torch. Nine people were killed. Later investigations by the Directorate of Naval Intelligence found links to the explosion with some members of the Irish Clan na Gael group and the Indian Ghadar Party. The Statue of Liberty's torch has been closed to tourist traffic since the explosion.

First Zeppelin Shot Down by a Plane: 2 September 1916

Lieutenant W. Leefe-Robinson of 39 Squadron RFC, flying a B.E. 2c twin-seater reconnaissance aircraft, shot down a Schütte-Lanz airship, in flight over Cuffley, north of London. He was promptly awarded the Victoria Cross. He had used a new, explosive bullet, the Pomeroy .303. It was filled with nitroglycerine and these bullets, fired alternatingly with incendiary bullets, tore open the exterior envelope and the interior gasbags of the airship, igniting the escaping hydrogen.

First Tank Attack in History: 15 September 1916

Tanks were first deployed as a surprise weapon in the third phase of the Battle of the Somme, which is known as the Battle of Flers–Courcelette. Twelve divisions and forty-nine tanks attacked the German front line and in three days the British captured over a mile of territory. However, a large number of the tanks broke down and the Army was unable to hold on to its gains. After an unsuccessful second attack on 25 September, the failed offensive at Flers and Courcelette was brought to an end.

The Oddest Regulation: 25 September 1916

Buying your round, or 'treating' as it was known, was considered to be a major factor in people drinking to excess. 'Getting them in' was normal as far as the average drinker was concerned, but it outraged others and the practice was outlawed across Leicestershire, Northamptonshire and Nottinghamshire from this date. The price of beer was also raised in the war, its strength was diluted and opening hours were restricted for the first time.

The Unknown Greatest Explosion: 10 November 1916

At Archangel, perhaps nine munitions ships exploded and the Bakaritsa harbour area was destroyed. The Russian authorities only admitted to 347 casualties, but British eyewitnesses state that thousands were killed. Eyewitnesses saw at least 2,000 corpses laid out, and initially the Archangel council gave deaths at 3,800, but they may have been higher. A Captain Pope reckoned that deaths were twice that amount. Captain Gwatkin-Williams, a British Naval officer of the White Sea Station, was there within a day of the explosion, writing, 'Never before probably has there been such an explosion as this one in Archangel. The death toll must have numbered several thousands, although, for official purposes, the Russian authorities gave out the number to be only one hundred and thirty. Whatever it was, approximately *thirty thousand tons* of munitions had gone up into the air.' Captain Pope commented that 'desolation was everywhere. All over the place were to be seen evidences of the freakish nature of the explosions. Ships were riven, cranes flung down, steel plates nearly an inch through were torn as though they were paper.' A Russian commentator, drawing on contemporary accounts, records as follows:

> On the day following, on 28th October [10th November N.S.], at the ruined wharves, as sailors stand posted in all corners of the port area of Bakaritsa, the Chinese stevedores dig out the corpses from under the rubble, and lay them in ranks along the wharf, either singly, or in groups; in one place the corpses numbered 100 ... Everywhere throughout the port area walk the Chinese, equanimous towards death. They move slowly, searching out corpses, they gather up the casings of unexploded shells. They die as shells explode. And the corpses keep on coming and coming. Some of us, more impressionable than others, having taken all this in, cannot eat, cannot drink. The corpses that the 'Chinamen' located and brought out were not human, but rather what remained of humans. On the wharf, a scene of horror – several hundred – corpses, burned over, giving off that odd indescribable smell of burn and decomposition.

First Bombing Raids on England from Planes: 28 November 1916

The main aircraft-based onslaught began when a lone German Gotha bomber dropped six bombs on London. The successful outcome of this opportunistic effort spurred the Germans into creating a special bomber squadron, dedicated to bombing England, named the 'England Squadron'.

Most Troops Killed in Avalanches and the Greatest-Scale Mountain Warfare in History: 17–19 December 1916

In three years of 'La Grande Guerra' on the Alpine Front, 60,000 soldiers were killed by avalanches. Another 60,000 died of cold-related injuries such as hypothermia. Trenches were used as high as 10,000 feet. Fighting could only be carried out in the summer months, when avalanches could easily be triggered by gunfire. On 13 December 1916, catastrophe struck the Austrian barracks below the Gran Poz summit of Monte Marmolada. This encampment had rock cliffs to shield from direct fire, and was out of high-angle mortar range. However, a landslide of 200,000 tons of snow and ice buried over 500 men. Only forty bodies were recovered of the estimated 300 who perished. Wind and snow accumulation had made the conditions critical, and from 17–19 December 1916 avalanches would take the lives of 9,000 to 10,000 Italian and Austrian soldiers. Communication lines, fixed ropes and climbing ladders were swept away, as were entire companies and batteries of men, guns and mules. In spring, their remains were found by the ravens.

The Second Unknown Great Explosion: 13 January 1917

The advance port of Archangel, Ekonomiia suffered probably an even greater explosion than that of 10 November 1916. There were three great detonations over eight hours. Casualties ran into the thousands and damage was worse than the previous explosion, but the Russian authorities only admitted 344 wounded and no deaths. It is estimated that in each incident around 30,000 tons of explosives were fired. Ekonomiia harbour was never used again, such was the damage.

Greatest British Explosion: 19 January 1917

A fire broke out at the Silvertown munitions factory on the outskirts of London, exploding 50 tons of TNT, killing over seventy people, destroying almost 1,000 properties, and damaging 60,000 more. The blast was so great that hot material was flung as far away as North Greenwich, where one piece of debris hit a gasometer and caused that to also explode, sending a massive fireball into the sky. A boiler from inside the factory, weighing a reputed 15 tons, was thrown out of the building and landed on the nearby road. Some 17 acres of warehouses in the area were destroyed by fires started by the falling burning debris. A munitions factory explosion at Faversham killed 105 in 1916, and another at Chilwell killed 137 workers in 1918.

First British 'Heavy' Bomber Goes into Action: 16 March 1917

Handley Page produced a series of heavy bombers for the Royal Navy to use in bombing the German Zeppelin yards of Berlin in revenge for the Zeppelin attacks on London. The Admiralty asked the company to produce a 'bloody paralyser of an aeroplane' for long-range bombing. The Handley Page O/100 biplane was sent to bomb a railway junction at Moselle. Initially, they were also used for daylight attacks, damaging a German destroyer on 23 April 1917, but the loss of an aircraft to fighter attack two days later resulted in a switch to exclusive night attacks. These were usually carried out by single aircraft against German occupied Channel ports, railway targets and airfields. O/100s were also used for anti-U-boat patrols. The improved, four-engined O/400 started to enter service in April 1918, being used for both support for the ground forces on the Western Front, and for strategic bombing. The O/400s could carry a new 1,650 lb bomb, which was aimed with a new bombsight. In service they were deployed in force, with up to forty aircraft participating in raids on the industrial zones of the Saar and the Ruhr in Germany. When the Armistice was signed, the RAF had 258 Handley Page aircraft on active service, some of which were modified for passenger transport.

First Purpose-Built Aircraft Carrier Ordered: April 1917
HMS *Hermes* was the world's first, although ships had previously landed on the *Ark Royal*, which was an Admiralty-requisitioned oil tanker. However, owing to design changes she was not commissioned until 1924, and was sunk by the Japanese in 1942.

Fastest Political About-Turn: 6 April 1917
Woodrow Wilson's campaign slogan for his second term was 'He kept us out of war'. About a month after he took office, the United States declared war on Germany.

The Americans Never Joined the Allies: 6 April 1917
The Allied Powers originally consisted of Russia, France, and Britain. Many other countries, including Belgium, Canada, Greece, Italy, Japan and Romania, joined later as associate powers. The United States never joined the Allied Powers, preferring upon principle to fight the Central Powers independently.

First Massed Bomber Raids on England: The First Civilian Bombings, 25 May 1917 Onwards
In September 1916, Germany abandoned raids by airship in favour of developing a heavier-than-air alternative. Operation Türkenkreuz – the 'Gotha Raids' were daylight bombing raids using Gotha G.IV bombers. In the first raid, twenty-three Gothas were to make a daylight raid on London but two were forced to turn back over the North Sea, and poor weather forced the remaining bombers to divert to secondary targets at Folkestone and a nearby Army camp. There were 95 deaths and 192 injuries, mostly in the Folkestone area. A second attack on 5 June 1917 was diverted to Sheerness in Kent. A third attack on 13 June resulted in the first daylight raid on London, causing 162 deaths and 432 injuries. Among the dead were eighteen children killed by a bomb falling on a primary school, and no Gothas were lost. In 1938, Air Commodore Lionel Charlton called this 'the beginning of a new epoch in the history of warfare'. A further Gotha raid of twenty-two aircraft was made on 7 July 1917, resulting in 54 deaths and 190 injuries. Many of these casualties were caused by falling anti-aircraft shells. Beginning in September 1917, improved British air defences forced the abandonment of daylight raids. Gothas carried out twenty-two raids

on England, dropping 186,830 lbs of bombs for the loss of sixty-one aircraft.

The First Anaesthetic Masks in Military Use: 1917
Sir Geoffrey Marshall (1887–1982) was the catalyst for development of anaesthesia and respiratory medicine, becoming doctor to both Winston Churchill and George VI. He first worked as commander upon an ambulance barge and then in the casualty clearing stations in the war, researching the increasing problem of surgical shock. Marshall wrote that 'with gas-oxygen we cut down the mortality from about 90 per cent to something like 25 per cent'.

The First Time a British Royal Family Changed Its Name: 17 July 1917
George V founded the Royal House of Windsor by altering its name from the House of Saxe-Coburg and Gotha. Actually, if we ignore this name change and give Charles, Prince of Wales, the real names of his mother and father (Prince Philip Mountbatten also changed his Germanic name), he is in reality not Charles Windsor but Charles of Schleswig-Holstein-Sonderburg-Glücksburg, Battenburg, Wettin and Saxe-Coburg and Gotha. In 1960, an Order-in-Council agreed that Queen Elizabeth's name was Windsor, but her descendants would be Mountbatten-Windsor. For some reason the sons of Charles, William and Henry, are known as William Wales and Harry Wales, not Mountbatten-Windsor.

The First Landing of a Plane on a Ship Under Way: 2 August 1917
Squadron Commander Edward Dunning DSC RN became the first person to land a plane on a moving ship when he landed a Sopwith Pup on the converted battle cruiser HMS *Furious*. Dunning calculated that, by combining his 40-knot stalling speed, the 21-knot top speed of the *Furious* and a 19-knot wind, he could hover relative to the ship. A party of officers rushed out and pulled him to the deck using some dangling ropes. He repeated the mission, and then gave orders not to touch his plane until it had touched down and he had come to a complete standstill. The wind blew the aircraft off the deck and he drowned.

The First Person to Receive Plastic Surgery: August 1917?
Walter Yeo (1890–1960) was wounded on 31 May 1916, during the Battle of Jutland, while manning the guns aboard the battleship

HMS *Warspite*. He sustained terrible facial injuries, including the loss of upper and lower eyelids. There is some uncertainty as to where he was first admitted to hospital, owing to poor documentation. He was treated by Sir Harold Gillies, the first man to transfer skin from undamaged areas on the body. Gillies opened a specialist ward at Queen Mary's Hospital for the treatment of the facially wounded. Walter Yeo is thought to have been one of the first patients to be treated with this newly developed technique, a form of skin transplantation called a 'tubed pedicle' flap. During the long process of surgery, a 'mask' of skin was transplanted across Yeo's face and eyes, including new eyelids. By July 1919, he was found to be fit for active service again and was recorded as having completed courses in September 1919. He underwent a further operation in August 1921, after which his disfigurement was recorded as 'improved, but still severe', and he was recommended for medical discharge, which took place on 15 December 1921.

First 'Blood Banks' and Portable Transfusion Units: 1917

Oswald Hope Robertson (1886–1966) was an English-born scientist who pioneered the idea of 'blood banks' in the 'blood depots' he established in 1917, during service in France with the US Army Medical Corps. In France he experimented with preserving human blood cells for use in transfusions and was recognised as the inventor of the blood bank. Geoffrey Keynes (1887–1982) was a lieutenant in the RAMC, acting as a consultant surgeon. His expertise in blood transfusion enabled him to create a portable blood-transfusion device which could store blood; this machine was recognised as saving thousands of lives.

The First Major Sealift, 1917

'Sealift' is the use of merchant ships for the deployment of military assets, such as weapons and troops. In the war, the USA bought, borrowed or commandeered vessels of various types, ranging from pleasure craft to ocean liners, to transport the AEF to Europe.

First American Troops Killed: 3 November 1917

During June 1917, 14,000 American troops had arrived in France for training. They had only two tanks, and for artillery had to rely on the French for guns and gunners. On 2 November 1917, an American infantry battalion took over from French soldiers in Barthelemont. The next morning, the Germans attacked an outpost of the battalion, killing three Americans, who were nearly decapitated with trench knives. The Germans took twelve prisoners and left the surviving

Americans in shock. An urgent inquiry was held and it was decided that the Americans were not yet sufficiently trained to take their place on the line and should be removed until properly trained.

Greatest Man-Made Explosion: 6 December 1917

The SS *Imo* and the SS *Mont-Blanc* collided in the harbour of Halifax, Nova Scotia. *Mont-Blanc* carried 2,653 tonnes of various explosives. After the collision the ship caught fire, drifted into town and exploded. The Halifax explosion was the largest man-made explosion until the atomic bomb was dropped on Hiroshima in 1945. About 2,000 were killed and over 9,000 injured. This was more than the number of casualties sustained in the 103 air raids on Britain. A large section of Halifax was completely levelled and buildings were damaged up to 12 miles away. The blast shook buildings 60 miles away and was heard over 160 miles away in Cape Breton.

World's Greatest Train Accident: 12 December 1917

A grossly overloaded troop train was derailed near the entrance of the station at Saint-Michel-de-Maurienne, after running away down a steep gradient from the entrance of the Fréjus Tunnel. The brake power was insufficient for the weight of the train. About 800 deaths were estimated, with 540 officially confirmed. The military had forced the driver to run the overloaded train.

First All-Metal Plane Developed: March 1918

Hugo Junkers, a professor of mechanics, designed the world's first all-metal plane, the Junkers D-1, in 1915, but his ideas were too advanced for his time. The prototype was built in 1917, and it did not begin full production until 1918. It was made from a lightweight form of aluminium called duralumin, as were Zeppelin airships. He also produced the Junkers CL-1, the best German ground-attack plane of the war.

After the Armistice Junkers established his own company, Lufthansa, and his aircraft factories produced civil and military planes. Hitler placed him under house arrest when the government took over his company.

First American Offensive of the War: 28 May 1918

This was thirteen months and three weeks after America declared war on Germany. The Battle of Cantigny was small in scale, and Americans went on to fight larger battles at the war's end. The most experienced of the seven American divisions, the First Division, in reserve for the

French Army near the village of Cantigny, was selected for the attack. The objective of the attack was to reduce a small German salient, but also to instil confidence among the French and British in the ability of the inexperienced American Expeditionary Force. US forces held their position with the loss of 1,603 casualties including 199 dead, and captured 250 German prisoners. It is interesting to note that the Americans only actually joined battle for the last three and a half months of the war. The Allies had fought for over fifty-one months at the war's end.

Formation of Long-Range Bombing Group: 6 June 1918
Britain formed the L.R.G. to engage in long-range bombings deep in German territory at industrial targets. The war ended before Britain's four-engined Handley Page V/1500 bomber, designed to drop a 7,500-pound bombload on Berlin, entered service. The British dropped 660 tons of bombs on Germany, more than twice the amount Germany had managed to drop on England.

First Parachute-Dropped Supplies of Ammunition: 4 July 1918
A constant problem that held up many an advance was the difficulty in keeping the forward troops supplied with ammunition and medical supplies. Not only were supplies heavy and bulky, needing many men and horses to transport them, but the supply routes were under fire, and were often over destroyed ground where roads were impassable. Rifle ammunition was now airdropped in cases, and supplies brought up by tanks, which led to the Australian capture of Le Hamel.

Last Cavalry Charge: 11 November 1918
On 28 November 1916, in the Prunari Charge in the Battle of Bucharest, the Romanian Second Rosiori Cavalry regiment charged German, Turkish and Bulgarian troops. Only 154 of 5,000 cavalrymen survived the charge, which enabled the escape and regrouping of a Romanian Army. An account reads, 'Behind fences, in brambles, in the windows of the houses and on the bridges, the enemy hid tens of machine guns, and threw a hail of bullets onto the mighty regiment. Horses and horsemen fell in a jumble over each other. Two hundred people remain on the field of battle, forming, together with the horses' cadavers, masses of bleeding flesh. Among them, all the officers of the regiment, starting with their brave commander.' On 31 October 1917, mounted infantry of the Australian 4th and 12th Light Horse charged across 2 miles of open terrain in the face of Austrian artillery and Ottoman machine gun fire. They captured the remaining trenches

defending Beersheba in Southern Palestine. The last cavalry charge of the First World War was by the British 7th Dragoon Guards in Belgium on 11 November 1918. They attacked German troops to capture the Lessines and Dender crossings in Belgium, the action being completed as the clocks struck 11 a.m. for the end of the war.

The Gung-Ho American: 11 November 1918

One American artillery captain kept his battery firing at the Germans until just minutes before 11 a.m. on Armistice Day, because he believed the Armistice was premature and the Germans needed to be truly beaten, not just defeated. Captain Harry S. Truman was to become President of the USA. His decisive character was emphasised by his momentous decision to use atomic bombs to defeat Japan in the Second World War.

Last Soldiers Killed: 11 November 1918

A German soldier by the name of Lieutenant Tomas was killed after the eleventh hour of the eleventh day of the eleventh month, by an American unit that apparently had not received word of the ceasefire. The final German killed before the eleventh hour is not known. The last British, French, Canadian and American men killed were the following: British cavalryman George Edwin Ellison, shot by a sniper around 9:30 a.m. while scouting around Mons; French soldier Augustin Trébuchon, killed at 10:45 a.m. while spreading the news that they would get hot soup after the eleventh hour; Canadian soldier George Lawrence Price, who died two minutes before the eleventh hour, just north of Mons; and the man believed to be the last killed in the war, American soldier Henry Gunther, sixty seconds before the eleventh hour. German soldiers were shouting and waving at Gunther and the others to go back. Hundreds of men died on this day, and one historian has calculated that there were 11,000 casualties on Armistice Day. Many were caused by commanders, who already knew that the Armistice would come into effect at 11 a.m., sending their men into action against the enemy.

Last Sailor Killed: 11 November 1918

Able Seaman Richard Morgan died aged twenty-six while serving on board the destroyer HMS *Garland* and is reputed to be the last British serviceman to die in the First World War. He is buried at Kilgwrrwg, Devauden, Monmouthshire.

Youngest British Soldiers

Myer Rosenblum of London joined the London Welsh Regiment in August 1914, aged thirteen years and nine months, but was 'claimed back' by his father in October. Undeterred, Rosenblum joined again and was wounded at Gallipoli in June 1915, and his father claimed him back again into civilian life. James Bartaby joined the 7th East Surreys on 20 January 1914, aged thirteen years and ten months. He was wounded in France and sent home in October. In October 1915, Arthur Peyman was in court, charged with being absent from his regiment since August. His mother produced his birth certificate. He was only fourteen years old and the case was dismissed.

Only in November 2013 was it discovered that the youngest British soldier was Sidney G. Lewis, who enlisted with the East Surreys in August 1915, five months after his twelfth birthday, and was fighting on the Western Front from June 1916. For six weeks he fought in the bloody Battle of Delville Wood in the Somme Offensive, until his mother belatedly wrote to the War Office. A fourteen-year-old boy, Henry Stevens, handed himself in at a police station at Ilford pretending to be his brother, a twenty-one-year-old wanted for desertion. Stevens then served, with no military training, with the 7th Northamptonshire Regiment at Harcourt in France, killing a number of Germans in 1918.

Oldest Soldiers and Sailors

In December 1915, James White of Sowerby was sent home from the Western Front. His mates had discovered that he had served in the Zulu War of 1878, and he was found to be seventy years old. In July 1916, Lieutenant Harry Webber was killed at the Somme and was found to be sixty-seven years old. The oldest Italian soldier was seventy-four and the oldest Frenchman seventy-eight. In the Royal Navy, a chief gunner had his left leg broken when his ship blew up in the Dardanelles. He had initially seen active service in the Crimea in 1853–56, and was eighty-four years old.

The Luckiest Village

Only fifty-two villages in England and Wales lost no men in the war, being later known as 'thankful villages' or 'blessed villages'. In France, where the human cost of war was higher than in Britain, Thierville in Normandy was the only village in all of France with no men lost from the First World War, nor any memorials constructed in the subsequent period. Thierville also suffered no losses in the Franco-Prussian War (1870–71), the Second World War (1939–45), the First Indo-China War (1946–54) or the Algerian War (1954–62), France's other bloody wars of the modern era.

The U-Boat Captain and *The Sound of Music*

Georg Trapp was born a Croat, and as an Austrian U-boat captain he married the granddaughter of the inventor of the Whitehead torpedo. At the end of the First World War, Trapp's wartime record stood at nineteen war patrols, with the sinking of twelve cargo vessels, a French armoured cruiser and an Italian submarine. For his service, Trapp was raised to the nobility and granted the right to use the word 'von' before his name. The end of the war saw Austria being reduced in size to its German-speaking core, losing its seacoast, and thus it had no further need for a navy. Von Trapp was unemployed, but his wife Agathe's inherited wealth was sufficient to sustain their family of seven children. In 1922, Agathe died of scarlet fever contracted from the children. Around 1926, one of the children, Maria, was recovering from an illness and was unable to attend school. Von Trapp hired a tutor, Maria Kutschera, from a local convent. Kutschera and Georg married in 1927, and had three further children. In the 1930s Georg lost all his wealth in the economic crash. Faced with an impossible economic situation, Maria took charge and arranged for the family to sing at various events to earn money. In 1938, the von Trapps, opposed to Hitler's annexation of Austria and having received offers to perform in the United States, left Austria and fled to Italy by train, not to Switzerland on foot as in the film. They escaped to the USA. This is the factual basis for the musical *The Sound of Music*.

First Votes For Women: 28 December 1918

Some women were allowed to vote in Britain for the first time, mainly as a result of women's role in the war.

The Downfall of Money and the Origins of the Second World War

The mark fell from 4.2 to the dollar in 1914 to 4.2 trillion in 1923. According to Frederick Taylor (*The Downfall of Money*, 2013), the great loser from this hyperinflation was the *bildungsbürgertum*, the classically educated Germany elite. Although it made up only 1 per cent of the German population, it was crucial to sound government. This upper class relied upon investment income, which fell from 15 per cent to 3 per cent of GDP between 1913 and 1924. The ruling elite became seriously impoverished, and its sense of grievance and injustice fertilised support for new parties on both right and left, with the Nazis surfacing as the strongest of these new movements.

The Longest Title of a War Leader

Nikolay Alexandrovich Romanov (1868–1918), Tsar Nicholas II, was the last Emperor of Russia, Grand Duke of Finland and titular King of Poland. According to the 1906 Russian Constitution, he was 'By the grace of God, Emperor and Autocrat of all the Russias, of Moscow, Kiev, Vladimir, Novgorod, Tsar of Kazan, Tsar of Astrakhan, Tsar of Poland, Tsar of Siberia, Tsar of Tauric Khersones, Tsar of Georgia, Lord of Pskov; and Grand Duke of Smolensk, Lithuania, Volhynia, Podolia and Finland, Prince of Estonia, Livonia, Courland and Semigalia, Samogitia, Bialystok, Karelia, Tver; Yugra, Perm, Vyatka, Bulgaria and other territories; Lord and Grand Duke of Nizhni Novgorod, Chernigov; Ruler of Ryazan, Polotsk, Rostov, Yaroslavl, Beloozero, Udoria, Obdoria, Kondia, Vitebsk, Mstislav and all northern territories; Ruler of Iveria, Karalinia and the Kabardinian lands and Armenian territories; hereditary Ruler and Lord of the Cherkess and Mountain Princes and others; Lord of Turkestan, Heir of Norway, Duke of Schleswig-Holstein, Stormarn, Dithmarschen, Oldenburg, and so forth, and so forth, and so forth.'

The First Communist State

The First World War was the catalyst that transformed Russia into the Union of the Soviet Socialist Republic (USSR). The creation of the world's first communist state began a new phase in world history, and many historians believe that this was the most important consequence of the First World War.

The Country That Suffered Most

Before the war, the Kingdom of Serbia had 4.5 million inhabitants. In 1915 alone, 150,000 people are estimated to have died during the worst typhus epidemic in history. The number of civilian deaths is estimated by some sources at 650,000, primarily due to the typhus outbreak and famine, but also due to direct clashes with the occupiers, especially the Bulgarians. Some 58 per cent of the regular Serbian Army of 420,000 men are said to have died in the war. The army shrank from this peak to about 100,000 by the end of war. The total number of casualties was over a million, taking away 25 per cent of Serbia's pre-war population and 57 per cent of its overall male population. In 1917, the Bulgarian Prime Minister said that 'Serbia ceased to exist'. These losses were mainly due to food shortages, epidemics and the Spanish flu, and there were 133,148 wounded. According to the Yugoslav government in 1924, Serbia lost 365,164 soldiers, or 26 per cent, of all mobilised personnel, while France lost 16.8 per cent, Germany 15.4 per cent, Russia 11.5 per cent, and Italy 10.3 per cent. At the end of the war, there were 114,000 disabled soldiers and 500,000 orphaned children in Serbia.

The Ten Bloodiest Battles
Casualties were roughly as follows: Hundred Day Offensive, 1,855,369; Spring Offensive, 1,539,715; Battle of the Somme, 1,219,201; Battle of Verdun, 976,000; Battle of Passchendaele, 848,614; Serbian Campaign, 633,500; First Battle of Marne, 483,000; Battle of Gallipoli, 473,000; Battle of Arras, 278,000; Battle of Tannenberg, 182,000.

The Bloodiest British War
While we often think that the First World War was the bloodiest for the British people, that honour goes to the 'War of the Three Nations', which this author used to know as the English Civil War (1642–49). Of a population of around 2 million men of fighting age, 85,000 died in battle and another 100,000 of wounds or disease. Around 500,000 men were forced to fight, so there was a 37 per cent mortality rate.

Who Won the War?
The First World War was a turning point for America economically. With war orders flooding in from Europe, American manufacturers grew rich, and American industrial might began to lead the world. The international financial system set up its capital in New York during this period, and the war catapulted America forever into a leading role in economic and military affairs. As in the Second World War, Britain had to repay all the money it owed to the USA, whereas the defeated nations, especially in Second World War, were often supported by new US investment.

Most Accurate Forecast I
In 1908, Admiral 'Jackie' Fisher forecast that the Germans would declare war when the Kiel Canal was completed, expected to be in October 1914. It was completed early, in August, and Germany declared war immediately.

Most Accurate Forecast II
Otto von Bismarck stated, 'Twenty years after I'm gone, it will all be over', referring to the German Empire. It fell in November 1918, twenty years and one month after Bismarck's death.

Most Accurate Forecast III: 28 June 1919

Marshall Foch considered the Treaty of Versailles to be 'a capitulation, a treason', because he believed that only permanent occupation of the Rhineland would grant France sufficient security against a revival of German aggression. As the treaty was being signed, owing to Germany being allowed to remain a united country, Foch declared, 'This is not a peace. It is an armistice for twenty years.' His words proved prophetic as the Second World War started twenty years and sixty-five days later.

Greatest Loss of Shipping in a Single Day: 21 June 1919

The Germans scuttled their High Seas Fleet, over 400,000 tons.

The End of the Four Great Dynasties

The Habsburgs, the Romanovs, the Ottomans and the Hohenzollerns all fell after the war. The Romanovs were rulers of the Russian Empire from 1613 to the Russian Revolution of February 1917. Russia is still the largest country in the world, despite in recent times losing its former possessions of Estonia, Latvia, Lithuania, Belarus, Ukraine, Georgia, Azerbaijan and Kazakhstan.

The Habsburgs were Holy Roman Emperors from 1438 to 1740, and produced kings for Germany, Hungary, Portugal and Spain. They ruled the Austro-Hungarian Empire, geographically the second-largest country in Europe after the Russian Empire, which included the modern states of Austria, Hungary, Slovenia, Bosnia and Herzegovina, the Czech Republic, large parts of Serbia and Romania, and smaller parts of Italy, Montenegro, Poland and Ukraine. Its dual monarchy was dissolved at the end of the war.

The Ottomans came from Anatolia, Turkey, and with the conquest of Constantinople (now Istanbul) in 1453, the Ottoman state became an empire, at times controlling the Balkans, Hungary and much of the Mediterranean Basin. The Armistice of Mudros of 30 October 1914 effectively partitioned the empire, and the rise of Ataturk led to a Turkish Republic, and the last Ottoman sultan leaving the country.

The Hohenzollerns were emperors of Germany, Prussia and Romania, originating in the eleventh century. The royal family abdicated during the November 1918 German Revolution, and the Treaty of Versailles in 1919 brought the end of the German Empire.

The Most Optimistic Name for a War

The First World War was known as 'the Great War' or 'the World War' at the time, owing to the nature of its global conflict. Because of 'the Second World War' it is generally now known as 'the First World War'. It could well have been called 'the Cousins' War', featuring the first cousins the Kaiser, Tsar and King of England. It was also known as 'the War of the Nations' and 'the War to Make the World Safe for Democracy'. However, such was the revulsion caused, and the desire never to see another such conflict, that it was very often referred to as 'the War to End All Wars'. It was thought that man could never be as stupid again. This may indeed have been the case for the Swiss, busily profiting by avoiding war since 1815. The First World War had been the deadliest military conflict in history, with over 100 million military personnel mobilised at one time or another during the war, and more than 60 million people losing their lives. Of this figure, one-third were military personnel and two-thirds were civilians. Sadly, 'the War to End All Wars' has been followed by continuous conflict across the world.

The Russian Revolution was still in progress after the war, but the following are just a sample of the successive wars, purges and ensuing deaths around the globe: 1915–20, Ottoman Empire kills 500,000 Armenians; 1916–23, Ottoman Empire kills 350,000 Greek Pontians and 480,000 Anatolian Greeks; 1917–21, Soviet Revolution (5 million+ dead); 1917–19, Greece–Turkey conflict (45,000 dead); 1919–21, Poland–Soviet Union conflict (27,000); 1928–37, Chinese Civil War (2 million+); 1931, Japanese Manchurian War (1.1 million); 1932–33, Soviet Union–Ukraine conflict (10 million); 1932 'La Matanza' in El Salvador (30,000); 1932–35, 'Guerra del Chaco' between Bolivia and Paraguay (117,500); 1934, Mao's 'Long March' in China (170,000); 1936, Italy's invasion of Ethiopia (200,000); 1936–37, Stalin's Purges (13 million); 1936–39, Spanish Civil War (600,000); 1937–45, Japanese invasion of China (500,000); 1939–45: the Second World War, including the Holocaust and the Chinese Revolution (55 million+); 1946–49, Chinese Civil War (1.2 million); 1946–49, Greek Civil War (50,000); 1946–54, First Indochina War (600,000); 1947, Partition of India and Pakistan (1 million); 1947–49, First Arab–Israeli War (21,000); 1947, Taiwan's uprising against the Kuomintang (30,000); 1948–1958, Colombian Civil War (250,000); 1949, Indian Muslims against Hindus (20,000); 1949–50, Mainland China invades Tibet (1.2 million); 1950–53, Korean War (3 million); 1952–59, Kenya Mau Mau Insurrection

(20,000); 1954–62, French–Algerian war (368,000); 1956, Second Arab-Israeli War (3,000); 1958–61, Mao's 'Great Leap Forward' (38 million); 1960–90, South Africa against Africa National Congress (?); 1960–96, Guatemala Civil War (200,000); 1961–98, Indonesia invades West Papua/Irian (100,000); 1961–2003, killing of Kurds in Iraq (180,000); 1962–75, Mozambique Frelimo against Portugal (10,000); 1962–75, Angola FNLA & MPLA against Portugal (50,000); 1964–73, Vietnam War (3 million); 1965, Second Kashmir War (7,000); 1965–66, Indonesian Civil War (250,000); 1966–69, Mao's 'Cultural Revolution' (11 million); 1966, Colombia Civil War (31,000); 1967, Third Arab-Israeli War (20,000); 1967–70, Nigeria–Biafra civil war (800,000); 1968–80, Rhodesian Bush War (11,000+); 1969, Philippines against the communist Bagong Hukbong Bayan/New People's Army (40,000); 1969–79, Idi Amin's reign, Uganda (300,000); 1969–98, The Troubles in Northern Ireland (3,000); 1969–79, Francisco Macias Nguema's reign, Equatorial Guinea (50,000); 1971, Bangladesh Liberation War (500,000); 1972, Moro insurgency in the Philippines (150,000); 1972, Burundi Civil War (300,000); 1972–79, Rhodesia/Zimbabwe Civil War (30,000); 1973, Yom Kippur War (20,000); 1974–91, Ethiopia Civil War (1 million); 1975–78, Ethiopian Red Terror (1.5 million); 1975–79, reign of the Khmer Rouge, Cambodia (1.7 million); 1975–89, Vietnamese 'boat people' exodus (250,000); 1975–87 civil war in Lebanon (130,000); 1975–87, Laotian Civil War (184,000); 1975–2002, Angola Civil War (500,000); 1976–83, Argentina's Dirty War (20,000): 1976–93, Mozambican Civil War (900,000); 1976–98 Indonesia occupation of East Timor (600,000); 1976–2005, Aceh insurgency (12,000); 1977–92, Salvadoran Civil War (75,000); 1979, Sino-Vietnamese War (30,000); 1979–88, Soviet war in Afghanistan (1.3 million); 1980–88, Iraq–Iran War (435,000); 1980–92, internal conflict in Peru (69,000); 1984, Kurdish–Turkish conflict (35,000); 1981–90, contras in Nicaragua (60,000); 1982–90, Hissene Habre's reign, Chad (40,000); 1983, Sri Lankan Civil War (70,000); 1983–2002, Sudanese civil wars (2 million); 1987–93 First Intifada (4,500); 1988–2001, civil war in Afghanistan (400,000); 1988–2004, Somali Civil War (550,000); 1989, First Liberian Civil War (220,000); 1989, Uganda against Lord's Resistance Army (30,000); 1991, First Gulf War (85,000); 1991–97, Congolese Civil War (800,000); 1991–2000, Sierra Leone Civil War (200,000); 1991–2009, Chechen–Russian conflict (200,000); 1991–94, Armenia-Azerbaijani War (35,000); 1992–96, Tajikstan Civil War (50,000); 1992–96, Yugoslav Wars (260,000); 1992–99, Algerian Civil War (150,000); 1993–2005

Burundian Civil War (200,000); 1994 Rwandan Genocide (900,000); 1995, Nepalese Civil War (12,000); 1997–99, Republic of the Congo Civil War (100,000); 1998, First and Second Congo Wars (3.8 million); 1998–2000, Eritrean–Ethiopian War (75,000); 1999, Kosovo War (2,000); 2000–03, Second Intifada (2,700); 2001, War in Afghanistan (40,000); 2001, Nigerian Sharia Conflict (1,700); 2002, Second Ivorian Civil War (1,000); 2003–11, Iraq War (160,000); 2003–09 War in Darfur (300,000); 2004, Shia insurgency in Yemen (?); 2004, South Thailand insurgency (3,700); 2007, War in North-West Pakistan (38,000); 2008, Gaza War (1,300); 2012, Syrian Civil War (100,000). More and more, war is shifting to religious differences being the cause. There is irony in this.

Greatest Epidemic of the Twentieth Century: 1918–19
The Spanish Influenza pandemic killed over 50 million people worldwide.

The Worst Post-Traumatic Stress Disorder
All the senior members of the Third Reich who were old enough, with the exception of Himmler and Goebbels, were veterans of the First World War. Himmler was a young reservist, and the war ended before he could fight. Goebbels tried to fight, but was rejected because of a limp. Hitler was a messenger well behind the front lines. Those who fought included Dietrich, Dönitz, Funk, Todt, Göring, von Schirach, Hess, Jodl, Raeder and von Ribbentropp. Some claim that they all displayed classic, untreated symptoms of PTSD. Perhaps 'emotional numbing' led them to not care about their treatment of Jews. Possibly, 're-experiencing' constant negative thoughts about the first war led them to want to reverse its results with a new, corrective war. Certainly, discontentment, irritability and angry outbursts were manifested in Hitler's behaviour.

Repayment of German Reparations – The Hard Way
The world's oceans contain around 20 million tons of gold. However, another estimate is 800 million tons. If all the gold suspended in the world's seawater was mined, each person on earth could have about 9 lbs of gold. Apart from the millions of tons dissolved in seawater, there are huge deposits underwater, for instance off Tonga, but these would have to be mined about a mile underwater. To help pay the German reparations for the First World War, Fritz Haber, as head of the Kaiser Wilhelm Institute, tried for six years to obtain gold from seawater. Previously, in 1910, he had invented a process for producing

ammonia from nitrogen and hydrogen, effectively killing off the guano trade. He then was in charge of production of poison gas and oversaw its use at Ypres. His wife, distraught, killed herself with his revolver. In 1918, the Allies wanted him tried as a war criminal, but in that year Haber was given the Nobel Prize for Chemistry.

17

War Terms and Slang

With people thrown together under conditions of stress, the war was a melting plot of classes and nationalities, and a creative time for language for all countries. Soldiers, sailors and airmen, at the end of the war, took their new terms back to the general population. Gallows humour abounded in all forces, most of it directed at officers rather than at enemy troops, for whom there was a grudging respect. Opposing soldiers were generally in the same terrible conditions, especially on the Western Front in its 'war of attrition'. Front-line soldiers often felt that they had more in common with the troops in the trenches opposite than with their own rear echelon troops and the people at home. The usual two-week stint in the front and reserve lines tended to leave soldiers covered with lice, unwashed, unshaven, and utterly exhausted. The German front-line infantryman would call himself a *frontschwein*, a front pig. The French soldier would be a *poilu*, literally a hairy beast as *poil* is used primarily for the hair of animals. Bleakly, the root of the German word *der Schützengraben*, their term for the trench, was *das Grab*, the grave.

Comrades who were killed were euphemistically said to be 'pushing up daisies', to have 'gone west', 'snuffed it', 'been skittled' or 'become a landowner'. Many more new terms came from the mix of nationalities thrown together by the war. The French *souvenir* replaced keepsake as the primary word for a memento. A plethora of phrases came from the war that refer to lice, their eggs and getting rid of them, such as 'you louse', 'nit-picking', 'going over with a fine toothcomb', 'chatting' and 'lousy'. The following words and phrases originated in, or first became popular in, the trenches of the First World War, and are still used today.

A-1 – On top form. By 1916, the British War Office had created an ABC system of classification for the Department of Recruiting. Each category was then graded on a scale of 1 to 3. A-1 men were fit for general service overseas. The Military Service Act 1916 gave classifications as A1 General Service; B1 Garrison Service Abroad; B2 Labour Service Abroad; B3 Sedentary Work Abroad; C1 Garrison Service at Home Camps; C2 Labour Service at Home Camps; C3 Sedentary Service at Home Camps. The physical standards defining each category were: A Able to march, see to shoot, hear well and stand active service conditions; B Free from serious organic diseases, able to stand service on the lines of communication in France, or in garrisons in the tropics; B1 Able to march five miles, and see to shoot with glasses and hear well; B2 Able to walk 5 miles to and from work, see and hear sufficiently for ordinary purposes; B3 Only suitable for sedentary work; C Free from serious organic disease, able to stand service conditions in garrison at home. A similar eighteenth-century system from Lloyd's of London was used for evaluating ships.

ABDUL – Anzac nickname for a Turkish soldier, as in 'Abdul did not seem to trust the situation and was pretty active in our sector'.

ABRI – Shelter or dugout, from the French.

ACCESSORY – British term applied to cylinder-discharged gas, used in orders and other communications to keep its use secret.

ACE – An outstanding pilot, as well as an excellent performer in any field. At first the term meant simply a 'high card' to play against the enemy. The French singled out those fliers who had downed at least five enemy planes as 'aces'. The nature of air combat in the First World War meant that it was very difficult to accurately record the true scores of the flying aces.

ACK-ACK – Anti-aircraft (AA) fire, from the military phonetic alphabet where A is represented by ack.

ACK EMMA – Morning, a.m.

ALF A MO (1) – One moment, please, from 'half a moment'.

ALF A MO (2) – A small moustache.

ALLEY – Go! Clear out! Run away! From French *allez*.

ALLEYMAN – German soldier, from French *allemagne*. 'If you want to see your dear Fatherland, keep your head down, alleyman' was a popular trench song of 1916.

ALLY SLOPER'S CAVALRY – Army Service Corps (ASC). From Ally Sloper, a character in popular pre-war papers. The ASC members, owing to their good pay, comfortable conditions and comparative safety, were regarded by the infantry as not 'proper soldiers'. When the ASC acquired their royal prefix in 1918, to become the RASC, their nickname was changed to 'Run Away, Someone's Coming!'

ALPHABET CODE – To ensure messages were correctly understood over a poor phone line, or when the noise of battle was near, men spelt out their sentences. The First World War British signalling code is reproduced below, with only 'Charlie' and 'X-ray' being used in today's globally standardised NATO code. The NATO Phonetic alphabet's full name is the International Radiotelephony Spelling Alphabet, developed in the 1950s to avoid the misunderstanding caused by poor radio acoustics, where an S and an F, for example, are easily confused. It replaced other phonetic alphabets, such as the RAF phonetic alphabet, Western Front slang or 'signalese', the Royal Navy phonetic alphabet and the US military 'Able Baker' alphabet. The First World War code is followed in brackets by today's NATO alphabet: A Ack (Alpha); B Beer (Bravo); C Charlie; D Don (Delta); E Edward (Echo); F Freddie (Foxtrot); G Gee (Golf); H Harry (Hotel); I Ink (India); J Johnnie (Juliet); K King (Kilo); L London (Lima); M Mike (Emma); N Nuts (November); O Oranges (Oscar); P Pip (Papa); Q Queen (Quebec); R Robert (Romeo); S Essex (Sierra); T Toc (Tango); U Uncle (Uniform); V Vic (Victor); W William (Whiskey); X X-ray; Y Yorker (Yankee); Z Zebra (Zulu).

AMMO BOOTS – Hobnailed boots, from 'ammunition boots, regulation issue'. They were so hard to break in that 'old sweats' gave new recruits the advice to urinate in them and leave them overnight. This would soften the leather and prevent blisters. A gunner recalled the first days of the BEF's advance into Belgium: 'They were getting more and more tired. The infantry were carrying about 100 lb. on their back, which made it worse. A lot of it was due to the fact that a number of them were reservists, and had been called up just prior to the outbreak of war. They were fitted out with kit, including "ammos" (that's the old Army word for boots) and they were very heavy. Before the war we were able to break them in, but they didn't get time. They were put straight on a march which lasted for about 150, 160 miles with only a very, very few rests, and if they got those boots off they couldn't get them back on again, consequently their feet were bleeding.' The French roads leading to Mons were cobbled, 'terrible to march on'.

ANGEL OF MONS – The Welsh writer Arthur Machen penned a short story for the *London Evening News* on 29 September 1914. He wrote that the ghosts of the bowmen of Agincourt had come to the aid of the beleaguered British troops at Mons in August. Around 10,000 Germans were said to have been killed in a shower of arrows, falling dead without a mark on them. Soldiers then wrote saying that they had seen angels at Mons. Perhaps they were hallucinating because of sleep deprivation and fear. The dead often had no marks on them, being killed in a shell blast or by a shell passing near them. See 'Wind of Ball'.

ANTI-FROSTBITE GREASE – This was issued on the Western Front because of the crippling cold, consisting mainly of pork fat. Whale oil was also issued, but hardly used because of its odour.

ANTONIO – Portuguese soldier.

ANZAC – Australian and New Zealand Army Corps.

ANZAC BUTTON/ANZAC NAIL – A nail used instead of a button to hold up one's trousers.

ANZAC SOUP – A shell hole full of water polluted by a corpse, originating in France when ANZAC troops moved there from Gallipoli.

ANZAC STEW – Any improvised meal the troops managed to prepare from their monotonous rations, e.g. a bucket of hot water with one rind of bacon in it.

ANZAC WAFER – a hard biscuit.

ARCHIE – Anti-aircraft fire or an artillery piece. The British forces nicknamed these guns 'Archie', from a music hall character. Both sides fired artillery rounds into the air, which released smoke clouds and shrapnel into the air on explosion.

ARMED BOARDING VESSEL – Civilian ship armed and taken into the navy.

ARMED MERCHANT CRUISER – Large civilian vessel armed as auxiliary cruiser.

ARMENTIÈRES – One of the more popular marching and front-line songs in the First World War was adapted by troops in the Second World War as 'The German Officers Crossed the Rhine, *Parlez-vous*' and is well remembered by this author from his rugby-playing days. (See Trench Songs.)

ARMOUR/IRON RATION – An emergency ration carried by soldiers.

ARSAPEEK – ANZAC term for upside down, comparable to 'arse over head'.

AUNTIE – ANZAC term for a Turkish broomstick bomb. Used as a warning, as in 'Auntie coming over!'

AUSSIE, AN or **AUSTRALIA, AN** – A sufficiently severe injury to be shipped back to Australia.

ATROCITIES – In *Catastrophe: Europe Goes to War 1914* (2013), Max Hastings makes the persuasive case that these were the doing of the Central Powers, for instance through the German policy of 'frightfulness' and the Ottomans' Armenian Genocide. Propaganda spread rumours of atrocities on all sides: for example, in the attack on the Hindenburg Line in 1918, Australian troops captured the entrance to the St Quentin Canal tunnel. Inside was a kitchen where German bodies were found, one of them in a cooking cauldron. There were wild claims that the enemy was boiling down the dead, and this was exploited by the Allied propaganda system. Anti-German sentiment was so strong that it was widely believed. An investigation soon proved that, during the fighting, a shell had exploded in an improvised kitchen, killing the unfortunate Germans and throwing one into a pot.

ATTRITION, WAR OF – War in which each side seeks to wear the other out, the expression dating from the war. Victory is determined purely by which side is better able to endure numerous and prolonged casualties, as opposed to a war in which victory is determined by accomplishing a specific objective, such as capturing a major city.

At the start of the war, the cavalry was still the premier branch of military service, and army commanders, nearly all ex-cavalrymen, believed that it would be like the last great European conflict, the Franco-Prussian War of 1870–71. Prussia had been a German principality until that war, when it united all of Germany into the German Empire, the first time in history that there had ever been a 'Germany'. The Franco-Prussian War had taught commanders that offence could beat defence, as an attacking army could outmanoeuvre a static enemy on the defensive.

AWOL – Absent without leave from the military. The first known use is in 1918. Of 3,000 British troops arrested for desertion, 10 per cent were shot. In the Second World War, Germany shot 15,000 men for the same offence, and Stalin personally signed the order in 1941 which led to 158,000 Russians being executed and their families being persecuted.

AXLE GREASE – ANZAC term for butter.

BABY KILLERS – Civilian casualties made the Zeppelins an object of hatred, widely dubbed as this.

BABY'S HEAD – Meat pudding, part of the British Army field ration, made with meat, flour, suet, onion, baking powder, pepper and salt.

BABY'S HEAD, TWICE – After the war, in London Docklands this was a lump of suet in gravy, followed by a lump of suet in custard.

BACKSHISH, BACKSHEESH, BUCKSHEE –Free of charge, or a tip. From Arabs begging for cigarettes or chocolate by offering free services as a guide, etc.

BAGS OF – ANZAC term for a great number or amount, e.g. 'We had bags of shrapnel on the beach last night.'

BALLOO – Bailleul, French town near the Belgian border, 12 miles south-west of Ypres.

BALLOON GOES UP – The beginning of just about any enterprise, originally referring to an observation balloon sent up to give gunners directions for firing.

BANGALORE TORPEDO – Explosive tube used to clear a path through a wire entanglement.

BANGER – Sausage.

BANJO – ANZAC term for a spade, entrenching tool.

BANQUETTE – Fire-step, the step incorporated into the front base of a trench that enabled its occupants to fire over the parapet.

BANTAM – Member of a battalion made up of men between the heights of 5 feet 1 inch and 5 feet 4 inches, previously too short to have been enlisted.

BARBED WIRE (1) – This was used by all sides to prevent movement of men. Entanglements were placed in front of trenches to prevent direct charges on men below, increasingly leading to greater use of more advanced weapons such as high-powered machine guns and grenades. A feature of these entanglements compared to modern barbed wire was that the barbs were stronger, longer and much closer together, often forming a continuous sequence. Barbed wire could be exposed to heavy bombardments because it could be easily replaced, and its structure included so much open space that machine guns or artillery rarely destroyed enough of it. 'It is simply murder at this part of the line. There is one of our officers hanging on the German barbed wire and a lot of attempts have been made to get him and a lot of brave men have lost their lives in the attempt. The Germans know that we are sure to try and get him in so all they have to do is to put two or three fixed rifles on to him and fire every few seconds – he must be riddled with bullets by now: he was leading a bombing party one night and got fixed in the wire – the raid was a failure.' From a letter by Private Jack Sweeney to his girlfriend.

BARBED WIRE (2) – By 1916, the staple of the German soldier's diet was a mixture of dried vegetables, mostly beans, that the *frontsoldaten* called *drahtverhau*, barbed wire, as it could cut a dry mouth.

BARKER (1) – A pistol, perhaps because it looked like a barking iron, a tool to take bark from trees, or from the noise a pistol makes when fired.

BARKER (2) – A sausage, from the uncertainty surrounding the meat content.

BARRAGE – An excessive number or quantity, after the massive artillery barrages of the war, which always seemed excessive. The

British and French each killed 75,000 of their own men with their artillery barrages, inappropriately named 'friendly fire'.

BASE RAT – A soldier perpetually at the base, therefore in comfort and safety. Also known as a 'base wallah'.

BASKET CASE – This term comes from the US military. In March 1919, the *Syracuse Herald* reported, 'By "basket case" is meant a soldier who has lost both arms and legs and therefore must be carried in a basket.' The term later came to be applied to someone in a hopeless mental condition.

BATTERIE DE CUISINE – French for cookware, referring to medals and decorations. As an interesting comment on the insignificance of medals to common soldiers, German *frontsoldaten* scathingly called all decorations *zinnwaren*, tinware.

BATTERY – A group of six guns or howitzers.

BATTLE BOWLER – A steel helmet, the 'tin hat' first introduced to British troops in February 1916. Term used mainly by officers.

BATTLE ORDER – British term for reduced infantry equipment. The pack was removed and the haversack put in its place, to reduce weight and facilitate movement in action.

BATTLE POLICE – Armed military police patrols deployed in the trenches following attacks, used to deal with stragglers and men who had refused to go over the top, possibly by summary execution.

BEER BOY – An inexperienced person, only fit for fetching beer, especially a poor flyer. RFC/RAF expression, possibly derived from the phonetic alphabet.

BEETLE – ANZAC term for a landing craft for 200 men.

BEF – British Expeditionary Force. After the bloodbath of Ypres, of the BEF's eighty-four infantry battalions of around 1,000 men each, seventy-five mustered fewer than 300 men. Eighteen were reduced to fewer than 100 troops.

BEFORE YOUR NUMBER WAS DRY – Expression used by more experienced soldiers to new recruits as a form of putdown, e.g. 'I was killing Germans before your number was dry' – i.e. before the ink on the junior soldier's enlistment papers was dry.

BELGIAN RATTLESNAKE – The Lewis gun, a .303-calibre light machine gun.

BELLIED – A term used when a tank's underside was caught upon an obstacle so high that its tracks could not grip the earth.

BELLY ACHE (1) – A serious, often mortal wound, usually a shot in the gut.

BELLY ACHE (2) – ANZAC term used as a verb: 'He was always bellyaching about the food.'

BELLY FLOP – To hit the ground quickly during an attack.

BERGOO – ANZAC term for porridge, possibly from Arabic.

BERM – Ledge on a trench parapet for storing ammunition and other equipment.

BERT – Albert was a large town in the Somme region of France, which remained in Allied hands throughout the conflict.

BIG ACK – The Armstrong Whitworth FK8, a general-purpose British aeroplane.

BIG BERTHA – Huge Krupp 42 cm siege guns used to attack the Belgian forts at Liège and Namur in the opening of the war, although the term generally applied to large German artillery pieces. They were made at the Skoda Works, run by Bertha Krupp (1886–1957), great-granddaughter of the firm's founder Alfred Krupp. In 1918, Paris was shelled by the 142-ton 'Paris' gun, which was also called Big Bertha.

BIG GAME HUNTER – Major Hesketh Vernon Hesketh-Prichard (1876–1922) was said to be the world's greatest marksman and an expert big game hunter. He organised and trained British snipers.

BIG PUSH – British reference to 1916 Battle of the Somme. Later the battle was known to troops as 'the Great Cock-Up'.

BIG SHOW – Americanism for the Meuse-Argonne Offensive, the largest American battle of the war.

BILLJIM – An Australian. Composite word formed from two popular Australian forenames, Bill and Jim.

BINGE – Originally a Lancashire term to describe overindulgence of alcohol, it came into national usage in the war.

BINT – A young woman. From the Arabic *bint*, meaning daughter. To 'go binting' meant to go on leave to Cairo to look for women.

BIRDIE – ANZAC nickname for General Birdwood, who, according to his troops, was a 'decent enough bloke'.

BIVVY – Short for bivouac, a form of temporary shelter. 'To bivvy up' was to set up shelter, usually for the night.

BLACK HAND – A nationalist organisation in Serbia, believed responsible for the assassination of Archduke Franz Ferdinand.

BLACK HAND GANG – A trench raiding party or a selected group engaged in some desperate enterprise.

BLACK STRAP – Coffee brewed and ready to be served.

BLANCO – Block used to whiten full-dress webbing. However, khaki blanco was used on service equipment.

BLANK CHEQUE – Kaiser Wilhelm's unconditional promise to defend Austria-Hungary if Russia attacked it while Austria-Hungary was invading Serbia. The guarantee was made on 5 July 1914, a week after Archduke Ferdinand's assassination.

BLIGHTY – England, home. This was the most well-known term derived from Hindi, coming from *bilati*, meaning foreign. When applied by Indians to Britons, it came to be perceived by Indian Army servicemen as the term 'British'. The British in India came to refer to Britain as Blighty and those in the trenches picked it up.

BLIGHTY ONE or **BLIGHTY WOUND** – A wound serious enough to require the recipient to be sent home to England. Self-inflicted 'blighty wounds' were a capital offence. Although none were executed, nearly 4,000 Britons were convicted of self-inflicted wounds (SIWs) and were sent to prison. In France, General Fayolle noted in a meeting of generals that General Pétain had ordered that twenty-five soldiers who had self-inflicted wounds should be bound and thrown into no man's land. In the French Army, the mail of soldiers was censored and analysed by the Postal Control of the Grand Quartier General. He reported in 1916, according to Richard Watt, that 'the man in the ranks is no longer aware of why he is fighting. He has lost both faith and enthusiasm. He carries out his duties mechanically. He may become the victim of the greatest discouragement, display the worst weakness.' Life in the trenches was becoming intolerable and dangerous. The German equivalent of the time was a *heimatschuss* (home shot), or an *urlaubschuss* (a leave shot), or even a *Deutschlandschuss* (a shot that gets one to Germany). Australians called it 'an Aussie'. The Americans had a comparable term during the Vietnam War. The USA was known as 'the world', and a 'blighty one' was known to US soldiers as a 'ticket to the world', i.e. back home.

BLIMP – RAF slang for their small, white, powered dirigible airships, used chiefly for submarine reconnaissance over the English Channel.

BLIND PIG – Mortar bomb.

BLIND SPOT – First World War pilots complained of 'blind spots', where they were unable to see other aircraft or ground anti-aircraft positions.

BLOCK HOUSE, PILLBOX – These were miniature reinforced concrete forts developed by the German Army to give their trench lines extra strength. 'Pillbox' was used by British soldiers as they were the same shape as the boxes in which chemists supplied tablets during the war. Pillboxes generally measured 30 feet along the front and were about 10 feet wide. German machine gunners were often housed inside pillboxes, which were difficult to destroy with artillery. During an enemy offensive, machine guns were placed either on the top or at the side of the pillbox. The British built very few machine gun pillboxes. Probably the reason was that the High Command feared that if the troops had such solid defences they would be less offensively minded.

Germans built machine gun block houses in large numbers all along the line at Ypres and Messines. Machine gunners were deeply hated by the infantry and they were more likely to be killed when captured than other soldiers.

BLOOD ORANGE – Nickname, probably from rhyming slang for the unpopular, rude and bullying Lieutenant-Colonel Sir George Gorringe (1868–1945). Unsuccessful in relieving Townshend at Kut, he was redeployed to the Western Front, and, unusually, was not promoted during the war.

BLOTTO – Pre-war slang for drunkenness, but during the war it referred to strong liquor.

BLUEBELL – A popular proprietary brand of metal polish. It was joked that the motto of the Brigade of Guards – '*honi soit qui mal y pense*' – could be freely translated as 'after you with the Bluebell, Rupert'.

BLUE CROSS – German respiratory irritant gases, from the marking painted on the delivery shell casing.

BLUE MAX – Nickname for German medal awarded to Rommel, von Richthofen, and others.

BOCHE – Disparaging epithet for anything German. It was used primarily by officers, as the infantry used 'Fritz'. Derived from French *caboche*, thickhead. Many popular songs were altered by troops, e.g. 'If You Were the Only Girl in the World' had the following first verse: 'If you were the only Boche in the trench,/And I had the only bomb,/Nothing else would matter in the world that day./I would blow you up into eternity./A Chamber of Horrors, just made for two,/With nothing to spoil our fun;/There would be such a heap of things to do,/I should get your rifle and bayonet too,/If you were the only Boche in the trench,/And I had the only gun.'

BOCHE-BUSTER – British 14 inch railway-mounted gun.

BODY-SNATCHER (1) – A stretcher bearer.

BODY-SNATCHER (2) – ANZAC term for a member of a raiding party, as they often had to try and bring in a prisoner for information.

BOKO – Much, plenty, from French *beaucoup*.

BOMBARDIER (1) – Potatoes, from the French *pommes de terre*.

BOMBARDIER (2) – A Royal Artillery corporal.

BOMBER – A soldier trained in using hand grenades, referred to early in the war as a grenadier. The Grenadier Guards protested to the War Office about the use of the term grenadier, claiming that the title was exclusively theirs, and in May 1916 'bomber' became officially used.

BON – Good, fine. From the French. When off duty, men would often be found having a 'bon time' at the local cafe. The opposite was 'no bon'.

BONK – To shell with artillery fire. Usually used in passive sense of being bonked, but later came to be used as slang for the sex act.

BONZER, BOSHTER, BOSKER, BONSTERINA, BONTOSHER – ANZAC term meaning very, very; expressing a superlative quality of something. A superlative of 'bon'.

BOOJUM – Tank.

BOOTLEG – Coffee.

BOURRAGE – Universally hated by French troops as '*bourrage de crone*' (head stuffing, i.e. false stories) and '*hurrah-patriotismus*' (hurrah patriotism), journalistic prose significantly shaped civilian attitudes about the war and soldiers' attitudes toward the jingoistic press. No journalist dared to really report the horrors of the front lines. French troops even called the official war bulletin '*le petit menteur*', the little liar.

BOX BARRAGE – Artillery bombardment on a small area.

BOYAU – Meaning 'gut' in French, a communication trench. The British called it a **BOY-OH**.

BRASS HATS or **BRASS** – High-ranking staff officers, from the gold decoration on the peaked cap. Also TOP BRASS – Highest-ranking officers.

BREAK NEW GROUND – To do something not done before, probably an allusion to digging a new trench.

BREEZE-UP – Variation of wind-up.

BRITISH WARM – An overcoat, knee-length and close fitting at the waist, worn by mounted troops and officers.

BRODIE – British steel helmet, introduced originally for snipers only in February 1916. The design can be traced back to the type of helmet worn by archers at Agincourt in 1415, and is named after its inventor, John L. Brodie.

BROOMSTICK BOMB – Turkish 4-inch cartridge filled with high explosive and metal scraps, with a percussion cap. It was placed on a 2-inch-thick and 5-foot-long stick and could be hurled a great distance.

BROTHELS – There was no discrimination between ranks in Paris, whereas in the British sector of France and Belgium as well as in the UK there were hotels and cafes for officers only, as well as brothels in France. The Army permitted troops to visit licensed brothels, as sex was considered a physical necessity for the men. The *maisons de tolérance* with blue lamps were for officers, and those with red lamps for the other ranks.

BUCK PRIVATE – Americanism for a private without any stripes.

BUCKSHEE – Free, spare. From Arabic/Hindustani *baksheesh*, or gratuity.

BUDDY – This term for friend became popular among Americans,

Burton Library
24hr Renewal Line
Tel: 0845 330 0740

Borrowed Items 22/09/2016 14:23
XXXXXXXXX2565

Item Title	Due Date
* Quest	13/10/2016
* Breverton's First World War curiosities	13/10/2016
* Big Sam my autobiography	13/10/2016

* Indicates items borrowed today
Thank you for using Self Serve

Thank you for visiting Your Library
www.staffordshire.gov.uk/libraries

probably deriving from the Welsh slang 'butty', formerly used down coalpits as a term for workmates, and still in use today.

BUGWARM – Small trench dugout.

BULL – Shortened version of Bullshit. Slang for unnecessary work, especially cleaning.

BULLETS IN A POT, or **REPEATERS AND PORK** – Pork and beans.

BULL RING – British Army training establishment such as those base camps at Rouen, Harfleur, Havre and Étaples. Men were posted here from the front line for refresher training, and to 'inculcate the offensive spirit', thereby suffering the full consequences of bullshit. The Bull Ring at Étaples was notorious for its severe discipline.

BULLSHIT – Nonsense; empty talk. Later to deceive a person or pull his leg. Probably of Australian provenance.

BULLY BEEF – Canned, 'corned', boiled or pickled beef, which was a staple in the British Army. It was the principal protein ration. 'Bully' is believed to be a corruption of the French *bouilli*, meaning boiled. As the war went on and German rations suffered, German troops rarely returned from trench raids without tins of bully beef. It was hated by the troops in Gallipoli, where it formed the main diet with hard biscuits. After being stored for a length of time on the beaches, it often turned into a liquid mass of fat. A well-known trench story has it that when supplies were thrown across no man's land to the Turkish positions, a tin of bully came sailing back. On it a scribbled note read: 'cigarettes yes, bully beef no'. The only exception to the rule was perhaps Maconochie's, a brand of tinned beef that was appreciated for its superior quality.

BUMBRUSHER – Anzac term for the personal servant of an officer, also known as a 'batman'.

BUMF – Toilet paper, or newspaper used for that purpose. Later it came to mean any excessive official documentation. It is still used today to describe bits of official paperwork that have only one practical use. From bum fodder, an eighteenth-century expression.

BUNDOOK – Rifle, from Arabic/Hindustani for firearm, originally meaning a crossbow. Native Egyptians once called Venice *Bundookia*, place of the big guns, from its Arsenal area.

BUNG – Cheese, as it was thought to cause constipation.

BUNKER – Fortification set mostly below ground level with overhead protection, probably from coal bunker.

BURGOO, BERGOO – Porridge, from Arabic/Turkish/Hindustani *burghul*, oatmeal porridge.

BUS – Royal Flying Corps expression for aeroplane, from the abbreviated form of omnibus.

BUZZ OFF – ANZAC term for going or running away.

C3 – Low-grade, worthless, from the lowest British Army classification of fitness – those fit only for base duty.

CAGE – Prisoner of war camp.

CAMEL DUNG – Egyptian cigarettes, from the smell, according to ANZAC troops.

CANARY – Instructor, often seen at the 'Bull Ring'. From the yellow armband they wore.

CANNED HORSE – US term for canned beef.

CANTEEN MEDALS – Beer or food stains on the breast of a tunic.

CASE-SHOT – Short-range anti-personnel artillery shell filled with pellets, chain links, etc.

CAVALRY – At the beginning of the war, mounted troops were still considered as the main component of offensive warfare. In battle, members of the cavalry carried a sword, rifle (for use when dismounted) and sometimes a lance. In 1914, most of the major armies had around a third of their strength in horsemen. Nearly all the senior officers all armies were ex-cavalry officers and it has been claimed that this explained the type of tactics used on the Western Front. Their reconnaissance value was rendered obsolete by aircraft.

CENTRAL POWERS – An alliance during the First World War that originally consisted of Germany and Austria-Hungary. Other nations, including Bulgaria and the Ottoman Empire, joined later.

CHAR – Tea, as in 'a nice cup of char', from Hindustani *char* or Chinese *ch'a*.

CHARPOY – Bed, from Hindustani.

CHAT – Body louse, possibly derived from chattel, personal belonging.

CHATBAGS – ANZAC term for underclothes.

CHATTING (1) – De-lousing. See also crumbing up.

CHATTING (2) – Conversing in an informal manner. Soldiers who spent many an hour removing 'chats' from the seams of their clothing passed the time in discussions with their mates. This led to the rapid popularising of the word chatting, which had been in use since the sixteenth century.

CHATTY – ANZAC term meaning verminous.

CHERB – Beer, from Hindustani.

CHEVEUX DE FRISE – Defensive barbed wire entanglement, sometimes with sharpened stakes. From French for frizzy hair.

CHINESE ATTACK – Fake attack. A preliminary bombardment would stop and the defending enemy would return to their trenches to face the presumed attack. Then the bombardment would start up again, catching the defenders out of their shelters.

CHIN-STRAPPED – Tired, exhausted. From the sense that a man could be so tired he was held upright only by the chinstrap of his cap or helmet. Generally speaking, chinstraps were employed only by mounted troops, other soldiers believing that if a bullet or piece of shrapnel were to strike their helmet, the chinstrap may cause choking or break their jaw.

CHIPPEROW – Quiet, shut up, from Hindustani *chuprao*.

CHIT – Note or receipt. To be excused duties, a soldier had to be in possession of a 'sick chit'. From Hindustani *cittha*, a note.

CHOCS – Members of the 8th Brigade AIF that arrived in Egypt just after the Gallipoli Campaign was over, and therefore did not take part in the fighting. This well-drilled brigade under Col E. Tivey were afterwards referred to by the Gallipoli veterans as 'Tivey's Chocolate soldiers', 'Tivey's Chocs' or 'Tivey's Pets'.

CHOKEY – Jail, from Hindustani *cauki*, a lockup.

CHOW – US term for food or rations. A chow hall is a military dining hall.

CHRONIC – Very bad. The correct meaning of this word is long-lasting, although seldom used in this way except perhaps by medical officers.

CHUB, CHUP – Abbreviated form of *chipperow*.

CHUM – Several phrases from the criminal underworld entered wider use, among them 'chum', formerly slang for an accomplice.

CIVILIAN CASUALTIES – Around 9 million civilians died during the war, and the following contemporary limerick succinctly summarises both the dangers of war and English attitudes to the bagpipes: 'There was a young lady of Wipers [Ypres]/Who was hit in the cheek by two snipers./The tunes that they played/Through the holes that they made/Beat the Argyll and Sutherland pipers.'

CIVVY – Civilian. To be 'in civvies' was to be dressed in civilian clothing, rather than uniform.

CLOBBER – ANZAC term for clothes.

CLOUT – ANZAC term for a wound.

CO – Commanding Officer. In the British Army, the term CO generally referred to the lieutenant-colonel in command of an infantry battalion or cavalry regiment.

COAL-BOX – Heavy German shell, usually a 5.9-inch, from the black smoke of the shell burst.

COAL SCUTTLE – German steel helmet, or *stahlhelm*, introduced at Verdun in January 1916. From the similar appearance to domestic fireside coal container.

COBBER – ANZAC term for a mate, a friend.

COFFIN NAILS – A term used by British soldiers to describe cigarettes.

COLD FEET – Cowardice. To become discouraged, possibly linked to trench foot or trench fever.

COLD MEAT TICKET – Identity disc. Men were issued with two of these, either of metal or red-and-green composite material. These gave the name, number, unit and religion of the holder. In the event of death, one disc was taken from the body (the cold meat) for records and one remained on the corpse for identification.

COLD STORAGE, IN – Killed in the bitter winter of 1916 or 1917.

COME UNSTUCK – Following exchanges with the French troops, officers who were sacked or demoted sacked were said to have 'COME UNGUMMED', from the French '*dégommér*', to dismiss. This quickly developed into 'come unstuck'.

COMIC CUTS – Corps Intelligence Summary, named after a kid's comic.

COMMISSARIES – US term for groceries.

COMMUNICATION TRENCH – Narrow trench constructed at an angle to a defensive trench, to permit concealed access to the trench.

COMSAH – Generic name for anything, from French *comme ça*, 'like that'.

CONCHIE – Conscientious objector.

CONK OUT – The dying sign of an engine, also referring to someone's death. It was the American Air Service expression representing the last sound of a disengaging aircraft engine.

CONSCRIPTION – In 1914, the British Army had approximately 710,000 men at its disposal. Lord Kitchener recognised that the British Army was far too small and wanted to build an army of seventy divisions. In August 1914, the government called for an extra 100,000 volunteer soldiers to come forward. They had 750,000 volunteers by the end of September, and by January 1915 more than a million had joined the armed forces. By mid-1915 volunteer numbers were falling fast and the National Registration Act was created. It was a list of all the men fit for military service who were still available. Conscription was introduced in January 1916, targeting single men aged eighteen to forty-one. Within a few months First World War conscription was then rolled out for married men.

CONSCIENTIOUS OBJECTORS – Men who were called up for service could appeal to a local Military Service Tribunal. Reasons included health, already doing important war work, or moral or religious reasons. The last group became known as the conscientious objectors. Some 750,000 men appealed against their conscription in the first six months. Most were granted exemption of some sort, even if it was only temporary. Only 2 per cent of those who appealed were conscientious objectors. Only 6,000 were sent to prison. Thirty-five received a death sentence but were reprieved immediately and given a ten-year prison sentence instead.

COOL – ANZAC term for someone reluctant to join the AIF, someone still living in Australia. Mostly used in plural form.

COOT, COOTIE – Body louse. Pre-war term, said to be derived from a titled lady who had suffered this misfortune. Brought by British Army from Malaya.

COPPING A CLOUT – Getting wounded.

CORKSCREW – Looped steel post, or picket, for staking barbed wire at night. The corkscrew shape at the end enabled the stake to be twisted quietly into the ground by wiring parties. Previously, the noise of hammering stakes in had attracted enemy fire.

CORNED BILL/CORNED WILLIE/SIR WILLIAM/WILLIE/BILL – Canned corned beef.

CORP – Corporal. Familiar term used by lower ranks.

CORPSE'S CLOTHING – German front-line troops called their uniform a *leichenkleid* (corpse's clothing), and their groundsheet a *leichentuch* (winding sheet) or a *heldensarg* (hero's sarcophagus).

COVERING PARTY – A detachment of soldiers protecting a working-party in the front line.

COW (1) – UK term for milk (UK).

COW (2) – ANZAC term for an obnoxious person in whose company a 'dinkum' soldier would not be seen.

CRAB – ANZAC term for a louse. Mostly used in plural form. See also 'chat'.

CRASSIER – Slagheap of mining spoil, such as those prominent on the battlefield around Loos and exploited to great effect by German observers and snipers. See also Fosse. From the French, who originally produced the trench maps of these areas.

CREEPING BARRAGE – Artillery bombardment with a range that was extended at timed intervals so as to avoid hitting one's own advancing troops.

CRICKET BALL (1) – British Number 15 hand grenade, a spherical bomb. Used with good effect in the Gallipoli Campaign, it was unsuccessful at the Battle of Loos in September 1915, because wet conditions rendered useless the external friction fuse igniter. It was superseded by the Mills bomb in late 1915.

CRICKET BALL (2) – Turkish hand grenade of that shape and size. Depending on the length of the fuse, it was often possible to hurl them back before they exploded in a trench.

CRUCIFIXION – If a man was sentenced while on active service, he became liable to a range of punishments, including 'Field Punishment Number One', popularly known as 'crucifixion'. The offender was kept in irons and attached to a 'fixed object' for up to two hours a day and for a period up to three months and the fixed object was not specified. The procedure was not standardised, and allegations arose that men were being attached to the wheels of guns in emplacements that were within range of enemy shellfire.

CRUMBING UP – De-lousing. See also chatting.

CRUMMY – To be itchy or lousy because of louse bites. A reference to the eggs of the lice, nits, being like crumbs of bread.

CRUMP – German 5.9-inch shell or the onomatopoeic burst it made. The **LAST CRUMP** referred to the end of the war.

CUBBY HOLE – Small dugout or shelter in the side wall of a trench. A 'funk hole' for those in a 'state of funk', possibly derived from cupboard.

CURIO – A battlefield souvenir, usually taken from a dead enemy. See also 'souvy'.

CUSHY (1) – Easy, pleasant. Soldiers would describe cushy, or comfortable billets, as well as cushy trenches, in quiet sectors. From Hindustani *khush*, pleasant.

CUSHY (2) – A minor wound necessitating some time away from the front line; perhaps a Blighty one. 'A bloke in the Munsters once wanted a cushy, so he waves his hand above the parapet to catch Fritz's attention.' – Pte Fry, Royal Welch Fusiliers.

DAISIES – Boots, from Cockney rhyming slang – daisy roots.

DAISY CUTTER – Shell with an impact fuse (graze fuse) designed to explode immediately on contact with the ground. Used in the clearance of barbed wire defences and also used as an anti-personnel bomb. Seems to have an ANZAC origin.

D-DAY – Initial day of a military operation, first used by American First Army at Saint-Mihiel on 12 September 1918.

DEEP THINKERS – Men belonging to reinforcements in the last stages of the war, mainly members of the General Monash's 'pampered' 3rd Division. Called thus because of the length of time needed to take the decision to join. The other four Australian divisions, all serving on the Somme, also called them **THE NEUTRALS**.

DEKKO – Look, observe. From Hindustani *dekho*, look, and *dekhna*, to see.

DERBY MEN, DERBY SCHEME – Men recruited under a voluntary scheme instituted by Lord Derby before conscription became law in 1916. Young and unmarried men were called for service before the others.

DER TAG – German for *the day*. From the German nationalist movement, in the First World War it came to refer to the day when conquest would begin.

DESPERATE FRANKIE – General Franchet d'Esperey.

DEVIL DODGER – Army chaplain.

DEVIL DOGS – Nickname given to the US Marines by Germans who faced them at Belleau Wood. The Germans in this sector had previously come to admire the huge mastiffs guarding a chateau in the nearby village of Belleau.

DICK SHOT OFF – The Distinguished Service Order, or DSO, an 'officers only' award. Ordinary soldiers substituted this disparaging phrase when referring to superiors who they disliked, e.g. General Rupert Fortescue-Smythe, Dick Shot Off. Over 9,000 were awarded in the war.

DIGGER (1) – Australian soldier.

DIGGER (2) – Less commonly, friend, chum. Originally from the miners of the nineteenth-century Australian gold fields. Resurrected by members of 1915 Gallipoli expedition who had to dig into cliffs to survive.

DIGGING IN – To establish one's position, as if digging a defensive trench.

DIG ONESELF IN – Establish one's position strongly, from entrenching.

DINGO – Mad, insane, from the French *dingot*.

DINKUM – Genuine, right, real, original, vintage. Something proper was said to be **FAIR DINKUM**. Among Australian troops, those who had served at Gallipoli were known as '**THE DINKUM**'. **DINKUMS** were Aussies. **FAIR DINKUMS** were volunteers. **DINKUM OIL** was true news, the truth. Also the name of a trench publication of the Australian 1st Division in June and July 1915.

DITCHED – A tank became ditched when the ground beneath became so soft or waterlogged as to prevent the tracks from gripping it and moving.

DIVISIONAL COMIC CUTS – Reports from Divisional Headquarters. These Corps Intelligence Summaries contained morale-boosting and often false information to increase morale for the troops and those at home. The serving troops realised this. *Comic Cuts* was a humorous paper of the time for children.

DIVVY – A division.

DIXIE – British camp kettle. Large, oval-shaped metal pot with lid and carrying-handle for cooking. The lid was often used for baking, e.g. bacon and biscuit pudding, while the pot itself was employed to brew tea, heat porridge, stew, rice, etc. From Hindustani *degchi*, small pot.

DOCK – Hospital. To **BE IN DOCK** was to be confined to hospital, due to wounds or sickness. From the nautical expression for ship repair yards.

DOCTOR'S ORDERS – See No. 9.

DODGING THE COLUMN – Shirking, the art of avoiding particularly dangerous or unpleasant duties. The expression originated in India and South Africa, a column being a body of troops sent forward into hostile territory.

DOG AND MAGGOT – Bread and cheese.

DOGFIGHT – Air combat at close quarters, based on the scrambling, twisting appearance of air warfare from the ground. The term dogfight originated during the First World War. The pilot had to turn off the plane's engine from time to time so it would not stall when the plane turned quickly and sharply in the air. When a pilot restarted his engine mid-air, it sounded like a dog barking.

DOGGO – In hiding and keeping quiet, probably from dog: 'All day we lie doggo in the dugout, partly because of the machine gun trained on the door, and partly because no good was to be got by going outside.'

DOG HOLE – Churchill remembered, 'There is a constant spice of danger. Daily shells, some very near; and a certain amount of risk in moving about by day and night. I have also had my tiny dog hole where I sleep in the line smashed up by a shell which, had it detonated perfectly, would have been the end of my chequered fortunes.'

DONKEY WALLOPER – British cavalryman, especially a member of the Household Cavalry. The expression originated among the regiments of British Foot Guards, the longstanding rivals of the Household Cavalry.

DOUGHBOY – U S soldier. Originally an American flour dumpling. Long a disparaging name for American infantrymen, its usage broadened and became far more positive in the war.

DRAFTEE – Conscript soldier (US). The aggregate of a call-up cycle became known as a draft, so draftee was the natural term for an individual who had been selected.

DRAW CRABS – To attract enemy artillery fire.

DRUM FIRE – Artillery barrage fired not in a salvo but by each gun in succession.

DRY RATIONS – A sermon.

DUCKBOARD (1) – Boards were laid in the bottom of trenches to try and keep the mud out of the soldiers' boots and allay trench foot and were used as walkways across muddy ground. Soldiers had felt like ducks, sloshing thorough the pools.

DUCKBOARD (2) – The ribbon of the British Military Medal, awarded for bravery in the field. The striped design of the ribbon resembled the wooden slats of duckboards.

DUCKBOARD HARRIER – Runner or messenger, from the term for a cross-country runner, originally derived from hare.

DUCKBOARD TRAIL – US term, as in 'someone hit the duckboard trail' – killed in action.

DUD (1) – A shell or bomb that fails to explode.

DUD (2) – Later, a person or enterprise that proves to be a failure, especially an officer. A soldiers' magazine had the following definition: 'DUDS – These are of two kinds. A shell on impact failing to explode is called a dud. They are unhappily not as plentiful as the other kind, which often draws a big salary and explodes for no reason. These are plentiful away from the fighting areas.' In 1918, J. F. C. Fuller wrote, 'Presumably victory is our object. This war is a business proposition; it therefore requires ability. Nevertheless, our army is crawling with "duds", though habitual offenders, they are tolerated because of the camaraderie of the old Regular Army: an army so small as to permit all of its higher members being personal friends. Good-fellowship ranks with us above efficiency: the result is a military trade union that does not pay a dividend.'

DUFF (1) – Pudding, especially boiled suet pudding.

DUFF (2) – To perform incompetently, or a useless person.

DUFF (3) – To beat up someone, as in 'duff up'.

DUGOUT (1) – An underground shelter, in a bank, side of a hill or more commonly a trench. In the wall of a trench, it could vary from a small area that could only accommodate one man (a **CUBBY HOLE**), to a deep dugout, 10 or more feet underground.

DUGOUT (2) – An officer who has been 'dug out' from retirement and recalled to active duty, usually much to his displeasure and the dissatisfaction of those under him.

DUG-OUT DISEASE – Term for fear, which kept those thus affected, including those of higher rank who had the choice, within the safety of their dugouts.

DUM-DUM – A split- or soft-nosed rifle round (bullet). The tip would open out on impact, causing horrific wounds. Named after the arsenal at *Dum-Dum*, a town near Calcutta.

DUMP – Temporary depot where supplies are left for distribution, from the US term for a pile of refuse.

EAT APPLES or **EETAPPS** – Étaples. French town between Calais and Boulogne, the site of many base depots and hospitals, and of the notorious 'Bull Ring'. Conditions within the town were so repressive that in 1917 a mutiny provoked by Military Police broke out among British troops stationed there.

EGG – German hand grenade, from the flattened spherical shape. Sometimes also a mine.

EGGS-A-COOK – Boiled eggs sold by Arab street vendors. Later on, in Gallipoli, it was used by the troops as a war cry when going 'over the top'.

ELEPHANT – Small dugout reinforced with semi-circular sheets of corrugated iron.

ELEVENTH HOUR – Just in time, at the last moment. The armistice of the First World War came into effect on the eleventh hour of the eleventh day of the eleventh month.

EMMA-GEE – Machine gun, from the phonetic alphabet of the time for the letters MG.

ENFILADE – To fire down a trench or at a row of men lengthways, rather than crossways.

EN-ZEDDERS – ANZAC term for New Zealanders.

ERSATZ – Substitute, artificial, substandard foods and materials. From German *ersetzen*, to substitute. Food progressively became worse as the war dragged on. In Germany, coffee began to be made with roast nuts flavoured with coal tar, then with roast acorns and beech mast. After an order that acorns had to be fed to pigs, coffee was made from turnips and carrots. Flour to make bread was obtained from peas and beans, with the addition of sawdust as a filler. Meat substitutes were developed, and substitute eggs made from a mixture of maize and potatoes. Basically, civilian hunger was far more of a German problem, exacerbated by the Allied blockade of food reaching its ports. It is a major reason for the Allied victory. In October 1917, British bakers were allowed to add potato flour to bread.

ESTAMINET – Building found in villages and minor towns for the purpose of eating, drinking and the general entertainment of troops. A typical *estaminet* would have a low roof, an open iron stove and wooden benches and tables. The proprietress would serve wine, cognac, thin beer, coffee, soup, omelettes and the most popular of all French dishes of the time, egg and chips.

EYEWASH – Tidying up for inspection.

FAG – This term for cigarette was a shortened form of 'faggot', a small stick used for kindling.

FANTI – Mad, insane, from Hindustani.

FASHY – Angry, from French *fâché*. 'Dinna fash thissen', don't get upset, was heard by this author until very recently in the north-east of England. 'Dinnae Fash Yersel and Keep Yer Heid' is even now the Scottish version of 'Keep Calm and Carry On'.

'FAT KING' –Major Ellis, known as 'the Fat King', set up a fat extracting factory in France, using the thousands of dead horses, old food and animal waste. It was sent to Britain to be processed into glycerine for making TNT explosives. Thus if a horse had been killed by a German shell, it might be returned to them in kind.

FED-UP – Disgusted. First used in the Boer War and carried into the First World War by the British Army.

FINI KAPUT – Definitely gone, emphatically finished, 'napoo'. From French *finis*, end, and German *kaput*, done for.

FICHE BLANCHE – White ticket or non-movable casualty.

FICHE ROUGE – Red ticket or movable casualty.

FIELD DRESSING – Small bag of bandages and pins carried by each man for application to small wounds.

FIELD PUNISHMENT NO. 1 – Punishment of soldiers that involved being tied to a gun wheel and being put on a bread-and-water diet. The soldier was lashed by the wrists and ankles for an hour in the morning and an hour in the evening for up to twenty-one days, the intention being to humiliate him.

FIRE-STEP – A step on the forward face of a trench, upon which men stood to fire or observe.

FIVE-NINE – German 5.9-inch artillery shell. 'All went lame; all blind;/Drunk with fatigue; deaf even to the hoots/Of tired, outstripped Five-Nines that dropped behind.' – lines from 'Dulce et Decorum est' by Wilfred Owen (1893–1918).

FLAK – Anti-aircraft fire. From German *Flieger abwehr kanone*, aircraft defence gun.

FLEABAG (1)– Sleeping bag.

FLEABAG (2) – An old, run-down hotel or accommodation.

FLYING PIG – British 9.45-inch trench mortar bomb.

FLYING RAZOR – The Fokker E-V/D-VIII was nicknamed this by Allied pilots, and was the last plane to score a victory in the air in the First World War.

FOKKER SCOURGE, FOKKER SCARE, FLYING GUN – This was the Fokker Eindecker (monoplane) fighter. With its synchronised machine gun, in 1915 it was far superior to the poorly armed Allied aircraft then in service, giving the Germans a huge technological and psychological advantage for many months.

FOOD – A total of 3,240,948 tons of food was sent from Britain to the soldiers fighting in France and Belgium during the First World War. The bulk of the diet in the trenches was bully beef, bread and biscuits. The catering staff put the food in dixies (cooking pots), petrol cans or old jam jars and carried it up the communication trenches in straw-lined boxes. By the time the food reached the front line it was always cold.

FOOTBALL – Trench mortar bomb, from the shape.

FOOT-SLOGGER – British infantryman, an eighteenth-century term originally used by cavalrymen.

FOSSE – Slagheap of mining spoil, from French.

FOUR-TWO – German 4.2-inch artillery shell.

FRAY BENTOS (1) – Corned beef, bully beef, named after the prevalent brand.

FRAY BENTOS (2) – Very good, very well, from a corruption of the French *très bien*.

FRED KARNO'S ARMY – Nickname given to the British Army raised after the start of the war, in allusion to Fred Karno, a comedian and producer of burlesque. Also known as Kitchener's Army.

FRENCH GOODS, or **GOUT** – Syphilis. Seamen often suffered from this, picked up in foreign ports. To be 'Frenchified' was to suffer from venereal disease. 'Frenchman' was before the war applied to any foreigner, and was again a synonym for syphilis. The prevalence of venereal diseases was often the main reason for wanting a doctor on board ship. Even in recent times VD has been a problem among sailors. Lady Astor, the first female MP, elected in 1919, proposed that merchant seamen should wear a yellow armband to identify themselves as potential carriers of the disease.

FRIENDLY 48½, THE – Nickname given by the Germans to their 49th Artillery Regiment, which had a reputation for firing short, onto German troops.

FRIGHTFULNESS – German policy of intimidating populations in occupied territories, a translation of *schrecklichkeit*. In August 1914, German troops shot and killed 150 civilians at Aerschot, as part of this war policy. Its purpose was to terrify civilians in occupied areas so that they would not rebel.

FRITZ (1) – Sympathetic nickname for German soldiers by Allies. From 'Old Fritz' a name for Frederick the Great of Prussia (1712–86), from the diminutive of Friedrich.

FRITZ (2) – Potato chips, from the French *frites*.

FROG'S PARADISE – US name for Paris.

FRONTSCHWEIN – Literally, front-line pigs. Implied is the imminence of being slaughtered. German soldiers referred to themselves thus as pigs ready for being killed.

FUNK – State of nervousness, fear or depression, dejected mood. To shrink from action.

FUNK-HOLE – Small dugout or shelter, just big enough to accommodate one or two men, usually scraped into the front wall of a trench. Soldiers could retire there if not on duty.

FUNKY VILLAS – Foncquevillers, French village in the Pas-de-Calais.

FURPHY – A term for camp rumours, stemming from Broadmeadows Army Camp in Melbourne. The name 'Furphy Shepparton' was found on water carts that visited the camp and therefore brought news from outside. The troops in the training camps would gather around these carts for a drink and to exchange information. The stories or rumours that circulated became known as 'Furphies'. Later the word was taken with troops to Egypt. The company that ran the water supply in carts also ran the sanitary carts down the back alleys to collect the sewerage when sewage/septic tanks were not available. A 'furphy' thus also became literally a load of 'sewage' or some such term.

GAFFS – Term for makeshift theatres built behind the lines to entertain the troops.

GALLIPOLI GALLOP – See Turkey Trot.

GAS BAG (1) – The cloth bag in which the respirator was carried.

GAS BAG (2) – An airship or barrage balloon.

GASPER – Cheap cigarette.

GASPIRATOR – British gas mask incorporating a filter, from a combination of gas and respirator.

GASSED – Slang for tipsy or drunk, from the disorienting effects of a gas attack.

GAWK – ANZAC term for an exhausting 'stunt', or small operation, that accomplished nothing as far as the troops could see.

GI CAN – GI was the abbreviation for galvanised iron during the war and a GI can was a large trash receptacle. This was then applied as a nickname to large German artillery shells.

GIEVES, MATTHEW & SEAGROVE – Naval slang for the trio of First World War campaign medals of the 1914–15 Star, British War Medal and Victory Medal. From the well-known firm of naval outfitters. See also Pip, Squeak & Wilfred.

GIPPO, GYPO – Egyptian.

GIVE HER THE GUN – Slang expression, still used to expedite accelerating an engine. From First World War air operations.

GLASSHOUSE – Military prison or detention centre.

GLORY HOLE – Dugout.

GOGGLE-EYED BOOGER WITH THE TIT – British gas helmet with goggles. The wearer had to breathe in through the nose from inside the helmet and breathe out through a valve held in the teeth.

GOLDFISH LOAF – US term for canned salmon, not a favourite dish.

GOOSEBERRY – Barbed wire entanglement or reel, from the prickly nature of the gooseberry bush.

GO PHUT – To stop functioning or to come to grief. Hindustani term used by Kipling in the nineteenth century.

GORBLIMEY – Peaked canvas service cap, made sloppy in appearance by removing the wire stiffener from the crown, not usually seen until after the end of 1914. Thus meaning generally scruffy or sloppy. A Cockney expression, a corruption of 'God blind me'.

GO UP – To go up the line, i.e. into the trenches.

GO WEST (1) – To be killed, to die. The most popular euphemism of this type. From 'Go west towards the setting sun'. 'He's hopped it' was another phrase meaning someone had died. There was a taboo in actually saying directly that someone had died.

GO WEST (2) – To go astray or be stolen.

GRASS-CUTTERS – Small anti-personnel bombs dropped from aircraft on to camps and bivouacs behind the lines. They were designed to burst on impact and scatter shrapnel balls at low level, with the intention to kill rather than to destroy material things.

GREAT WAR, THE – The First World War. Formerly used for the Napoleonic Wars, it was first applied to the events in the October 1914 issue of *Maclean's* magazine.

GREEN CROSS – German phosgene gas, from the marking painted on the delivery shell casing.

GRENADES – German hand grenades, which had handles, quickly became known as 'potato mashers'. The oval hand grenades of France and Britain were called *les tortues*, turtles, by the French and *Ostereier*, Easter eggs, by the Germans.

GREYBACK (1) – British Army shirt, with sharp-edged tin buttons.

GREYBACK (2) – A louse.

GREY HEN – A grey-and-brown earthenware jug which contained the rum ration, usually Royal Navy Pusser's rum.

GRIFFIN – The bottom line, confidential information or warning of trouble to come.

GRUBBER – ANZAC term for a spade or entrenching tool.

GRUNGEY, GRUNGE – ANZAC term for a self-made dish consisting of bully beef, biscuits, onion, water and salt, served hot.

GUFF – Rumours.

GUM BOOTS – Rubber boots or waders sometimes worn in wet trenches.

GUNFIRE – Strong tea, usually laced with rum.

GÜTEN MORGEN – Usual term for 'Good morning' in Germany. Was universally replaced with **GOTT STRAFE ENGLAND**, God punish England. The greeting was rubberstamped on letters, printed on postcards and engraved on badges and gifts. German troops were issued with belt buckles stamped with **GOTT MIT UNS** – God is with us.

HARD TACK, TEETH DULLERS, SHEET IRON – British Army hard biscuits often accompanied bully beef and raw onions, but the French were known to use the biscuits as firelighters.

HARNESS – Infantryman's equipment, the two basic types being brown leather and khaki webbing. Although the webbing did not cut into the shoulders as much as the leather, it was considerably heavier when soaked with rain.

HATE – A bombardment. Troops in the trenches often had to endure a morning 'hour of hate', meaning an hour of artillery bombardment.

HAYBURNERS – US term for army horses and mules.

HEDGE-HOP – Flying near the ground.

HELLO GIRLS – American women who served as telephone operators for Pershing's forces in Europe. In 1979, the US Army finally gave war medals and veteran benefits to the few 'Hello Girls' who were still alive.

HIPE – Rifle. Derived from a drill sergeant's habit of malforming the last word of an order on the parade ground, as a way of achieving a crisper, sharper delivery. 'Slope arms!' became, in some cases, 'Slope hipe!'

HITCHY-KOO – Itchy from louse bites, from the chorus of a popular pre-war music hall song. This author remembers seeing Small Faces perform 'Itchycoo Park', based on a piece of wasteland full of nettles in Ilford. As kids they used to hang out there and received itches from the nettle stings.

HOLY JOE or **SKYSCOUT** – US term for a chaplain.

HOM FORTY – French railway carriage used for troop transportation, average speed one and a half miles per hour. From the load capacity stencilled on the side of the carriage: *Hommes* 40, *Chevaux* 8. The horses were an alternative not an additional load.

HOMME MORT – 'Dead man' was the name given to the hill to the north-east of Verdun, and it rose 7 feet because of the build-up of dead bodies as both sides tried to hold the high ground.

HUN (1) – German. On 27 July 1900, Kaiser Wilhelm urged his troops to behave like the Huns of old in order to instil fear into the enemy. The German Expeditionary Forces was on its way to China to defeat the Boxer Uprising. He shouted, 'Should you encounter the enemy, he will be defeated! No quarter will be given! Prisoners will not be taken! Whoever falls into your hands is forfeited. Just as a thousand years ago the Huns under their King Attila made a name for themselves, one that even today makes them seem mighty in history and legend, may the name German be affirmed by you in such a way in China that no Chinese will ever again dare to look cross-eyed at a German!' This notorious *Hunnenrede* (Hun speech) was picked up by the British press, and the name was further popularised by British soldiers.

HUN (2) – RFC instructors' name for their pilot pupils, who were more dangerous to their life than the real enemy.

HUNTLEY & PALMER – Royal Flying Corps term for twin Lewis machine guns, named after a well-known biscuit manufacturer.

HUSH-HUSH – First used in the First World War to describe top-secret operations.

HUSSIF – A 'housewife', a small canvas roll containing needle, thread, buttons, etc., used for the personal maintenance of a soldier's kit.

HYMN OF HATE –The German people and their soldiers for the war adopted a new national anthem, one in stark contrast to the British songs. It was written in 1914 to stir up wholesome hatred against the English. The second verse is translated as:

> Take you the folk of the Earth in pay,
> With bars of gold your ramparts lay,
> Bedeck the ocean with bow on bow,
> Ye reckon well, but not well enough now.
> French and Russian, they matter not,
> A blow for a blow, a shot for a shot,
> We fight the battle with bronze and steel,
> And the time that is coming Peace will seal.
> You we will hate with a lasting hate,
> We will never forego our hate,
> Hate by water and hate by land,
> Hate of the head and hate of the hand,
> Hate of the hammer and hate of the crown,
> Hate of seventy millions choking down.
> We love as one, we hate as one,
> We have one foe and one alone –
> ENGLAND!

IDDY UMPTY – Signaller. 'Iddy' and 'umpty' were verbal ways of expressing the dashes and dots of Morse code. 'Most of [the signallers'] trench time was spent in their own dugout, testing lines and sharing private jokes on technicalities with other iddy umpties.' – Denis Winter, *Death's Men: Soldiers of the Great War* (1988)

IGGRY – Hurry up, from Arabic. One particular crossing in Bullecourt was named 'Iggry Corner' by the Australians.

IMSHI – Go, be gone, shoo, from Arabic.

INTERIOR ECONOMY – Quiet periods when men would turn their attention to personal matters, writing letters, sewing on buttons, darning socks, etc.

IRON RATION – Emergency ration of corned beef, tea, sugar and biscuit, carried by all soldiers in case they were cut off from normal food supplies.

JACK JOHNSON – Large German shell bursting with black smoke. After the boxer (1878–1946), who was the first African American world heavyweight champion (1908–1915).

JACKO, JOHNNY, JOHNNO – ANZAC term for a Turk.

JACKS – Military Police.

JAKES – Latrines, an expression dating back to Elizabethan times.

JAM-TINS – Originally, homemade or improvised bombs made from jam tins, mainly used before widespread introduction of the Mills bomb. Later on in the war, however, jam was issued in cardboard tubes. The expression was also used as a nickname for the No. 8 and No. 9 Double Cylinder grenades of late 1914 and early 1915 due to their resemblance to jam tins.

JANKERS – A minor punishment, fatigues, usually performed while confined to barracks.

JAPAN – Bread, from French *pain*.

JERICHO – Severe bombardment. 'This Hun Archie [anti-aircraft battery] spotted us and opened fire and gave us Jericho for five minutes – the best shooting I have seen so far!' – 2nd Lt Gerard Robin, 41 Squadron, RFC.

JERRY – German. The expression became popular later in the war, eventually coming into its own during the Second World War. Possibly because the British thought the German helmets looked like chamber pots, also known as jeroboams, abbreviated to Jerries.

JERRY UP! – Warning exclamation that a German aeroplane was overhead and may drop bombs.

JILDI – Quick, hurry up, from Hindustani.

JIPPO – Juice or gravy, especially of bacon. Also the shout given by Army Service Corps cooks to announce mealtimes.

JUDAEANS – 38th to 42nd battalions of the Royal Fusiliers, consisting of Jewish officers and men. The regiment was able to provide the necessary dietary and other religious conditions required by members of the faith.

JUMPING THE BAGS – Going over the top, i.e. attacking over the sandbags of the trench parapet.

JUMP OFF – To begin an attack. The jumping-off point was the start line of the attack in the front-line trench.

K, or **K OF K** – Kitchener or Kitchener of Khartoum. Field Marshal Lord Horatio Herbert Kitchener, 1st Earl Kitchener of Khartoum, was appointed Minister for War at the outbreak of hostilities. He was greatly successful in recruiting volunteers for the New Armies, his finger-pointing picture on thousands of recruiting posters being one of the most famous images of the twentieth century. He drowned, along with 642 other souls, when the cruiser *Hampshire* struck a mine off the Orkneys on 5 June 1916.

KAMERAD – Friend, comrade, from German.

KAPUT – Slang for ruined, broken, not working, from German *kaputt*, done for.

KICK THE BUCKET – To die. Although dating from at least 1780, it became common among English-speaking soldiers in the First World War. It probably originated from someone standing on a bucket to be hanged before the bucket was kicked away.

KILOMETERSCHWEIN – Kilometre pig, as the German infantrymen, tired of marching, referred to themselves.

KILTIE – A soldier of a Scottish regiment.

KITCH – British soldier. Australian and New Zealand slang, from Kitchener.

KITCHENER'S ARMIES – Refers to British enlistees who responded to Lord Kitchener's 1914 appeal for volunteers. This group provided the machine gun fodder for the disastrous 1916 Battle of the Somme.

KITE BALLOON – Observation balloon controlled by a cable from the ground.

KIWI (1) – A New Zealand soldier.

KIWI (2) – Ground crew of the RFC or RAF – implying an similarity with the flightless bird.

KNIFE-REST – Portable barbed wire entanglement, stretched on an X-shaped frame and used for quickly stopping gaps in no man's land.

KNOCKED – ANZAC slang for killed or wounded, from 'knocked out'.

KNOCKED OFF – This is one of several phrases from the criminal underworld that rapidly spread among the forces; it meant stolen. To 'GET KNOCKED OFF' was thus to go missing, i.e., dead.

KNUT – Person, usually an officer, who took particular care over his appearance. From the popular music hall song *Gilbert the Filbert, the Colonel of the Knuts*.

KRAUT – Derogatory term for anything Germanic, from German food *sauerkraut*.

LA CROIX DE BOIS – French for wooden cross, meaning killed or dead – 'He earned the wooden cross.'

LAKENPATSCHER – Puddle splasher, one of the names German infantrymen used for themselves.

LANCE CORPORAL BACON – ANZAC term for very fat bacon, with only one streak of lean running through it. A comparison to one stripe on uniform.

LANCE-JACK – Lance-corporal, a junior NCO having one chevron. This was an appointment and not a rank.

LAND CRAB, LAND CREEPER – Tank. 'Sunday 10th September, 1916: Walked … to see the Land Creepers. They look wonderful things but rather vulnerable.' – Capt Sir Iain Colquhoun, 1st Scots Guards

LANDOWNER – Dead. 'To become a landowner' was to be dead and buried.

LANDSHIP – This was the official Army name for a tank, which was also known as a whale, willie, slug, tortoise, toad, land crab, land creeper, boojum, behemoth and wibble-wobble.

LAUGHING MURDERER OF VERDUN – Crown Prince Wilhelm (1882–1951) was one of the more aggressive of the military cabal, and the nickname was applied because of his command of the costly German offensive at Verdun in 1918. However, he is said to have argued against prolonging it. Also known as 'Little Willie' – his father the Kaiser was 'Big Willie'.

LEAPFROG – System of assaults in which the first wave took the first objective and the second wave passed through them to take the second objective.

LÉGUMES – Staff officers, to the French front-line soldier, because they never saw any *légumes* (vegetables). Generals were *grosses légumes*, great legumes.

LIBERTY SAUSAGES AND DOGS – In the USA, because of anti-German war feelings. Frankfurters, which were named after Frankfurt, Germany, were called 'liberty sausages', and dachshunds similarly became 'liberty dogs'.

LID – Steel helmet.

LIFTING BARRAGE – An advancing bombardment.

LINSEED LANCERS – The Royal Army Medical Corps. It was also applied to Australian Field Ambulance men.

LISTENING POST – Advanced post, usually in no man's land, where soldiers tried to find out information about the enemy.

LITTLE WILLIE (1) – Crown Prince Wilhelm of Germany.

LITTLE WILLIE (2) – The first tank prototype, built by William Tritton and Walter Wilson in 1915. In 1916, General Haig's aide-de-camp said, 'The idea that cavalry will be replaced by these iron coaches is absurd. It is little short of treasonous.'

THE LIVE BAIT SQUADRON – Three old cruisers were commissioned from the Reserve at the beginning of the Second World War. Known as the 7th Cruiser Squadron, it was patrolling the Dutch coast at 9 knots, in line abreast, with no destroyer escort. Around 6 a.m. the *Aboukir* was torpedoed by *U-9* and began to sink. In response to her distress, the other two cruisers stopped to give assistance. Around 6.45 a.m., the *Hogue* was almost cut in two by two torpedoes, and began to sink. At 8 a.m. the *Cressy* was torpedoed through the magazine and she sank almost immediately. The casualties of this passive action on 22 September 1914 were 1,400 men, 60 officers and 13 cadets out of a total of 2,200 seamen, more than the losses sustained at Trafalgar.

LOOEY/LOUIS – Second Lieutenant.

LOOPHOLE – Gap in the parapet of a fire trench enabling shooting to take place whilst providing head cover.

LOOSE – Larceny, a thief, from Hindustani *lus*.

LOUSY – Infested with lice. It came to mean contemptible, contaminated, unethical, etc.

L PIP – Listening post (LP), usually located in a sap, from the phonetic alphabet.

MACARONI – An Italian soldier.

MACONACHIE – Canned British ration of beef, potatoes, beans, onions and carrots in gravy.

MACONACHIE MEDAL – Military Medal (MM). The inscription on the back of the MM says for bravery in the field, and some soldiers maintained that the Maconachie ration was so terrible that only a brave man would eat it and thus be awarded a medal for doing so. Alternatively, an allusion to the notion that the Military Medal was given out so often that it 'came up with the rations'.

MACHINE GUN – The Germans generally used the acronym MG for *maschinengewehr*, although *stottertante* (stuttering aunt) and *nuhmaschine* (sewing machine) were current. They also called it a mowing machine or reaper and the *fleischhackmaschine,* flesh grinder.

MAD MINUTE – Firing off fifteen (or more) rounds of rapid-fire aimed shots from a bolt action .303 Lee-Enfield rifle in one minute and hitting a 1-foot-wide target at 200 yards. This would include at least one five-round clip being loaded during that minute.

MAFEESH – Nothing, all gone, from Arabic. *Mafeesh* was used by troops in Egypt, Gallipoli, Mesopotamia and Palestine in the same way that *napoo* was used by those on the Western Front.

MAFFICKING – Celebrating. From the general air of excitement that followed the relief of Mafeking during the Boer War.

MATE – Aussies did not have friends, they had 'mates'.

MATLOW – Sailor, from French *matelot*, although the expression is pre-war.

MAXIM – What the Allies called German machine guns. In 1910, the director-general of the French infantry stated that the invention 'will change absolutely nothing'. Such was Haig's opinion that in 1915 he called it an 'overrated weapon', ordering that 'two per battalion is more than sufficient'. At this time the British had suffered massive and virtually unsustainable casualties from Maxims.

MAXWELL'S PINK-EYED BASTARDS – The Australian troops of the 17th Battalion AIF, who were proud that none of them had taken part in the '2nd Battle of the Wazzir' (a riot in the Cairo brothel area) and therefore received congratulations from the British Government in Egypt. When they landed in Gallipoli afterwards, this fact earned them their nickname.

MEATHEAD – Military Police.

MESOPOLONICA – Hypothetical posting in the East, regarded by those on the Western Front to be a comparatively safe destination. The word is a composite of Mesopotamia and Salonica.

MICK – A soldier in an Irish regiment. 'The Micks' is also the nickname of the Irish Guards.

MICKEY – Louse. This is the origin of the phrase 'taking the mickey', to tease.

MILLS BOMB – British No. 5 grenade. Invented by William Mills (1856–1932) in 1915, it remained in service in a modified form with the British Army until the 1960s.

MINE – Subterranean passage made to extend under an enemy's works or position, for the purpose of securing access or depositing explosives for blowing up a military position.

MINNIEWERFER – 'Mine Thrower', a German trench mortar. A variety of calibres were employed. The British called its whistling shells 'singing Minnies' or 'moaning Minnies' from their noise in flight.

'**MIRACLE ON THE MARNE**' – The German march on Paris was brought to a halt in 1914, not so much by divine intervention as by the Germans outrunning their supplies.

MOB – One's battalion or another unit.

MOCKUP – A near full-sized, non-working model of a new design, derived from practices in the new aircraft industries.

MONKEY MEAT – Nickname for French canned beef from Madagascar. Also, for the Americans, a canned beef and carrot mixture ration from South America.

MONTY BONG – Montauban, a French village in the Somme region.

MOTHERS – 5.7-inch British guns; WIVES were 9-inch British guns.

MUCK ABOUT – To wander aimlessly. Used by Kipling and adopted by the BEF.

MUCKIM – Butter, from Hindustani.

MUD VALLEY – To pitch camp in any wet, muddy place.

MUFTI – Civillian clothes, from Arabic.

MUTT & JEFF (1) – First World War campaign medals (British War Medal and Victory Medal) given to those who served from 1916 onwards. Named after the cartoon characters created originally in the United States by Bud Fisher, but popular in Britain by 1920, the time when campaign medals were being sent out.

MUTT & JEFF (2) – Deaf, from Cockney rhyming slang.

NAPOO, NAIPOO, NARPOO, NAHPOO – Gone, finished, no way, taken from the French *il n'y a plus* meaning that there is no more. British troops in Russia or who had returned from German prisoner of war camps often used *nichevo*, a Russian word with the same meaning. Some of us remember the tune to this front-line song that features the word *napoo*:

> Brother Bertie went away, to do his bit the other day.
> With a smile on his lips and his lieutenant pips upon his shoulder bright and gay.
> As the train moved out he said: 'Remember me to all the girls'
> And then he wagged his paw and went away to war shouting out these pathetic words:
> 'Good-bye-ee, good-bye-ee, wipe the tears, baby dear, from your eye-ee.
> Though it's hard to part I know, I'll be tickled to death to go.
> Don't cry-ee, don't sigh-ee, there's a silver lining in the sky-ee.
> Bon-sewer old thing, cheerio chin-chin, napoo, toodle-oo, good-bye – ee.'

NEST, MACHINE GUN – Strong point of multiple machine guns with overlapping fields of fire.

NEVER LIGHT THREE CIGARETTES WITH A SINGLE MATCH – This unlucky superstition lasted for decades. It was thought that a spotter would sight the first light, the second light would allow the sniper to set his sights, and the third light would be accompanied by a bullet. Soldiers never lit fires in front-line trenches for a similar reason – artillery would be directed at them.

NIGGER JACK – General John Pershing (1860–1948), commander of the American Expeditionary Force, had commanded a troop of the 10th Cavalry, a regiment of African American soldiers in the 1890s. Later, when an instructor at West Point, his extremely harsh discipline caused the recruits to call him 'Nigger Jack'. American reporters altered this to 'Black Jack' when the US entered the war.

NO-EYES – Soldier blinded at the front.

NO MAN'S LAND – The desolate territory between the hundreds of miles of opposing Allied and German trenches. The distance between could be as short as 30 yards or as far as half a mile, but probably averaged around 300 yards. The term dates from the 1300s, when it meant the waste ground between two kingdoms, and it did not acquire its military meaning until the First World War. The periscope was the only safe method for viewing the area. At night flares briefly illuminated the scene, trying to catch enemy patrols and bring them under fire.

NON-STOP – Enemy shell that has passed well overhead.

NOSEDIVE – Sharp descent or decline, originally a description of fighter pilots' tactic of pouncing down on the enemy from above.

NUMBER 9 – Sick. The British Army's No. 9 was a laxative pill. This gave rise to the bingo caller's expression, 'Doctor's orders – number nine', the game being a popular pastime among soldiers.

NYD – Medics had to attach a signed note to the wounded and ill, as they were left by the side of the road or made their way back for help; without a note they could be shot as deserters. If in a hurry, or unsure, they scribbled NYD, for 'Not Yet Diagnosed'. With typical gallows humour, troops referred to this as 'Not Yet Dead'.

NYDN – In 1917, the term 'shell shock' was no longer allowed. Men were classified as Not Yet Diagnosed Nervous (NYDN). The men bleakly called it 'Not Yet Dead Nearly'.

OBAT – 'Order of battle' defines the structure and organisation of the British Army, and can be confusing, for instance the word 'corps' is used in three different ways. Very generally, an infantry soldier in the First World War was part of a battalion (around 1,000 men). The battalion is subdivided into companies, which are subdivided into platoons, which are subdivided into sections. Several battalions form a Brigade (around 5,000 men), and several brigades become a division (around 20,000 men). Several divisions are under the command of a corps, and several corps make up an army of around 400,000 men. For instance, the maximum deployment on the Western Front was five armies, making up 2,046,901 men.

O. C. DUNKS – ANZAC term for the quartermaster responsible for battery mules. From Officer Commanding Donkeys.

OCEAN VILLAS – Auchonvillers, a village in the Somme region of France, just north of Albert.

OIL – ANZAC term for authentic, the truth.

OLD – This became a popular form of approval during the war, as with beloved cartoon character 'Old Bill'.

OLD BEAN – Form of address which started in the Royal Navy about 1914 and spread to other services.

OLD CONTEMPTIBLES – Nickname for British Army regulars who formed the original BEF. Few survived the war. The name comes from Kaiser Wilhelm's comment that his forces in Belgium were being held up by 'Sir John French's contemptible little army'.

OLD SWEAT – An experienced soldier.

OMG – This phrase was first used by Admiral Jackie Fisher in a 1917 letter to Winston Churchill, which ended, 'I hear a new order of Knighthood is on the tapis [tapestry or carpet] – O.M.G! (Oh! My God!) – Shower it on the Admiralty!! Yours, Fisher.'

ON THE MAT – To be called before the Commanding Officer to answer a minor charge.

O-PIP – Observation post, from the phonetic alphabet.

OUTED – ANZAC term meaning killed, taken care of.

OVER THE TOP – Make an attack, go over the top of the trench parapet, or **OVER THE BAGS** (sandbags). In civilian use it was extended to mean taking the final plunge and doing something dangerous or notable.

PALS BATTALIONS – For the Kitchener armies, men from the same town or trade were allowed to enlist and serve together. This was potentially catastrophic for a community when a Pals unit took heavy casualties.

PANZER – German tank, from German *sturmpanzerkampfwagen*.

PARIS GUN – Krupp artillery piece designed to fire over 75 miles to bombard Paris, sometimes confused with Big Bertha. The first time the shells landed, air-raid sirens sounded in Paris because they did not realise a gun could fire that far.

PARADOS – The side of a trench farthest from the enemy.

PARAPET – The side of the trench facing the enemy.

PARNEE – Water, from Hindustani.

PENINSH, THE – The Gallipoli Peninsula.

PERISHER – Trench periscope.

P GAS HELMET – With glass eyepieces, this was introduced in November 1915. However, the Phenate Gas helmet did not protect adequately against phosgene, and was replaced by the PH (Phenate-Hexamine) helmet from January 1916. From August 1916, the PH helmet itself was replaced by the small box respirator, which, although an unwieldy design, gave protection against the different gases in use.

PICKELHAUBE – German spiked helmet used in first half of the war, from the German *pickel* (point or pick axe) and *haube* (hat). The basic *pickelhaube* was made of hardened leather, given a glossy black finish, and reinforced with metal trim. This was usually plated with gold or silver for officers, and it included a metal spike at the crown. These helmets were sometimes referred to as 'lobster-tail helmets' by Allied forces due to their distinctive curved neck guard. All helmets produced for the infantry before and during 1914 were made of leather. As the war progressed, Germany's leather stockpiles dwindled. It was soon discovered that the *pickelhaube* did not measure up to the demanding conditions of trench warfare. The leather helmets offered virtually no protection against shell fragments and shrapnel and the conspicuous spike made its wearer a target. Beginning in 1916, the *pickelhaube* was slowly replaced by a new German steel helmet, the *stahlhelm*, intended to offer greater head protection against shell fragments. The German steel helmet decreased German head wound fatalities by 70 per cent.

PICKET (1) – Metal post used for staking out barbed wire.

PICKET (2) – Sentry-party or patrol.

PIGGY-STICK – The wooden handle or shaft of an entrenching tool.

PILL – ANZAC term for a bullet. **TAKEN A PILL** meant taken a bullet.

PIP EMMA – Afternoon, p.m., from the phonetic alphabet.

PIPPED – To be hit by a bullet.

PIP, SQUEAK & WILFRED – Nicknames for the trio of standard-service First World War campaign medals, the 1914–15 Star, British War Medal and Victory Medal. Named after popular *Daily Mirror* cartoon characters of the time.

PIPSQUEAK (1) – Small, insignificant person.

PIPSQUEAK (2) – Any 2nd Lieutenant.

PIPSQUEAK (3) – A small German trench gun.

PLONK – Cheap wine. From French *vin blanc*, white wine, although the expression may also be derived from the firm of Plonques, importers of a particularly poor Algerian red wine.

PLUG – To shoot, to 'plug with lead'.

PLUGSTREET – Ploegsteert, a Belgian village north of Armentieres.

PLUM AND APPLE – Only tins of this type of jam were normally sent to the trenches, and it was universally hated. Troops used the tins to make grenades. 'Oh! It's a lovely war!' was a 1917 music hall song sung by troops and refers to the jam:

Up to your waist in water,
Up to your eyes in slush
Using the kind of language,
That makes the sergeant blush;
Who wouldn't join the Army?
That's what we all inquire
Don't we pity the poor civilians sitting around the fire.

Oh! Oh! Oh! it's a lovely war,
Who wouldn't be a soldier eh?
Oh! It's a shame to take the pay.
As soon as 'reveille' has gone
We feel just as heavy as lead,
But we never get up till the sergeant brings
Our breakfast up to bed.

Oh! Oh! Oh! it's a lovely war,
What do we want with eggs and ham
When we've got plum and apple jam?
Form fours! Right turn!
How shall we spend the money we earn?
Oh! Oh! Oh! it's a lovely war.

Come to the cookhouse door boys,
Sniff at the lovely stew,
Who is it says the Colonel gets better grub than you?
Any complaints this morning?
Do we complain, not we
What's the matter with lumps of onion floating around your tea?

POILU – Front-line French soldier, literally 'hairy one' (like an animal).

POM – The term was first recorded in 1916 among troops, and D. H. Lawrence wrote, in 1923 in his novel *Kangaroo*, 'Pommy is supposed to be short for pomegranate. Pomegranate, pronounced invariably pommygranate, is a near enough rhyme to immigrant, in a naturally rhyming country. Furthermore, immigrants are known in their first few months, before their blood "thins down", by their round and ruddy cheeks. So we are told.' Thus 'Pommy Grant' replaced the older nickname for an immigrant as Jimmy Grant, as the sun turned the skin of the pale English 'pomegranate red'.

POP – Poperinghe, Belgian town in West Flanders. Captured from the Germans in October 1914, it remained in British hands until the end of the war.

PORK AND BEANS – Portuguese. From the observation that British Army ration pork and beans contained very little, if any, pork, and therefore alluding to the fact that the Portuguese had very few troops on the Western Front.

POSH – Smart. From the obsolete English use of posh to refer to a dandy, but often said to be an acronym of 'Port Out, Starboard Home', the optimum (i.e. shaded) position of a cabin in British ships sailing to and from the East.

POSSIE, POSSY – ANZAC term. A firing position, but also a hole excavated in the side of a trench to rest.

POTATO MASHER – German stick grenade.

POZZY – Jam. Issued as part of the British Army field ration, tinned plum and apple pozzy was much in abundance in the early years of the war, being supplemented later on by such exotic mixtures as gooseberry and rhubarb.

PROPAGANDA – This was extreme on all sides during the war, especially regarding alleged atrocities such as bayoneting babies. The Allies exploited the belief that Germans were rendering human bodies to make oil, having seen a newspaper report on the Western Front in April 1917: 'We are passing the Kadaver Exploitation Department of this Army group. The fat that is won here is turned into lubricating oils and everything else is ground down in the bone mills into a powder which is used for mixing with pig food – nothing can be permitted to go to waste.' However, *kadaver* is not the English cadaver, a human corpse, but an animal corpse. The Germans were melting down dead horses.

PULL-THROUGH – A tall, thin person. From pull-through, the device used to clean inside the barrel of a rifle.

PUMP SHIP – Urinate, from the naval expression.

PUNK – US term for soft bread.

PURPLE HEART – United States military decoration awarded in the name of the President to those wounded or killed while serving on or after 5 April 1917. Taking the form of a heart made of purple cloth, the Purple Heart is the oldest military award that is still given to members of the US military, the only earlier award being the obsolete Fidelity Medallion.

PUSH – A large-scale attack on enemy positions.

PUSHING UP DAISIES – Dead and buried.

Q-SHIP – Antisubmarine armed vessel disguised as a merchant steamship.

QUARTER BLOKE – Quartermaster. Officer usually commissioned from the ranks and responsible for the supply of accommodation, food, clothing and other equipment to the unit, via the Company Quartermaster Sergeants. When an issue of new kit was requested, the Quarterbloke's stock answer would usually be: 'Stores is for storing things; if they was for issuing things then they would be called issues.'

QUICK FIRER – Field Service Post Card (Army Form A2042). The card consisted of a number of pre-printed sentences which could be deleted as appropriate. Nothing, except the address of the recipient, was to be written on the post card in order to alleviate the problems of censorship.

RACE TO THE SEA – When they first started digging trenches, each side tried to outflank the other and they kept on digging and digging in what became known as 'the race to the sea'.

RAMC – The Royal Army Medical Corps was nicknamed Rob All My Comrades due to the practice of removing injured men's possessions before medical treatment. Also known as the Linseed Lancers, Run Away, Matron's Coming, Rats Ate My Cheese and Can't Manage A Rifle (RAMC backwards).

RANK AND FILE – Its general usage stems from soldiers returning from the First World War. The rank and file are the individual members of a political organisation or union, exclusive of its leadership. The phrase originated in the military, denoting the horizontal 'ranks' and vertical 'files' of foot-soldiers, exclusive of the officers and is still sometimes used to refer to the bulk of lower-ranking troops.

RAPE OF BELGIUM – The name given by British propaganda to alleged German atrocities in Belgium early in the First World War. As a neutral country in 1914, Belgium tried to stay out of the war, but German forces invaded and, according to the Allies, raped and plundered their way through the country.

REAR ADMIRAL – The soldier whose duty was to empty latrines.

RED BADGE OF FUNK – In the British Army, staff officers were distinguished by the wearing of bright-red shoulder tabs and hat bands. The colour constituted a visible symbol that the wearer did not belong to the colourless khaki world of the front, where distinguishing marks had been abolished because they made good targets for snipers. The front-line troops soon dubbed the tabs 'the Red Badge of Funk'.

RED BARON AND HIS FLYING CIRCUS, THE – Manfred von Richthofen (1892–1918) was the most successful ace of the First World War, with over eighty credited air victories. Von Richthofen began the war as an artillery spotter. In 1915, he joined a new German flying unit and began his career, developing the 'Flying Circus', a new type of mass air attack that confounded the Allies for years. Von Richthofen's famous Fokker triplane, which was painted red to help his fellow Germans identify him, is the iconic figure of a plane in the First World War. The Allies dubbed him 'the Red Baron' out of respect for his skills. After he was killed in action on 21 April 1918, the Australian unit that retrieved his body gave him a full military funeral, later dropping propaganda with pictures of the ceremony over German lines.

REDCAP – Military policeman, said to be the most despised men on the Western Front. From the red covering to their field service caps.

RED LAMP – Brothel. Sometimes licensed and under police surveillance. From the red light outside, the recognised symbol.

RED TAB – British staff officer, from the red gorget patches on the collar. Rear-echelon officers wore bright-red shoulder tabs and hat bands. See also **RED BADGE OF FUNK**.

REGIMENTAL – A real mess, a monumental failure. Short for Regimental Foul-Up or Fuck-Up.

REGIMENTAL NICKNAMES – Most were known by nicknames, which are outside the scope of this book, but some include: 'Sight-Seeing Sixth' – the 6th infantry division of the AEF, as they only saw a month of action at the end of the war; Queer Objects On Horseback – Queen's Own Oxfordshire Regiment; the Sweeps – 95th Rifles, Rifle Brigade – from black facings on their uniforms; the Stink – Special Brigade, Royal Engineers, responsible for poison gas and flame attacks; the Mounted Micks – 4th Royal Irish Dragoon Guards; the Mutton Lancers – Queen's Royal West Surrey Regiment, from their Paschal Lamb and Flag badge; the Comical Chemical Corporals – Special Brigade, Royal Engineers, responsible for poison gas and flame attacks (men with knowledge of chemistry were immediately promoted to corporal); the Cat and Cabbage – York and Lancaster Regiment, from the regimental badge, which was a royal lion atop a stylised

Tudor Rose; Agile and Bolton Wanderers – Argyll and Sutherland Highlanders. The Welsh Regiment 1st Battalion (41st Foot) was raised as a regiment of invalids in 1719, and it was for a long time known as the 1st Invalids, appearing as such in most of the old 'Army Lists'. Also in the Welsh Regiment, the 2nd Battalion (the 69th Regiment) was known as 'the Old Agamemnons'. They were thus called by Lord Nelson at the naval battle of St Vincent, from the name of his ship, the *Agamemnon*, on which the regiment served as Marines. They were also known as 'the Ups and Downs' from the fact that their regiment number, 69, can be read either way up.

RESPIRATOR – Gas mask in which air was inhaled through a metal box of chemicals.

REST CAMP – Cemetery.

RFC – Royal Flying Corps, which became the RAF on 1 April 1918.

ROCK-CHEWER – ANZAC term for a dry biscuit, responsible for many broken teeth and dentures, a problem that was aggravated by the fact that originally there were no dentists with the medical services on Gallipoli. 'I broke my dentures – my top plate – on an army biscuit. So then I had to manage these iron biscuits with only my bottom teeth. I used my entrenching tool to powder them as best I could.' – John Skinner, Otago Infantry Battalion

ROOKIE – A recruit or newcomer, probably a corruption of recruit.

ROOTI – Bread, from Hindustani *roti*.

ROOTI GONG – British Army Long Service & Good Conduct Medal. This stemmed from the belief that they were so easily obtained that they were brought in with the bread ration, or could be earned by eating Army rations for the required number of years.

ROUGH HOUSE – A fight or disturbance, so called from the type of public house where this type of behaviour could arise after drinking.

ROUGHNECK – US term for an artilleryman.

RUMBLED – Several phrases from the criminal underworld entered wider use, among them 'rumbled', to be found out when up to no good.

RUM JAR – Mortar bomb, from the shape. The rum ration was issued to the troops in earthenware jars, stamped with the initials S. R. D. This stood for Supply Reserve Depot, but was called Service Rum Diluted by the troops. Soldiers also argued that this actually stood for Seldom Reaches Destination or Soon Runs Dry.

RUNNER – Soldier who carried messages by hand.

RUPERT/RODNEY – Slang for an officer, usually one new to the service or of low rank who was a little naive.

RUSSIAN SAP – Narrow trench dug below ground like a mineshaft, so that the surface of the earth was not disturbed. A sap trench helped raiders to approach enemy lines without being detected.

SALIENT – Trench system projecting towards the enemy.

SALISBURY STEAK – During the First World War, American hamburgers, named after the German city of Hamburg, were renamed 'Salisbury steak' because of anti-German war feelings. Dietician Dr James Salisbury had recommended a diet of three daily meals of beef 'patty' i.e. a hamburger, with a glass of hot water.

SANDBAG – Sack usually filled with earth, from which defences were built. Churchill impressed his men with tough but fair discipline and attention to their living conditions. One officer reported, 'To see Winston giving a dissertation of the laying of sandbags ... rendered you certain that Wren would have been proud to sit at his feet.' Because burlap and earth (or sand) cost little, big protective barriers can be erected cheaply. The friction created by moving the sand grains or soil, along with the multiple tiny air gaps, means that sandbags are an effective dissipater of any explosive blast. The most common sandbag size was 14 by 26 inches, which was light enough to lift and use to make an interlocked wall. Sandbags were used to provide troops with protection at both the front (parapet) and rear (parados) and were generally stacked 2 to 3 feet deep. A First World War bullet would only penetrate 15 inches into a sandbag.

SAN FAIRY ANN – It doesn't matter, it makes no difference, from French '*ça ne fait rien*'.

SAP (1) – A listening post in no man's land, connected at 90 degrees to the fire trench by a narrow communication trench.

SAP (2) –Anything that was not regarded as a regular (firing) trench. During an advance, saps were often joined together to make the new front-line trench. A sap could be a short part of a trench branching off into no man's land for observation, a big communication trench leading to the lines, or a shortcut between different trenches. 'The Big Sap' was the big seaside communication trench that connected Anzac Cove to the 'Outposts'.

SAPPER – Equivalent to a private in the Royal Engineers, originally a digger of saps.

SARDINES – French brigadiers. Their stripes of rank looked like sardines, suggesting a small, smelly fish.

SARNT – Sergeant. Sarge was never permitted.

SATURDAY NIGHT SOLDIERS – Members of the Territorial Battalions. Originally a derisory name, until they proved their worth.

SAUSAGE (1) – Barrage balloon.

SAUSAGE (2) – German mortar bomb.

SCRATCHER – An Army term for bed or place to sleep, especially in the field.

SCHRAPNELLES – French soldier's name for the undercooked peas or beans which were regular items in his diet, along with lentils, known as *punaises* (bugs).

SCREAMING SHELL – See **WHISTLING WILLIE**.

SCROUNGING – Foraging for food, such as wild rabbits, thought to have derived from the north of England.

SCUTTLEBUTT – Rumours shared among American sailors, and then soldiers, around the water barrels or scuttlebutts. Originally a naval term, and known as Furphys by ANZAC forces.

SEVEN, 'IT'S ALL IN THE SEVEN' – Expression used by regular soldiers who had enlisted for seven years.

SHACKLES – Soup made from leftovers.

SHELLS – In French, a similar shell to the 'coal box' was *un gros noir*, a big black, and one that exploded with greenish smoke was *un pernod*, named after the popular drink. Others were *saucissons,* sausages filled with entrails, '*sacs B terre*', sandbags, and '*marmites*', named after a large, deep cooking pot. Germans called a heavy shell an '*aschpott*', ash pot or a '*marmeladeneimer*', jam pot.

SHELL SHOCK – To suffer from an acute neurasthenic condition due to the explosion of shells or bombs at close quarters. It was an early description of combat fatigue and Post-traumatic Stress Disorder.

SHIPS – Lloyd George, in a speech welcoming America into the war in 1917, said, 'The road to victory, the guarantee of victory, the absolute assurance of victory is to be found in one word – ships; and a second word – ships; and a third word – ships. And with that quickness of apprehension which characterises your nation, Mr Chairman, I see that they fully realize that, and today I observe that they have already made arrangements to build one thousand 3,000-tonners for the Atlantic.'

SHIT HOT – Unpleasantly enthusiastic, credited to the Canadian forces.

SHOOT DOWN IN FLAMES – To refute the argument of an opponent completely, a metaphor borrowed from aerial warfare.

SHORT ARM INSPECTION – Medical inspection of the privates' private parts to look for cases of VD, especially when stationed in Egypt.

SHRAPNEL (1) – Shell for anti-personnel use, designed to burst in the air and eject a number of small projectiles. From General H. Shrapnel (1761–1842), the English Army officer who invented it during the Peninsular War.

SHRAPNEL (2) – The metal pieces, often lead, contained therein.

SHRAPNEL (3) – Any metal splinter from a shell.

SHRAPNEL (4) – Used for the chickpeas that Australian POWs in Turkey sometimes found as an addition to their daily ration of boiled wheat.

SIDE-DOOR PULLMANS – American term for railway carriages or boxcars that took eight *chevaux* or forty *hommes*, eight horses or forty men.

SIGARNEO – OK. From a corruption of 'All Sir Garnet', named after Sir Garnet Wolseley (1833–1913), Commander in Chief of the British Army from 1895 to 1899.

SIGNALESE – The phonetic alphabet used in the war.

SILENT DEATH – The practice of waiting quietly at night in no man's land for the advent of a German patrol. The patrol was then dispatched in hand-to-hand combat as quickly and silently as possible by the use of trench knives. Much favoured by the Canadians.

SILENT PERCY – Artillery piece firing at such long range that it could not be heard.

SILENT SUSAN – High-velocity artillery shell.

SINKERS – US term for dumplings.

SIX-BOB-A-DAY TOURISTS – ANZAC nickname for members of the 1st Division.

SIW – Self-Inflicted Wound. Faced with the prospect of being killed or permanently disabled, soldiers sometimes hoped that they would receive what was known as a 'blighty' wound, and be sent back home. George Coppard was shot by mistake by one of his men and was suspected of being guilty of SIW: 'Transferred to an ambulance car, I became puzzled to find myself the only casualty in it. Finally I arrived at the 39th Casualty Clearing Station. Next morning I discovered that there was something queer about the place which filled me with misgivings. None of the nursing staff appeared friendly, and the matron looked, and was, a positive battleaxe. I made anxious inquiries, and quickly learned that I was classed as a suspected self-inflicted wound case. Unknown to me, the letters SIW with a query mark added had been written on the label attached to my chest.' Some men killed themselves rather than carry on in the trenches. The usual method of suicide was to place the muzzle of the Lee-Enfield rifle against the head and press the trigger with a bare big toe. In some cases, when men could endure no more, they stood up on the trench fire-step and allowed themselves to be shot by an enemy sniper.

SKEE – US term for whiskey or any hard booze.

SKILLY – Thin stew, gruel.

SKIPPER – Officer's informal expression for a captain commanding a company.

SLACK – Small pieces of debris thrown up by a shell burst. From slack, small pieces of coal with a high ash content.

SLAPJACKS – American term for pancakes.

SLING THE BAT – To speak in slang.

SLUM, SLUMGUM – A thin stew of meat, potatoes, onions and tomatoes eaten by American soldiers.

SLUM IN A FULL PACK – Slum with a dough crust baked over it.

SMOKO – ANZAC term for a cigarette break.

SNAPSHOT – A quickly taken rifle shot.

SNIPE – To shoot at the enemy from a hidden position. In general, a sniper worked together with a 'spotter', who was equipped with a trench periscope. 'Sniping' was originally used for a rifleman expert enough to shoot the erratic snipe in India.

SNOB – Soldier employed as a cobbler.

S.O.S. – American acronym for 'shit on a shingle' – creamed, chipped beef on hardtack.

SOUP TICKET – Medal citation. A small card presented to soldiers recommended for a gallantry decoration, usually a DCM or MM, giving some details of the act.

SOUVENIR – To steal, from French *souvenir*, to remember. The word came to replace keepsake as the main word for a memento. To try and find battlefield trophies after an engagement. To try and steal something useful, for instance from an army dump.

SOUVY – ANZAC version of **SOUVENIR**.

SOW BELLY – American term for bacon.

SPINNING INCINERATOR – The Aerco DH.2 was a single-seat fighter plane. It had sensitive controls and, at a time when service training for pilots in the RFC was very poor, it initially had a high accident rate, gaining the nickname 'the Spinning Incinerator', but as familiarity increased it was recognised as relatively easy to fly. The rear-mounted rotary engine made the DH.2 easy to stall, but also made it highly manoeuvrable.

SPOTTED DOG – Currant pudding.

SPOUT – Rifle breech. Soldiers often loaded the .303 Lee-Enfield rifle with ten rounds in the magazine and one up the spout. **UP THE SPOUT** then became a term for being pregnant.

SPUD (1) – Potato.

SPUD (2) – Nickname given to a person with the surname Murphy.

SPUD (3) – Metal shoe affixed to a tank's tracks to provide better grip in muddy conditions. From 'spudde', a fifteenth-century word for a digging tool.

SPUDHOLE – The guard room.

SPURIOUS, *OUTRAGEOUS* AND *UPROARIOUS* – Nicknames given to three battle cruisers – *Furious*, *Courageous* and *Glorious* – built during the war, on account of their perceived uselessness by many naval men. HMS *Furious* had two 18 inch guns fore and aft, the largest guns in the world.

SQUADDIE – Soldier. From squad, but also said to be a corruption of 'swaddy', an eighteenth-century word for bumpkin.

SQUAREHEAD – German, from the shape of the M.1916 German steel helmet.

SRD – This stands for Supply Reserve Depot, the inscription found on large rum jars supplied to the troops. It was also known as 'Service Rum, Diluted'. The sergeant who served it out to a company might say, 'I'll have mine with you', before going to supply the men in another part of the trench, where the same might occur. By the time he reached the last men, he may have drunk their share. Thus SRD came to mean 'Seldom Reaches Destination' and was applied to other useful supplies. The sergeant stealing men's rum was the subject of a popular song in the trenches:

> If the sergeant drinks your rum, never mind
> And your face may lose its smile, never mind
> He's entitled to a tot but not the bleeding lot
> If the sergeant drinks your rum, never mind
>
> When old Jerry shells your trench, never mind
> And your face may lose its smile, never mind
> Though the sandbags bust and fly you have only once to die,
> If old Jerry shells the trench, never mind
>
> If you get stuck on the wire, never mind
> And your face may lose its smile, never mind
> Though you're stuck there all the day, they count you dead and stop your pay
> If you get stuck on the wire, never mind
>
> If your mate just lost his sight, never mind
> And he screamed the whole damned night, never mind
> Though they'll send him home it's tough, he'll be great for blind-man's bluff
> So if your mate just lost his sight, never mind
>
> If the sergeant says you're mad, never mind
> P'raps you are a little bit, never mind

Just be calm don't answer back, cause the sergeant stands no slack
So if he says you're mad, well – you are.

STAND-TO – Period when troops in the front line were required to man the fire-step of their trench, fully armed, in case of enemy attack. Routinely done at dawn and nightfall when enemy attacks were most likely to occur.

STAR – Badge of rank, or pip, worn by British officers on the sleeves or epaulettes of the tunic.

STARS AND STRIPES – American term for beans and bacon. The diet of American troops was considerably better than that of all the other forces in the war.

STAR SHELL – Artillery projectile consisting of a magnesium flare and a parachute, intended to illuminate the battlefield during night operations. Coloured star shells, not always incorporating the parachute, were used for signalling purposes.

STAY-AT-HOME, STAY-AT-HOMER – ANZAC term for someone reluctant to enlist.

STEEL JUG – Steel helmet.

STICK BOMB – German grenade with a wooden handle that allowed it to be thrown further. Also known as a potato masher.

STIFF – ANZAC term for a corpse, a dead soldier.

STIFFS' PADDOCK – ANZAC term for a graveyard.

STINK – Soldier of the Royal Engineers employed on gas duties.

STINKER – British Army goatskin or sheepskin jerkin, first issued in winter 1914. From the smell, especially when wet.

STOP ONE – To be hit by a bullet, shell fragment, etc.

STORMTROOPER – Specially trained German assault troops used in Germany's 1918 offensives. The nickname was later adapted by Nazi Brown Shirts.

STOUSH, STOUCH – To fight, hit, kill or use violence in general. ANZAC derivation, leading to the term **REINSTOUSHMENTS** – reinforcements.

STRAFE (1) – To machine-gun troops on the ground, especially from the air.

STRAFE (2) – General bombardment. From German *strafen*, to punish. '*Gott Strafe England*', God punish England, was a popular song and greeting in Germany during the war years.

STUFF – Shellfire.

STUNT – ANZAC term for a performance of outstanding skill or effectiveness, on a large or small scale.

SUICIDE CLUB – Bombing or raiding party.

SUICIDE DITCH – Front-line trench.

SUICIDE SQUAD, THE – Machine Gun Corps. A total of 170,500 officers and men served in the MGC, of which 62,049 were killed, wounded or missing.

SUMP HOLE – Small holes dug at intervals in the base of a trench for collecting water. Sump holes made the baling out of flooded trenches somewhat easier.

STRAW AND MUD – German food was even worse than that of the Allies. Culinary delights included *stroh und lehm*, literally straw and mud, which was yellow peas with *sauerkraut*. *Schrapnellsuppe* or shrapnel soup was undercooked pea or bean soup. They had the same term for butter as the Allies: *wagenschmiere*, axle grease.

SWEATING ON THE TOP LINE – Hopeful. To be expectant of a forthcoming victory, derived from the popular game of Bingo or House, where numbers are called out and marked off in lines on a card.

SWEET FANNY ADAMS, S. F. A. – Nothing at all. Originally nineteenth-century naval slang for tinned cooked meat, from the notorious murder and dismemberment of a girl so named. The initials **S. F. A.** were, by the time of the First World War, also allocated to the expression Sweet Fuck-All, and Sweet Fanny Adams was a bowdlerised version of this phrase.

SWIPE – Slang derived from Canadian troops for acquiring something by unofficial means.

SYNCHRONISE WATCHES – American order for all officers to set their watches to the same time, ready for an offensive.

TAILSPIN – Out of control, about to crash, from aircraft spinning towards the ground.

TAKE HIS NAME AND NUMBER – Place on report.

TAMBOO – Small trench dugout.

TANKS – Armoured, self-propelled vehicle first used in the Battle of the Somme, 1916. As a deception, the original shipping crates of these vehicles were labelled water storage tanks and the name stuck. Tanks were initially called landships.

TAPE (1) – Chevron or stripe worn on the uniform sleeves by non-commissioned officers.

TAPE (2) – Line of tape used to indicate the starting line of an attack or the direction it should take.

TAUBE – German aircraft. Although a Taube was a specific make, British troops referred to all German aircraft as Taubes.

TEDDY BEAR – British Army goatskin jerkin, first issued in winter 1914.

TERRIER – Member of the British Territorial Force, a pre-war expression.

THINGUMMYJIG – Many of the technical devices encountered by soldiers could be quite baffling and hard to describe, which helps to explain the widespread emergence of the word 'thingummyjig'.

THIRD MAN – To go too far. The most popular superstition on the Western Front was that the third man to light his cigarette from the same match would inevitably be killed soon after. This was derived from the story that enemy snipers would, at night, use the flame of the match to find a target – the first light alerted the sniper, the second allowed him to aim, and the third time he fired.

THREE BLUE LIGHTS – Something highly improbable. From a story that peace would be signalled by the firing of three dark-blue signal flares, which would, of course, be invisible against the night sky.

THROW A SEVEN – ANZAC phrase, meaning to get killed, probably from playing dice. When playing with two dice, a seven is the most common number to be thrown.

TICKED OFF (1) – Chastised or told off. Of UK military origin, the earliest known citation of it in print is in a 1915 letter published in Wilfred Owen's *Collected Letters*: 'He has been "ticked-off" four or five times for it; but is not yet shot at dawn.' To tick off, in the sense of reprimand, presumably refers to the image of an officer going through a list of the subordinate's faults and deficiencies, ticking them off as he goes along.

TICKED OFF (2) – US term for angry, annoyed.

TICKET – Official discharge from the Army, especially for medical reasons, before the full period of service had been completed. To 'work one's ticket' was to scheme to get out of the Army.

TICKLER'S (1) – Jam, pozzy. From the brand name of Tickler's, a company in Hull, Yorkshire, but synonymous with jam whatever the brand.

TICKLER'S (2) – Improvised hand grenades, usually made from old jam tins packed with nails, glass and explosives. These were made and used extensively before the Mills bomb became widespread in 1915.

TIC-TAC – Signaller.

TIME-SERVING MAN – Regular soldier who had enlisted for a definite period, usually seven years, as opposed to a conscript or one who had volunteered for the duration.

TIN HAT, SHRAPNEL HELMET, TOMMY HELMET, DOUGHBOY HELMET, TIN PAN HAT, DISHPAN HAT, WASHBASIN, BRODIE HELMET, KELLEY HELMET, BATTLE BOWLER (when worn by officers) – British steel helmet. The French Army was the first to introduce steel helmets for protection against shrapnel, and by December 1915 more than 3 million distinctive Adrian helmets had been manufactured. The War Office Invention Department was ordered to evaluate the French design and decided that it was not strong enough and too complex to be swiftly manufactured. British industry was not geared up to an all-out effort for war production in the early days of the First World War, which also led to the 1915 shell shortage. A design patented in 1915 by John Brodie could be pressed as one piece from a thick sheet of steel, giving it added strength. It resembled the medieval infantry 'kettle hat', with a shallow, circular crown, a wide brim around the edge, a leather liner and a leather chinstrap. The helmet's 'soup bowl' shape was designed to protect the wearer's head and shoulders from shrapnel projectiles bursting from above the trenches. This made it more resistant to projectiles, but it offered less protection to the lower head and neck than other helmets like the German, which was based upon the medieval 'sallet' design. It was first used in 1916, and American troops also used the design. The German Army called it the *salatschüssel*, salad bowl.

TIN OPENER – A bayonet.

TOASTING FORK – A bayonet, but often used for this purpose.

TOC EMMA – Trench mortar (TM), from the First World War phonetic alphabet.

TOFFEE APPLE – Mortar bomb with attached shaft.

TOILET SHEDS – These were constructed behind the front lines, communal toilets where twenty men would sit in line while others queued outside. They were subject to bombardment in the early morning when the enemy knew they would be occupied. In the trenches, buckets were used for defecation. A soldier was instructed after dark to leave the trench, dig a hole and bury the contents of the buckets, but as often as not they just tipped them into a nearby shell hole. Some soldiers lit cigarettes to disguise the smell, and were then subject to being shot by a sniper. Soldiers in the trenches urinated in bully beef tins and threw the contents out of the trenches.

TOMMY – British Army soldier. From Tommy Atkins, a name sometimes used on specimen forms to represent a typical British Army private soldier.

TOMMY BAR – Spanner or wrench for unscrewing the base of Mills bombs, to adjust the timing fuse.

TOMMY COOKER – Small, portable, oil-fuelled stove.

TOOTHPICK – A bayonet.

TOOT SWEET – Quick, quickly, from French *toute de suite*.

TOUR – A period of front-line service.

TOURIST – ANZAC term for a member of the 1st Australian Division.

TRACER – Rifle or machine gun round which can be observed in flight by the (usually) red phosphorescent trail it leaves in its wake. Used chiefly at the time by airmen. The rounds are identifiable by the red-painted tip, and some soldiers and gunners loaded a tracer as the penultimate round in their magazine or ammunition belt, in order to indicate that a reload would then be necessary.

TRAVERSE – Trenches were not straight ditches, since this would have made them far too vulnerable to enfilade fire. Instead, they had traverses built in. This also reduced the effect of shells when they landed in the trench.

TRAY BON – Very good, from French *très bon*. After the spontaneous Christmas Truce of 1914, Private Ronald MacKinnon wrote home to his family: 'Here we are again as the song says. I had quite a good Xmas considering I was in the front line. Xmas Eve was pretty stiff, sentry go up to the hips in mud of course ... We had a truce on Xmas Day and our German friends were quite friendly. They came over to see us and we traded bully beef for cigars ... Xmas was "tray bon", which means very good.' He was killed in the Battle of Vimy Ridge in April 1917.

TRENCH – The long, narrow excavations built to shelter troops from enemy fire on all First World War battlefields. The use of trenches to conceal military forces long predates 1914.

TRENCH COAT – Short waterproof overcoat, belted and double-breasted, with straps on shoulders and arms. Originally worn by officers in the First World War, they are still in fashion. Trenches were frequently, if not always, wet and muddy. Officers were able to purchase this specially tailored coat.

TRENCH DISEASES – Trenches were built for protection, but were not necessarily places of safety. Artillery and gunfire caused one-third of the casualties suffered in the trenches, as disease was endemic. Then there was the smell – rotting flesh, stagnant water, overflowing latrines, unwashed bodies, gunpowder, cigarette smoke, mouldy sandbags, etc.

TRENCH FEVER – A louse-borne relapsing febrile disease which struck soldiers of the First World War; characterised by fever, weakness, dizziness, headache, severe back and leg pains and a rash. Also called Wolhynia Fever, it is treated with antibiotics today.

TRENCH FOOT – Common disabling problem among First World War soldiers. Also called Immersion Syndrome, it is caused by overexposure to cold, damp conditions. It is treated, like chilblains, by rapid warming. This fungal infection of the foot could become gangrenous.

TRENCH MOUTH – Formerly called Vincent's Infection and

characterised by painful, bleeding gums and bad breath, this was another common affliction among front-line soldiers. It was caused by poor oral hygiene and nutrition, heavy smoking and stress.

TRENCH RABBIT – US term for a rat.

TRIPEHOUND – The Sopwith Triplane.

TRIPLE ALLIANCE – A pre-war alliance between Germany, Austria-Hungary and Italy, formalised in 1882. Italy dropped out of this alliance at the start of the First World War, initially maintaining a neutral position.

TRIPLE ENTENTE – A vaguely defined pre-war alliance between Russia, France and Britain, finalised in 1907.

TRIPWIRE – Anything which might catch someone or trigger a response.

TUNE UP – Many early cars' magneto ignition systems were very simple, with one ignition coil for each sparkplug. Each coil needed to be adjusted to provide the same spark intensity for better idle and acceleration. As these coils worked, they made a buzzing sound. When adjusted properly, they all buzzed in tune, thus coining the term 'tune-up'.

TURKEY TROT – Diarrhoea, also known as 'the trots', 'the runs' and the 'Gallipoli gallop', derived from dysentery among ANZAC forces at Gallipoli. The turkey trot was a dance made popular in the decade from 1900 to 1910, performed to fast ragtime music. It lost favour to the foxtrot by 1914, but was picked up by Goffin and King, the writers of Little Eva's 1963 pop song 'Let's Do the Turkey Trot'. Presumably they were unaware of this alternative meaning of turkey trot, referencing running to the latrines while suffering from diarrhoea. The following lines are from the song: 'Do some turkey trottin' and a/All your cares will be forgotten yeah/Come on let's turkey trot/Shoo-shoo gobble-gobble diddle-ip/Let's give it all we've got/Shoo-shoo gobble-gobble diddle-ip.' They rarely write songs like this anymore, except in the Eurovision Song Contest.

TURNIP JAM – In the German Army, this 'jam' became standard issue after the blockade and crop failures created severe shortages. Spread on ersatz bread made with sawdust and other fillers, it was neither appetising nor nourishing.

TURNIP WINTER – In the terrible winter of 1916–17 this was the only food which was plentiful for German civilians and troops alike. People ate horse if they were lucky, and also dogs and cats. Even the kangaroos in Berlin Zoo were eaten.

TYPEWRITER – ANZAC term for a machine gun.

U-BOAT – Submarine, from German *unterseeboot*.

UNCLE CHARLIE – Marching order with full equipment.

UNDEAD – The concussion from shell blasts could stop a man's heart or rupture internal organs so that he died with no obvious external trauma. Even a passing shell could kill a man stone dead, much as wind turbine blades do with bats today, with no external sign of injuries.

UP AGAINST THE WALL – In serious difficulties. Those facing a firing squad are placed against a wall.

VAMOOSE – To go quickly. From Spanish *vamos*, let us go.

VELVET – Good. To be 'on velvet' was to be in exceptionally fortunate and comfortable circumstances.

VERMOREL SPRAYER – An agricultural spraying tool, used in the trenches to spray dispersal chemicals onto low-lying pockets of gas.

VERY LIGHT – A flare or coloured light fired from a Very pistol for signalling at night. After the inventor, Edward W. Very (1852–1910), a US naval ordnance officer. 'When Irish Eyes' became:

> When Very lights are shining,
> Sure they're like the morning light
> And when the guns begin to thunder
> You can hear the angels shite.
> Then the Maxims start to chatter
> And trench mortars send a few,
> And when Very lights are shining
> 'Tis time for a rum issue.
>
> When Very lights are shining
> Sure 'tis like the morning dew,
> And when shells begin a bursting
> It makes you think your times come too.
> And when you start advancing
> Five nines and gas comes through,
> Sure when Very lights are shining
> 'Tis rum or lead for you.

VICTORIA CROSS – The British Empire's most honourable medal for valour was first instituted in 1856 for participants in the Crimean War. Since then, the medal has been awarded 1,357 times to 1,354 individual recipients. Of these, 633 members of the armed forces were awarded the Victoria Cross during the First World War. Of these, 187 had been killed during their act of heroism. Over twenty winners will not be commemorated upon memorial slabs in their home towns in 2014, because they were born abroad, although they were British and brought up in Britain. Two men won the VC twice, both members of the RAMC: Lieutenant A. Martin-Leake (in 1902 and 1914) and Captain N. G. Chavasse, MC. In 1916, Chavasse was hit by shell splinters while rescuing men in no man's land. It is said he came as close as 25 yards from the German line, where he found three injured men, and he continued rescuing men throughout that night, under a constant rain of sniper bullets and bombing. He performed similar heroics in the offensive at Passchendaele, where he was wounded, and gained a second VC to become the most highly decorated British serviceman in the war. Although operated upon, he was to die of his wounds in 1917.

WAD – Sandwich.

WALLAH – Chap, or person in charge of a particular object, duty or task. It is used in conjunction with appropriate word. For example, the soldier unfortunate enough to be on latrine duty was invariably known as the shit-wallah. From Hindustani *wala*, man or protector.

WANGLE – To acquire, through some sort of trick or clever scheme.

WASH OUT – Described a process by which aspiring officers who failed their commissions and were sent back to their regiments, or 'washed out'. By 1915, the term was being used to signify any kind of failure.

WASTAGE – Used by politicians and generals as a euphemism for soldiers being killed or wounded. Sometimes used to differentiate casualties in the presumably less productive interim periods from the major battles.

WAZZAH – Dugout, derived from the Haret el Wasser, the red-light district in Cairo.

WEARY WILLIE – German shell passing safely, although rather slowly, overhead. The expression was first used in 1914, from a pre-war *Comic Cuts* character of the same name. The expression was also used in Gallipoli as a term for shrapnel.

WESTERN FRONT – Some 400 miles of opposing trenches, sometimes only yards apart. Before an infantry or offensive attack, a great deal of preparation took place. Extra troops were brought up to the front line, extra ammunition and supplies were needed, but also many coffins had to be prepared. The coffins were placed on the roadside, in plain view of the soldiers heading to the trenches. However, the enemy had planes that flew over the battlefield and observed what was going on, dropping warning messages for their troops. However, the greatest clue to a future attack did not come from increased plane activity but from the heavy artillery bombardments beforehand. 'Our High Command had not advanced beyond the tactics of the Stone Age. They could not think of any other form of warfare, except to throw into battle large numbers of men month after month.' – Infantryman Lovatt Fraser. A German soldier on the front wrote home, 'Lice, rats, barbed wire, fleas, shells, bombs, underground caves, corpses, liquor, mice, cats, filth, bullets, fire, steel: that is what war is. It is the work of the devil.'

WET, A – A cup of tea or coffee.

WHACK, A FAIR – Derived from when parcels from home were shared among friends or 'whacked round'.

WHIPPET – Specifically a name for the medium Mark A British tank first seen in 1917, but later applied generally to any type of light tank, including the French Renault. From the breed of dog noted for its speed.

WHISTLE – They were used primarily to initiate a pre-set plan, so that all men within earshot would move simultaneously. As at sea, whistles could be heard over loud noise. Officers would synchronise their watches and return to their posts to blow whistles, signalling for all troops along a broad stretch of trench to attack at the same time.

WHISTLING WILLIE – A shell, and this or Willie (q.v.) is the origin of 'giving the willies'. This was the German 8-inch 'Screaming Shell', known among the British troops as the 'Whistling Willies'. These shells screeched like sirens, and were designed to unnerve the men in the trenches.

WHITECAP – Royal Air Force (RAF) policeman, also known as a **SNOWDROP**.

WHITE FEATHER – Vice-Admiral Charles Cooper Uniacke-Penrose-Fitzgerald, nicknamed 'Rough' (1841–1921), was seventy-three years old and had never seen much action by 1914. In August 1914, he founded the Order of the White Feather. With the support of leading women, the organisation encouraged women to give out white feathers to young men who had not joined the British Army. Many soldiers home on leave in 'civvies', recuperating, or men in restricted occupations were mistakenly given these. The government responded by issuing a badge which could be worn by civilians occupied in war work. Men home from the war were virtually forced to wear their tattered uniforms to avoid facing abuse in the streets.

WHITE HANDKERCHIEF – Sergeant Thomas Painting of the King's Royal Rifle Corps remembered, 'We were not allowed to have white handkerchiefs in case we used them as a white flag. We had to go out and buy a red handkerchief. I remember the first bit of French I learnt was "mouchoir rouge", handkerchief red.'

WHITESHEET – Wytschaete, a Belgian village on the ridge just north of Messines.

WHITE STAR – A German mixture of chlorine and phosgene gas, from the identification marking painted on the delivery shell casing.

WHIZZ-BANG – High-velocity shell, from the noise of the rapid flight and the explosion, originally applied to shells from the Skoda 77 mm field gun. A trench song had the lyrics, 'I don't want to go in the trenches no more,/Where the whizz-bangs and shrapnel they whistle and roar.' The word later became synonymous with excellent or top-notch.

WHOLE NINE YARDS – The term 'I gave it the whole nine yards', meaning one did one's best, perhaps originated from the fact that the machine gun ammunition belts in aircraft were about 9 yards long.

WIBBLE-WOBBLE – Tank.

WILLIE (1) – Tank, from the prototype British tank, 'Little Willie'. It may well be that 'Give them the willies', i.e., to make someone scared, and 'get the willies' come from the use of tanks in the War.

WILLIE (2) – American term for canned corned beef.

WIMP – Whinging Incompetent Malingering Person, a First World War term, probably first seen in print in 1920. It may have originally come from someone who whimpered before action, becoming known as a whimperer and then a wimp.

WIND-UP TUNIC – A British officer's tunic with the stars worn on the shoulders instead of the sleeves, a standing order in some regiments even during the early stages of the war. The practice of wearing the badges of rank on the epaulettes was favoured by many officers as it made them less conspicuous to the enemy, and after the war the wearing of rank badges on the sleeves was discontinued. The same officers often carried the .303 Lee-Enfield rifle into battle in preference to the standard-issue service revolver for the same reason. However, some senior officers disapproved of this practice, viewing it as a case of an officer 'with the wind-up' (see **WINDY**).

'WIND OF BALL' – This phenomenon was seen frequently in sea battles in the Napoleonic Wars. This was death or injury from a cannon ball passing close to, but not actually hitting, the body. 'Wind of ball' that passed the head often meant survival; if it passed close to the stomach, death was almost always the result. The same phenomenon later happened with artillery shells. We see it today when bats pass the tip of a wind turbine blade, which spins at around 160–180 mph. They fall out of the sky with their internal organs damaged, but, as with humans, there are no obvious causes of death.

WINDY, BE; HAVE THE WIND UP – Afraid, nervous. Such a person was said to have the wind-up. The origin seems to have been flatulence due to nerves. Churchill recommended laughter to prevent men becoming 'windy' or afraid. His advice to his officers was, 'Don't be careless about yourselves – on the other hand not too careful. Keep a special pair of boots to sleep in & only get them muddy in a real emergency. Use alcohol in moderation but don't have a great parade of bottles in your dugouts. Live well but do not flaunt it. Laugh a little & teach your men to laugh – great good hum'r under fire – war is a game that is played with a smile. If you can't smile, grin. If you can't grin, keep out of the way till you can.'

WIPERS – Ypres (Flemish Ieper) was a Belgian town in West Flanders. From the pronunciation of a literal 'Y' at the beginning of the word.

WIRELESS – It was obvious from the outbreak of war that wireless had become a technology of great strategic importance. The British government immediately took control of parts of the Marconi Company, such as its latest transatlantic stations in Wales and its factory in Chelmsford, and the company established an ambitious training programme for wireless operators. The demands of war – from land, sea and airborne services – meant that technical developments were accelerated. Wartime priorities emphasised the potential for counter-offensive inherent in wireless communication. Signals could be intercepted, for example, and direction-finding techniques could locate and destroy the positions of enemy transmitters. Once it was possible to locate trench wireless sets, enemy troop positions could also be known, as well as those of Zeppelins and other hostile aircraft. It was detection of wireless traffic that alerted the Royal Navy to the movements of the German fleet and precipitated the Battle of Jutland in May 1916.

WONKY – Defective.

WOODBINE – The most common brand of cigarettes used by the British.

WOOFS – German 4.7 inch high explosive and shrapnel shells.

WOOLLY BEAR – German shrapnel shell, bursting with a cloudlike explosion.

WAZZIR – Cairo's red-light district, Haret el Wasser. Two 'battles' were fought there by drunk ANZAC troops, the first one on 2 April (Good Friday) 1915 and the second one by the 2nd Australian Division some months later. They were caused by the high prices being charged by prostitutes, and the rumour that they were intentionally infecting the men with sexually transmitted diseases. On both occasions a great deal of damage was done in the district.

Local people were molested, furniture was thrown out of windows and houses were even set on fire. One slang phrase, going 'to the top of the Wazir', or Wozzer derives its meaning of doing something to excess from these riots.

WRITE-OFF – Bad casualty, corpse or a ruined military vehicle.

YELLOW CROSS – German gas, from the identification marking painted on the delivery shell casing.

YPERITE – French name for mustard gas.

Z-HOUR – Zero hour, the time that an attack was to commence.

ZINNWAREN – German for tinware, a term for medals and decorations.

Select Bibliography

Over 300 books and over 200 websites have been used, of which the following are recommended as a starting point.

Books

Arthur, Max, *Forgotten Voices of the Great War: A New History of WW1 in the Words of the Men and Women Who Were There* (Ebury Press, 2003)

Ellis, John, *Eye-Deep in Hell: Trench Warfare in World War I* (Johns Hopkins, 1989)

Ellis, John, and Cox, Mike, *The World War I Databook: The Essential Facts and Figures for All the Combatants* (Aurum, 2001)

Fussell Paul, *The Great War and Modern Memory* (Oxford University Press, 1975)

Gilbert, Martin, *The First World War: A Complete History* (2nd ed., Holt, 2004)

Hart, Peter, *The Great War: A Combat History of the First World War* (Oxford University Press, 2013)

Hastings, Max, *Catastophe: Europe Goes To War* (Collins, 2013)

Keegan, John, *The First World War* (Vintage, 2000)

Liddell-Hart, Basil Henry, *The Real War (1914–1918)* (1930)

MacMillan, Margaret, *The War that Ended Peace: The Road to 1914* (Profile, 2013)

Meyer, J. G., *A World Undone: The Story of the Great War 1914–1917* (Delacorte, 2007)

Neiberg, Michael S., *Fighting the Great War: A Global History* (Harvard University Press, 2005)

Pope, Stephen and Wheal, Elizabeth-Anne (eds), *The Macmillan Dictionary of the First World War* (MacMillan, 1995)

Röhl, John, *The Kaiser and His Court: Wilhelm II and the Government of Germany* (Cambridge University Press, 1996)
Simkins, John, *First World War Encyclopaedia* (Spartacus Educational, 2013)
Tuchman, Barbara, *The Guns of August* (Ballantine, 1952)

Websites
All of the following are superb resources, leading you in many intriguing directions for further research:
www.1914–1918.net
www.firstworldwar.com
www.worldwar1.com
www.ww1facts.net
www.spartacus.schoolnet.co.uk/FWW.htm

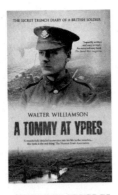
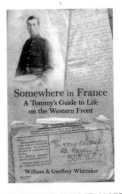